THE
URBAN FARM
HANDBOOK

Date: 11/6/13

THE
URBAN FARM
HANDBOOK

City-Slicker Resources for Growing, Raising,
Sourcing, Trading, and Preparing What You Eat

· ·

ANNETTE COTTRELL AND JOSHUA MCNICHOLS | PHOTOGRAPHY BY HARLEY SOLTES

SKIPSTONE

For my grandmother—baker, beekeeper, gardener, canner, and chicken slaughterer. She taught me to always follow my heart. *(AC)*

To Emily, Gavin, and Luella, for exploring this world with me, even if I have to coerce some of you with Legos and check marks. *(JM)*

Published by Skipstone, an imprint of The Mountaineers Books

Printed in the United States of America
First printing 2011
14 13 12 11   5 4 3 2 1

Copy Editors: Joan Gregory, Barry Foy
Designer: Heidi Smets Graphic Design, heidismets.com
Cover photograph: Harley Soltes
Illustrations: Joshua McNichols

ISBN (paperback): 978-1-59485-637-2
ISBN (ebook): 978-1-59485-638-9

Library of Congress Cataloging-in-Publication Data
Cottrell, Annette
  The urban farm handbook : city-slicker resources for growing, raising, sourcing, trading, and preparing what you eat / Annette Cottrell and Joshua McNichols ; photography by Harley Soltes. — 1st ed.
     p. cm.
  ISBN 978-1-59485-637-2
  1. Organic gardening. 2. Organic living. I. McNichols, Joshua. II. Title.
  SB453.5.C67 2011
  630.973'091732--dc23
                    2011029263

Skipstone books may be purchased for corporate, educational, or other promotional sales. For special discounts and information, contact our Sales Department at 800-553-4453 or mbooks@mountaineersbooks.org.

Skipstone
1001 SW Klickitat Way, Suite 201
Seattle, Washington 98134
206.223.6303
www.skipstonebooks.org
www.mountaineersbooks.org

♻ Printed on recycled paper   LIVE LIFE. MAKE RIPPLES.

contents

acknowledgments

Thanks to Marc Ramirez for discovering me, and Kate Rogers for her persistence and faith in this project. Thanks to Will Allen, Alleycat Acres, Sue McGann, Eddie Hill, and Stephanie Snyder Seliga for making food sovereignty something that is not reserved for the upper classes. Thanks to Charmaine Slaven, Lacia Bailey, and the other Seattle Farm Co-op mentors for giving so much of their time and knowledge to build Seattle's urban farming community. Thanks to Skeeter for a lifetime of teaching others to grow food, feed friends, and make this world a more loving place. Thanks to Joshua for helping to make this dream a reality. And thanks especially to Jared, Max, and Lander for putting up with my crazy bus. *(AC)*

A book about a food community wouldn't succeed without the generosity of so many farmers, producers, friends, and neighbors. Without their stories, this would be just another how-to book. Special thanks to René Featherstone and Michael "Skeeter" Pilarski, the "monks" of our personal food community.

Thanks to our editors at Skipstone: Kate Rogers for finding us, Joan Gregory for hammering our work into shape, Barry Foy for his ironclad recipe standards, Heidi Smets for her excellent eye, Margaret Sullivan for her expert facilitation, and Anne Moreau for her last-minute cleanup. Thanks to Harley Soltes, who turned out to be a mentor as well as an outstanding photographer.

Thanks to the family members who helped proof various bits and pieces of text, to the editors at KUOW who taught me how to locate a person's quest, and to Philip Lee for his occasional guidance. Thanks to P-Patch and Seattle Tilth for teaching me how to steward the soil. And finally, thanks to Annette, without whose engine this train would never have left the station. *(JM)*

Annette's entry table.

how it all began

Annette

For four years, beginning in 2006, I spent every spare minute working in my yard. I eradicated dandelions, ivy, blackberries, and plantain, and did all I could to nurture the dead lawn back to life. I had a landscaper create plans for a formal ornamental garden. I spent hours, my baby in my arms, gazing out the window and dreaming of fountains and boxwoods and flowers.

But midway through this all-consuming project, I suddenly had a change of heart. Soon I was ripping it all out like a woman possessed. What in the world happened?

My first son, Max, had terrible acid reflux as an infant, and my concern for him led me to spend hours researching the connection between diet and health. As he grew into a highly intense toddler, my focus expanded to include the effects of diet on behavior.

When Max's weight plummeted from the ninety-fifth percentile of average body weight for his age group to the fifth (he had a habit of boycotting food), I reached a turning point.

Our pediatrician sent us to Children's Hospital for help from a nutritionist. Her advice was to feed Max special canned drinkable meals made entirely of synthetic ingredients. I listened politely, but when I got home I was irate. How could isolated synthetic nutrients compare to the natural nutrients humans had evolved with? I knew that what Max needed didn't come in a can. I crumpled up the nutritionist's recommendation slip and threw it away.

Instead, I set out to create my own special diet for Max. Rather than synthetics, this one was loaded with rich organics: butter, heavy cream, pastured bacon, egg yolks. I served them in forms that no toddler could refuse, such as eggnog, pudding, and smoothies.

In no time at all, Max's weight was back up. At the same time, he started trying new foods, and from there he has never looked back. Now he'll try anything once, and he's come to love anything sour or salty or sweet or all of the above. He sips shots of local apple cider vinegar like a wine connoisseur and craves pickled or lacto-fermented foods.

Max's younger brother, Lander, was a different story: He started off as a great eater but at some point just stopped. He reached a stage where he would eat any kind of processed snack food but steadfastly refused meals. But with the peanut recalls, and more and more snack products being added to the daily recall list, I stopped buying snack foods entirely.

As a result, Lander unwittingly became my second mentor in the search for the most nutrient-dense foods possible. With snack foods unavailable, he refused to eat anything but pancakes. I decided that if he was going to eat only pancakes, then I would make them the most nutritionally packed pancakes possible. Only I didn't yet know how to make pancakes without a mix.

My research into diet and health continued, and eventually I arrived at the conclusion that it was impossible to buy processed foods with entirely benign ingredients, regardless of corporate stewardship pledges or organic labels.

I resolved to look for a different framework: I was done supporting the mainstream food industry, both conventional farmers and the large organics that operated like them. No more giving money to companies whose processed foods contained ingredients I couldn't buy myself, or livestock raisers who didn't pasture their animals or feed them based on the animal's natural diet. I vowed from that moment on to grow as much of our food as possible and buy the rest from local farmers.

My husband, Jared, referred to this scheme as my "Crazy Bus." Still, he agreed with me in principle and consented to take out the lawn and replace it with what a neighbor dubbed my "midlife crisis garden." Labeling his sketches "Experience Garden Project," after Seattle's Frank Gehry–designed Experience Music Project museum, Jared created plans for the new fence and the garden boxes. Every time I came up with a new idea, such as putting fruit trees in the side yard, he would mutter something like, "Next stop on the Crazy Bus." But he never stood in the way of my scheme . . . even if he was pretty adamant about not getting chickens.

That was two years ago, and now the dream of a strictly decorative garden is long gone. These days when I look out the window, I see a garden bursting with enough fruits, vegetables, and berries to open a greengrocer's stand. Bees busily pollinate herbs and make honey for winter. Composting worms quietly turn the garden's excess biomass into nutrient-rich soil. Chickens and ducks patrol for garden pests, and a corner of the coop is in the process of being converted into a rabbit hutch, while the children's play fort is slated to become a dairy goat pen. Instead of a koi pond with water lilies, I now dream of a pool growing dinner tilapia and watercress.

The transformation doesn't stop at the yard. Inside the house, the chest freezer has ceded its industrial-sized plastic bags of ravioli and dinosaur-shaped chicken nuggets to paper-wrapped primal cuts of animals purchased directly from local farmers. My downstairs pantry shelves are lined with home canned goods, all from the garden or local farms.

My mother-in-law came to visit not long ago, took one look in the kitchen cupboard, and said in shock, "You have no food!" But believe me, we have plenty of food. In fact, for once we have nothing *but* food. The cupboard's contents may not be loaded in comparison with the average grocery store shelf, but those canning jars brimming with whole grains, dried

Annette and her son Lander shucking corn.

fruits, beans, granola, homemade fruit leather, and beef jerky are a treasure trove of nutrients. And now that I find myself with more than enough cupboard space, it's because real, nutrient-dense food turns out to be quite compact—who knew?! (So if you feel like your kitchen pantry is too small maybe you should consider optimizing for nutrients instead of for space.)

I clearly remember that first January Saturday after making my decision to go local. For the first time ever, I bundled up and went shopping at the farmers market. The first order of business was applesauce for the kids, and I snatched up what boxes of fruit were available in midwinter. Over the next few weeks I would put up eighty pounds of apples, freezing the sauce. Then I set to work finding a source for local grains.

There were still three months left until spring, lots of time to convert what was recently lawn into my family's private grocery store. I had never gardened for true sustenance before, so this would be one heck of an experiment. Could a small-scale gardener manage to grow enough food to feed the whole family year-round? I was about to find out.

deciding not to leave the city

Joshua

When Gavin turned one, my wife, Emily, and I bought a house with a yard. In the brief two-hour window during Gavin's daily afternoon naps, I planted nearly a dozen apple, pear, and plum trees by growing them flat against the property lines. I created a blueberry patch and a kitchen garden. When Gavin woke up, I'd set him down in the garden and lie next to him in the grass. I'd watch as he wandered through the garden rows, eating snap peas out of hand. Over the course of the summer, we spent almost every afternoon in this fashion. After the snap peas, he moved on to shelling peas, then blueberries, strawberries, and tomatoes. Gavin brought me berries and bugs. He watched ants and dug holes. His simple joy made me feel at peace.

A few years later, the global economic crisis kicked us in the butt. Our work dried up and we started eating through our savings. We considered dropping out of society and moving to a farm, to live off the land as many others had before us. We now had a second child, Luella. We imagined a farm would give our kids room to run freely, instead of being confined to our small city lot. But moving to a farm would have meant permanently abandoning our careers, as both our jobs were tied closely to the city.

Each evening after the kids went to bed, we combed online real estate maps looking for a way out. Within our internet browser window, we'd fly high above an agricultural community, then drop down out of the sky onto a farm for sale. "Do you think we could live there?" I'd ask, pointing at a property near the meandering oxbow of a river in the middle of an agricultural valley. Emily zoomed in until we could make out a quaint farmhouse and a big red barn. From the realtor's photographs, the fields appeared to be overgrazed, with patches of weeds poking through. "We could restore the pasture, let a few other organic farmers lease the land, open a small bed and breakfast. We could help turn the area into a hub for agritourism."

"That property looks like it floods every year," said Emily.

"Oh, you're probably right. Not a good thing for a bed and breakfast, huh?"

Emily zoomed out and we retreated back to our view from the sky. We flew around the state like birds looking for a nesting site. We imagined lives filled with a small barnyard of animals and a field full of fruit trees.

But even as we dreamed, we knew this wasn't right. It felt like retreating, like entering an early retirement. And we knew that waves of city folk dreaming of the country would only contribute to suburban sprawl, a blight that threatens to turn our agricultural land into cul de sacs.

One night, I lay in bed with a copy of the poems of Edna St. Vincent Millay. There was a poem in there I'd read once, that had been nagging me for some time.

> *The trees along this city street*
> *Save for the traffic and the trains,*
> *Would make a sound as thin and sweet*
> *As trees in country lanes.*
> *And people standing in their shade*
> *Out of a shower, undoubtedly*
> *Would hear such music as is made*
> *Upon a country tree.*
> *Oh, little leaves that are so dumb*
> *Against the shrieking city air,*
> *I watch you when the wind has come,*
> *I know what sound is there.*

Careful not to wake Emily, I grabbed a flashlight and walked out the back door in my slippers. As I opened the door, I heard Luella stir. She has no tolerance for parents leaving the house, for any reason. When she made no further noise, I crept across the back deck, through the yard to the southern property line. There our first crop of apples slowly ripened on carefully espaliered apple trees. The French method of pruning fruit trees flat allowed us to fit in several heirloom varieties without giving up much garden space. I pulled an apple off the tree and examined it in the moonlight. It was a Karmijn de Sonneville. An unusual apple, with a bizarre extra set of chromosomes and an intense flavor to match. The apple's interior was ripe and delicious. I bit carefully, avoiding a small worm that had eaten a trail to the apple's core and back out the other side. I crunched through the spots where the flesh had crystallized, like old honey, creating the aberration prized by Japanese apple connoisseurs. My grocery store had nothing like this.

In the western United States, there's always somewhere less developed where you can project your dreams. There are empty places that look, upon first glance, to be unshaped, to be big enough to accept the expansive life we want to live. My ancestors left Europe, left the Oklahoma dust bowl, followed the military, followed the jobs. It's the history of the West. From the gold rushes to the back-to-the-land movement in the 1970s, from Henry David Thoreau to Barbara Kingsolver, people in this country leave. They move on. They plant their dreams in a new plot of ground, new to them but abandoned by someone else. It's a nonstop game of musical chairs.

Could I stay? Could we live off *this* land? This little 5,000 square foot lot? That seemed a bit of a stretch. Could we even afford to eat healthy food in the city?

Just then, my neighbor pulled into his driveway, his headlights washing over me. I froze, embarrassed to be standing outside in my pajamas, eating an apple in the middle of the night. I clicked off my flashlight and padded quietly back to bed without brushing my teeth. I lay there, enjoying the apple's aftertaste, until I fell asleep.

Not long after that, I discovered we weren't alone in our ambitions. Someone started a forum online for Seattle backyard farmers and the membership exploded. We realized there were people like us, rejecting unhealthy factory-processed food, all over the city, many of them right in our neighborhood.

And that's where I met Annette Cottrell. Annette had been living without visiting the grocery store for well over a year. She offered to give us a locavore makeover, to teach us how to return to real food and ditch the grocery store.

Annette is one of those people who appears not to sleep. When she decides to do something, she's like a police dog on a criminal's leg. When she decided to change her family's diet, she turned her life upside down, and her family's life too.

As she discussed with me the problems with the American diet, I saw the truth in much of what she said. Internet research pushed me further into her world, to the point that I came to feel ill at ease in grocery stores. I'd lost my appetite for their stiff green bananas and vast banks of frozen pizzas. One day, I stood still in middle of the grocery store with an empty cart. I had thirty minutes until dinner and I couldn't think of anything I wanted to buy.

In some ways, this is what it means to be human in the twenty-first century. We know too much about the problems of the world around us. We know about the giant islands of plastic in the middle of the ocean, the swimming polar bear looking for an ice floe to land on. We can't go back to accepting the world as it is. The burden of this responsibility can paralyze us. And so, we look for ways to move forward.

My mother, a marriage and family therapist, talks a lot about "good enough parenting." By that she means, do the best you can and forgive yourself the rest. Researchers in her field, including Dr. John Gottman, have discovered that being a good parent just 30 percent of the time is enough to help your kids develop emotional maturity. I decided to apply this attitude to what I'd learned about food from Annette. If I could feed my family this way just 30 percent of the time, we'd be better off than if I'd done nothing.

Then, a surprising thing happened. We got into the habit of grinding our own grains and

Joshua and his wife, Emily, barter with friends.

found a way to do it nearly every day, even with busy schedules. We found that cooking with scratch ingredients costs less than eating from grocery stores and restaurants. We found sources of high-quality, sustainably raised meats for less money than you'd pay at the store. Shopping and cooking this way is addicting, and we believe you'll feel the same.

Annette and I have come to appreciate each other's limitations, to understand that our different levels of commitment make our strategies more accessible to others. Annette chooses to knead all her own bread by hand, whereas I use a bread machine. Annette prepares different gourmet meals almost every night, whereas we've simply replaced a limited roster of quick meals we used to buy at the grocery store with home-grown versions of the same.

Whether you choose to dabble in these ideas, or take them much further than we do, there's a place for you in this book.

. . . .

OPPORTUNITIES FOR CHANGE

Throughout the book, we highlight what we call "Opportunities for Change." You might think of these as "different levels of crazy." Choose the level that fits your personality. Joshua is crazy. Annette is very, very crazy. Sometimes we reverse positions, just to try on each other's shoes. We're never too proud to make fun of ourselves. Sometimes, you'll want to join in the fun. You may want to set off the "crazy alarm," as Annette's husband, Jared, did when she presented him with a salad made from hairy old dandelion leaves (before she knew the correct variety for eating). But that's part of making change. We push ourselves, sometimes going over the edge, in order to locate the cliff.

. . . .

WINTER

It may seem strange to begin with winter, when spring is typically considered the start of life, of seasons, and of planting calendars. But I believe that the seeds of lasting transformation take root best during a period of dormancy—just as a caterpillar transforms itself within the dormacy of a cocoon. Winter is when we have time to read, to reflect, and to reinvent.

When the subject of food comes up with a new acquaintance, and I tell her I don't shop at the grocery store, her thoughts inevitably leap to a garden bursting at the seams with fresh produce ready to be canned in a steamy kitchen. And she's not wrong: Home gardening, with all its rich visual and tactile elements, is one way—the most common way—of avoiding the grocery store.

But it is not the only way. After all, you don't need to garden or put up your own fruits and vegetables to buy organic meat, eggs, dairy, and produce at farmers markets, with a focus on eating in season. How far you go with the process is up to you, whether it's buying a grain grinder and baking your own bread, or handing your lawn over to dairy goats, or simply shifting your buying dollars from

what we are eating now

Brussels sprouts
Cabbage
Carrots
Collard greens
Dandelions
Kale
Mâche
Parsnips
Rutabagas
Salsify
Storing apples
Storing carrots
Storing garlic
Storing onions
Storing pears
Storing potatoes
Storing squash
Turnips

big-box grocery stores to farmers markets and giving up some processed foods. There is no one correct answer and no one correct path.

Winter is when you have the least pressure from local crops coming ripe or gardens needing urgent attention. It's the perfect time to practice baking, when a warm oven and the smell of home-baked goods is most inviting, or for ripening homemade cheese in a garage that is the same temperature as the ideal cheese cave. It's the best season for stepping back and rethinking your shopping and eating habits.

Winter is the perfect time to plan for a new beginning—from the ground up. *(AC)*

recipes for a winter meal

Long winter nights call for something warming, like this backyard rabbit stew prepared in the style of Provence. Full of earthy stored carrots, onions, and garlic, the stew incorporates home-canned tomatoes to round out its flavors. Polenta made from dried, stored corn and enriched with creamy homemade chèvre makes the perfect foil for the stew's rich juices. We've paired this dish with oven-roasted Brussels sprouts sweetened by winter frosts, and stored sweetmeat squash adds complexity to a crème brûlée to finish the meal.

Lapin en Daube à la Provençale Rabbit with Vegetables and Provençal Herbs
Makes 6–8 servings
This is the perfect recipe for older rabbits: Low and slow stewing in acidic wine helps dissolve any toughness. It is equally suitable for a pot roast or stewing hen.
Note: You can make this in a slow cooker, cooking all day on low or 5 hours on high.

Legs and saddle meat from 2 rabbits
1½ teaspoon salt
½ teaspoon freshly ground black pepper
1 tablespoon bacon grease or lard
12 cloves garlic, peeled and sliced
1 cup dry red wine
2 cups chopped carrots
1 large onion, peeled and chopped
1 cup beef bone broth (recipe page 291)
1 tablespoon tomato paste or ½ cup pasta sauce (recipe page 241)
1 teaspoon chopped fresh rosemary

1 teaspoon chopped fresh thyme
1 pint canned tomatoes (recipe page 235)
1 bay leaf

1. Preheat the oven to 300°F.
2. Rub salt and pepper on rabbit pieces. Heat bacon grease or lard in a heavy-bottomed stockpot over medium-high heat. Add rabbit meat and garlic, cooking until meat is browned on all sides, about 5 minutes.
3. Add remaining ingredients, scraping bottom of pan with a wooden spoon to loosen any browned bits.
4. Bring mixture to a boil, then cover and bake for 2½ hours. Remove bay leaf before serving.

Roasted Brussels Sprouts with Bacon
Makes 4–6 servings
In the wintertime, my body craves these little beauties. I try to wait until they are the size of a bouncy ball, but sometimes I harvest them when they are no bigger than marbles.

2 stalks Brussels sprouts
3 or 4 pieces of smoked bacon, chopped (recipe page 286)
2 tablespoons bacon grease or lard
½ teaspoon sea salt

1. Preheat the oven to 400°F.
2. Trim sprouts from stalk, reserving large leaves from stalk for another meal. Remove any scruffy outer leaves from sprouts and wash well.
3. Melt bacon grease or lard on a jelly roll pan. Place sprouts and bacon on pan, sprinkle with salt, and roll to coat in grease.
4. Roast for 30 minutes, shaking pan from time to time to brown sprouts evenly.

Chèvre Polenta
Makes 6–8 servings

1 tablespoon butter
3 cups water
¼ teaspoon salt

1 cup freshly ground dent corn, ground on a medium-coarse setting
½ cup chèvre (recipe page 90)

1. Preheat the oven to 300°F.
2. Coat bottom and sides of a shallow gratin dish with the butter.
3. In a medium saucepan, bring water and salt to a boil. Add polenta in a thin stream, whisking constantly. Continue to whisk over medium heat for 5 to 7 minutes, until it reaches the consistency of Cream of Wheat.
4. Stir in chèvre, then let stand for 10 minutes to thicken. Pour onto plates, and top with rabbit and fresh thyme.

If you double or triple this recipe, plan on 45 minutes to an hour of constant stirring. However, you can begin it on the stovetop and then move it to the oven to bake alongside the rabbit for the last hour. That will free up your time for more important things, like firing up your biochar oven (see page 128) to celebrate the winter solstice.

Variation: Baked Swiss Chard and Polenta. Spread one-half the cooked polenta in a casserole dish. Top with braised and chopped Swiss chard, spread a layer of crème fraîche (recipe page 88) or chèvre (recipe page 90) on top, then finish with the other half of the polenta. Bake at 400°F for 20 minutes. Let stand 10 minutes before serving.

Variation: Grilled Polenta. Spread cooked polenta in a lasagna dish and refrigerate overnight. The next day, slice into rectangles, brush with olive oil, and grill on the barbecue about 3 minutes per side, until grill marks appear and polenta is heated through. This is wonderful served with braised greens, poached eggs, and pasta sauce (recipe page 241).

Variation: Polenta Fries. Spread cooked polenta in a lasagna dish and refrigerate overnight. The next day, cut into 1 by 4-inch rectangles. Brush rectangles on all sides with olive oil, sprinkle with salt and optional garlic powder, and place on a cookie sheet. Place cookie sheet about 4 inches from preheated broiler. Turn pieces over after 10 minutes, then continue baking until golden, another 5 to 10 minutes.

Sweet Meat Squash Crème Fraîche Brûlée
Makes 6–8 servings

This is no ordinary crème brûlée: It's richly flavored with heirloom sweet meat squash and homemade crème fraîche. You can make the brulées days ahead and torch the sugar topping in front of your eager guests.

3 cups sweet meat (or really any) squash puree*
1 cup organic sugar
1 tablespoon molasses
2½ teaspoons ginger
2½ teaspoons cinnamon
1 teaspoon freshly ground nutmeg
Pinch of ground clove or ground allspice
½ teaspoon salt
1 cup crème fraîche (recipe page 88)
½ cup milk
4 backyard egg yolks

1. Preheat the oven to 325°F.
2. Put on a kettle of water to boil. Combine squash, sugar, molasses, nutmeg, spices, and salt in a food processor, blender, or mixer bowl, and mix well.
3. Pour mixture into a heavy-bottomed saucepan and simmer over low heat until thickened, about 10 minutes. (This step removes moisture from the squash and results in a creamier dessert.)
4. Add remaining ingredients and stir well. Set empty individual ramekins or small gratin dishes in a large lasagna casserole. (The greater the surface area, the more burnt sugar on top.) Pour mixture into ramekins, then carefully pour boiling water into casserole until it reaches halfway up sides of ramekins.
5. Bake just until brulée is set around the edges but still trembling in the center, about 40 to 45 minutes. Refrigerate ramekins for 3 hours or up to several days. To serve, remove ramekins 30 minutes before serving and sprinkle custard surface thickly with organic sugar. Melt sugar with a kitchen torch or under a broiler until it forms a crispy top, but be careful not to burn the sugar.

*To make squash puree, split squash in half, remove seeds, and roast cut-side down in a jelly roll or casserole pan at 350°F until soft. Scoop out squash meat and puree in a blender or food processor.

chapter 1
it all begins with grain

My journey began with grain. That makes sense, because grain is the food from which we've become most disconnected. It's easy to buy local meats and vegetables from butchers and farmers markets, but finding a source for local grains can be a bigger challenge. And yet, a shift from processed, grain-based foods—things like crackers, bread, and breakfast cereal—can lay the foundation for your transition away from the grocery store.

Two years ago, I had never made pancakes from scratch or a successful loaf of 100 percent whole wheat bread. But on January 1, 2009, I began by learning how to bake with whole grains. In the coming months, I experienced quite a few bread-making flops, but each week I improved, and soon I was creating amazing fresh-baked bread that brought everyone in the house running to the kitchen when I pulled it piping hot from the oven. I frequently shaped half the dough into a loaf and let the kids turn the other half into

GRAINS

annette's grocery list

ORIGINAL LIST

Baking powder
Baking soda
Bread
Breakfast cereal
Crackers
Croutons
Flour
Frozen pizza
Frozen waffles
Hot dog buns
Oatmeal
Pancake mix
Salt
Yeast

REVISED LIST

Baking powder
Baking soda
Local grains
Salt
Yeast (unless making sourdough)

cinnamon rolls or breadsticks. They loved this new, edible play dough, and I loved the way it connected them with their food.

With a husband who likes toast for breakfast and sandwiches for lunch and dinner, and two kids who revere bunny crackers, breakfast cereal, pizzas, and pancakes, keeping my household supplied with all those grain products can be challenging. But think of all the food additives and energy-intensive manufacturing, packaging, and transportation that that effort replaces: It represents all that is wrong with our outlook on food, all the bad things we are doing to the planet and to our bodies.

Before learning to bake, I was buying whole wheat bread from a local bakery that used only a few pure ingredients. But I was paying six dollars a loaf, and the grains weren't even local. Now a loaf of bread costs me about fifty cents. Plus, I don't have to make a trip to the bakery, with its window counters full of saucer-sized cookies that tempt both me and my children.

Not long into my bread-making adventures, I started wondering about the age, nutritional content, growing conditions, and high price of the flour I was using. The more I looked into that store-bought flour (even whole wheat, "organic" flour), the less enamored of it I became.

So I took the next logical step: purchasing a grain mill, finding local sources for heirloom grains, and baking my own. It turned out to be both easy and economical—and what a difference it made in my breads!

Baking with your own locally sourced flour, especially if you grind it yourself, will probably be the single biggest food change you make (and have the greatest financial benefits). It's also rewarding and fun. But, more important, it may be your gateway to opting out of processed foods. *(AC)*

. . . .

OPPORTUNITIES FOR CHANGE
GRAINS

🌾 Buy organic bread from a local bakery.

🌾🌾 Buy whole-grain flour, bake your own bread.

🌾🌾🌾 Buy a grain mill, source local grains, grind your own flour, bake your own bread.

. . . .

why you should grind your own flour

Fee-fi-fo-fum,
I smell the blood of an Englishman.
Be he alive or be he dead,
I'll grind his bones to make my bread!

In medieval times, it was a common occurrence to grind bones along with grain in order to stretch flour. And even today, store-bought flour is likely to contain more than just grain: In the United States, a regulated percentage of bug parts and rodent hairs is allowed in all ground flour.

Grain is a commodity in the United States—grown on mono-crop farms and sold to the cooperative running the grain elevator. Mingled with grain from other farms, it sits in the silo until beckoned by the call of the mill. Having perhaps come in damp from the field, it may begin to mold, before being fumigated to prevent that mold from spreading throughout the silo. In the meantime, the grain's sweet smell attracts bugs and rodents. One can only hope that inspectors will spot most of the moldy kernels, bugs, and rodent hairs before milling.

Then there is the question of oxidation. You've seen what happens to an apple when you cut into it: Immediately it begins to oxidize, turning brown before your eyes. Just like that apple, once the bran is removed and the germ separated from the surrounding endosperm of a grain berry, flour begins to oxidize and its volatile oils begin to dissipate.

Twenty-five years ago, coffee grinders were rare; we all drank canned, preground coffee unquestioningly. Today many coffee drinkers keep coffee grinders at home, and espresso drinkers consider them a necessity. What changed? Among other things, Starbucks showed American coffee consumers the value of grinding fresh coffee beans, and I tip my latte to them. Grocery stores now carry an overwhelming variety of coffee, by region or blend or flavor or roast, water or chemically decaffeinated, "fair trade," shade grown, organic. We've come a long way from the cans of Folgers, Yuban, and Chock Full o'Nuts that once lined those shelves.

Unfortunately, the grain industry has no similarly passionate champion. Thanks to federal subsidies on traditional wheat, we don't pay fair trade prices for grains. Few people know of heritage grains like spelt, emmer, and einkorn. No one has stood up to show you the value of grinding grain at home. We hope to do that in this book.

When you grab a bag of flour off a grocery store shelf, you support the grain elevator. But when you buy your grain from a local farmer and grind it yourself, you help that farmer remain independent of the elevator, allowing him to set his own price, to choose which heirloom grains to raise, and even to choose organic growing over conventional. Buying your own grains also keeps you aware of their age; you can grind your flour and use it before it begins to oxidize.

For many people the idea of a home grain mill is farfetched. So when I show them mine, with its simple hopper at the top for the kernels (picture a large funnel) and the opening at the bottom where the flour pours into my waiting bowl, they almost seem disappointed. It's simpler than a coffee grinder and just about as loud, and it will save you more money than any other appliance in your kitchen. At my neighborhood grocery store, organic whole-wheat flour costs about a dollar sixty per pound. But I can buy organic wheat berries for fifty cents per pound (or less) from a local farmer, and he's happy to get that price because it's miles above what the grain elevator pays him.

In my own small way, I am creating an heirloom grain industry, providing local grain farmers a fair living, maximizing nutrition and food purity, and saving a load of dough. By grinding my own flour and making my own bread, crackers, and pancakes from scratch, I avoid contributing to the mountain of packaging and food additives, the distribution of products, and the waste that then needs to be carted off and dumped or recycled.

If you make only one change in your food-buying habits, do this: Learn to bake. Find a farmer to sell you grain. Grind your own. *(AC)*

grinding your own

Once I had decided to bake bread using my own home-ground flour, I needed to find a grain mill. After many late nights of online research, I ordered Jupiter Mill (also called a Family Grain Mill; see Resources, page 370) with a motorized base and an optional manual crank. I chose this particular grinder because of its small footprint, since I have a tiny kitchen. I also love that it allows me to grind grains into flour or merely crack them into cereal, like steel-cut oats. It has an optional flaker attachment that lets me roll grains into flakes like oatmeal, and a manual crank that the kids like to use.

But quiet she's not. Imagine the high-pitched whir of a vacuum cleaner overlaid with a lot of cracking and grinding noises. It's enough to send my husband running for the basement and start the kids shouting that they can't hear themselves. She works great, though, and is a nice, compact appliance that I now can't imagine being without.

Once I ordered my grinder, I realized I had no clue where to get the grains or what to do with them. So I placed a large order with Bob's Red Mill, which wasn't local for me, but it was organic and the bulk prices were amazingly cheap (see Resources, page 370).

The shipment arrived before the grain mill, and the box weighed eighty pounds. I was

Hand cranking—fun for kids, but definitely a novelty. If you want efficiency, go electric.

floored at how much grain I got for a mere hundred dollars. After having paid six dollars a loaf for whole wheat bread, this was a boon.

As I baked my way through that first order of grains from Bob's, I followed a rabbit trail of local grains, from emails to farming extension offices to interviews with local farmers, then online searches, then phone calls to friends of farmers and friends of friends of farmers. I even contacted local bakeries purporting to use local grains and begged them for the farmers' names. Soon I was fairly well versed on which grains grew in Washington State, and was regularly meeting René of Lentz Spelt Farms in a grocery store parking lot to score fifty-pound bags of local heirloom grains from him.

My friend Joshua also has two small children and also has struggled with buying processed food for them. He's an avid gardener and canner who values real food. When I told him about my stash of grain and my grinder, he asked to come tour my food stores, check the grinder out, and pick my brain.

Joshua came on a rainy Wednesday. We chatted about grains—what to do with things like dent corn, emmer, spelt, kamut, barley, oats, and rye; the different types of wheat (soft, winter, spring, white, red); and where to get them locally.

I took Joshua to my utility room in the basement, where I house my treasured stores of grains. "It's so simple!" he remarked on seeing it. On the floor is a row of five-gallon buckets. Each sports a different-color lid, to identify the grains I buy in twenty-five- or fifty-pound increments: hard red wheat for bread, soft wheat for muffins and scones, spelt for pancakes and cookies, hard white wheat for pizza dough, and oats and emmer for crackers and hot breakfast cereal.

I spun the top off of one of the bins and invited Joshua to fill a Mason jar. He plunged it in. It disappeared under the grains, and then came up a few seconds later full of golden treasure. One by one I opened the other bins, showing him how each kind of grain had its unique shade, shape, scent, and flavor. Even though I didn't grow those grains myself, I had bought them from a local farmer, and I knew their history and the land on which they were grown. I felt connected with them in a way I could never feel about a box of store-bought crackers.

My grain stores make me feel rich and self-sufficient. I sometimes imagine that if, like the Ingalls family in *The Long Winter*, we were snowed in for seven months, we could survive on nothing but pancakes and bread from these grains.

To seal the deal, I sent Joshua home with some freshly ground dent corn grown in Dufur, Oregon. I knew that, once he discovered how sweet and pure freshly ground corn tastes, he would be hooked. *(AC)*

grain mills: a worthwhile investment

A week after meeting with Annette, after adding and deleting it from my online shopping cart over and over again, I ordered a grain mill. It felt like a huge expense, one of those big appliances that might sit around and never be used. But my fears were unfounded: Within a month, we fell into the habit of grinding our own grain every day.

We ordered a micronizer, a type that grinds a little finer than Annette's and makes even more noise. To start us off, Annette gave us about twenty pounds of grains. When I offered to pay her she refused, saying, "That was only a few dollars' worth of grain."

Before the grain grinder, we used to eat store-bought breakfast cereal every morning. Now we make pancakes or muffins or waffles from whole grains almost every day, taking a breakfast cereal break only once or twice a week.

Every evening, I pour one-and-a-half cups of grain into the mill for tomorrow's baking. I vary my grains from day to day, dipping my scoop in emmer farro, or Black Nile Barley, or plain old soft white wheat. One day I'll add corn, the next I'll add buckwheat or spelt or oats. Every day, something different.

QUICK FACTS ABOUT GRAINS

What we mean when we say "whole grains": The complete kernel, or flour made using the complete kernel without the bran or germ removed.

How to get them

› For small quantities, look in the bulk food bins at the grocery store; they're also increasingly available at farmers markets. Remember, though, that in small quantities heritage grains can be expensive.

› Buy larger quantities (25- or 50-pound bags) directly from the farmer. Arrange a group buy with friends to get wholesale prices. You will use that entire bag before it molds. Just take the plunge and enjoy the savings. (For more information, see Resources, page 370, and "Buying Clubs and the Law," page 257.)

› If you can't find a farmer selling the kind of grain you want, buy directly from independent distributors such as Bob's Red Mill or Azure Standard (see Resources).

How much they cost

› Prices range from about 40 cents a pound for organic hard red wheat to as much as $2.50 a pound for newly revived heirloom grains.

How to store them

› For grains purchased in 25- or 50-pound bags, use 5-gallon buckets with standard pry-off lids or easy-to-remove, screw-top "gamma seal lids" (available from Azure Standard online; see Resources). Store grains purchased in 5-pound quantities in large jars with sealable lids.

› Grains will keep for years if kept in airtight, water- and insect-proof containers.

How to grind them

› Dump the grains in the mill and turn it on. In a minute or two, harvest your freshly ground flour. It's that easy! If you have recipes with weights listed, keeping a digital kitchen scale next to the grinder and weighing before grinding streamlines the process.

Flour's shelf life

› Try to use your flour within a day or two, as it begins to oxidize once ground.

I put on my protective earpieces and turn on the machine. The grains slide down the little chute. They land on the spinning micronizer blades and shatter into flour.

For the one-and-a-half minutes the grinder runs each evening, there is no conversation, only the screaming sound of this mechanical beast, with its insatiable appetite for

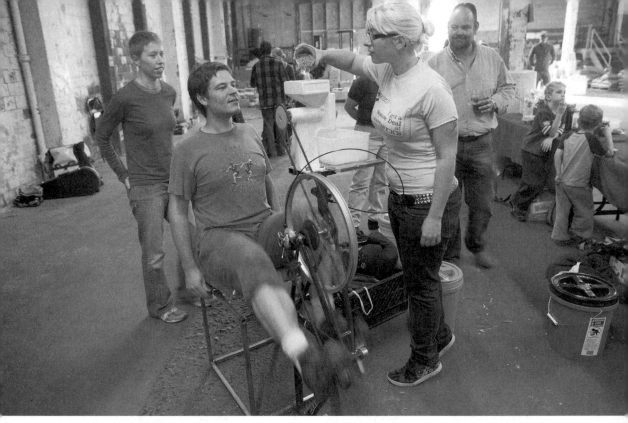

Scott Behmer hacked this hand-cranked Country Living Mill to run on bike power.

destruction and radical transformation. My kids love it. They revel in the anarchy of that nightly moment, squealing and running around upstairs. For a minute and a half their parents offer no instruction, no critique. Someone will get tickled. Prized pieces of furniture will tip over.

Then I turn the mill off and open the flour canister. The flour sits in a little mound, peaceful and quiet as freshly fallen snow. Upstairs, the tickle party ends. The kids snuggle up with their mother.

I pour the flour into the bowl of my KitchenAid mixer, where I combine it with some dechlorinated water (created by letting tap water sit around in an old milk container in the pantry) and a little whey or yogurt. I stir it briefly with a silicone spatula. A long overnight soak in a slightly acidic environment will improve the grain's texture, flavor, and nutrition. In ten or twelve hours I'll add baking powder, baking soda, salt, eggs from our backyard hens, oil, vanilla, cinnamon, and a little sugar if the kids behave. A quick beating from the KitchenAid will turn it into pancake batter.

For around a hundred days in a row, we made nothing but pancakes for breakfast. Then Gavin decided he'd had enough.

"Oh, no—are we going to have pancakes again?" he complained.

"How about muffins instead?" I asked.

"Muffins!" he squealed delightedly.

I greased some muffin tins and poured in the pancake batter.

About a hundred days later, he started complaining again. I added a little more oil to the recipe and made waffles. "Waffles!" he clapped.

Waffles turned out to be the easiest breakfast of all. No muffin tins to grease, no burned pancakes. While the waffle iron cooked them one by one, I dressed Luella, took a quick shower, put on my shoes and belt.

These days we alternate between pancakes, muffins, and waffles, often allowing our kids to choose the form. When I feel organized, I mix the baking powder, soda, salt, sugar and cinnamon beforehand, so I can save about two minutes during the morning rush to get the kids out the door. Sometimes I premix six or seven little cups' worth, so I'm ready for the whole week.

It's evening now, and my chore of preparing the grains for tomorrow is done. The whole business took me about ten minutes. I leave the soaking grains on the counter and return to the kids, now giggling and wrestling on the floor. It's my night to read bedtime stories. *(JM)*

selecting a grain mill

A good grain mill will cost you over two hundred dollars. But if you want to feed your family healthy food, it is one of the most important investments you can make. We use our mills almost every day. Grain mills come in two types: burr grinders and impact mills.

burr grinders

In this type, two coarse "stones" turn in opposite directions, just as in the old wind-powered mills of yesteryear. But unlike the old mills, these ones are compact enough to fit on your counter. Also, most of the "stones" are made of metal, textured with rough burrs. You can adjust the distance between the metal plates to change the coarseness of your flour. Burr mills produce flour a little coarser than impact mills, from bread flour to cracked grains for making hot cereals like Irish oatmeal.

Many burr grinders can accommodate alternative sources of power, but while we like having the option of going green, we don't recommend cheaper mills that rely on hand power alone. It's easy to underestimate the effort it will take to crank out flour by hand.

Recommended burr grinders:

Family Grain Mill (also sold under the name "Jupiter"). This grinder attaches to a motorized base that is sold separately. A flaker is available to fit the same motorized base, if you want to make rolled oats (you can flake just about any grain in the same way). Alternatively, skip the motor and crank it by hand. This is Annette's mill of choice, though she dreams about Country Living and KoMo mills.

Country Living Grain Mill. This hand-cranked model has a large flywheel. Handy people can attach it by belts to any power source they choose, from an old washing machine motor to a bicycle!

KoMo Mill (also known as the Wolfgang Mill). This is a beautifully made and more expensive electric grain mill from Europe. It's like a piece of fine furniture on your countertop.

impact mills

These are the micronizer-type mills that Joshua uses. They feature a series of concentric toothed metal rings that spin inside each other, like Russian nesting dolls with chainsaws. The grain doesn't stand a chance: It explodes like a pigeon in a jet engine. Of course, they're all electric—these monsters don't mess around with hand cranks. Impact mills can produce flour much finer than can burr mills, but can't do coarse grinds or cracked cereals, despite what you may read online. Fine flour isn't necessarily better; it's just a matter of taste.

Recommended impact mill:

Nutrimill. This is Joshua's mill of choice. Rugged and reliable, it's the only impact mill we can recommend without reservation. It sounds like the devil's vacuum cleaner, so don't forget ear protection.

producer profile: Lentz Spelt Farms

When René Featherstone plans a trip to Seattle, he calls those of us who organize group purchases of his grains. He usually catches me at breakfast, serving waffles to my children, waffles made with his grains. When I get off the phone, I tell my kids, "Well, that was the farmer who grew these grains. He wants to know if we need any more." My wife, Emily, and I grin at each other, then laugh. Sometimes our lives feel like a *Saturday Night Live* sketch about the local food movement.

René insists he is not a farmer. He rarely drives a tractor. But I can't help referring to him that way. He's had more impact on my diet than any farmer I know; René and Lentz

Spelt Farms brought a number of ancient grains to the Pacific Northwest and taught me why they mattered.

After leaving Germany in 1970, René spent decades living in a tepee in the American woods. He camped in Eastern Washington, he picked up work in the nearby apple orchards, and later started typing out agricultural articles on an old typewriter.

While working on a story about draft horses, he learned that the farmers fed their horses a curious grain called "spelt farro," sometimes referred to simply as "spelt." While the grain dated back to biblical times, the only people still growing it were old-school horse ranchers and the Amish. Spelt had been completely ignored by industrial agriculture. René would return to spelt later, in a big way.

René Featherstone delivering spelt farro grain to Erin Wilson.

Another theme that interested René was that of farmers who grew subsidized crops such as wheat. To make a living growing subsidized commodity crops, farmers must hold vast plantings. In the region around Lentz Spelt Farms, wheat farms average 3,000 acres. "The farmer can't pay attention to that much land," René told me, "so he cuts corners wherever he can. That's not a good way to farm." These farmers exploit the land and grow inferior grains,

grains selected to serve the white flour industry and bread manufacturers such as the makers of Wonder Bread. The system helps keep food cheap, but it doesn't make food any better.

When René joined Lena Lentz-Hardt to form Lentz Spelt Farms, he hoped to correct the problems he'd seen as an agricultural journalist. Lena had inherited 240 acres of her family's nonirrigated land, less than a tenth the size needed to profitably grow commodity wheat. René and Lena decided to grow spelt, and over many years, the pair would introduce the Northwest to one heritage grain after another, eventually expanding their operation to include many independent farmers on 800 acres. René had discovered a narrow, winding trail by which a small farmer could make a living and enjoy some self-respect. Today, several farmers grow heritage grains in Washington State. They all walk in René's footsteps.

I met René in a cafe near Seattle's Tall Grass Bakery, where he'd just delivered ten bags of spelt. "It's incredible," he said as we sat down. "All those young people in there baking with ancient grains."

I asked him to explain why bakers would like ancient grains. He drew a grain of wheat on a napkin.

"Look at a wheat kernel." René tapped his pen in the middle of the drawing. "You've got the inner part—that's called the endosperm. It's mostly carbohydrates, not much else. White flour is nothing but ground endosperm, and these other parts are thrown out. The germ, that's where most of the protein is—gone. The bran, where you'll find most of the vitamins, minerals, and antioxidants—gone. These nutritious parts, they mean little to the white flour industry. They feed them to the cows. They say, 'We can add vitamins to the mix later. Right now, we want it white, white, white.' So over the years they've been breeding a thinner and thinner bran, while pumping up the endosperm."

The whole wheat flour you buy in the grocery store corrects some of these problems. At the end of the milling process, the millers recombine some of the nutritious parts with the white flour. But once it's milled, the flour spoils quickly.

Stone-ground flour is not separated and recombined in this way, and lasts slightly longer. But neither whole wheat nor even stone-ground whole wheat addresses the core problem with modern wheat. Even if I start with the hard red wheat from which these mainstream flours originate, even if I grind that grain in my grinder at home and consume it before it spoils, I'm at the mercy of poor genetics. These wheat plants consistently thrive only when pumped up on chemical fertilizers, when protected from wheat rust by fungicides, and when isolated by herbicides. René says modern wheat is "as far removed from the ancient grains as the poodle is from the wolf."

By growing spelt farro and, later, emmer farro, René tapped into a culture dating back to ancient Mesopotamia and the dawn of civilization. Now, even as genetic engineers are promising to help wheat evolve further, René is following an even older farro grain deeper into the past, into the long slog of prehistory, the age of stone tools and woolly mammoths.

That's where you'll find the ancient grain einkorn farro, scattered around Stone Age fire rings buried under 19,000 years of sediment. Archaeologists discovered einkorn in the pockets and stomach of "Ötzi the Iceman," an Iron Age man mummified for several millennia in an ancient glacier. Ötzi fell prey to pursuers who shot him with arrows and finished him off with a heavy stone—perhaps he shouldn't have dawdled at the village storehouse, filling his pockets with einkorn.

An agricultural researcher gave René a tiny handful of einkorn seeds, not much more than Ötzi had carried, and he planted them in a small plot on Lena's farm. Over the seasons, he slowly increased his stock of the prehistoric grain. "It took a bit longer than it should have," René said. "One year, birds descended on the crop and ate all but the bottom three or four kernels from every plant. That set us back a whole year." This year, René managed to plant a few acres of einkorn farro, the first in the United States. For the first time ever, he'll have enough to sell.

All this history piqued my curiosity. I asked him: "So what do you do with einkorn?"

"We've already lost 75 percent of our food crops," he explained. "People talk about biodiversity in nature. We used to have it on the farm."

I pressed him: "But how does it taste?"

Again he dodged my question. "It's about variety. Different grains have different nutritional benefits. You wouldn't want to eat spelt every day of your life, would you? Just like you wouldn't want to eat wheat every day of your life."

"Yes, but I want to know how you cook it."

He paused for a moment. "I have no idea."

"You mean you haven't tried it yet? You're banking on selling this grain and you don't even know if it's any good?"

"Those seeds were precious," he said. "We had to save every one, until this year."

I wasn't satisfied, so he continued. "Einkorn is already popular in Europe. This is what happened with spelt twenty years ago: It gained a reputation in Europe, and then spread here to the United States."

René once told a reporter for *The Furrow* magazine that people don't want to just buy a product anymore, they want a story. I like a good story too. I asked René to reserve me a fifty-pound bag of einkorn. (*JM*)

a guide to grains

Rye can be cooked whole and used in grain salads, soups, and risottos. When flaked, it can be cooked as a hot cereal or ground to make crackers. Rye is lower in gluten than wheat, so 100 percent rye bread will come out dense and crumbly but taste wonderful. Used traditionally in pumpernickel and Swedish *limpa*.

Oats can be flaked into oatmeal, cracked for unrolled, coarse-cut groats ("steel-cut" or Irish oats), or ground for unleavened baked goods like pancakes and scones. Annette adds a few cups of ground oats to her sandwich bread recipe to sweeten it. Oats contain very little gluten, so add them sparingly to yeasted items such as bread.

Barley has a sweet flavor, especially when roasted. Make sure you purchase hulled barley, as it sometimes is sold with the hull (you need not remove the hull for sprouting). Barley makes a lovely addition to soft white wheat graham crackers, scones, and cookies, and can be cooked whole and added to soups and stews. Avoid pearl barley, as it lacks the germ and much of the bran.

Purple hull-less barley can go directly from farm to table without being processed, since its thin hull may be eaten. If you find this rare grain, give it a try. Lentz Spelt Farms sells a related grain under the name "Black Nile Barley."

Hard white wheat is high in gluten, so it makes excellent yeasted breads. The white wheat has a sweeter flavor and slightly less color than red wheat. Because of this, it may be easier to transition your family from white flour to flour made from whole white wheat by substituting hard white wheat for 25 percent of the all-purpose flour your yeasted bread recipe calls for. Over time, increase the percentage of whole wheat flour. Annette prefers this grain for pizza dough and sweet rolls.

Hard red wheat also contains a high amount of gluten. Annette prefers this grain for yeasted sandwich bread. It makes a nutty and sweet-tasting, high-rising loaf with a full-bodied wheat flavor.

Soft white wheat contains much lower gluten levels and thus is better as a pastry flour, when you want your baked goods flaky, crispy, or chewy like a cookie and not springy like bread. Substitute this for all-purpose flour in any unyeasted item.

Spelt farro is one of three ancient hulled grains that once nurtured civilizations but have been completely overlooked by modern agriculture. This omission is due to slightly more complicated processing requirements and slightly lower yields than wheat. The other two grains in this class are emmer farro and einkorn farro (see below). Spelt has a sweet taste that lends itself well to pancakes, waffles, and cookies. It can be cracked and cooked as a hot

René inspecting his grains.

cereal, cooked whole for grain salads or soups, or ground into flour. It can be used to make bread, but unlike wheat it will tolerate only about 4 minutes of kneading before the delicate gluten breaks down. It also makes a much denser, crumbly loaf. Annette prefers this grain for pancakes and cookies.

Emmer farro has a nutty taste and makes a wonderful cracked-grain hot cereal. It can be cooked whole in the style of a risotto, added to hard wheat in bread recipes, or used to make pasta.

Einkorn farro is the most recently revived of the three ancient hulled grains. And frankly, because it is only just now becoming available, we can't tell you much about it yet. Keep an eye on Annette's website, www.SustainableEats.com, for recipes using einkorn.

Kamut is a patented variety of wheat that predates modern wheat breeding. Like emmer, it makes nice pasta.

Buckwheat is not a grain at all but the triangular seed of a broad-leafed plant related to rhubarb. It used to be common in the United States but fell out of favor when it failed to respond well to modern nitrogen fertilizers. Toasted, it has a nutty flavor favored for French crêpes and makes a wonderful addition to pancakes or cookies. Buckwheat contains no gluten.

Dent corn can be nixtamalized and cooked in posole or ground in a food processor to make masa for tortillas or tamales. Nixtamalization is a traditional process similar to the soaking process we use (see "Unlocking the Nutrition in Your Grains," below), but it involves a basic medium (pickling lime and water) rather than an acidic medium, to draw nutrients from insoluble plant fibers. Dent corn can be ground into cornmeal or cracked into polenta.

. . . .

WEIGHING GRAINS—AN OPTION FOR PERFECTIONISTS

Because grains have different sizes and shapes, and flours can be ground to different levels of fineness, you cannot rely on measuring cups to provide you with an accurate measure of home-ground flour. If you prefer precision in your recipes, you may wish to invest in a small digital kitchen scale (under twenty dollars). Weight provides a more accurate measure than volume, and this will allow you to weigh grains before grinding, so you grind only what you need.

The following list shows how widely the weight of one cup of grain can vary, depending on how it's processed.

Product	Weight
Hard red wheat berries, unground	6.2 ounces
Hard red wheat flour, finely ground in a Jupiter, or Family Grain Mill	4.85 ounces
Hard red wheat flour, coarsely ground in a Nutrimill	4.41 ounces
Hard red wheat flour, finely ground in a Nutrimill	3.7 ounces
Hard red wheat flour, store-bought	4.3 ounces

Most of our baking recipes provide both weights and volumes so you can measure flour in the way most comfortable for you. We follow a 4.85 ounces-per-cup standard, since we recommend the Jupiter (Family Grain Mill) above other grinders. To use freshly ground flours in recipes from cookbooks that do not provide flour weights, begin by assuming the recipe is based on a store-bought weight of 4.3 ounces. This will give you a target weight to shoot for, rather than the less accurate target volume.

. . . .

unlocking the nutrition in your grains

By selecting heritage whole grains and grinding them yourself, you'll end up with more nutrients in your flour. But your body can't benefit from those nutrients unless you properly prepare your grains and flours by soaking or sprouting them. To understand why, you need to know something about what happens to those grains in nature.

Shelling and drying backyard corn.

> Grains are seeds.

> Seeds must be protected as they go through an animal's digestive tract.

> Chemical compounds in the seed help it resist digestion as it passes through an animal. The most significant of these compounds is known as phytic acid.

> Phytic acid breaks down naturally as a seed prepares to germinate. This allows the developing seedling to access the store of nutrients present in the seed.

> In our own bodies, phytic acid can create indigestion and inflammation and can prevent absorption of many of the nutrients in seeds.

> By artificially creating conditions right for germination, we can break down these chemical compounds manually, unlocking the nutrition in our grains and flours. Here are our favorite methods for making our grains and flours as nutritious as possible:

Soaking in an acidic medium: Soaking grains in an acidic medium overnight breaks down phytic acid. Acidic mediums can include buttermilk, yogurt, whey, lemon juice, or vinegar, often diluted in water. Because we use most of our grains for baking, we generally soak our grains as flour overnight after grinding them. (See "Power Pancakes," below, for an example of how to soak flour.)

Sprouting: This method follows nature's path by simply letting the seeds germinate. After they sprout little tails, you can dry them and grind them into flour. However, sprouting is a little more work, so we save it for special occasions (see "Making Sprouted Grain Flour," below). *(JM)*

making sprouted grain flour

When making leavened breads and griddle-fried foods, it's easy to unlock the grain's nutrients by soaking the flour the night before. But when you bake things with little added liquid, like cookies and crackers, it's a different story. I've found that low-liquid recipes work best if you first sprout your grains, dry them, and then grind them into flour.

As with soaking, sprouting breaks down phytic acid and releases nutrients. But it also increases protein quality and essential fatty acids, so I find it well worth the time it takes. If you can't manage to do this yourself, you can find sprouted flour online, or, to keep costs down, purchase it through buying clubs. One benefit of a buying club is that you can split a large bag of flour with others, and so go through your supply much faster. That is good, since grain degrades in quality once ground into flour.

I typically sprout flour for cookies and muffins, so I use soft white wheat grain; however, you can make sprouted flour from any grain. Here's how:

1. Cut a piece of fine mesh screen that will fit over the mouth of a quart-size canning jar.
2. Place 2 cups of grain in the jar.
3. Place a screen over the jar's mouth, and secure it with the jar's screw-on ring.
4. Add enough water to rinse the grain, swirling to moisten thoroughly.
5. Tip the jar upside down and drain the water.
6. Set the upside-down jar in a bowl (to catch any further drips) and leave it on a countertop or windowsill.
7. Repeat rinsing twice daily.

In a day or two, you should see little tails emerging from your grains. Once this happens, spread the grains on a cookie sheet, and dry them, at your oven's lowest possible temperature, until they feel hard to the touch. This can take up to 8 hours, so it's nice to make a large batch. (You can also dry the grains in a dehydrator.) Once the grains are dry, store them in a jar in the freezer until you are ready to grind them. *(AC)*

grain recipes

Power Pancakes
Makes about 24 pancakes
At my house, we call these "power pancakes" because they are as nourishing as it gets: free-range eggs, whole grain, and coconut oil, with the grain soaked in buttermilk overnight to maximize nutrients. My son Lander (a.k.a. "Pancake Boy") swears by them.

This recipe makes a *lot* of pancakes, because, well, why wouldn't you? They freeze fabulously and can be popped into a toaster if fruit or cocoa nibs weren't added, or a toaster oven if they were. One nice thing about soaking the flour is that you don't have to worry so much about toughening up the batter if you overmix it: The gluten has already developed and rested, so it's a little more flexible. We prefer the nutty, sweet flavor of spelt for pancakes, but you can make this recipe using any combination of grains. Each grain will have its own unique flavor profile—we hope you will have fun experimenting with them all!

2 cups (about 9.75 ounces) any combination soft wheat, oat, or spelt flour
2 cups buttermilk
2 tablespoons organic cane sugar
2 teaspoons baking powder
1 teaspoon baking soda

¼ teaspoon sea salt
½ cup coconut oil or butter, melted
4 free-range eggs

1. Mix flour and buttermilk, and let sit covered on counter for 12 to 24 hours.
2. When buttermilk and flour mixture is ready, combine sugar, baking powder, baking soda, and sea salt in a small bowl.
3. In another bowl, beat together melted oil and eggs.
4. Make a well in the middle of the batter, and stir in eggs and oil until combined. (After the overnight soak, the batter will be almost gelatinous and difficult to mix with the other items.)
5. Sprinkle dry-ingredient mixture evenly over surface of batter, and stir to thoroughly incorporate. Note: The leavener will begin to bubble immediately, so leave this step until you are ready to cook. Adjust batter to desired consistency by adding water, buttermilk, or flour.
6. Heat a cast-iron skillet or griddle over medium heat. When a drop of water sizzles on skillet, grease with additional butter or coconut oil. Ladle batter onto skillet. Add fruit, nuts, berries, or cocoa nibs, if desired, by gently pressing them into batter.
7. When edges begin to bubble and bottoms are brown, flip pancakes and cook for a couple more minutes.

Whole Grain Sandwich Bread

Makes 2 loaves bread

This is an extremely forgiving loaf with a nice crumb structure and a sweet whole-wheat flavor. You can substitute spelt, rye, or ground oat groats (another name for oat berries) for up to one-half of the hard wheat. If you go much beyond that, though, your bread will become crumbly and dense.

Play around with the ingredients to get the flavor, structure, and schedule you prefer. Raw honey will make your loaf denser, while sugar will make it lighter. Buttermilk or kefir will give your bread more of a tang than the whey and milk. Using less yeast will lengthen the rising time, reducing the gluten and giving you a longer-keeping bread with a different flavor profile. A finer grind of flour will give you a taller, lighter loaf, while a coarser grind produces denser bread that makes for sturdier sandwiches.

This recipe calls for both a sponge (a bit of dough with yeast added to it) and a soaker (a mixture of flour, liquid, and, in this case, salt). The sponge, also called a pre-ferment, begins an overnight fermentation process that activates enzymes and develops the loaf's flavor.

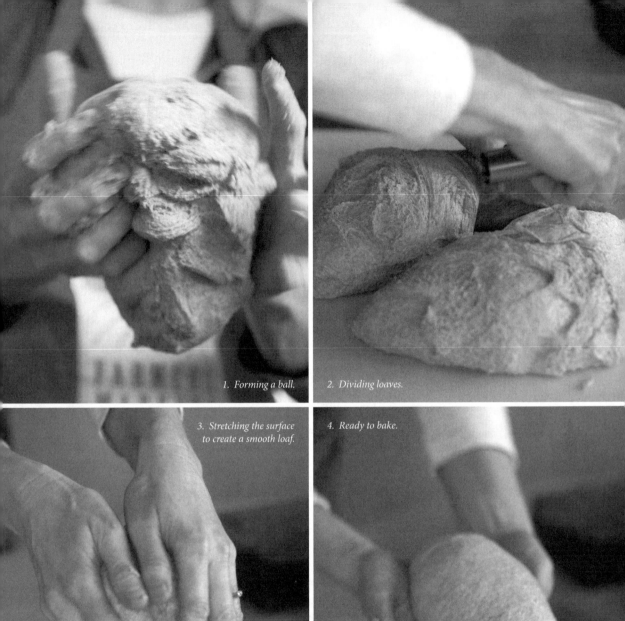

1. Forming a ball.

2. Dividing loaves.

3. Stretching the surface to create a smooth loaf.

4. Ready to bake.

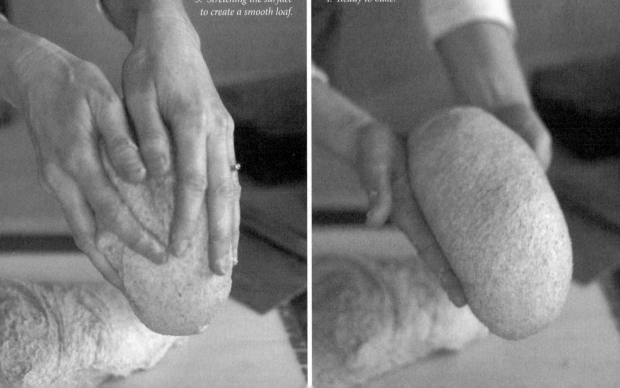

The soaker hydrates the full-fiber flour and improves the texture of the loaf, but we have added enough salt to the soaker to thwart premature enzyme activity. Enzymes are tiny digesters that turn starch molecules into simple sugars. By slowing down the enzyme activity, you ensure there will be plenty of starch left for the yeast in the pre-ferment to feast on when the sponge and soaker are combined in the morning. If you don't somewhat thwart this activity during the overnight soak, there would not be enough structure left in the morning to support a lovely rise. It is a little more work to make two doughs, but I've tried this recipe every which way, and I can assure you that making a separate sponge and soaker will take your bread to new heights. It's well worth the extra few minutes.

This makes two 9-inch loaves or three 8-inch loaves. You can also use the dough to make hamburger buns, cinnamon rolls, or breadsticks.

For the soaker

 1½ cups minus 2 tablespoons milk
 2 tablespoons whey or vinegar (or substitute one-half buttermilk, yogurt, or kefir for
   milk and whey for a tangier bread)
 3½ cups (about 17 ounces) whole grain flour (I use hard red wheat)
 1 teaspoon sea salt

Combine all ingredients. Cover bowl with a plate and let sit on the counter overnight.

For the sponge

 3½ cups (about 17 ounces) whole grain flour (I use half hard red wheat and half rye,
   spelt, or emmer)
 ¼ teaspoon yeast
 1½ cups filtered water
 2 tablespoons whey or vinegar

1. Combine all ingredients in the bowl of a stand mixer. Using dough hook, knead for several minutes until dough forms. Turn off mixer, let rest for 5 minutes to allow dough to hydrate, then knead for 1 more minute. (This gives the high-fiber flour a chance to absorb the liquid.)
2. Cover bowl with a plate and refrigerate overnight.

If you won't be making bread the next day, the soaker and sponge will keep in the fridge for several days. But be sure to allow a few hours for them to reach room temperature before using.

For the finished loaf

    1 quantity soaker
    1 quantity sponge
    1 teaspoon sea salt
    2 tablespoons butter (optional)
    Up to 5 tablespoons honey or organic cane or brown sugar, to taste
    2¼ teaspoons instant yeast

1. Combine all ingredients in the bowl of a stand mixer. If you are using honey you may need up to an extra cup of flour. Begin with the quantities in the recipe and add just enough extra flour to make the dough manageable. Using dough hook, knead for 6 to 8 minutes. (Alternatively, knead by hand for 10 to 15 minutes.) Wait until kneading is about two-thirds done before adding more water or flour to modify texture. Dough should stick to your hands a tiny bit but remain easy to knead by hand. If using a mixer, dough should stick to bottom of bowl but not sides and once it has formed a cohesive mass will begin to develop "arms" near the top of the dough mass. If your dough does not have stubby arms it will not have enough structure to support a high rise—add more flour a bit at a time until you see stubby arms appear while the mixer is running

2. Check final dough by performing a "windowpane test" with a small piece. Dough should be elastic enough to stretch, creating a window you can see light through without tearing. This ensures the gluten in the bread has developed enough to create a nice loaf.

3. Shape dough into a ball and return to bowl. Cover with a plate and let rise in a draft-free place. (I let mine rise in the oven with the light on for warmth, but you can also let it rise on the counter; it just takes longer.) Dough is ready when you can poke your finger into it and the indentation does not immediately fill in. Mine takes about 1½ hours for the first rise in a 66°F house. If you find it is taking too long for you, next time try increasing the amount of yeast.

4. After first rise, shape loaves (see photos on page 43), then cover with tea towel and let rise again, about 45 minutes. (They will continue to rise in the oven.)

5. Remove tea towel and turn oven on at 350°F. Once oven is up to temperature, set a timer for 35 minutes, for a rough idea of when bread should be done. Place bread in oven (if it's not there already). When there is 5 minutes to go on the timer, brush top of both loaves with a little water, then continue baking. When loaves cool they will have softer crusts, more like store-bought loaves. Loaves are done when they are

richly browned and sound hollow when thumped on the bottom. The edges should pull away from the sides of the pan slightly, like a cake does, and a thermometer stuck into the loaf bottom should register 190° to 195°F.

6. Remove loaves from pans and cool completely on a wire rack before slicing.

With experience, you'll figure out how high the loaves should get before baking. For example, if your bread develops large holes in the top, you'll know you let it rise too long. A too-dense crumb, on the other hand, means it did not rise long enough. You may end up with several loaves that are only good for making breadcrumbs, bread pudding, or croutons, but the value of the experience you gain is immeasurable. If you do happen to let the bread rise too long, try slashing the tops with a serrated knife before baking, to keep them from rising any more.

Homemade bread will last for several days and then may start to mold, so be sure to pre-slice and freeze any bread you don't plan on eating within that time frame. You can pop it in the toaster to thaw and/or toast when you want it.

. . . .

NO TIME TO BAKE? ADAPT YOUR BREADMAKING SCHEDULE TO SUIT YOU

Even if you're short on time, there are things you can do to fit homemade bread into your schedule. Any of these three strategies can give you more control over your bread-making timetable:

› Use a bread machine (see "Joshua's Bread Machine Loaf," below).
› Decrease the amount of yeast in the recipe, increase the amount of salt, or lower your rising temperatures. All these steps will result in a slower rising loaf.
› Try turning your overnight soak into a workday soak. When you get home from work, mix your dough and let it go through the first rise. Shape the loaves when the dough looks ready, then put them in the refrigerator until you get home from work the next night. Move them directly from the refrigerator into the hot oven (but please not in glass bread pans, since the change in tempera-ture might crack them!). Your bread will take a few more moments to cook this way but should otherwise come out fine. Note that for a longer rise like this you will want to use sugar instead of raw honey to sweeten the dough: Raw honey (much like cinnamon) will impede a nice rise.

Joshua's Bread Machine Loaf
Makes 1 loaf bread
This recipe takes some cues from Annette's techniques and radically simplifies them for a bread machine. The resulting loaf is rustic and dense, but also flavorful and packed with nutrients.

3½ cups (17 ounces) freshly ground hard red wheat flour
Pinch yeast plus ¼ teaspoon yeast (use "instant" or "bread machine yeast")
2 tablespoons honey

3 tablespoons whey OR 2 tablespoons vinegar plus 1 tablespoon filtered water
1 cup room-temperature water
1 tablespoon oil, such as olive oil
1 teaspoon salt

› In the early evening, stir all ingredients except ¼ teaspoon of the yeast and salt into a bowl. Mix until it forms a ball. Dump the dough ball into the bread machine pan. Now the dough is ready to soak overnight.
› Add salt to top of dough, forming it into a little volcano. Inside volcano, put remaining ¼ teaspoon yeast. Set bread machine to Whole Wheat setting, and adjust timer so that bread will be completed when you wake up in the morning.

Troubleshooting: Baking bread by hand allows you to correct dough moisture as you go along, but with bread machines, we tend to start the program and walk away, leaving overly dry or wet doughs to bake into bricks or burst like balloons. Measuring flour by weight rather than volume can resolve many bread machine problems. Also, remember every bread machine is different—you may need to experiment in order to adapt the recipe to your machine.

. . . .

100% Whole Wheat Pizza Crust

Makes 4 medium-size pizza crusts

Pizza is one of those compromise foods we make as a family. I'm pretty picky about it: I like it in Rome and Florence, and I liked it from Seattle's now-defunct Fremont Trattoria, a neighborhood joint. Generally, though, you can pretty much keep your pizza, as far as I'm concerned.

But since my family loves pizza, I've been working on it for years. I want a crust that uses 100 percent whole-wheat flour but doesn't overpower the toppings (which should be minimal). I want the crust to be crunchy on the bottom but still have some toothiness and chew, and I want it thin but with pockets. I want the toppings to change frequently, since I don't like to eat the same thing more than a few times a year. I'm not easy to please.

I think I've probably tried every pizza dough recipe I've come across and then some. Here's the one I finally settled on. It's not at all authentic, because it's whole wheat and contains a bit of oil. But I feel like it's pretty darn good.

The recipe calls for an overnight soak in an acidic medium, 100 percent hard white winter wheat flour ground as fine as possible, and it's got some nice tricks to get you good bubbles in a home oven. If the whole wheat comes across as too strong for your liking, substitute all-purpose flour for all or part of the whole-wheat flour.

4½ cups (about 21.85 ounces) hard white whole-wheat flour
2 teaspoons salt

1 teaspoon yeast

3 tablespoons of whey, combined with enough filtered water to make a total of 1¾ cups liquid

2 to 3 tablespoons olive oil (not required, but this helps tenderize the dough so it's soft inside yet crunchy on the bottom)

1. Combine flour, salt, and yeast in the bowl of a stand mixer. Add liquid and olive oil, if using, and mix using dough hook about 3 minutes, until dough comes together.
2. Turn off mixer, and let dough rest 10 minutes. Turn on mixer and knead for another minute or two. By this time, the flour will have absorbed the moisture, and you'll be able to tell if the dough needs more flour or water. It should be fairly wet and sticky—a little tricky to work with, but necessary in order to get the right texture. Leave dough in mixing bowl covered with a plate and put it in the refrigerator overnight.
3. In the morning, divide dough into 4 pieces, rubbing each one with olive oil to keep it from drying out. Place each in a small lidded container to refrigerate or freeze. If the dough has been frozen, remove it from the freezer and let it thaw in the refrigerator overnight. Remove dough from refrigerator several hours in advance to allow it to come to room temperature; otherwise, it will be difficult to work with.
4. To bake: About 30 minutes before making pizza, preheat oven (with a pizza stone in it) to the highest temperature it will reach. Mine goes to 550°F, but if you have a wood-fired oven in the backyard, 800°F is ideal.

If you are using white flour, stretching instead of rolling does make a difference, but we've found that with whole wheat it really doesn't matter. What does matter is that you get your dough as thin as possible by hook or crook. We sprinkle our pizza peel with semolina to keep the dough from sticking, and then roll it out as thin as possible.

I prefer pizza dough with a crispy bottom and just a bit of softness inside, ideally with nice bubbles. But you don't want bubbles so large that you end up with pita bread, so the secret with 100 percent whole-wheat dough is to gently dock (poke holes in) your crust with a fork and prebake it naked (without toppings).

Once your dough is sufficiently rolled and docked, use a deft flick of the wrist to shake it off the peel and onto the preheated pizza stone. If that doesn't go so well the first time, keep at it—eventually it will work. Prebake the dough for 3 minutes, remove it from the oven, and poke any bubbles that approach pita bread size with a fork. Then add toppings.

Pizza sauce doesn't have to be the traditional tomato-and-oregano kind. Try cheesy white sauce, garlicky olive oil, taco sauce, or barbecue sauce to complement seasonal toppings. Hold off on any fresh toppings that will singe in the oven, such as basil or other leaves, fresh herbs, or fresh tomatoes.

Return the dressed pizza to the oven and bake for another 3 minutes, until the cheese is bubbly and the bottom is darkened and crunchy. Remove it from the oven, then top it with the fresh ingredients. Let the pizza sit for 5 minutes before slicing, to meld the flavors and set up.

Crisp Whole Grain Crackers
Makes two sheets of crackers
These crackers come together easily and are reminiscent of Partners crackers made in Kent, Washington. This is a large recipe, so either bake half the dough now and freeze the rest for later, or bake it all and freeze half the finished crackers.

> 2½ cups (about 12 ounces) sprouted (or unsprouted) hard wheat, spelt, or emmer flour
> 2 tablespoons organic sugar
> 1 teaspoon salt
> 1 teaspoon instant yeast
> ¾ cup filtered water

1. Combine flour, sugar, salt, and yeast in the bowl of a stand mixer.
2. Add water, and knead using a dough hook until you have a smooth dough. You may need to add a tablespoon or two more water, but the dough should be fairly stiff.
3. Divide dough into 3 balls, and cover them with an overturned bowl when not working with them.
4. Preheat the oven to 350°F. Line a baking sheet with a silicon mat or parchment paper, then roll dough as thinly as possible to cover. Personalize them, if you like, by sprinkling dough surface with salt, seeds, or herbs and then rolling them in. Poke holes all over the dough with a fork, then let rise for about 30 minutes.
5. Once dough has risen for 30 minutes, use a ravioli cutter or pastry scraper to cut into squares or diamonds. Bake for 20 minutes, until crackers are crisp and edges begin to brown. Turn off oven but leave crackers in for another 15 minutes to further crisp.

Because these contain no preservatives, they will last just a few days stored in a sealed container, and it is best to freeze them. Before serving, place frozen crackers on a cookie sheet and pop them into a 350°F oven for 5 minutes. This will crisp them back up, but watch them closely so they don't burn.

. . . .

A SIMPLE WAY TO MAKE WHEY

If you don't make cheese, you may wonder where you can get the whey called for in many of our recipes.

If you make yogurt from our recipe (see page 88), you've probably already seen whey pooling in your yogurt. To harvest whey from your yogurt, place a colander over a bowl. Line the colander with cheesecloth or a tea towel, add yogurt and place the bowl in the refrigerator. In a few hours, you'll have plenty of whey in the bowl. The yogurt in the bag will have turned to yogurt cheese, which can be used like cream cheese or quark. You can do this same thing with dairy kefir. If you don't have homemade yogurt, you can also extract whey from store-bought plain yogurt. Look for yogurts with live, active cultures, but without scientific-sounding ingredients, as these ingredients may be "binders" that prevent yogurt and whey from separating.

You can also make you own curds and whey from raw milk. See "Curds and Whey" on page 84 to learn how.

. . . .

Spelt Tortillas
Makes 12 tortillas

When my son Lander decided to add cheese quesadillas to his diet, I was ecstatic—until I read the list of ingredients on the tortilla package. I will never understand how products with partially hydrogenated oil can sport "trans-fat free" labels. Now I don't need to, thanks to Oregon blogger Wardeh Harmon, who developed this recipe. The kids love helping me roll these out. Sprinkling a small amount of rice or potato flour on the counter makes this simple for them to do.

> 6 cups (about 29 ounces) sprouted spelt flour
> 1½ teaspoons Rumford baking powder. (Rumford baking powder does not contain genetically engineered corn.)
> 1½ teaspoons sea salt
> ½ cup lard
> 2 cups filtered water

1. Put flour, baking powder, and salt in a food processor or bowl, and cut in lard until mixture resembles coarse meal. Sprinkle water over surface and mix until it forms a smooth dough. Divide dough into 12 balls and cover with a moist kitchen towel while you shape and fry them, one at a time.
2. Preheat an ungreased cast-iron skillet over medium-high heat. Roll each tortilla out as thin as possible, and fry for about 30 seconds on each side, until surface begins to blister and brown. Stack fried tortillas on a plate, covering top tortilla with a damp towel. As they steam they will become soft and pliable.

These will keep only 3 or 4 days in the refrigerator, but once they cool, you can freeze them.

chapter 2
the chicken and the egg

Once I had eliminated the need to stop by the store for a loaf of bread, I was eager to cross eggs off my grocery list. I had read a lot of arguments about why it's cheaper to buy store-bought eggs than to keep backyard hens. And that is true, as long as you are content with eggs from caged hens or from farms that keep their birds in cramped quarters and feed them genetically modified corn and soy. Sadly, even most of those "free-range, organic" eggs at the farmers market—the ones that cost five to seven dollars a dozen—cannot hold a candle to backyard eggs.

EGGS

annette's grocery list

ORIGINAL LIST

Eggs

REVISED LIST

Chicken Feed

If you're looking for the most nutrient-dense eggs possible, filled with naturally occurring omega-3 fatty acids, you want eggs from healthy hens that don't have soy or genetically modified grains in their diet, hens that have room to spread their wings and walk around in the sunlight, eating greens and bugs.

Unfortunately, you cannot buy eggs like that at any price. Most farmers markets sell pastured eggs and/or organic eggs, but none that I know of sell soy-free, organic, pastured eggs. The only way to control the contents of the laying hens' feed and the manner in which they are raised is to get your own backyard chickens.

Many cities' ordinances, including Seattle's, allow for a small flock of backyard laying hens or ducks. While I've never been much of a bird person, our family uses a lot of eggs, and there was something pleasingly pastoral about the thought of chickens in my backyard. And of course the kids were all for it. So chickens became my gateway into the world of urban livestock. *(AC)*

● ●

OPPORTUNITIES FOR CHANGE
EGGS

◯ Buy organic, free-range eggs.

◯◯ Buy organic, pastured eggs at the farmers market.

◯◯◯ Get your own chickens.

● ●

what's in an egg?

Buying eggs these days can be highly confusing. When I do venture into the store, I see eggs labeled "organic," "vegetarian," "cage-free," "natural," and "omega-3 enhanced." But what does it all mean? Let's look at the terms used to label eggs—and meat birds too.

Organic. USDA standards dictate that eggs (and meat) labeled organic must come from chickens whose feed is grown using no synthetic fertilizers, pesticides, or animal by-products. The chickens are given antibiotics only in the event of infection, and the feed cannot be genetically modified. This feed is almost certainly soy- and corn-based, but because corn is wind pollinated (meaning wind carries pollen from one plant to the next), organic corn is sometimes contaminated by pollen from conventional corn. Since 86 percent of American-grown corn is genetically modified (according to the USDA), there is a high likelihood that corn grown organically in an area where conventional corn is grown will be contaminated.

Organic chickens are required to be cage-free and have access to a small patch of outdoors, but don't assume that patch is populated with grass and bugs. Also, organic standards do not allow arsenic in chicken feed (another startling ingredient in conventional feed, which helps chickens grow faster, but readily passes into the eggs and from there into human bodies).

Vegetarian. This term means that the feed does not contain by-products of the meat industry. However, laying hens have a relatively high protein requirement, and if they're not allowed access to a continual supply of bugs or fed animal scraps, the protein must come from somewhere else, which is generally soybeans. Ninety-three percent of American-grown soybeans are genetically modified, so conventional chicken feed has a high likelihood of containing GM soy.

Cage-free, free range, pastured. None of these chickens are raised in cages—though they may be raised in a crowded warehouse. Free-range chickens also have daily access to a small yard, but that yard may well be cement, or the same overcrowded hoop house or tent that the chickens are raised in. In other words, "free range" doesn't necessarily mean the chickens have access to fresh grass, sunshine, or bugs; chickens raised on dirt or cement end up getting the majority of their diet from feed.

Natural. This label means nothing. There are currently no guidelines governing its use in marketing.

Omega-3 enhanced. These chickens are fed a diet that contains some specific source of omega-3 fatty acids. This makes them somewhat healthier than conventional eggs.

getting to yes

I ventured into the world of chicken raising very delicately at first. Whenever possible, I brought up the subject in a roundabout way with my husband, mentioning the price of eggs or the deplorable conditions laying hens typically live in. I would point out that we had no idea what those chickens were fed or what kind of access to fresh greens, bugs, and sunshine they had. I would end the conversation with something vague like, "I'd like to get chickens this spring," to which he would roll his eyes discouragingly and reply, "When we have more time."

Gradually, I started getting into the particulars of how we might convert our unused doghouse into a chicken coop by adding nest boxes. After a few months, my husband stopped replying, which I took as quasi-assent. When spring came around and the kids and I happened to be running an errand up north, I rationalized, "Hey, we're practically to Monroe" (a small, rural town north of Seattle)—even though we were still twenty miles away.

We drove to the Monroe feed store just to see what kind of chicks they had, and one hour later, we were Seattle-bound with a box full of chirping chicks, a bag of feed, a bag of wood chips, some grit, and a chick-sized plastic water and feed container. I had spent around forty dollars on equipment and birds.

We borrowed a warming light from a neighbor and situated the chicks on the dining room table, in a cardboard box with a chicken wire roof. The kids immediately set about naming them: Pot Pie, Drumstick, Wishbone, and McNuggett (who later turned out to be a rooster).

When, instead of the smell of dinner cooking, my husband came home to the scent of pine shavings and baby chicks, he realized my food journey wasn't going to stop at garden boxes and grain mills.

Our girls grew quickly, their peeps getting louder by the day. Likewise, our dog grew increasingly frantic, circling the dining room table, overturning dining room chairs, and leaving trails of saliva on the floor. Eventually I got tired of the relentless peeps waking me in the wee hours and the overturned furniture, so we moved the chicks into the utility room downstairs.

At around five weeks old, they went outside for good.

We cleaned out our old wooden doghouse (long since rejected by the dog) and, using scrap lumber, bumped out nest boxes. We covered up part of the original front opening to make a chicken-size door, then attached another board (for a working door) with hinges and a latch. We cut a clean-out door into the back and built a raised platform to elevate the house so I didn't need to bend down to clean it out. The platform also provided a dry place to put the feeder under. Finally, my husband built a ramp from an old two-by-four, with cross ties made from leftover floor molding, to help the chickens get in and out of their coop. He notched the top of it so it attached firmly inside the front door opening. We remove it each night to close and lock the door when we "tuck the chickens in." I suspended tree branches inside for roosts, installing them with closet rod holders.

A well-handled chick will grow into a patient hen.

After two days and about twenty more dollars, our chickens were happily housed in their new home. We hung out on the patio watching as the hens pecked gleefully away at the lawn. Now all we had to do was wait for the eggs. *(AC)*

a rude awakening: chicken noises and neighbors

"What are you doing?" Emily asked.

"Oh, I'm just perusing this list of heritage chicken breeds."

This was a lie. I was not perusing, I was consuming, with every ounce of my soul, every word about every chicken breed known to mankind. There were the huge Brahmas, with their fluffy feathered feet; beautiful tiny Japanese bantams, with long tail feathers; the classic American Barred Rock, with its beautiful black-and-white stripes, developed by a man who attempted to seize control of the Mormon church after Joseph Smith's assassination. And there was the Rhode Island Red, the only chicken to achieve the status of state bird. Chickens had come a long way from their roots as jungle fowl.

To make space for my coop, I sank a few hundred dollars into renting jackhammers and concrete saws to bust up part of my driveway. Once construction began, I sawed wood late into the night, calling it quits only when my neighbor's bedroom light finally switched off, just the other side of the fence.

One rainy spring day, I drove two-year-old Gavin to the feed store in nearby Woodinville. Inside, a crowd was gathered around the giant galvanized feed troughs full of chicks. We chose three healthy-looking ones: a Buff Orpington, a Barred Rock, and a Rhode Island Red. We drove home with three tiny chicks inside a box beside Gavin's car seat. "I hear dem peepin' in dere!" he exclaimed.

As the hens outgrew their box in the garage and moved into their coop, their tiny peeps evolved into awkward, adolescent squawks. And then one day, at the breakfast table, we heard a loud squawk outside, as if one of the hens were being eaten alive by a raccoon. "SQUAWK! SQUAWAWAWK!!" Alarmed, I ran outside to see what was the matter. Lottie, the Buff Orpington, had hopped from her nest, leaving behind a beautiful brown egg. I removed it from the nest—still warm.

But the treasure came at some cost. Chickens can drop their daily egg at any hour. They stop only for darkness. In the summer here in the Pacific Northwest, dawn can come fairly early, and sometimes I'd wake up at five-thirty in the morning with a faint feeling of dread. A moment later I'd hear the relentless five-minute SQUAWK! indicating, *"Holy sh*t, I'm laying an egg!"*

All the beautiful magazine articles about urban chickens advise you to ply your neighbors with eggs. I complied enthusiastically, bringing my neighbor half a dozen eggs once or twice. That's why I was surprised when he appeared at my front door one day with a stack of papers about the legality of chickens. He told me he was sick and tired of the noise. He traveled a lot and needed to sleep in on weekends. "I want you to move your chicken coop," he said. Having spent hours building the coop on freezing winter nights, I didn't relish that idea. My neighbor handed me the stack of papers. I noticed a few magazine articles in the stack, including the ones that recommended offering eggs as bribes. I'd been caught!

Within a couple of weeks, I had insulated the coop, in hopes of absorbing some of the noise. I knocked on my neighbor's door, to see if he'd noticed any difference. He told me he wouldn't be happy until I moved the coop. "I just don't understand why people want to keep chickens in the city."

"For the eggs," I explained. "The eggs are better."

At this, he became visibly irritated. "That's B.S.! You can get great eggs at the farmers market for only a few dollars more. The eggs!"

A free-ranging hen looks for bugs in the lawn.

He told me that the noise ordinance required quiet until 7:00 AM on weekdays, 9:00 AM on weekends.

"I wonder," I ventured sheepishly, "if you could just keep a pair of earplugs by your bed?"

"I can't ask everyone in my house to wear earplugs!"

I looked over at my chicken coop, just behind the fence. He's right, I thought, my suggestion was a little rude. I turned back to say something. The door was already closed.

I realized that the time had come for action. The police could show up this Saturday morning with decibel meters. In desperation, I decided to cover the coop windows with a dark tarp, in hopes of tricking the hens into thinking it was night. By 8:00 AM, my family had finished a leisurely pancake breakfast. I peeked out the window at the chicken coop in the driveway: No visible activity. Not a peep.

It worked on Sunday, too. The hens seemed to operate on some sort of invisible solar panel. By keeping the tarp over the coop, I could keep them quiet as long as I liked. At 9:01, I threw off the tarp.

Over the next week, I built shutters over the windows of the chicken coop. I got in the habit of closing the hens in at night and waking them up in the morning. Every once in a while I forgot to wake them and returned home after work to find them still asleep on their roost—what that does to their biorhythms, I have no idea.

A month later, I ran into my neighbor's wife as she swept brown rhododendron leaves from our driveway.

"Do you still hear the chickens in the morning?" I asked.

"Oh, no, they don't bother me at all anymore."

I breathed a sigh of relief. *(JM)*

selecting your chickens

Chickens need companionship, so plan on buying enough chicks to end up with at least three mature hens. Three mature hens will give you between six and eighteen eggs a week, depending on breed, diet, temperament, and daylight hours.

›   Assume that roughly half your chicks will turn out to be roosters, which are illegal in many cities. You can buy sexed chicks to reduce your chances of getting a rooster, but the methods for male chick disposal are often cruel. (Ironically, it may be less cruel to eat them when they first crow.)

›   Plan what you'll do with older hens once their egg laying slows down. The stew pot is one option.

> Know the law. In Seattle you may keep eight hens and no roosters. In Portland, Oregon, three hens and no roosters. In Vancouver, B.C., Canada, four hens and no roosters. Visit www.TheCityChicken.com for more information.
> For a list of online resources to help you make your selection, see Resources.

. . . .

SHOULD YOU NAME YOUR HENS?

We named our first set of hens Lottie, Fannie, and Henny Penny. When Henny Penny died, perhaps from some poisonous weed I'd thrown her, perhaps from an egg that failed to eject properly, we let Gavin name her replacement. He chose the name Bear.

Although Bear appears to have brain damage and walks on crumpled legs, she's somewhat special to us. And not because she lays an egg every day, despite her deformity. (She achieves this humble act in the only way she can, laying her simple brown egg on the floor below the nest boxes.) No, Bear is special for another reason: She's the last hen we ever named.

When Seattle raised the legal limit on hens from three to eight, I quickly bought a supplemental batch. I thought we'd raise them in my garage until they'd grown enough to survive the brutal initiations expected from their veteran coop mates. We planned to observe them in their cardboard box and watch for the unique behaviors that would inspire us to name them. But the naming ritual never happened; we just kept putting it off. Eventually, we simply forgot about it.

I can't help thinking this was no accident. Our relationship with the hens was changing. We would still care for our hens, give them the best food we could grow and buy. I would stay up late with an egg-bound hen, massaging her vent with olive oil over a steaming pot of water, worrying that I'm accidentally massaging her butt instead of her egg-hole. But make no mistake about it, a vision had formed in my mind, a vision that betrayed the distance between our species: Someday, friend, I'm gonna eat you. *(JM)*

. . . .

making your chickens a home

Chickens need a **coop**, a **run**, and **food and water**.

the coop
Build or buy a coop that provides the following:
> Protection from rain, wind, and predators. Some ventilation is important, but you don't want wind whistling across the bodies of your sleeping hens. Keep vents up high or down low.

› About 4 square feet of area per chicken. (If your chickens have constant access to a run, the coop can be about half this size.)
› A dry roost for the chickens to sleep on. A roost looks like the rod in your closet where you hang your clothes.
› Dry, cozy nest boxes. Given the chance, chickens like to do other things besides lay eggs in the nest box (like sleep and poop), so you need to make the roosts more attractive as a place to sleep than the nest boxes. That means the roost should be significantly higher than the nest box and draft-free.
› A dry place to hang or mount the chicken feed dispenser. Alternately, the feed dispenser may be kept in the run, but only if protected from rain and predators.
› A warm place for water (or you'll be thawing it on winter mornings). In the mild Pacific Northwest, putting the water inside the coop is usually enough to keep it from freezing.

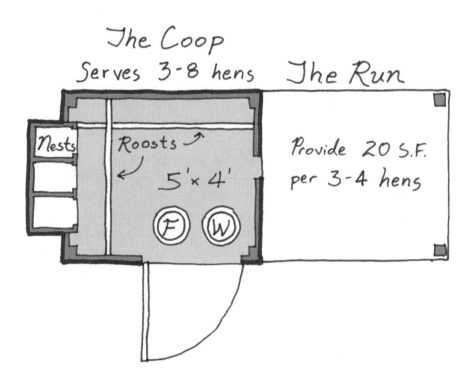

the run

The run is the hens' outdoor play and forage area; it's where they can stretch their legs and work out their petty squabbles. Create a run that provides the following:

›   Access to sunlight.

›   Room for the hens to run around. On a farm, this may be the entire farm, and in the city the run can be an entire backyard. But hens wreak havoc on garden seedlings and may be consumed by wandering predators, so you might want to enclose your run. An enclosed run should provide a minimum of 5 square feet per hen, though more is better. If you plan on using the deep litter system (see below), provide at least 6 or 7 square feet of run per bird.

›   Good drainage and/or a cover to keep out excess rain. Your hens shouldn't stand around in puddles. If you plan to use the deep litter detailed below, drainage and a roof are especially important, as wet litter is difficult for hens to dig through. Providing them with a dry place will allow them to take dust baths, which help prevent mites.

›   Protection from predators. If you plan to keep the door between coop and run constantly open, you'll want to enclose the run in half-inch galvanized hardware cloth. You'll also want to bury hardware cloth around the perimeter, extending outward about 12 inches. This will not only keep out raccoons and dogs, but also rats that would raid your chicken feed.

food and water

Chickens need different sorts of feed at different stages in their lives. When they're growing, they need extra protein and must eat "grower feed." When they're laying, they need extra calcium, and must eat "layer feed."

›   You can buy chicken feed through farm co-ops, at feed stores, and even at some pet stores. For a list of recommended outlets for buying chicken feed, see Resources, at the back of the book.

›   Supplement the feed with fresh greens from your garden (weeds are fine) and with healthy table scraps. Chickens can eat meat in moderation, vegetable peels, burnt toast, sour milk, almost everything from your kitchen. Avoid potato peels and baked goods made from white flour, which is only slightly healthier for them than sugar. Toss them a handful of grit every day or two to aid their digestion, and for strong eggshells, throw in a handful of oyster shell. (The oyster shell and grit also come from feed stores.) If your hens are allowed constant access to your yard, they will find grit on their own. Some people grow forage crops just for their chickens, as it elevates the healthiness of their eggs above and beyond anything you can buy. For a list of forage crops to grow for hens, see Plants for Livestock, page 365.

› Provide fresh water every day or two. Keeping water fresh helps protect the health of your hens.

› You can find galvanized hanging food and water dispensers at feed stores. Feed dispensers come ready to be hung, water containers do not. Drill a small hole through the handle of your water container so you can hang it in your coop by a wire, or place it on masonry blocks.

deep litter: an easier way to keep chickens

Back when I was still waiting for the day when chicks would arrive in feed stores, I obsessed about my chicken coop design. Questions would swirl around in my head, keeping me up at night until I rose and posted them on internet discussion forums. How big should the nest boxes be, and where to position them? (One cubic foot, and lower than the roosts.) Should the chickens have permanent access to the run? (Sure, as long as it's predator proof.) And so on.

Feeding scratch (treats) to the hens.

Six months later, I finished the coop (where the chickens eat, sleep, and lay eggs) and the adjacent run (where they scratch around during the day). I wrapped the whole enclosure in half-inch hardware cloth to keep out rats and raccoons, and buried an apron of the same stuff around the perimeter of the run to keep out digging raccoons and possums. It seems these predators dig straight down when they hit a wall, and when they hit metal, they give up. This simple method is so effective, it's used in zoo design to contain even the most aggressive burrowing animals.

Inside the coop, I set up the essential elements: food, water, nest box, and roost. I was clever in making the best of a tight space, or so I thought, by spanning the roost (a recycled closet rod) above everything else.

But not long after the chicks outgrew their box under a heat lamp in the garage, they proved how much I had to learn about chicken coop design. They loved their roosts—so much that they'd put themselves to bed there every night. In the morning, I'd find their food, water, and nests covered with poop.

This was a puzzle. Through trial and error, I calculated the poop zone to be within about eight inches of either side of the roost. In a coop this narrow, that would mean I needed to dedicate one end of the coop to the roost and the other to the food, water, and nests. A simple enough theory, but difficult to achieve. I remodeled the coop half a dozen times, shuffling and reshuffling the elements like the squares of a Rubik's Cube. In my dreams, chicken poop rained down like Tetris pieces.

Finally, I conceded that there just wasn't enough room, and I built a nest box that hung off the side of the coop. When I removed the old nest box from the coop, I noticed the coop floor inside. At one end of the coop, Henny Penny had dug herself a hole in the bedding and was pecking at some food she'd found there. In another corner, Lottie had dug another hole down to the dirt layer and was giving herself a dust bath, fluffing up her feathers and tossing dirt over her back to discourage parasites. As for the bedding itself, what had once been eighteen inches of mixed straw and leaves was now rich compost. This was the stuff I'd been waiting for!

Essentially, I had a working compost pile on the floor of my chicken coop. I had nitrogen from the chicken poop, and carbon from the bedding. I had ground moisture from the dirt floor below, along with worms and other decomposers. And my heritage hens, with their strong foraging instincts, kept the pile aerated by constantly digging deep into the litter in search of bugs and worms. I extended this system into my run, and today, harvest wheelbarrows-full of compost at a time.

The bedding that I harvest from my coop isn't completely composted, so I age it a bit longer before putting it on the garden. But it's much, much further along than the soiled bedding scraped from coops by my friends with more conventional coop designs and wooden floors. And whereas they must clean their coop floors every month or so, I never have to clean my coop floor. As long as I add enough carbon, it never smells.

In time, I came to understand this as the "deep litter system." I learned never to step in the coop, as this compacts the soil and makes it impossible for the chickens to dig. I learned the importance of good drainage and a solid roof in the coop and run, as chickens cannot dig in heavy, wet litter. I learned to keep plenty of fresh organic straw or leaves nearby, since chicken waste falling on bare soil begins to stink. Every fall I collect bags and bags of fallen leaves from friends and neighbors and dump them in the coop (choose small leaves, as these are easier for chickens to turn). In the summer I refresh the coop with straw. If they get lazy about digging, I toss them a little scratch. My chickens do the rest.

I use this aged, composted bedding as fertilizer for my garden. Unlike chemical fertilizers, compost releases nitrogen slowly, feeding a whole community of soil microorganisms that make soil nutrients available for plants. The soil, amended in this way, has turned rich and dark. The plants, once limited to the thin layer of soil beneath what was once lawn, now send their roots deep, following tunnels left behind by worms, worms fed in part by the organic matter in the compost.

The deep litter system can fail under certain circumstances. If the soil doesn't drain properly, or if the brown leaves you use as bedding are too big to be tossed around by chicken feet, or if the run is overcrowded with chickens, then the bedding can become matted and the chickens will not turn it. But even with the extra effort of carefully selecting light and fluffy bedding (chopped straw tossed with small leaves makes the best combination), I spend less time managing my chicken coop than many other urban chicken owners. *(JM)*

conventional chicken bedding material

If you don't want to use the deep litter method, you can always switch to conventional bedding. To raise chickens on conventional bedding, you'll want to provide a wooden floor at the bottom of the coop to keep the bedding dry, rather than the dirt floor required for deep litter. Whenever the bedding becomes wet or smelly from droppings, replace it with new bedding, adding the old stuff to the compost pile.

As for the run, even conventional chicken owners tend to use a modified version of the deep litter method, without realizing it. As with deep litter, they start with a dirt floor and add more bedding whenever the run becomes smelly. But unlike a deep litter system, these owners do not expect their chickens to turn the litter. These owners can crowd their runs with chickens a bit more, without fearing the litter will be compacted from the weight of so many hens (5 square feet of run per hen, rather than 6-7 in the deep litter system). When the litter becomes too deep, these owners start over with new bedding material, tossing the old bedding into the compost bin.

After spending four months in your compost bin, and if kept as damp as a wrung-out sponge, composted chicken bedding should be mellow enough not to "burn" plants and pathogen-free enough to use in the garden. For more on this process, refer to the composting sections in Chapter 5, "It's All in the Dirt."

bugs and worms make good eats

Chickens evolved scratching in the dirt in search of their favorite meal: bugs. But city chickens are often safest in predator-proof coops and runs, which limit their access to bugs. You can solve this problem by raising bugs or worms for your birds.

red wiggler worms: vermiculture

A worm bin is a great way to generate amazing vermicompost (a rich fertilizer for your garden, full of worm castings), vermicompost "tea" (made from vermicompost, for watering seedlings and using as a foliar spray, i.e., topical fertilizer), and worms for your chickens—all from junk mail and kitchen scraps. Worms are the ultimate in low-maintenance pets, able to fend for themselves for weeks or even months at a time.

You can make an easy worm bin by drilling small air holes into the sides of a plastic storage tub, lining the bottom with a 6-inch layer of bedding, such as bark, damp leaves, or moistened shredded newspaper (no glossy ink please), and covering that with a layer of moistened compost or dirt. Your dirt should be about as damp as a wrung-out sponge. Be sure to maintain that moisture level: Worms must have some moisture to survive, but too much will kill them.

Add red wiggler worms (see Resources, page 370), kitchen scraps, and a final 2-inch layer of shredded junk mail or leaves to discourage fruit flies. How many worms and how large a bin depends on you. If you provide them with enough food and a happy, damp home they will multiply quickly. Snap on the container lid and you are good to go. Add food scraps, coffee grounds, and junk mail on a regular basis, and periodically check the moisture level of your soil. In a few months you'll have a rich vermicompost that is ideal for adding to your seedling mix for baby spring greens and other plant starts.

To create vermicompost tea, buy two plastic storage containers of the same size (the kind that can nest). Drill small holes in the sides and bottom of one, and cover the bottom with fine-gauge screen fabric. Place two bricks or old pieces of four-by-four in the bottom of the undrilled container (to create spacing between the two), and set the drilled container inside it. Fill the top container as described above, and place a lid on it. You now have a system for producing vermicompost tea, which will collect in the bottom container. It will be so thick and rich—almost like syrup—that you'll want to dilute it by adding only a few drops to a small spray bottle filled with water.

Because red wiggler worms are not as hardy as the Northwest's native night crawlers, they cannot stand freezing temperatures. I keep my worm bin outside the backdoor after the last freeze of spring and bring it into the garage with the first frosts of fall. I don't recommend keeping it inside the house, because it's the perfect breeding ground for fruit flies, and that is one type of bug you don't want to be breeding!

To harvest worms for the chickens (or castings for growing seedlings), I simply scoop out a container full of compost and put it where the chickens can get it. They gleefully clear out the worms, and then I am free to add the castings to my garden soil or return it to the bin for another day.

Vermicompost from food scraps and junk mail.

mealworms

You can also raise mealworms in your house. (*What?! Mealworms in my house?*) Someone once asked if I was afraid they would get into the cupboards. I replied that at my house, the mealworms are more likely to be eaten by chickens than to find boxes of processed foods to get into! You can raise mealworms (see Resources, page 370) in just about any container with good airflow, but I prefer the old cracked aquarium that I got off the Freecycle group website (www.freecycle.org) because it allowed us to observe the grubs, pupas, and beetles too.

I left the plastic cave and seaweed inside the aquarium, filled the bottom with oatmeal, and gave the mealworms a small piece of carrot for moisture. The transformed aquarium became an endless source of fascination for my kids. In just a few short weeks, the mealworms changed from grubs to pupas and then to adult dark beetles. They are like those sea monkeys kids sometimes send away for, only more interesting. Whenever we have a surplus of beetles or grubs, we release some for the chickens and ducks. *(AC)*

. . . .

WHAT TO DO WITH ALL THOSE EGGS

While certain breeds of hens (and ducks) may lay only two eggs per week, others can lay six per week for most of the year. Wondering what to do with all those eggs? Some city ordinances allow you to sell them, and they make great gifts for unconvinced neighbors. However, even with five chickens and two ducks, I rarely end up with more eggs than I can use. I'm always coming up with new recipes (see some favorites below), and if my pickiest child is going to eat only one meal in a day, I make sure it contains as many of those nutrient-rich eggs as I can cram in. Persuading my son Lander to eat egg dishes hasn't always been easy, but I stumbled on a tactic based on his favorite video game, "Super Mario Brothers." By telling him these foods were "power-ups" that he needed in order to complete each new level, I got him to take that first bite. After that, I was home free, and the word "power" before each food stuck. I love the word "power" too, because these are truly powerful foods—full of nutrient-dense backyard eggs and local dairy products, and with minimal sugar.

› Crème brûlée and flan (recipe page 20)
› Hard boiled, omelets, eggnog (on its own or as a smoothie ingredient (recipe page 71))
› Ice cream (recipe page 69)
› Pancakes (recipe page 41)
› Pudding (recipe page 69)
› Soufflé (recipe page 98)

. . . .

egg recipes

Pudding and Custard-Based Ice Creams

The list of ingredients on the back of a pudding box or ice cream container sounds mysterious and synthetic. But you don't need those fancy chemicals, or the special packaging they come in, to make your own pudding or ice cream. In fact, you probably already have the necessary ingredients in your pantry and fridge. Making your own lets you control the amount of sweetener and supply growing children or nutrition-conscious adults with nutrient-dense calories. And it's easy!

Pudding and ice cream are normally eaten as dessert, but they can easily be turned into breakfast by increasing the number of egg yolks and cutting back on the sugar. Try making a bacon-and-maple-syrup–flavored ice cream for breakfast. The beauty of cooking from scratch is that you are limited only by your imagination.

You can create endless flavor possibilities by adding various extracts in place of the vanilla (think orange, coconut, mint, almond), or steeping herbs and spices for 30 minutes in the warm milk before making the pudding (think mint, lemon verbena, anise hyssop, coffee beans, tea with chai spices, cinnamon, or even garlic, curry, rosemary, or basil), or adding solids (citrus zest or pureed pumpkin), or substituting another liquid at the end as part of the total liquid in the recipe (think rum or scotch). And you can dial up or down the sweetness and fat to your own personal preference, since the sugar and butter have nothing to do with getting the pudding to set (although they do contribute to a nicer texture).

And really, there's always room for pudding and ice cream—everyone knows that.

Master Recipe for Pudding and for Custard-Based Ice Cream
Makes about 8 servings

> 1½ cups whole milk
> ¾ cup organic sugar
> ¼ teaspoon salt
> 3 tablespoons organic cornstarch (omit for ice cream)
> 1½ cups heavy cream
> 3 egg yolks (add more for ice cream if you want to make it really rich)
> 3 tablespoons butter, divided into 3 parts (omit for ice cream)
> 1 teaspoon vanilla extract

If you plan to steep herbs or spices in the milk, gently warm the milk, add the spices, and then turn off the heat and let the milk sit for 30 minutes. Strain and discard the herbs or spices before using the milk as directed below.

1. In a saucepan, whisk together sugar, cornstarch, and salt. Add egg yolks and one-half of cream, and whisk until smooth. Whisk in remaining cream and milk.
2. Place pan over medium heat and bring to a boil, stirring constantly once mixture thickens. Boil for 1 minute, then remove from heat and stir in butter, along with any extracts (such as vanilla), liquors, or chocolate chips, until mixture is smooth.

For pudding: Pour into individual serving dishes, place dishes on a cookie sheet, cover with another cookie sheet, and place in refrigerator. (Covering the pudding helps prevent a skin-like layer developing on the surface. Using cookie sheets is my alternative to using plastic wrap) Pudding will set as it chills.

For ice cream: Omit cornstarch. Pour into an ice cream maker, and freeze according to manufacturer's directions.

Flavor Variations

Chocolate: Add 3 tablespoons unsweetened cocoa powder along with sugar. Once mixture is cooked and you've removed pan from heat, stir in about ½ cup of chocolate chips or chopped baking chocolate. Cinnamon, mint, orange, coffee, Kahlua, or rum are all great additions to this chocolate variation.

Butterscotch: Substitute ¾ cup packed brown sugar for granulated sugar. Once mixture is cooked and you've removed pan from heat, stir in 2 to 3 tablespoons scotch along with vanilla.

Rum raisin: Add ¼ cup raisins to mixture with sugar and eggs, and cook as directed. Once mixture is cooked and you've removed pan from heat, stir in 2 to 3 tablespoons of rum along with vanilla.

Chai: Steep 1 tablespoon black or rooibos tea along with 3 cardamom pods, 3 black peppercorns, ½ stick cinnamon, 6 cloves, and a pinch of dried ginger in milk as discussed above. Proceed with master recipe.

Lemon verbena or mint: Steep ½ cup freshly picked mint or lemon verbena leaves in milk as discussed above. Proceed with master recipe.

Eggnog, the Drinkable Omelet

Makes 3 cups

Why buy eggnog when you can get high-quality local dairy and eggs, perhaps even from your own backyard, and make it yourself? When you think about it, eggnog is really just an omelet in disguise, with added spices and sweetening. Consider making a large batch to keep on hand in the refrigerator, ready to use as a welcome, nutrient-dense addition to any smoothie or breakfast shake.

When making eggnog I use only yolks. Save the whites for pancakes and baked goods, for angel food cake or meringues. If you plan to add this to fruit smoothies, you may choose to omit the spices, to make it more flexible. Do you have a toddler who won't eat? Make this eggnog using only whipping cream, to increase his overall daily calories.

> 2 cups milk
> 1 cup whipping cream (or use all milk for a less creamy end result)
> ⅓ cup organic sugar, honey, or maple syrup
> 1 vanilla bean, cut lengthwise, or ½ teaspoon vanilla extract
> ¼ teaspoon cinnamon
> 1 pinch grated nutmeg (optional, but I'm a nutmeg fiend)
> Dash sea salt
> 3 egg yolks from pastured eggs

1. In a pan over medium heat, combine milk and cream, sweetener, vanilla bean or extract, spices, and salt. Place egg yolks in a small bowl.
2. When milk mixture is almost boiling, pour a little into egg yolks, stirring continuously. This will warm yolks, so they won't congeal when added to the hot milk. If you add them cold, they will turn into the kind of omelet you eat with a fork, which is not what we're shooting for.
3. Add egg yolk mixture to milk in pan in a slow stream, whisking continuously. Cook, stirring, until mixture coats the back of a spoon, or reaches 170°F.
4. Let mixture cool to room temperature. Remove vanilla bean and reserve for another use.

chapter 3
dairy dilemma

Once I had eliminated bread and eggs from my grocery list, I wanted to cross off milk and other dairy products as well. Our family of four was consuming three gallons of milk a week in addition to yogurt, ice cream, and cheeses, and I wanted to know the source of it all. Most dairies pool milk from many different farmers and sell it under one label.

Why does that matter, you may ask? Because as dairies have become bigger, sanitary milking conditions have suffered, and grains, supplements, and medicines have become a bigger part of dairy cows' diets. As a result, dairy pools now have to not only pasteurize but *ultra* pasteurize their milk to maintain a safe product.

I vowed to skip the dairy pools, find a local dairy source for raw milk, and learn to craft my own kefir (yogurt's drinkable cousin), yogurt, buttermilk, sour cream, and cheeses. I knew I could buy some marvelous artisan cheeses from local, reliable sources, but once I started making my own dairy products I never looked back. There was not only an immense cost savings (if you've priced artisan cheeses, you

DAIRY

annette's grocery list

ORIGINAL LIST

Butter
Cheese
Ice cream
Kefir
Milk
Sour cream
Yogurt

REVISED LIST

Alfalfa hay or pellets

Black sunflower seeds

COB (corn, oats, and barley)

Goat mineral supplement (usually kelp and probiotics)

One time purchase of yogurt and buttermilk cultures

One time purchase or gifting of dairy kefir grains

One time purchase of Flora Danica and mesophilic cultures

Rennet

know what I mean), but there was the pleasure of creating a grocer's aisle of unique flavors in my own kitchen from just a handful of ingredients.

You will need to make your own decisions about pasteurized milk versus raw milk. I decided it was important for my family to support small farmers producing quality raw dairy. Although the FDA's website states that "research shows no meaningful difference between the nutrient content of pasteurized and unpasteurized milk," "no meaningful difference" wasn't good enough for me. Just as cooking destroys some nutrients and enzymes in food, pasteurizing destroys some nutrients, enzymes, and proteins in milk.

Also, as a cheesemaker, I learned that many of the bacteria that create those wonderful flavor nuances are killed off at temperatures above 115°F. So how could milk heated to 176° (pasteurizing) or, even worse, 280° (ultrapasteurizing) possibly be the same as milk that has never been heated at all?

Need another reason to support small, independent dairies? Consider this: By turning milk into nothing more than a commodity, dairy pools have done to dairy farmers what the grain elevator did to wheat farmers.

Buying raw milk is possible in many states, Washington and Oregon among them. It is much richer and fresher than pasteurized milk, and many people with lactose sensitivities have fewer troubles drinking it. (To find out about the laws in your area, visit www.realmilk.com.)

This doesn't mean there aren't significant dangers in using raw milk from dairies that don't guarantee healthy cows and sanitary milking and bottling conditions. Therefore, if you decide to source raw cow's milk, ask to tour the farm, see the milking shed, and interview the farmer. Also, make sure that the animals' diet comprises mostly grass and hay, with limited grains. Visiting farms and questioning growing practices should be something we all do anyway, but it's more important with some foods than with others.

You may even want to go a step further. If you want ultimate control over the milking and handling conditions and nutritional composition of your dairy products (by controlling the animals' diet), consider buying a few miniature dairy goats to round out your growing urban barnyard. In some cities, such as Seattle, mini-goats fall under the small animal ordinance and can be licensed as pets just like dogs and cats. *(AC)*

Buy organic milk.

Buy organic (good), unhomogenized (better), or unpasteurized (best) milk from a local farmer.

Raise dairy goats.

. . . .

producer profile: Pav Cherny

Pav shapes cheese balls.

For cheesemaker Pav Cherny, food is something you share. "In the United States, there's this concept of eating alone. If it's time for lunch or dinner, you just go off by yourself and make some food."

Pav shakes his head. "I know people who do that. To me, it's very bizarre. It's rude, frankly. You don't eat by yourself. You find a friend. You call him up. You make a meal with someone, or for someone. And if you don't have anyone to love, find someone."

Pav's ideas about food stem from his upbringing in a devout community of evangelical Baptists in Ukraine. His country forbade religious expression at the time, arresting or killing those who admitted being Baptists. His father was a minister, and conviction bound their community tightly together. When one of them needed something, they shared.

"We didn't really have a concept of food ownership," he explained. "In my church, we were motivated by the idea of radical sharing of one's substance. In the early Christian world, all these people literally sold their entire estates—if they were rich or not. They gave over the money and they went and lived together and shared food together in communities."

Given this family history, it's no surprise that the first thing Pav did once he finished college and made a little money was start to build a community around food. Having studied chemistry, engineering, physics, and molecular biology, he dedicated several years of his life to the study of cheese. He spent thousands of hours making cheese and reading books and academic papers on the subject. "I'm hypertechnical," he explained. "It's just my personality."

Pav poured that cheesemaking knowledge into a small but dense website for professional and amateur cheesemakers. He offered cheesemaking classes and made beautiful cheeses to share with others. When he talks about sharing his cheese knowledge, he sounds like a minister, maybe like his father. "When you empower a person with information, you start something wonderful everywhere. Because then they can share it with others. Then it transforms communities."

Annette first met Pav at Lacia Bailey's Goatfest, an ad hoc fundraiser for the Seattle Farm Co-op designed to showcase city goats. Pav was demonstrating how to make mozzarella, a notoriously tricky cheese popularized by grocery store cheesemaking kits and various books.

Annette had set up a chèvre-making demonstration at the same festival. Over the course of the weekend the two discussed other types of cheeses, and Annette pressed Pav for tips on how to avoid some of her previous cheesemaking flops. Though drawn to the flavor and aging qualities of pressed cheeses, she had come to realize that they all required more time and attention than she could spare. She challenged Pav to come up with an artisan cheese that did not require special equipment or precise timing.

He accepted the challenge, and a few weeks later, Annette found an email from Pav in her inbox. "I'm onto something," he wrote. "I just need to perfect the recipe." Finally, he sent her the recipe for a tasty little cheese he called "Annette."

The real Annette whipped up a batch, aged it a few weeks, and invited Emily and me over to try it. It had a soft, spreadable texture. And the flavor, well, had I no family obligations or other responsibilities, I just might have dropped everything then and there and left it all behind to raise goats. After years of grocery store Camembert, this cheese was a revelation.

"I started with the premise of the simplest kind of cheese," Pav explained later, "a drained clabber. Like a yogurt that you drain, or a chèvre that you drain and it's done." Unlike a chèvre, which is designed to be eaten fresh, this cheese includes a culture. You can eat it fresh, but it will develop complex flavors as it ages. You can change up the flavor by rubbing different herbs and spices on the outside, even wood ashes or beer. The flavor even varies throughout the year, depending on what the animals eat. "I love it best in the summer," says Pav, "when your animals are eating a wide variety of greens and herbs. You can really taste those flavors in the cheese. The terroir."

Pav kept expanding the range of variations on his "Annette" cheese. To show us its potential, he brought over a dozen wheels, each one slightly different from the other. One he'd rolled in ash, another in dried herbs, another he'd rolled in curry, and another in paprika. Velvety white molds had just started to bloom on the cheeses' surfaces.

He left us each with a couple of wheels of "Annette." They sat on beds of straw in vented plastic containers. "I call these 'portable cheese caves,' but they're really just inexpensive lettuce keepers," Pav said. "You can buy them anywhere. I have many more at home."

"And the straw?" I asked.

"It helps keep the humidity consistent and adds thermal mass to more closely imitate a real cave." I poked at the straw. "You can age these in your basement," he explained. Over the next few days, he told us, the tiny colonies of mold would spread until they covered the cheese entirely. That's good: The mold outcompetes harmful organisms and gives the cheese its flavor. "Flip the cheeses every day," he instructed. "In another three weeks you'll start getting that rich, ripe flavor."

Pav started another batch, in Annette's kitchen, then showed us how to pour the curds into cheese molds. "Or, you can just hang the curds from a pillowcase," he told us, "and then roll them into little balls." Pav demonstrated his rolling technique, his hands covered in white cheese. He told us we could age these little balls if we wanted, just like a cheese wheel. "Or you can just pop them into your mouth now, and eat them fresh like chèvre."

Pav dipped a few fresh curd balls into a medley of dried herbs from Annette's backyard. Annette pulled a couple of sheets of homemade crackers from the oven and a jar of apple-pepper jelly from her fridge. The three of us sat together on her back steps, enjoying our impromptu, farm-fresh picnic.

You can find the recipe for "Pav's Bloomy Rind Cheese ('Annette')" on Annette's website, www.SustainableEats.com. *(JM)*

. . . .

PAV'S WORDS OF CHEESEMAKING WISDOM

› Use the best milk you can find and afford. Fresh, raw milk is best; homogenization and pasteurization both decrease the quality of your cheese curd. Pav prefers raw goat milk.

› Find a mentor. If you can't, take a class or join a local organization such as the Washington Cheese Guild (see Resources).

› Keep a journal and take detailed notes about your cheesemaking. That way you can learn from your mistakes.

› Focus on one style of cheese at a time. Once you have the technique down, work on variations, or use the new skills to venture into another style of cheese.

. . . .

backyard dairy

My vow to no longer support milk pools made knowing which animals our milk came from especially appealing. Imagine being able to control the diet of the animal whose milk you consume! So when I learned that mini-goats are allowed under the Seattle small animal ordinance, I casually mentioned the idea at dinner one night. Wouldn't it be fun to have dairy goats? Unfortunately, no one else saw the potential I did. My husband said absolutely not, and the kids refused to give up their backyard playfield and fort. So I put the goat idea on hold. And then one day a friend who lives not far from me decided to take the plunge and brought home two mini-Nubian goats, Mona the Milker and Baby Bessie. I fell in love with them instantly and offered to milk them whenever she needed help.

Milking Mona intimidated me at first. I soon realized that goats have personalities just like dogs do, and Mona frequently flexed hers. She tested my resolve by refusing to go up or down the stairs to the milking stand or deciding to lie down during milking. I'd coax her back up with new kibble and resterilize her udder and teats just in time for her to lie back down again.

Bessie the mini-Nubian goat enjoying a good scratch.

After a few cycles of this, I resorted to inserting my shoulder underneath her belly and jacking up all sixty-five pounds of her for the entire milking session. Whenever she wouldn't come back down the stairs and I pulled her along by the collar in frustration she would stiffen, and the next time I came she would refuse to look at me, deliberately turning her head the other way when I spoke to her or tried to catch her eye.

Eventually, though, Mona would forgive me and produce a tail wag and nuzzle. And once she and I had worked through our issues, we fell into the comfortable partnership of an old married couple. She chewed my foraged blackberry canes happily while I sang or spoke softly to her, listening as the ping of the milk on the sides of the steel milk pail became gradually lower in tone and then finally faded away as the bucket went from empty to full. I loved to put my ear against her stomach and hear the magnified sounds of chewing and digestive gurgles. She smelled like sweet hay and on chilly mornings offered my nose and ears warm respite.

At the end, there would be a treat of dried fruit to coax her down the stairs and back to her paddock, and a warm, foamy pail of fresh, creamy milk for me to take home. Since I wasn't milking regularly, it usually wasn't enough for a full batch of cheese unless my friend was on vacation, so my treasured bucket of goat's milk most often became golden cajeta (a goat's milk version of *dulce de leche*; see recipe on page 89).

Milking Mona convinced me that someday soon I would like dairy goats of my own. It may not be this year, (or even in this house), but I'm preparing my goat entrance strategy for when the time comes. Here's how it might go:

I will first scatter books on raising dairy goats around the house (or perhaps under my spouse's pillow to plant the seed.) If I can't convince my spouse and family, right off the bat, of how important it is to have dairy goats for the pure milk and the opportunity to make cheese ("Cheese! You all love cheese, right?"), then I'll begin telling them how I pine to have a hobby farm. Once they've spent all summer driving around the state with me on property-finding excursions, the idea of staying in the city and giving up some turf to a pair of dairy goats probably won't seem like such a bad idea. *(AC)*

getting started with dairy goats

Forget everything you know about goat's milk: Unlike the stuff in the grocery store, backyard goat's milk tastes like fresh, creamy cow's milk. Imagine getting fresh, raw milk from your own backyard! Enough to experiment with cheeses and yogurts… until the cows come home.

But dairy goats require much more work than chickens, even the miniature goats we recommend for city dwellers. They need daily milking. They jump over low fences and might eat the siding off your house. And because they must "kid" (have babies) periodically to continue producing milk, you'll get to enjoy the messy miracle of birth. But for many urbanites the rewards justify the labor.

Following are some basic facts about miniature dairy goats, so you will know what you're getting into.

› Goats need companionship. Expect to keep two. You might start off with two kids, or a mom and a kid, to ease into things.

› We recommend the Mini-Nubian and Mini-La Mancha breeds for urban goat keepers because of their docile nature, their milk's high butterfat content, and their high feed-to-milk ratio. Mini-Oberhaslis also make great urban dairy goats. However, goat personalities and decibel levels vary with each animal. Be sure you spend some time with your future goats before you bring them home, to be sure their particular bleats will not give your neighbors reason to complain. Also expect them to be louder when in heat, just after kidding, and when weaning.

› Two goats can yield well over a gallon of milk a day.

› Every year or two, you'll need to take them to a stud service. You'll be able to milk the mothers within two weeks of their giving birth. Seattle laws allow you to keep three small animals, including dehorned mini-goats. Males must be castrated. Offspring may be kept while nursing up to 12 weeks of age. In Portland, Oregon, you can keep three goats. Many cities do not allow goats, but you can help change that (see the profile of backyard producer Jennie Grant, page 82).

what goats need
Goats need a **shed**, an **outdoor enclosure**, and **food and water**.

a shed
A goat shed should have the following features:
› Protection from rain and wind.
› About 50 square feet (6 feet by 8 feet) of area for a pair of goats and any kids.
› A hay manger.
› A dry floor for the goats to sleep on.

an outdoor enclosure
Create an outdoor enclosure that includes:

> An excellent fence—goats are talented escape artists.
> About 400 square feet for two goats and any kids.
> Good drainage. Goats are prone to hoof infections and shouldn't have puddles in their pens. A nice, thick bed of wood chips can help keep goats' feet dry.
> A manger or a pair of stock panels (from a feed store) or welded wire mesh panels (such as used to reinforce concrete slabs) mounted on poles or a fence, for holding fresh browse (such as blackberry vines). Goats should not (and won't) eat food off the ground.

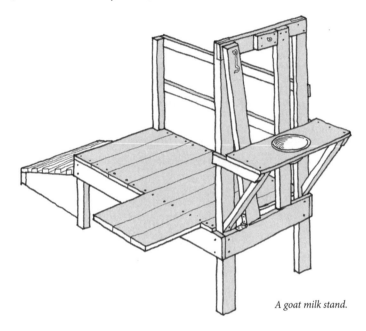

A goat milk stand.

> A milking stand, protected from rain. The stand should include some way to restrain the goat's head (like the stocks used by the Puritans to humiliate evildoers!), but your goats won't mind, because they get to eat kibble from a bucket while you milk them.
> Hay storage (a shelter big enough for one or two hay bales).
> An old picnic table or large rock to climb on. Goats like to climb things—they'll thank you for it.

food and water
> Alfalfa (hay or pellets, available at feed supply stores).
> All the fresh browse you can find, taking care to avoid plants poisonous to goats (see Plants for Livestock, page 365).

> Limited corn, oats, and barley, along with mineral supplements. These can be used as a reward or bribe for good behavior, or an enticing snack during milking and hoof maintenance.
> Fresh water every day.

backyard producer profile: Jennie Grant

When Jennie Grant was turned in for owning goats within the Seattle city limits (illegal at that time), she didn't pout. Instead, she led the charge to change the law. She never expected to become the unofficial spokesperson for a movement to legalize goats in cities across the country.

The whole thing began when she wrote to Seattle City Council member Richard Conlin. Conlin had voiced an interest in food security issues, and Jennie saw her access to fresh milk under threat. Conlin sent his staff member Phyllis Shulman to meet with Jennie. "If you can demonstrate community support," Shulman advised, "we can work on some legislation that would legalize goats."

In the months that followed, Jennie printed up petitions promoting the formal legalization of goat ownership. She handed them out to friends, who'd bring them to work or to the rowing club. At first the signatures dribbled in, ten or twenty at a time. She set up tables at her neighborhood farmers market, often accompanied by her goat Brownie. "I'd tell them, 'I'm trying to legalize goats in the city. We want to reclassify them as small animals so you can have a goat just like a dog.' Most of the time they'd say, 'Well, that sounds fun.' But when I had my goat with me on a leash, they'd say, 'That sounds *really* fun!'"

Jennie observed, from watching her audience's response, that cuteness sells. She started bringing along her six-year-old son, Spencer, who pleaded, "We want to keep our goat!" When she brought both Brownie and Spencer to Seattle Tilth's Harvest Fair, she garnered a landslide of signatures.

Jennie rebranded her wonky-sounding "Society for the Legalization of Mini Goats" as "The Goat Justice League" and promoted what she called "stylish urban goat living." She printed up a T-shirt featuring a mini-goat in a cape, flying above the city like Superman.

Over the following months, Richard Conlin's office took the ball and ran with it, drafting legislation and setting up public hearings, even as they were mocked. Meanwhile, Jennie helped shape the press coverage by the force of her personality. Before her campaign, goat owners had been seen as backwards and desperate. Jennie represented a new kind of goat owner: charismatic, educated, and comfortably middle class. Reporters adored her. When she encountered sincere critics of her movement, she found the most effective response to be, "Golly, I just think it would be fun to keep pet goats, milk them, and make cheese. My goats don't bother you, do they?" And she did have her critics, among them those concerned about abused goats being kept in condos, or about goat feces being tracked into restaurants on patron's feet.

But when the vote finally arrived, the City Council came down on the side of dairy animals—for the first time in a century. That vote marked a shift in how we define "city living" in this country. After all, social progress in most American cities has been associated with leaving our rural past behind us. In his fantastic page-turner of a dissertation, "Cows in the Commons, Dogs on the Lawn," historian Fred Brown chronicles Seattle's changing relationship with animals. He says that in the city's earliest days, cows roamed the streets freely; their right to graze on anyone's front lawn was protected by law, a law modeled on rural rights granting cattle access to public rangeland. As late as 1900, Brown calculates, backyard cows still produced a third of Seattle's milk. In suburban neighborhoods like Georgetown and West Seattle, he says, most milk "was furnished from one neighbor to another."

Jennie with Snowflake and Maple.

As rail lines were created, connecting Seattle with its countryside, it became possible for suburban dairies to replace the backyard cow. That's when the arguments of real estate developers began to stick: Cows were not a symbol of utilitarian industry, they were a public nuisance. In Brown's words, people "complained that cattle broke fences, ate flowers, and trampled truck gardens and lawns. They broke through wooden sidewalks. They collided with streetcars and trains, damaging the machines and injuring passengers."

Seattle began excluding cows from its downtown core, and the cow-free zone crept slowly outward from there. By 1907, the city had banned wandering cows from every neighborhood except the isolated Magnolia peninsula.

But it took a while for dairies to completely replace the backyard cow. People couldn't trust far-off dairies like they could trust a neighbor. Scandalous rumors circulated about milk having some of its butterfat removed or being watered down, about dairy cows fed on a diet of "swill," a by-product of the brewing industry. Not until the regulatory infrastructure improved and inspectors were dispatched to enforce quality control did dairies completely replace the urban cow.

This gradual banishment of dairy animals happened in many cities across the country. And in almost every case, it was women who held out the longest. For women in families of limited means, cows offered income and with it a degree of independence. Keeping cows was considered woman's work. It was men—the real estate developers, bankers, and businessmen—who led the drive to eliminate farm animals from the city.

It doesn't surprise me that it would be women who finally reversed this trend. Women like Jennie Grant, who influence or control their households' diets; women who've used the local food movement as a tool for transforming food security into everybody's concern. *(JM)*

Whey drips from curd in a pillowcase.

dairy recipes

Curds and Whey

One of the simplest things to make if you have raw milk is curds (solid milk proteins that clump together) and whey (the semiclear liquid that remains after you strain out the curds). The lactic bacteria present in raw milk will cause it to first sour, then thicken, and finally separate into curds and whey.

To make this happen, pour two cups of raw milk into a quart-sized Mason jar, cover the top with a paper towel affixed with the jar ring or a rubber band, and let it sit on the counter for several days, until separation occurs. The separation of the watery whey from the heavier milk solids will be obvious once it is done. (In other words, if it's not obvious, it's not done.) Strain the contents of the jar through a fine mesh strainer or tea towel.

Rich in lactic acid, the whey can be used as a starter when fermenting foods, or as an acidic medium when soaking grains and beans to reduce the phytic acid. You can also add it to smoothies in place of the whey powder sold as a nutritional supplement.

Use the curds like quark or cream cheese when baking, or in spreads or dips. It will have a strong, cheesy smell, so adding salt and herbs may make it more palatable for you.

Note: You cannot do this with pasteurized or homogenized milk. Instead of souring, thickening, and separating, the milk will go rancid. Another method for getting whey is to harvest it from yogurt. See "A Simple Way to Make Whey" on page 50.

. . . .

BACTERIA AND CULTURES AND MOLD, OH MY!

Working with dairy products is a balancing act, between eliminating the microorganisms that can harm you and nurturing the ones that are desireable.

To remove any harmful microorganisms, it's critical to start off with clean equipment. Sterilize all your pots, utensils, plastic molds, etc., either by rinsing with a weak bleach solution (1 tablespoon bleach to ½ gallon water) or by boiling a large pot of water, turning off the heat, and placing them in the lidded pot for 5 minutes. If you are using bleach, be sure to rinse everything off thoroughly afterward, or the chlorine may end up destroying the very bacteria you are trying to propagate.

A very different crop of microorganisms comes into play once you start making your products. A culture is a specific strain of bacteria that will flavor and thicken your milk. Each bacterium thrives in a different temperature range and imparts unique qualities to the milk, helping you shape the flavor and texture of the end product.

Mesophilic cultures are typically used for cheeses for which the milk is kept in the range of 77° to 86°F, while *thermophilic* strains are used for the 95° to 140° range. The two cheese cultures we call for in this book are both mesophilic: Flora Danica and a general mesophilic blend (see Resources).

Molds are used in making moist cheeses like Brie and Camembert, to create their characteristic fuzzy and flavorful rinds. In moist conditions, wild molds can take over very quickly, so adding specific strains to these cheeses helps us control which molds we'll end up with. In the recipe "Pav's Bloomy Rind Cheese ('Annette')," we call for *P. candidum* and *Geo. candidum*. (Find recipe on Annette's website, www.SustainableEats.com.)

. . . .

Dairy Kefir

One item on my recent winter reading list was the book *Wild Fermentation: The Flavor, Nutrition, and Craft of Live-Culture Foods*, by Sandor Ellix Katz. Inspired by the section on dairy kefir, I eventually discovered an Australian kefir Yahoo! group. And through that group, based all the way on the other side of the world, I made a connection with a wonderful woman who lives right at my doorstep, in the Seattle suburb of Bellevue, Washington.

Charlotte met me at the University District farmers market one Saturday in January, with a gift of free dairy kefir grains. Before then, I had been buying dairy kefir at the grocery store for the amazing amount of probiotics it contained. What I hadn't noticed was how loaded with artificial flavoring and high-fructose corn syrup it was.

As it happens, kefir is simple to make at home once you've got your starter grains. The grains are odd to look at, like gummy cauliflower nodules. A combination of bacteria and yeasts, they are one of the most beneficial foods for increasing gut flora, which is thought to be an integral part of the immune system.

To make kefir, you simply soak the grains overnight in milk, in a jar covered with a paper towel to keep the fruit flies out. When your kefir is as thick and tangy as you like it, just strain out the grains. I follow the constant-brew method, whereby I strain out my kefir every day or so and begin a new, small batch, so it is perpetually brewing. If you need to take a break from kefir-making, you can either freeze the grains or put them in fresh milk, cap the container tightly, and refrigerate up to several weeks.

I have found kefir grains to be extremely forgiving, lasting for days on the counter (long past the point where the curds separated from the whey). If they develop orange mold on top, I simply scrape off the mold layer and feed it to my chickens or compost, strain the kefir through a mesh strainer, and start over again.

Working the milk proteins through a fine strainer with a spoon will give you a thicker kefir, and longer brewing will make it more sour and effervescent. Adjust the texture and flavor to your family's preferences. You can also sweeten it with honey or fruit syrup as you are introducing it to your family, then gradually reduce the level of additives as they become accustomed to the taste. *(AC)*

Butter

Makes ½ pound

Butter is another thing that is easy and fun to make at home; the hardest part may be finding an affordable source for heavy cream. You can make butter either by shaking the cream in a jar or by using a mixer.

1 pint heavy cream, or 1 gallon whole, nonhomogenized milk strained to make
   about 1 pint of heavy cream
½ to 1 teaspoon salt

If starting with whole milk, first strain off cream. To do this, leave milk undisturbed in refrigerator for several days. Cream will rise to top, and you will see a distinct line separating it from milk. Using a turkey baster, carefully draw off just the top cream layer.

In a mixer:
Pour cream into a mixer bowl and whip as for whipped cream. Continue to whip long after peaks form, until cream begins to change color and lose volume. Stop churning when whipped cream begins separating into butter and buttermilk.

In a jar:
Shake jar until cream begins to separate into butter and buttermilk.

Final steps for mixer or jar method:
1. Strain butter through a tea towel or a piece of buttercloth (a more finely woven version of cheesecloth) or muslin. Save buttermilk for baking.
2. In a bowl, continue working butter with hands or a spoon, until all milky water has been squeezed out. Place in a fine strainer, and rinse until runoff is completely clear. Any remaining milk in butter will cause it to go rancid much more quickly.
3. Add ½ to 1 teaspoon of salt to butter, kneading in thoroughly. (This will help extend its life.) Refrigerate.

Variation: Cultured Cream Butter. Add a pinch of Flora Danica culture to your cream and let it sit out, covered, overnight. Proceed with the butter recipe. This will change the flavor of your butter and increase its shelf life.

Cultured or Clabbered Buttermilk

I always used to buy cultured buttermilk for baking, and it would always go bad before I used the whole carton. But it's so easy to make your own cultured buttermilk, using a small amount of store-bought buttermilk starter, that you'll kick yourself for not having tried it sooner.

To make cultured buttermilk, combine 1 pint milk and 3 tablespoons good quality store-bought buttermilk in a pint jar and stir well. Cover the jar with a kitchen towel to keep the bugs out but allow it to breathe, and let it sit until it's cultured to your liking (longer culturing time will result in a more sour flavor). Cap tightly and refrigerate. Every week or two, use 3 tablespoons of your cultured buttermilk to make a new pint. If you are diligent about making it at least twice a month, you should be able to make cultured buttermilk forever. Just to be safe, though, freeze 3 tablespoons of it in case you forget about it so long that it molds. Frozen starters will last 6 to 12 months before losing their effectiveness, so be prepared to replace any unused ones twice a year. Make a note on your calendar so you don't forget.

You can try using cultured buttermilk in place of the mesophilic culture in the following recipes, but the curds may take a little longer to set and the flavor will be a little different. However, if you are reading this and suddenly get the urge to try your hand at soft cheeses, this is one way to start right now!

Crème Fraîche
Makes 1 pint

Crème fraîche is a much thicker version of sour cream, made from whipping cream instead of light cream. You can easily make either one at home using Flora Danica or another mesophilic cheese culture. Try replacing the mayonnaise in any recipe with crème fraîche: It makes a great dip or salad dressing base and adds an ethereal touch to scalloped potatoes.

To make crème fraîche, gently warm 1 pint of heavy cream to 80°F, then pour it into a bowl. Sprinkle the surface with ⅛ teaspoon Flora Danica or other mesophilic cheese culture, then stir it gently using an up-and-down motion. Cover the bowl with a lid, and leave it on the counter for 48 hours before refrigerating. It will continue to thicken over the next 24 hours, but you can use it at any point. This will last 1 to 2 weeks in the refrigerator.

Sour Cream
Makes 1 pint

To make sour cream, gently warm 1 pint of heavy cream to 80°F, then pour it into a bowl. Sprinkle the surface with ⅛ teaspoon Flora Danica or other mesophilic cheese culture, then stir gently using an up-and-down motion. Cover the bowl with a lid, and leave it on the counter for 24 hours before refrigerating. This will last for 1 to 2 weeks in the refrigerator.

Yogurt

Yogurt is almost as easy to make as buttermilk. One way of flavoring yogurt is by adding flavoring to the milk first. You can flavor with plants like lemon verbena or anise hyssop, with cinnamon or chai spices. Muddle the leaves in the milk or add the spices, then steep overnight in the fridge. Make the yogurt the next day as directed below.

Some yogurt cultures, such as viili and piima, set up at room temperature (though you can also use less culture to produce a more runny buttermilk substitute). If using viili, simply add 2 tablespoons of culture to a quart of milk in a jar, cover the top with a dish towel to keep fruit flies out but allow air to penetrate, and wait until it sets up.

You can buy many other specialty yogurt cultures (see Resources, page 370), or simply use a few tablespoons of any high-quality plain store-bought yogurt. Some produce a milder flavor and a thicker, smoother texture than others, so it's good to read reviews online and decide which culture will be most appealing to you. Note that cultures will cross readily in the kitchen, so if you have a small kitchen you may be limited to having just a few cultures at a time.

The Bulgarian- and Greek-style yogurts that we are accustomed to buying at the grocery store require a little more effort. Essentially you need to heat your milk to 180°F to destroy any bacteria that might compete with the culture. Cool the milk to 115°F as quickly as possible by placing the pan in a bowl of ice cubes, then add the culture, mix well, and maintain a temperature of 110° to 115°F for 4 to 6 hours. You can accomplish this by placing your yogurt container in a thermos, an ice chest, a closed dishwasher, or an oven with the light on or set to 110°, or by first boiling some water in the microwave and then putting your container of yogurt in the microwave with it. Check the warm environment every so often, and adjust the temperature as needed. Refrigerate the yogurt once it begins to set up. It will thicken further over the next 12 hours.

Cajeta
Makes 1 quart
You can increase this recipe, but that will lengthen the cooking time. Since cajeta requires near-constant attention, it's best to make it in small batches.

> 1 quart goat's milk
> 1 cup sugar
> 2 teaspoons organic cornstarch
> Pinch of baking soda

1. Pour milk and sugar into a heavy-bottomed saucepan. Sprinkle surface with cornstarch and baking soda, and stir well.
2. Bring ingredients to a boil over medium-high heat, stirring frequently. You can choose how thick you want cajeta to be, from a thin and runny syrup for flavoring steamed milk to a thick and chewy candy. I prefer to stop cooking when it oozes

lazily off a spoon, which seems to be the best texture for pouring on ice cream. If you have the time, you can cook it longer until it thickens substantially, then roll small balls of it in crushed local hazelnuts.

cheese recipes

I lusted after the cheeses from the farmers market; their full-bodied flavors had my number. But while their captivating nuances beguiled my senses, their prices soon curbed our relationship. So I thought I'd try making my own.

After staying up until 3:00 AM nursing curds that turned into monumental flops, I gave up. Those beguiling cheeses were fussy, expensive to make, and a huge time commitment. They required a cheese press and an aging cave. And when they failed I wanted to cry.

I've settled instead on some simple, nearly foolproof varieties that require little to no equipment and can easily fit a normal schedule. Each step in making these cheeses is a large window of time, so your odds of hitting each phase correctly are much higher than when making other cheeses. They are also all low-temperature types, none of them being heated beyond 86°F, so they are great raw cheeses to make at home. In other words, these are approachable and forgiving cheeses.

Be prepared: It takes a lot of milk to make a little cheese. I typically get about a pound of cheese for every gallon of milk. This makes home cheesemaking an expensive hobby if you can't find an affordable source of local milk, but the benefits are highly rewarding.

If you can't find affordable local milk, don't despair. Many smaller-scale cheese artisans have wholesale buying clubs and will sell at what they consider restaurant price if you buy in sufficient quantity. Check with your local cheesemakers, then find as many friends and neighbors as necessary to meet the minimum.

Chèvre, Fromage Frais, and Cream Cheese

Makes roughly ¼ gallon chèvre or fromage frais or 1 pint cream cheese; results will vary based on butterfat percentage in milk or cream

These cheeses all follow the same technique, but the ingredients differ slightly. Chèvre is a soft, spreadable cheese made from goat's milk; fromage frais is a soft, spreadable cheese made from cow's milk; and cream cheese is a stiff, spreadable cheese made by using equal parts cow's milk and heavy whipping cream. You can use the same mesophilic culture and rennet for all three.

These cheeses are great mixed with garlic and herbs as a dip, crumbled into salads or over polenta and braised winter greens, as a topping for crostini or pizza, or baked into quiche or cheesecakes.

You can purchase special chèvre molds, or use small yogurt containers with holes poked in the sides to let the whey drain out as the cheese sets up. If you plan to make a spreadable cheese or roll it into balls when done, you can also simply drain it into a tea towel–lined colander, tie up the four corners of the towel like a hobo sack, and let it hang from the sink faucet or a wooden spoon laid across a deep container like a stockpot to drain further.

For this recipe you will need three molds (if using), one cookie rack, one jelly roll–type pan to catch the whey, a 5-quart or larger stainless steel or enamel pan, a cooking thermometer, a long-handled spoon for stirring, and a slotted spoon or spider for scooping out the curds. If you are not using molds, you'll need a colander and a tea towel to hang the cheese.

Ingredients for chèvre
  ½ gallon goat's milk
  ⅛ teaspoon Flora Danica or other mesophilic culture
  1 drop liquid rennet

Ingredients for fromage frais
  ½ gallon cow's milk
  ⅛ teaspoon Flora Danica or other mesophilic culture
  1 drop liquid rennet

Ingredients for cream cheese
  1 quart cow's milk
  1 quart whipping cream
  ¼ teaspoon Flora Danica or other mesophilic culture
  2 drops of liquid rennet

1. Heat milk to 72°F. Gently stir in starter.
2. Dilute rennet in 2 tablespoons filtered water, add to pot, and gently stir for about 1 minute. Let mixture sit, covered, for about 12 hours depending on room temperature, until it coagulates.
3. If not using molds, line a colander with a tea towel, and set colander over a bowl to catch whey. Scoop curds into colander and let drain for about 6 hours. If using molds, place a cookie rack over a jelly roll pan to catch whey, and set molds on cookie rack. Scoop curds into molds using a slotted spoon, and let drain for several days until they have reached the desired texture. Alternatively, you can hang them inside the tea towel to drip for the same amount of time.

This cheese gets drier the longer it sits in the mold, so you can remove it at any point to determine its consistency. I like to unmold the cheese when it is still slightly moist and just beginning to flake, although either softer or firmer is equally good.

For chèvre or fromage frais, unmold the cheese and sprinkle dried herbs and/or salt on it; the cheese will absorb the flavor of the herbs and salt. You can also layer dried herbs into the molds as you are scooping in the curds. Some of my favorite embellishments are chives, cracked peppercorns, rosemary, lavender, nuts, or a combination of finely chopped dried apricots and hot peppers.

For cream cheese, remove it from the colander and knead in 1 teaspoon of salt. Soft cheeses will last a week or two in the refrigerator.

Feta
Makes 1–2 quarts, results will vary based on butterfat percentage in milk
Feta is a versatile cheese that you can use on pizzas and grain salads. It's also simple to make at home. A large stockpot, a long-handled spoon, a long knife, a thermometer, a colander, and a tea towel are the only equipment you need.

> 1 gallon goat's or sheep's milk
> $\frac{1}{16}$ teaspoon mesophilic culture
> ⅛ teaspoon liquid rennet

1. Warm milk to 86°F, then sprinkle culture over top. Using an up-and-down motion, gently stir in culture. Cover and let sit for 1 hour while maintaining a temperature of 86°F. In the summer that's fairly easy to do, but in winter you may have difficulty. Try setting the milk pot inside a larger pot or baking dish so that 86° F water comes up the sides; check the water temperature and adjust by adding warm water. You can also place a heating pad under and around the sides of the pot, or put your pot inside a cooler that has previously been warmed with a heating pad or hot water bottle.
2. Mix rennet with ¼ cup filtered water and add to milk, gently stirring using the same up-and-down motion. Cover and let sit for 30 minutes or until you reach "clean break." To test, insert a long knife in top. If cheese has thickened like gelatin and you are able to cut it, then you have achieved "clean break."
3. To cut curds, use a long-handled knife or offset spatula. Starting with the side of the pot farthest from you, cut curds vertically into ¾-inch strips. Turn pot 90° and once again cut ¾-inch strips. You should end up with ¾-inch squares. Finally, insert knife into same cuts at a 45° angle. Allow curds to "heal" for 5 to 10 minutes, then gently

stir for 20 to 30 minutes, depending on how hard you want your cheese to be. A longer stirring time makes for a firmer cheese.

4. Line a colander with a dish towel, and set colander over a bowl to capture draining whey. Pour curds and whey into dish towel. Gently take up all four corners of towel, and tie into a hobo sack. Suspend sack from a wooden spoon stretched across a deep container like a stockpot, or tie to kitchen faucet and place bowl underneath in sink. Save whey that drips during first 30 minutes for fermentation projects or smoothies, or use it in your garden as fertilizer. It will also jump-start your compost pile, or you can feed it to livestock.

5. Drain cheese at room temperature for 24 hours. Cut curds into cubes, sprinkle with salt to taste, and store in refrigerator. Over the course of 3 or 4 days, curds will develop more flavor and soak up salt.

SPRING

After what felt like an eternal winter of eating cabbage and kale from farmers markets, I was ecstatic to see the first spring greens begin to trickle in: purslane, chickweed, and arugula. My family, longing instead for tomatoes and broccoli, did not share my excitement.

My husband Jared's support dipped even lower one night when I served him a bowl of spring green and parsnip soup. Halfway through eating it, he threw his spoon down in horror. There in the curve of the spoon lay half of a chickweed-green caterpillar, plumped up from cooking and bearing teeth marks where it had been bitten in half.

Jared grabbed his throat as if suffocating. Unfazed, I searched his bowl. "I can't find the rest of it. You must have eaten it," I said. Jared covered his mouth with one hand and pushed the bowl away with the other. "I'm not hungry anymore," he said, still ashen.

It reminded me of a story I once read about vegetarian Indians who became anemic after emigrating to London. Apparently, the English food supply was so clean that the rice and legumes were free of the insects their former diet

what we are eating now

All herbs but basil
Asparagus
Beets
Broccoli
Cabbage
Carrots
Cauliflower
Early potatoes
Fiddlehead fern
Green garlic
Horseradish
Leeks
Mustards
Nettles
Peas
Parsnip
Radishes
Rhubarb
Salsify
Scallions
Sea beans
Spring greens
Strawberries (June)

had contained. But I chose not to share that story with my husband.

"Do you want me to go back to shopping at the store?" I asked, trying to sound supportive while visions of my treasured garden plans went up in flames. "No," he replied, "but I don't ever want to eat green soup again."

Afraid that Jared would change his mind about ceding the front lawn to garden space, I decided to rip it out as quickly as possible. I had dabbled in gardening for many years and loved harvesting herbs, lettuce, and tomatoes, relishing the fresh flavors and the sense of self-sufficiency. But I had never considered it possible to grow all our produce on our small, in-city lot. That prospect seemed so monumental that it bordered on lunacy—and I looked forward to the challenge.

There is a sense of finality when you create a garden. It's like waving a flag for all to see, boasting of your commitment to fresh, organic produce. Ripping out the lawn was a definitive moment, like Scarlett O'Hara clenching that fistful of dirt and vowing, "As God is my witness, I'll never be hungry again." Only for me, it was a vow never again to support seed companies I disagree with, or processed food companies, or pesticide companies. I'd keep that vow by buying or growing heirloom organic vegetables and making my own food. If that meant I no longer had time to watch TV, then so be it. No one ever changed anything by watching TV anyway.

If you have the luxury of adequate space and free time, grow your own produce in tune with the seasons. You can select varieties of vegetables and herbs not often available from local farmers (because they're not economically viable on a large commercial scale), such as broccoli raab, chervil, and watercress. Growing your own will save you money and allow you to harvest food just when you need it, at the peak of perfection. After all, raspberries begin perishing within hours of picking, and the sweetness of Brussels sprouts starts to disappear within minutes. An heirloom tomato picked the day before being shipped to market can't compare with one picked in full sun on a lazy afternoon and sliced into the lunchtime salad.

What I like best about growing my own is that I don't have to shop. Instead of getting up early to hit the Saturday morning farmers market, I can stay in my toasty bed, knowing that no matter how lazy I am, those Brussels sprouts will be in my garden, waiting for me to harvest them ten minutes before I'm ready to cook them. Even in the dead of winter I can pick cabbage, carrots, turnips, or collard greens at my leisure. No lines to wait in, no stacks of candy tempting my kids at the checkout stand, and no produce rotting in my refrigerator. Yes, I spend time working in my garden and harvesting produce, but I would choose that over shopping any day of the week. *(AC)*

Previous page: Winter harvest.
This page: Preparing rabbits.

Opposite page, top: Lena and René of Lentz Spelt Farms.
Opposite page, bottom: Modern motorized grain grinder.
This page: Old-fashioned hand-crank grain grinder.

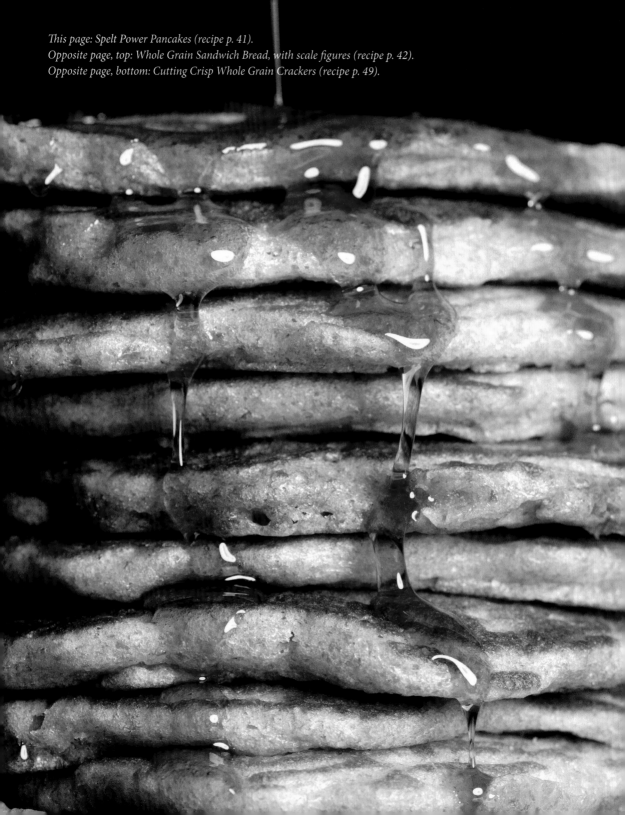

This page: Spelt Power Pancakes (recipe p. 41).
Opposite page, top: Whole Grain Sandwich Bread, with scale figures (recipe p. 42).
Opposite page, bottom: Cutting Crisp Whole Grain Crackers (recipe p. 49).

Top: Backyard eggs with golf ball.
Bottom: A hen-pecked dog retreats.
Opposite page: Lottie, an American
Barred Rock, rules the cover crop.

Mona, the mini-Nubian, gives three quarts of milk daily.

Top: Molded chèvre on a cheese mat (recipe p. 90).
Bottom left: Chèvre.
Bottom right: Backyard gouda, kefir, and yogurt.

Top: *Spring Green and Parsnip Soup (recipe p. 97).*
Bottom: *Rhubarb Custard Pie (recipe p. 100).*

Making biochar in a stove from SeaChar.

Opposite page, top: At the farmers market.
Opposite page, bottom: Planting signs and squash harvest at Marra Farm, a community garden.

Top: Starting corn in an egg carton.
Bottom: Inspecting the chemical-free beehive.
Next page: Overwintered onion and scooter.

recipes for a spring meal

A celebration of fresh greens and eggs! A green chickweed and parsnip soup starts off mini arugula and goat cheese soufflés (which we can make now that the hens are laying after their long winter's rest). Young asparagus spears are drizzled with Rockridge Orchard young balsamic vinegar and Samish Bay Montasio cheese curls. Dessert is a custard-based rhubarb pie.

Spring Green, Parsnip, and Caterpillar Soup
Makes 4–6 servings

> 1 large leek, woody ends trimmed, cut in half lengthwise and sliced into thin crescents
> 2 tablespoons butter (recipe page 86) or ghee
> 2 parsnips, diced
> 1 apple, peeled and diced—the oldest, mealiest one from the bottom of the box in the garage
> 1 quart chicken bone broth (recipe page 291)
> 1 quart of any spring green (chickweed, sorrel, and spinach are my favorites)
> ½ cup cream or whole milk
> ¼ teaspoon freshly ground nutmeg
> ½ teaspoon salt (assuming chicken broth is not salted)
> Pinch of ground white, Tellicherry, or sancho peppercorns. (Sancho peppercorns grow well in the Pacific Northwest.)
> Caterpillar (optional)

1. In a heavy-bottomed stockpot over medium-high heat, cook leeks in butter or ghee until translucent. Add parsnips, apple, and broth, and cook 15 minutes. Add greens and cook until just done, about 3 to 5 minutes depending on what kind of greens they are.
2. Using an immersion blender, puree soup just enough that some chunks remain. Add cream, nutmeg, salt, and pepper. Serve with herbed cheesy breadsticks made from pizza dough (recipe page 47).

Mini Arugula and Goat Cheese Soufflés

Makes 7 servings

> 1 tablespoon + 3½ tablespoons butter
> 3 tablespoons bread crumbs (make by whizzing a piece of stale bread in a blender
>   or food processor)
> 4½ tablespoons flour
> 1½ cups whole milk
> 6 backyard egg yolks
> 1 cup crumbled gorgonzola
> ¾ cup blanched arugula
> ¼ teaspoon freshly grated nutmeg
> Pinch of paprika
> 7 egg whites
> Pinch of salt

1. Preheat the oven to 400°F.
2. Butter 7 10-ounce ramekins, and sprinkle bread crumbs on sides and bottom. In a heavy-bottomed saucepan, melt 3½ tablespoons butter over medium heat. Add flour and stir until it resembles mashed potatoes. Add milk a little at a time, stirring until it's incorporated before adding more. Cook until mixture comes to a complete boil and thickens, about 1 minute.
3. Remove pan from heat. Let it cool for five minutes, then whisk in egg yolks one at a time. Return pan to heat for 30 seconds, then remove and let cool to lukewarm. Add crumbled cheese, arugula, nutmeg, and paprika.
4. Beat egg whites with pinch of salt until they form stiff peaks. Add one-quarter of egg whites to soufflé base. Gently fold in remaining egg whites, and turn mixture into prepared ramekins.
5. Turn oven down to 375°F, and put soufflés on middle rack. Bake for about 20-25 minutes, until a skewer stuck in center of soufflés comes out clean.

Variation: Substitute any grated or soft cheese for the gorgonzola, and omit the greens.

Roasted Asparagus with Young Balsamic Vinaigrette and Cheese Curls

Makes 6–8 servings

The sweet-sour of balsamic vinegar plays well against the concentrated sugars of roasted

Roasted Asparagus with Young Balsamic Vinagrette and Cheese Curls.

asparagus. Rockridge Orchards releases a small number of bottles of their *balsamico,* called Rocksalmic, each year. Order yours early, because they sell out quickly!

2 pounds fresh asparagus
2 tablespoons bacon drippings or olive oil
Salt
2 tablespoons balsamic vinegar
2 ounces dry grating cheese, shaved with a vegetable peeler to make curls

1. Preheat the oven to 450°F.
2. Snap off woody ends of asparagus spears, peeling lower halves of thicker spears.
3. Melt bacon drippings, if using, and drizzle drippings or olive oil on a jelly roll pan. Turn asparagus spears in drippings or oil to completely coat. Sprinkle with salt and roast for 5 to 15 minutes, until they soften somewhat and are easily pierced with a fork.
4. Plate asparagus spears, drizzle with balsamic, and top with Parmesan curls and sea salt.

Grandma Judy's Rhubarb Custard Pie

Makes 8 servings

Whether you are a hard-core rhubarb-strawberry fan or a rhubarb purist, you must try this pie. The addition of the creamy custard and nutmeg just might win you over.

1 Easy as Pie Crust (recipe opposite)
Enough finely diced rhubarb stalks to fill the pie crust
3 eggs
Scant 2 cups sugar
½ cup cream
3 tablespoons flour, cornstarch, or potato flour
1 teaspoon vanilla extract
½ teaspoon salt
½ teaspoon, plus a little extra, grated nutmeg
¼ teaspoon mace

1. Preheat the oven to 425°F.
2. Set aside one-quarter of pie dough. Roll out remaining dough 1½ inches wider than pie plate. Fit dough into pie plate, fold edges under and flute them. Refrigerate pie crust for an hour before baking, to prevent from shrinking.
3. Blind-bake piecrust: Poke all over with a fork to prevent it from bubbling up, line with parchment paper or aluminum foil, and fill with dried beans to weigh down crust. Bake for 15 minutes. Remove from oven, and reserve beans and aluminum foil for another use. This can be done the day before baking the pie.
4. While crust is baking, roll out reserved one-quarter dough and cut into small shapes. If you don't have a tiny cookie cutter, hand-cut into circles or diamonds.
5. Fill crust with rhubarb. In a bowl, combine all remaining ingredients except extra nutmeg, and pour over rhubarb. Arrange dough cutouts in a circle on top. Sprinkle with sugar and extra nutmeg.
6. Bake pie for 10 minutes, then reduce heat to 325°F and bake for 1 more hour. If dough edges start to get too dark, cover with aluminum foil.

If you have any extra filling, pour it into a ramekin and bake until the edges are done and the middle is still wiggly like gelatin. Then eat it before anyone catches you.

Easy as Pie Crust

This pie crust employs a trick or two to make a normally tricky crust easy as pie. The vodka or brandy will evaporate during baking, leaving open pockets that make for a flaky crust, and the rice or potato flour will keep your crust from sticking, which means you will be less likely to overwork the dough or add too much flour to it. You can mix this either in a bowl using a fork or in a food processor. Use the least amount of processing possible to keep the dough cool. The crust freezes well for months, frozen in a disc or rolled out in a pie plate but left unbaked. If you use it rolled out but unbaked, add an extra 5 minutes to the baking time.

1¼ cups all-purpose, soft wheat, or spelt flour, divided
1 tablespoon sugar (omit for savory pies)
½ teaspoon salt
¾ cup butter or chilled lard, or a combination of the two, cut into small pieces
2 tablespoons ice-cold water
2 tablespoons vodka or apple brandy
Potato or rice flour for rolling

1. Measure out ½ cup of the flour and set it aside. In a bowl or food processor, combine remaining flour, sugar, salt, and butter or lard, and process using a fork until all the butter or lard is incorporated and all the flour has been coated. Add the remaining ½ cup flour and process just a few seconds. Sprinkle the water and vodka over the top of the flour mixture and combine just until you get a shaggy dough ball. Flatten the dough into a disc, wrap in plastic wrap or put in a tight fitting, reusable container to reduce airflow around the dough, and refrigerate at least 30 minutes or overnight.

2. When ready to roll out the dough, take it out of the refrigerator and let it sit for 10 minutes to soften. Sprinkle potato or rice flour on the counter and on top of the dough. Roll the dough evenly, picking it up and rotating it a quarter turn every few rolls to keep it round. Add more rice or potato flour as needed. Place an overturned pie plate on top of the dough and trim the dough so it is ½-inch larger than the pie plate. Transfer the crust to a cookie sheet and store it in the refrigerator while you make the pie.

chapter 4
growing your own

So you've decided to grow your own food. Congratulations! You are on the path to self-sufficiency and to discovering the pleasures of eating homegrown vegetables, fruits, and herbs. And your actions may even inspire others down that same path. But where do you start? First, you need to decide *what* you want to grow. Do you want to focus on specialty items such as heirloom tomatoes? Maybe you'd rather emphasize workhorse produce such as lettuce and kale. Or maybe you want to preserve foods that frequently ripen at the same time, such as cucumbers, beans, and peas.

Maybe you live in an apartment but have a small gardening space in a family member's yard or a window herb garden—and a plan to supplement your harvest with visits to farmers markets and U-pick farms. Or maybe you have a large garden and plenty of time and want to grow it all!

PRODUCE

annette's grocery list

ORIGINAL LIST

Fresh and dried herbs

Fresh, canned, and frozen fruit

Fresh, canned, and frozen vegetables

Herbal extracts and essential oils (mint extract, lavender essential oil, etc.)

Honey

Pepper

Tea

REVISED LIST

Year 1: Fruits and berry rootstock, seeds, peppercorn and tea plant, manure, beehives.

Successive years: A handful of seeds.

Begin by creating a "produce eating plan," a chart showing the varieties and quantities of produce you typically eat, by season (see the chart "Sample Produce Eating Plan," next page). At the left of the chart, create a column listing items that you like to eat and that grow well in your climate. To the right of that, make four sets of two columns each, a pair for each season. The first column of each pair shows how much of each produce type you use in a typical week. Multiply that weekly figure by 12.9, the number of weeks in a quarter, and you'll arrive at your seasonal quantity. Insert the seasonal total into the second column of each seasonal pair. Finally, at the far right of your chart, make a column for the total annual amount of each type of produce used (or do this in a computer spreadsheet and let it do the calculations for you).

Now you have an overview of how much produce you will need in a year. It should make certain things clear. For example, it may show you that, to have as much broccoli and tomatoes as your family would like, you'd have to fill up your entire garden space with those plants. It may make more sense to focus on more productive plants like kale, and buy those nice big heads of sprawling broccoli and those tomatoes at the farmers market instead.

Once you know what you want to grow, determine how to stagger your planting schedule so your plants don't all mature at the same time. Of course, this always works better on paper than in the garden: Spring storms, uncooperative sunshine, and/or voracious slugs can delay or even destroy your first round or two of plantings. So be sure to round out your plantings with hardy, fail-proof varieties, just in case. (For instance, I can get beet and lettuce seeds in the ground fairly early, but if the spring sun decides to make its debut in June rather than April, we won't be eating baby beets and tender young greens in our salads. On the other hand, we'll get by just fine on overwintered mâche and arugula.)

To schedule your harvest, check each seed packet for the first and last planting dates and days to harvest. Create a spreadsheet whose columns represent seed varieties and whose rows represent sowing and harvesting times. (See a sample spreadsheet under "Selecting Winter Varieties," page 206.) This will give you a visual tool for counting back from planned harvest date to planting date, so you can stagger your sowings. At a glance, you will be able to see if you have enough types of produce coming ripe at the right time to keep you and your family supplied with fresh, seasonal produce all year. *(AC)*

sample produce eating plan

	Winter Week	Winter Quarter	Spring Week	Spring Quarter	Summer Week	Summer Quarter	Fall Week	Fall Quarter	Total Annual
Kale (bunch)	1	12.9	1	12.9	0	0	1	12.9	38.7
Onions (each)	3	38.7	1	12.9	0	0	1	12.9	64.5
Carrots (bunch)	2	25.8	1	12.9	1	12.9	2	25.8	77.4
Parsnips (bunch)	1	12.9	0	0	0	0	1	12.9	25.8
Tomatoes (each)	0	0	0	0	10	129	10	129	258
Garlic (head)	1	12.9	1	12.9	1	12.9	1	12.9	51.6
Celery (head)	0	0	0	0	1	12.9	1	12.9	25.8
Celeriac (each)	1	12.9	0	0	0	0	0	0	12.9
Broccoli (head)	0	0	1	12.9	1	12.9	0	0	25.8
Cabbage (head)	2	25.8	1	12.9	0	0	2	25.8	64.5
Brussels sprouts (stalk)	1	12.9	0	0	0	0	1	12.9	25.8
Cucumbers (each)	0	0	0	0	20	258	0	0	258
Swiss chard (bunch)	0	0	0	0	2	25.8	2	25.8	51.6
Beetroot (bunch)	0	0	10	129	0	0	10	129	258
Beet greens (bunch)	0	0	2	25.8		0	2	25.8	51.6
Mustard greens (bunch)	2	25.8	2	25.8	1	12.9	2	25.8	90.3
Turnip greens (bunch)	2	25.8	2	25.8	0	0	1	12.9	64.5
Turnips (bunch)	2	25.8	0	25.8	0	0	1	12.9	64.5
Collard greens (bunch)	2	25.8	0	0	0	0	2	25.8	51.6
Salad greens (bunch)	0	0	4	51.6	5	64.5	3	38.7	154.8
Kohlrabi (each)	1	12.9	0	0	0	0	1	12.9	25.8
Broccoli raab (bunch)	0	0	2	25.8	0	0	2	25.8	51.6
Peas (quarts)	0	0	4	51.6	0	0	0	0	51.6
Beans (quarts)	0	0	0	0	3	38.7	3	38.7	77.4
Corn (ears, fresh & dried)	4	51.6	0	0	12	154.8	4	51.6	258
Winter squash (each)	1	12.9	0	0	0	0	1	12.9	25.8
Zucchini (each)	0	0	0	0	2	25.8	0	0	25.8
Potatoes (pounds)	4	51.6	2	25.8	0	0	4	51.6	129

Create a container garden.

Arrange a garden share with a neighbor.

Rip out part of your lawn and plant a summer garden.

Rip out your entire lawn and plant a four-season garden.

• •

designing your garden

Now that you know what you want to grow and when to plant and harvest it, you can start designing your garden.

Begin by considering how much free time and yard space you want to devote to raising food. If you're a new gardener, you may want to start small. The job of planting, maintaining, and harvesting a large garden can be overwhelming.

The first year, consider simply peppering an existing flowerbed with leafy greens, carrots, and some cherry tomatoes. That way you will master a few crops and build on those successes the following season. A garden doesn't need to be large to be successful: A well-planned 4 x 4-foot bed can yield three seasons of carrots, peas, beans, tomatoes, cucumbers, lettuce, corn, and pumpkins and get you some good gardening experience.

But what if you already have some gardening experience and are determined to grow as much of your own food as you can? Start by mapping your property on grid paper, with one square equaling one square foot. Shade in your house and any other structures, as well as areas that are off limits or unusable for gardening (a driveway or patio, a steep slope, your children's favorite play area). But don't completely write those areas off, because they may work great for chickens or honeybees, dairy goats or mushrooms, a compost bin or a water catchment system. Mark off your potential garden beds, then make four copies of your property map so you'll have one for each season.

Next, spend some time determining how much sun your garden beds will receive each season. Will that area be in the shade when the large maple leafs in? Does that part of the yard get parched under the summer sun? Will the side yard receive sunlight in the winter but be shadowed by the house during spring and summer? Label the garden beds in each of your four drawings with the appropriate sun description for the season (or use colored pencils, designating one color for full sun, another for part sun/part shade, and another for dappled shade/full shade).

Now, beginning with the items you most want to grow and using the lighting and spacing guidelines from your seed packages, start filling your diagram with crops. For example, broccoli and cabbage need full sun and a square foot of space each. My family eats broccoli four times a month in the spring and summer, so I put twenty-four broccoli plants in a full-sun garden bed in my spring diagram and twelve plants in the same bed in my summer diagram (by summer we would have already eaten the other twelve). Because I try to keep plant families grouped together, I add other brassica crops from my produce eating plan (such as broccoli raab, kohlrabi, collards, cabbage, Brussels sprouts, and cauliflower) to the remaining free space in that bed.

Understanding just how much (or how little) you can grow will make your expectations realistic. Knowing that you have space for only three heads of cabbage but could fit a half-dozen "cut-and-come-again" Lacinato kale and lettuce plants in the same space may make you decide to buy cabbage at the farmers market and grow your own kale and lettuce. It's better to know these things now than to find them out at the end of the season! *(AC)*

Starter plans for a 4 x 4 bed.

Spring

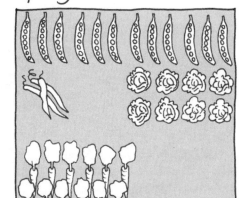

4'x4' garden including
Peas, beans, carrots, lettuce

Summer

4'x4' garden including
Corn, beans, tomatoes, lettuce,
basil, cukes, carrots, pumpkins

garden infrastructure

Irrigation systems, raised beds, and formal pathways all can make your garden easier to manage, but they also lock you into a garden layout. Don't be afraid to keep things simple, investing in infrastructure as you gain confidence as a gardener.

Joshua reclaims part of the driveway for a new garden bed.

to irrigate or not to irrigate?

That garden that was such a joy in June can quickly turn into a ball and chain in August, when it needs careful watering. If you plan to travel during the summer months and don't have someone to water for you, you should give some thought to irrigation before you build your garden beds. It's simple, in a small garden, to put a sprinkler on a timer and program it for twenty minutes twice a week, but a large garden may need a more sophisticated system.

There are many types of irrigation, from simple octopus-style sprinklers to pop-up sprayers to soaker hoses that can be buried beneath ground cover. The latter have the benefit of both conserving water and keeping plant leaves dry, which can help reduce mildew and soilborne diseases such as blight. Finer garden centers and online sources such as DripWorks and Drip Depot (see Resources, page 370) have tutorials and catalogs that can help you decide which style is best for you and your budget. The costs add up quickly, so plan and price out your entire system before deciding. You may find it cheaper to hire a neighbor kid to water for you while you are gone.

Another option is to practice dry gardening techniques if it's a drought year. In the summer when things start to dry out, mulch heavily, and increase the spacing between plantings so they are not competing with other plants for the same amount of soil moisture. Group plants by water needs so you don't end up watering the entire yard equally, and, if possible, let a section of the garden (or better yet, your lawn) go fallow for the season. This has the added bonus of helping you break the cycle of soilborne pests and diseases.

build pathways

Whether or not you use raised beds (see below), your garden should have clearly designated paths to keep you and others from walking through your beds and compacting your soil. Establishing paths can be as simple as laying down cardboard, wood chips, or old two-by-fours to discourage weeds from growing, and making it clear to all just where they should walk. Or you can construct permanent pathways with recycled bricks, concrete, gravel, flagstones, or urbanite (broken, recycled concrete). There is a natural beauty to a simple wood-chip path and a defined elegance and heat-retaining capability to a flagstone path. If you are just starting out, consider installing temporary pathways, knowing you can change them later.

to raise or not to raise?

Although raised beds aren't absolutely necessary, here in the Pacific Northwest they do help with poor drainage and heavy, clay soils. They also prevent your carefully amended soil from washing away during winter and spring rains. If you build your raised beds at least eighteen inches high, you can even garden over contaminated land. Another advantage of

Succession planting in a raised garden bed.

raised beds is that many beginning gardeners find squares and rectangles easier for planning and planting. If you use simple rectangular beds the first year, you can always build something more intricate the following year.

You don't need to be a carpenter or spend a lot of money to build raised beds. Use materials as simple as salvaged two-by-fours nailed into rectangles, or salvaged urbanite (concrete). I've even seen temporary raised beds held together by six-inch-high lengths of tree trunks split in half and then turned face out, or even old wine bottles embedded in the dirt. Simple plastic lawn edging held in place with rebar or stakes works too.

protecting garden beds in high foot traffic areas

In the city, most of us don't have to build fences to prevent deer and elk from eating our plants. However, we do need to keep out pathogens from animal (or human) feces or from litter and garbage. Some of us must also contend with unwanted harvesters.

Fences can range from simple plastic netting and metal U-stakes to more permanent wood structures. If you don't want to fence in your garden, try containers or raised beds tall enough to keep out animals. In the end, though, if you don't feel you can adequately protect your garden, it may be best to seek out produce from local farmers and make your own sprouts indoors.

WHAT ABOUT HARVESTING RAINWATER?

Rain barrels fill up during a single deluge—sometimes in less than two hours—so they can't store all of winter's rains. You can store a bit more by installing rain barrels in a series, but once the rains stop, you'll use up your stored water very quickly. You don't want to eat plants steeped in water that has run off from your roof. Even if you don't have asphalt shingles (and the toxins these bring), you do have bird droppings and thus dangerous bacteria levels. You can get around this by using stored rainwater in ornamental beds rather than in vegetable gardens.

. . . .

grow your own without a yard

What if you want to garden but have no yard? No problem: With just a few square feet of balcony or patio, you can raise vegetables in pots.

There's no doubt that gardening in containers is more difficult than gardening in the ground. All the problems associated with poor soils increase dramatically in containers. Containers experience extreme moisture and temperature fluctuations. Nutrients drain away quickly with the water.

But it's still quite possible. Your job as a container gardener is to provide good potting soil with enough organic content to help buffer the plants against these extreme soil conditions. The limited space makes it easier to observe your plants for signs of stress. And there are practical advantages to container gardening too. For instance, fruits such as tomatoes tend to ripen earlier when grown in containers, since the soil warms up rapidly.

Conventional potting soil mixes rely on peat and vermiculite to make the soil light and fluffy—a necessity for containers, since worms can't survive in pots long enough to aerate the soil. Peat, however, is an unsustainably harvested product, and vermiculite may contain trace quantities of asbestos.

You can create a more environmentally friendly potting soil by mixing your own. Dr. Rita Hummel, a horticultural professor at Washington State University, studies alternative growing media. She recommends a potting soil mix consisting of one part finely shredded Douglas-fir bark (available from nurseries) and one part finished compost.

To Dr. Hummel's mix I would add 1½ cups of complete organic fertilizer (see page 131) for every 3 gallons or so. If you want to get radical, you can add a half-gallon of crumbled biochar (see "Making Biochar in your Backyard," page 128) soaked in liquid organic fertilizer. *(JM)*

choosing a container

To minimize nutrient loss (leaching), choose containers that allow you to water from below, such as the planters made by EarthBOX. If you choose a more conventional planter, you'll need to apply diluted liquid organic fertilizer every two weeks during the summer to make up for nutrient loss. Recommended liquid organic fertilizers include fish emulsion, kelp emulsion, or homemade teas from compost or worm castings.

Some compaction is inevitable in a pot, as the pot lacks the soil critters that help aerate the soil naturally. At the end of the season, remove obvious clumps of dead plant material. It's okay to leave some roots if you chop them up, but don't let root material overwhelm the soil mix. Dump the soil into a 5-gallon bucket, and amend it with compost until the volume will again fill the potting containers. Apply 1½ cups of complete organic fertilizer for every 3 gallons of potting soil. Mix it all up, refill the containers, and protect them from rain until you plant again next spring.

Even if you have nothing more than a part-shade apartment balcony, you can still have a worm bin and grow salad greens, cherry tomatoes, strawberries, columnar apples, carrots, early potatoes, and herbs. Not a bad start to self-sufficiency!

. . . .

GOOD PLANT CHOICES FOR CONTAINERS

Artichokes	Fig trees	Onions
Beets	Garlic	Potatoes
Broccoli	Hardy ginger	Rhubarb
Cabbage	Herbs	Strawberries
Cardoons	Horseradish	Swiss chard
Carrots	Kale	Tomatoes
Columnar apple trees	Leafy greens	Turnips
Compact blueberry bushes	Miniature eggplants	

. . . .

community gardens

At the edge of the community garden known as Marra Farm, in South Seattle, runs a little stream. Once, the stream was covered with garbage. But environmental activists cleaned it up and raised hell when water runoff from a nearby construction project clouded the water. Today the stream gurgles through brambles under an open sky.

On the day I visited, I found a Laotian-American woman named Tunh walking gingerly out onto the log that spanned the little stream. She bent down carefully and scooped a handful of greens from the water. "You can eat it," she told me, handing me a bunch. It tasted like watercress. After a brief tour of her garden plot, I went home with seeds for a purple corn brought over from Laos.

Every time I visit a community garden, I learn something new. Gardens like this act as universities of the soil: Older, more experienced gardeners teach the youngsters how to view the garden as a place of opportunity and delight.

One of my first community gardens was in the densely packed Seattle neighborhood of Capitol Hill. At one end was Randy, snipping the heads off spent daffodil flowers and tying the leaves into attractive little bundles. The leaves continue to feed the bulb, he explained to me, but there's no reason they have to look messy.

On the other end of the garden, a formidable, ornery woman named Sandy stuffed tufts of cat hair and dryer lint between the branches of woody shrubs. For the birds to line their nests, she explained.

While gardens like this helped me find my inner gardening style (I'm more of a cat-hair stuffer than a daffodil bundler), they're increasingly seen as vital to what's known as a city's food security, a trendy term that measures whether all people can access and afford healthy food. Seattle's P-Patch community gardening program has moved aggressively into under-served communities, and gardens like Marra Farm go further by providing thousands and thousands of pounds of produce to food banks and senior citizens.

Similar programs exist in most major cities. You may have to join a waiting list. If you can't find any gardens nearby, consider starting one yourself; most community garden programs are hungry for volunteers willing to help locate and build new garden sites.

You may lack garden space, a yard, all the accoutrements of an urban garden lifestyle in the city. But here's a tip for you apartment dwellers, you students in studios: The secret to enjoying gardening in the city is not having private space. It's having the companionship of other gardeners. *(JM)*

garden sharing

Sometimes people without space can garden in someone else's yard. Many people enjoy a garden, but can't find the time or strength to maintain one.

After Emily and I had moved to Seattle's Fremont neighborhood, we gardened in the backyard of a gregarious vegetarian named Griggs. He lived just down the street from my new P-Patch plot and offered to split his yard between myself and a silent British gentleman. This holding tripled my garden space. When combined with a few containers on my condo's patio for growing shade-tolerant crops, we had as much garden space as our friends among the landed gentry.

Garden sharing has become more popular in Seattle and a growing list of other cities thanks to a website called UrbanGardenShare.org. The site matches up gardeners and willing yard owners.

Because garden shares occur on private property, you'll want to respect your host's personal boundaries. On occasion I've felt I crossed those boundaries, such as when I'd show up at Griggs's garden to find him hosting a dinner party on his back deck. While my host didn't seem to mind my intrusions, you may feel more comfortable if you establish some ground rules with your host in advance. Here are some questions to discuss:

› When is it not okay to visit the garden?
› Does your host expect to receive a portion of the produce?
› Does he use chemical pesticides or fertilizers in his yard?
› Can you (the gardener) bring in soil amendments? If so, is there a place where it's okay to dump compost, while you move it by wheelbarrow to your plot?
› Are there any tools on site that you can use? If so, how can you get access to those tools while remaining respectful of the host's privacy? *(JM)*

gardening with kids

When I decided to rip out the lawn and put in an edible garden, I wanted to instill in my two young sons a love for all the beauty a garden holds. I wanted to share with them the sense of wonder in watching a seed sprout and begin to unfurl its first leaves, to see their amazement as a spider pounced upon its unsuspecting prey and then wrapped it neatly in homespun packaging to enjoy later.

But my boys shared none of my vision; they seemed more interested in jumping off the retaining wall and heading for open traffic. Still, I persisted. My children, I was determined, would come to know good food, to enjoy a crisp carrot plucked straight from the damp earth, to taste a fat pod bursting with sweet peas only seconds after harvest. They would learn valuable life lessons by selling succulent strawberries and dinner salads from a wagon in exchange for toy money.

Early childhood education recognizes the fact that children learn best through activity, and what better place for learning than a garden? Following are some activities you might try with your kids. They have enthralled my children in the garden over the years; I hope they will do the same for yours.

› Dedicate a section of the garden to each child, and let the child choose what to grow and harvest.

Examining baby heirloom carrots.

> Plant some things you don't mind your children destroying: daisies for counting, top-heavy flowers like alliums for beheading, or bushes that can serve as dragons for slaying.

> Include carefree annuals or perennials that children can harvest and put to use in the kitchen: sunflowers for seeds, mint to flavor ice cream, chamomile for sleepy time tea.

> Plant blueberries, strawberries, and peas for your kids to forage at will.

> Plant things that taste like candy: stevia, angelica, anise hyssop.

> Build up your soil. Healthy soil increases the natural sugars (and nutrition) in your peas and carrots, and kids prefer sweeter-tasting vegetables.

> Make spider web frames from sticks and jute and place them around the garden. Ask your children to check daily for new spiders-in-residence.

> Have your kids construct fairy houses from rocks, sticks, moss, and leaves to encourage garden-protecting fairies.

> Construct a homemade rain gauge or wind sock.

> Install a homemade sundial.

> Make a bug book with pictures from the Internet, to help your children identify both good and bad bugs. Then give them a canning jar with screened lid and magnifying glass, and send them on a scavenger hunt.

› Build an earth spiral, a small mound of dirt with an indented track spiraling down the sides. At the base of the track, dig a depression. Let your children pour water at the top of the mound, watching as it travels down and fills the depression. Then let them dig in the mud. (We even have a small "oven" made of salvaged bricks that my sons use for baking mud pies.)

› Give kids a spray bottle of water and ask them to make the leaves shiny.

› Hit up yard sales and thrift shops for garden art, or save up scrap wood and doodads. Give kids paint, a hammer, and some nails and let them construct garden signs and artwork of their own.

› Let them create stepping-stones out of plaster of paris, using plastic plant saucers for molds. Have them make handprints or designs with rocks and marbles before the plaster dries.

The more you let your children shape the garden, the more they will delight in sharing it with you. *(AC)*

Put the kids in charge of harvesting vegetables, even if they won't eat them.

KIDS AND VEGETABLES

Once you've taught your kids to enjoy spending time in the garden, you're halfway to success. But my children still needed coaxing to learn to enjoy vegetables.

In a world dominated by television ads for Pop-Tarts and candy bars, you need not feel shame in deploying whatever means necessary to get your kids comfortable with vegetables. Here are some strategies that have worked for me:

›   I pay my kids a nickel for each head of lettuce harvested (price increases with age). Then I let them prepare a salad for me, scattering vegetable ingredients to satisfy their own creative impulses. As they watch, I visibly enjoy my salad. I express my delight a hundred times, until they ask to try a single leaf dripping with dressing.
›   I offer vegetables as part of a balanced meal, but I don't force my kids to eat them.
›   I offer them a single Lego block from a set for every serving of vegetables consumed.
›   I prepare pesto, grinding the basil less and less finely each time and slyly substituting other greens, until eventually I'm serving my kids pasta with braised greens.
›   I feed rejected vegetables to the chickens. At least my kids will get some of those nutrients through their eggs. *(JM)*

chapter 5
it's all in the dirt

Have you ever known someone with a green thumb? Someone who could grow just about anything? Many of those green-thumbed gardeners will tell you that their secret lies not in how they treat their plants, but in how they build up their soil. Plants grown in poor soils quickly fall prey to insects and diseases, because so much of a plant's strength comes from the ground.

In the city, we often begin with poor soils. In this chapter we'll explore how to build and rebuild good soil structure (called "tilth") using traditional techniques like composting alongside recently rediscovered ancient techniques like biochar. We'll feed the soil with organic fertilizers and protect it with mulches, and explore the multifunctioned miracle of cover crops.

If you reclaim a patch of earth from beneath a driveway or under a neglected lawn, you're likely to find bare mineral soil. You may find clay, you may find sand. They both make a fine starting point for garden soil, but sand doesn't hold water or nutrients worth a damn, and clay, while it holds water and nutrients better, introduces other problems. Both of these mineral soils improve dramatically when you add organic matter.

Organic matter has lots of holes, like a sponge. It soaks up water and nutrients and keeps them there, until plants send their roots into every nook and cranny looking for sustenance.

Organic matter feeds billions of microscopic creepy-crawly things. It contains energy—energy from the sun, harvested and locked away by plants using photosynthesis. The energy hides in carbon rings, along with countless other nutrients needed to sustain life. When microorganisms eat those carbon rings to get the energy, they release the nutrients slowly by dying or pooping. These nutrients hide in the nooks and crannies of soil organic matter until they're needed by another organism—a worm, or a carrot.

Because microorganisms consume organic matter, farmers and gardeners need to replenish some of it every year. You could use manure, but in the city, the most convenient form of organic content is compost. *(JM)*

. . . .

OPPORTUNITIES FOR CHANGE
DIRT

Buy compost and fertilizer.

Buy compost and fertilizer and plant cover crops.

Plant cover crops and make your own compost from kitchen scraps, garden waste, and manure from backyard animals.

Plant cover crops and make your own compost from kitchen scraps, garden waste, and manure from backyard animals; also get a worm bin.

Do all of the above and also make your own biochar.

. . . .

compost

Composting is all about breaking things down, and incorporating them back into the earth. It's about taking the detritus in our lives and converting it into something wholesome and life giving.

Municipal composters like Cedar Grove digest Seattle's yard waste with great efficiency. Their piles get hot—up to 180°F, very close to the temperature at which milk is pasteurized. This sterilizes the compost, killing most plant diseases and weed seeds, and all but the most heat-tolerant microorganisms.

Your own backyard compost pile will be rich with all kinds of microorganisms, from primary decomposers like bacteria to secondary decomposers like worms, slugs, centipedes, and potato bugs. I rely on municipal compost for volume. I use my homegrown compost to inoculate that stable, sterile compost with life.

Backyard compost bins won't get hot enough to kill most plant diseases or insect pests. But generally I've chosen not to worry about that. In the city, diseases and pests will find your plants no matter what you do. Better to build the soil with compost, increasing your plants' resistance to these threats.

The ingredients that go into compost fall into two categories: greens and browns. Greens contain lots of nitrogen and include stuff like lawn clippings and weeds. Browns contain mostly carbon and include things like autumn leaves and straw. Most green garden waste turns brown if you leave it to dry.

To make compost, you combine equal volumes of greens and browns. You put them in a big pile, add water, and leave them alone to rot. If you're lazy, you can leave it at that. If you're a busybody like me, you can fuss with your pile to hurry it along.

At Annette's house, Jared, her husband, adds a layer of greens to the compost pile every time he mows the lawn. Then Annette adds a layer of browns when she cleans out the chicken coop bedding or rakes up some leaves. When she needs compost, she pulls aside the new material on top and harvests finished compost from the bottom of the pile.

In contrast with this, my compost pile is a compost factory. I use a classic "three-bin" system consisting of three 3-foot cubes. A three-bin system lets you move things along faster, by turning compost with a pitchfork back and forth between the first two bins every two weeks or so. This keeps the compost loose and full of air. Microorganisms work faster when they have easy access to oxygen. A well-turned, well-built compost pile will grow so warm that you could climb inside and survive a winter's night, like Luke Skywalker inside his tauntaun on the icy planet Hoth.

To increase the volume of compost I produce, I suck up all the organic waste I can find in my neighborhood, such as by bumming lawn clippings and fallen leaves from the neighbors. One year, my son and I filled my pickup truck with free pumpkins from the

Chopping compostables with a machete in front of a three-bin system.

grocery store on the day after Halloween. We had a grand old time smashing them in the driveway.

A couple of weeks later, however, the pumpkins attracted rats. That taught me a valuable lesson: Food scraps (including smashed pumpkins) don't belong in the urban compost bin (unless it's rat proof). And so today, we divert our table scraps to one of two buried rat-proof enclosures called "green cones."

We keep a green cone just outside our front door and use it like a garbage can for food. We use it for things our chickens don't eat, such as coffee grounds and potato skins. It's the ultimate low-maintenance system: We never aerate it, we just let the worms do the work for us. When it gets full, we switch to green cone number 2. After six months, the table scraps in the first cone have turned to worm poop—gardener's gold.

You can make a homemade green cone at your house by drilling holes in a small metal garbage can and burying it two-thirds of the way in the ground.

Whether you use a lazy compost pile or an efficient three-bin system, you probably can't make enough compost to feed impoverished urban soils. And so you'll have to buy some. *(JM)*

• •

HOW TO BUILD ANNETTE'S LAZY COMPOST PILE

› Pile up organic materials in a forgotten corner of the yard.
› Add new materials to the top of the pile.
› If you can, alternate layers of greens and browns.
› Harvest finished compost from the bottom of the pile.

• •

HOW TO BUILD JOSHUA'S EFFICIENT COMPOST PILE USING A THREE-BIN SYSTEM

› Chop up green and brown ingredients with a machete.
› Mix greens and browns thoroughly on a tarp, moistening them as you go. Toss them into bin 1. Cover the pile with a moist burlap coffee bag.
› In two weeks, toss the pile with a pitchfork from bin 1 to bin 2. In another two weeks, toss it back into bin 1. Repeat until the pile appears uniformly brown. Periodically water the pile. Keep it moist as a wrung-out sponge.
› Use ½-inch hardware cloth to screen finished compost into bin 3. It's now ready to bury in your garden! What didn't pass through the screen can return to a new, working pile in the first two bins.

• •

where to buy compost

All affordable composts utilize some waste stream or other. In Seattle, Cedar Grove Composting uses material from the curbside yard and food waste recycling program. Other recyclers use agricultural or industrial waste streams, such as poultry or cow manures mixed with bark, wood chips, or sawdust.

These companies vary dramatically as you travel from city to city, and many of them deserve praise for helping us recycle our own waste. Still, I'd want to see any compost before ordering a truckload. Give it a good look: Does the material appear to have been fully composted? There should be no visible fresh wood or white chicken waste; the whole handful should be uniformly brown and should smell neutral, sweet, or even slightly burnt. Your local nursery is a good place to start researching the composts available in your area. If the nursery doesn't offer a brand in bulk, you may be able to order it directly from the manufacturer.

You can also find horse manure wherever horses are kept outside the city. Sometimes it needs more time to become fully composted, and sometimes it contains weed seeds. Sometimes it's mixed with conventionally grown straw, which can contain residual pesticides. But under the right conditions, horse manure can be a valuable and nearly free soil amendment.

For a list of compost manufacturers and resources for finding manure in the Pacific Northwest, consult the Resources section at the end of this book.

. . . .

HOW MUCH COMPOST DO I NEED?

YEAR 1 Use this equation to determine how many yards of compost to make or buy when preparing neglected urban soil for a new garden:

A (area of garden in square feet) x 0.015 = C (cubic yards of compost required)

For example, to improve a 10 by 10-foot patch of barren soil, you need 1.5 cubic yards (usually referred to as, simply, "yards") of compost. This will spread out to about 5 inches of compost.

YEAR 2 After the first year of soil building, you can get by with about an inch of compost every year. Use this formula:

A (area of garden in square feet) x 0.003 = C (cubic yards of compost required)

YEAR 2 ALTERNATIVE For such a small amount, you may prefer to buy compost in bags, which are labeled in cubic feet. In that case, use this formula:

A (area of garden in square feet) x 0.081 = C (cubic feet of compost)

For the same 10 by 10-foot garden, you would only need 0.3 cubic yards or 8.1 cubic feet.

. . . .

why is compost so important?

Before the industrial revolution, aged manure, a form of compost, provided much of the nitrogen needed to amend soils. British sodium nitrate mines in Chile provided another source of nitrogen for fertilizer. Byproducts of the coke and steel industry provided yet another source of nitrogen. But until some chemists in Germany developed a method of harvesting nitrogen (in the form of ammonia) from natural gas, most farmers husbanded organic matter in the soil carefully in order to make the most of their available nitrogen.

Ammonia has a secondary use as an inexpensive explosive. During the two World Wars, production of ammonia by the German method ramped up. After the wars, the bomb manufacturers needed a market for all their nitrogen, and they started cranking out chemical fertilizers for farmers. I can just imagine the chemists pitching the idea to farmers over a stein of beer: "Just think—you'll never have to haul manure again. You can provide all the nitrogen your plants need, whenever they need it." The German chemists won Nobel prizes, and their work led to a "green revolution." Eventually, the global population would explode as a result of all the inexpensive food grown from cheap nitrogen.

But this chemical dependency led farmers to undervalue soil organic matter, and as soil microorganisms consumed most of the organic matter in the soil, the side effects of industrialized agriculture began to show. Plants grown on industrial fertilizers were bigger, but they weren't necessarily more nutritious. The protein was there, but the ammonia did not also provide a similar increase in micronutrients, so the resulting plants were less nutritious than their ancestors. *(JM)*

. . . .

LET YOUR KIDS PEE ON THE COMPOST PILE!

Urine contains lots of nitrogen, so why flush it down the toilet? Pee comes out too strong for plants (you need to dilute it 16:1 to use it for fertilizer), and if applied to a barren soil incapable of holding on to that nitrogen, it can get into the groundwater and feed algae blooms that rob lakes and streams of oxygen.

But a compost pile is a machine for holding on to nitrogen. Technically, everybody should pee on the compost pile. But we don't. Grownups find it socially awkward, girls find it physically awkward. But young boys can get away with it. So if you have young boys, locate your compost pile in a private corner of the yard and let them have sword fights there with their pee. If your neighbors catch on, you can always just shrug and grin. After all, boys will be boys.

. . . .

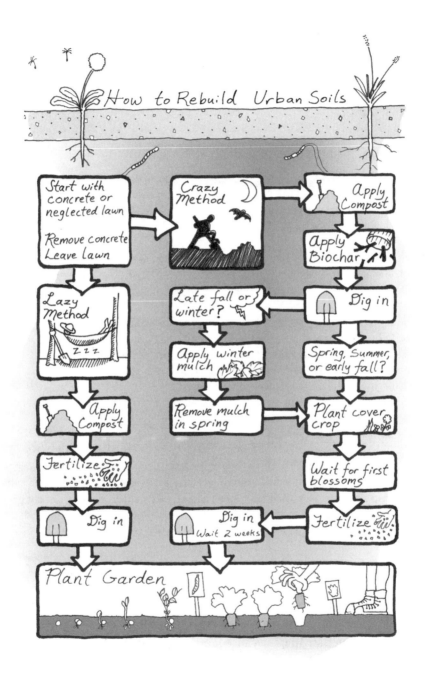

How to Rebuild Urban Soils

Start with concrete or neglected lawn

Remove concrete
Leave lawn

Crazy Method

Apply Compost

Apply Biochar

Lazy Method
Zzz

Late fall or winter?

Dig in

Apply winter mulch

Spring, Summer, or early fall?

Apply Compost

Remove mulch in spring

Plant cover crop

Fertilize

Wait for first blossoms

Dig in

Dig in
Wait 2 weeks

Fertilize

Plant Garden

Abundant synthetic nitrogen introduced logistical problems too. Wheat, for example, grew too tall. Like a genetically modified dinosaur with ballerina legs, it collapsed in the field. Breeders had to develop short, stubby new strains just to cope with the problem. To further complicate life on these chemically dependent farms, plants grown without healthy soil ecosystems at their roots proved more vulnerable to drought, more prone to diseases and insect predators.

• •

TEST YOUR SOIL

Before you grow your own food, have your soil tested for contaminants. The University of Massachusetts and many local agricultural programs offer low-cost soil testing (see Resources). Be sure the test checks for heavy metals; while you may feel empowered by growing your own food, you don't want your plants taking up toxic chemicals from the soil.

If you find contaminated soils in your garden, it's not the end of the world. (Certain areas of my yard contain lead, arsenic, and other such substances.) But those areas will need special care. Bury them under deep organic mulches, and plant edibles that don't uptake toxic chemicals.

The following areas of your yard probably contain some toxic chemicals:
› Soils next to buildings constructed before 1978 (when lead paint was banned)
› Soils next to busy highways or railroad tracks (may contain lead or oil)
› Old orchard sites (an old pesticide contained both lead and arsenic)
› Soils downwind of metal smelters (may contain arsenic)
› Soils near treated lumber, including creosote railroad ties and a few (especially older) pressure-treated lumbers
› Soils near abandoned heating oil tanks.

Some plants are safer than others for growing in contaminated soils, because when pollutants do show up in plants, they tend to find expression in the green, leafy parts rather than in the fruits. Plant likely polluted areas with blueberries and espaliered fruit trees. If you want to grow vegetables in an area that's likely to be contaminated, make your raised beds 24 inches high; vegetable roots typically don't reach deeper than 18 inches.

• •

Today, many food consumers have begun seeking what they call "nutrient-dense" food. Understanding what cheap nitrogen does to food, it's no mystery why these people favor old-style organic agriculture. That's because food grown more slowly, in concert with a full orchestra of soil microorganisms, provides more nutrition.

But it's not enough just to grow organically, as that method only addresses some of our system's deficiencies. What we need now is a revolution in farming methods, a way to feed the world while rebuilding our soils. Recently, traditional agriculture has started to respond to the crisis of soil degradation. Many land-grant universities now push progressive farming methods that reincorporate agricultural waste directly into the soil by either tilling it in or leaving it there to rot.

As an urban gardener, you have an advantage. Big industrial farmers have thousands of acres of soil to improve. But you only need to rebuild the soil on your own property. *(JM)*

biochar

Biochar is charcoal intended for burial. You create biochar by burning organic waste in a carefully controlled fire until it turns to charcoal. You douse the fire before it consumes the charcoal, let it steep in diluted fertilizer for a day, and bury the charcoal in your garden. It's a fancy way to convert some of your waste stream into something that helps your garden grow. Plus, it's carbon negative (more on that below).

Biochar has a huge surface area. When buried in the soil, it provides billions of nooks and crannies for critters and nutrients to hide in. It has a slight negative charge, allowing it to hold on to positively charged water and nutrient molecules. Compost has similar qualities, but unlike compost, the carbon in biochar can't be consumed by soil microorganisms, not for tens of thousands of years. Compost must be added to your garden every year. After you've added biochar to your soil, though, you can sit back and enjoy the benefits for the rest of your life.

Today, biochar has environmentalists excited, because burial of charcoal removes carbon from the carbon cycle and thus helps fight global climate change. In the carbon cycle, plants inhale carbon from the atmosphere. After the plants die and fall to the ground, they decompose, and eventually the carbon returns to the atmosphere. The carbon cycle itself is "carbon neutral." If you remove anything permanently from that cycle, then that's "carbon negative."

As for the fire used to make biochar, it is only environmentally sustainable if it meets two conditions. First, it must not pollute. Second, it must run on garden waste: garden stakes or arborist's chips, things that would have decomposed within a few years. If you burn firewood, that's not sustainable; wood is relatively stable and does a fine job locking up carbon without passing through a biochar fire.

making biochar in your backyard

In order to create biochar sustainably, you need an efficient cookstove, a stove that gets so hot it burns the smoke, virtually eliminating pollution. Because they're efficient, such stoves run on garden waste—things like old bamboo stakes, corncobs, and dry rabbit poop.

I learned how to build a biochar stove at a stove-building workshop hosted by the non-profit SeaChar.org. SeaChar's "Garden Master Stove" does a good job of burning the smoke, eliminating pollution. But there's an even simpler stove you can build on your own, if you'd like to experiment with biochar.

How to Make Biochar from Garden Waste

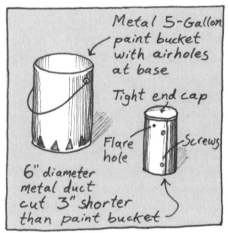

Metal 5-Gallon paint bucket with airholes at base

Tight end cap

Flare hole

Screws

6" diameter metal duct cut 3" shorter than paint bucket

Pack duct with dry garden waste

and place upside-down in paint bucket

Build fire around and atop duct inside bucket

Burn 45-60 minutes until gas stops flaring from flare hole

Dump hot coals from both containers into water plus liquid organic fertilizer

Bury finished biochar in garden

Because all fires produce smoke, many people don't understand how biochar production can be carbon negative. And although it's true the fires themselves produce smoke, the carbon sent into the atmosphere is mathematically much lower over a 2–4 year period than would have occurred had the garden waste decomposed naturally.

Still, there are ample reasons, especially in the city, to curb smoke pollution. You can upgrade your simple biochar stove by adding a chimney. Take the original paint can metal lid or garbage can lid and cut a 6-inch circle cut out of the center (a difficult task—make friends with a metal worker). On top of this hole, attach another length of 6-inch-diameter duct as a chimney. Though you will need to remove this lid periodically to feed the fire, much of the smoke will combust within this chimney. You can further improve your stove by adding a corrugated metal sleeve around the outer can (for insulation) and wooden handles (to facilitate dumping the contents).

Create up to one pound of biochar for every square foot of barren soil you want to amend. *(JM)*

fertilizer

Compost probably won't supply all your plants' nutritional needs. Chances are, you'll need to apply fertilizer as well. Instead of resorting to a chemical fertilizer (such as Miracle-Gro), choose an organic fertilizer derived from plant or animal products. To understand why, consider the following illustration.

Say you're going to run a marathon tomorrow. What do you want for dinner tonight, a lollipop or pasta? Too easy? Okay, say it's a really big lollipop, one that contains the same number of calories as the pasta dinner. For most of us, the answer is obvious: We'd choose the pasta dinner, because we know it's not just the calories that are important, it's the sustained pace at which they become available to the body. The lollipop would give you a rush of energy at the beginning, then leave you crumpled and depressed at the ten-mile mark. The pasta dinner would take you farther—heck, you might even finish!

Chemical fertilizers are like lollipops for your garden. Their water-soluble nutrients surge through the soil. The plants grab what they can, and the rest washes out to sea, where it does all kinds of damage. Eventually the plants require another fix. When that happens, you'd better be there, armed with a backup gallon of the chemical fertilizer.

Organic fertilizers contain much lower percentages of water-soluble nutrients, so they don't wash away with the first rain. As in compost, microorganisms and fungi help release the nutrients slowly. If you've amended your soil with compost, your compost will help hold on to these fertilizers, even as they break down and become water soluble. Plants grown in this kind of soil receive a slow trickle of essential nutrients, much like the runner who ate pasta the night before the race.

The term "organic" confuses many gardeners because organic fertilizers include minerals that don't come from living organisms. For example, agricultural lime comes from mines. However, organic fertilizers, whether mined or derived from plants and animals, share a common function: They build healthy soils.

You may be able to grow bigger, greener plants by pumping them full of chemically derived nutrients. But when it comes to healthy, productive plants, organic fertilizers prove that slow and steady wins the race. *(JM)*

dig it in

If you leave all your compost and fertilizer on the soil surface, plants won't have much reason to send their roots deep. When the summer drought arrives, their shallow roots won't have access to the water reserves held in the subsoil, and the plants will die. This is why we dig: to mix fertilizers and compost down to about eighteen inches, so that roots will grow deep.

At some point, plants will encounter a division between amended soil and subsoil. As a digger of gardens, you should try to blur the division between those two layers so your plants won't notice the difference.

When I turn in my compost, fertilizer, or biochar, I like to work with a wheelbarrow at my side. This lets me store a little of the excavated soil. When I've excavated to somewhere between twelve and eighteen inches, I poke holes into the bare subsoil with a piece of rebar or a pick. Next, I alternate shovelfuls of new material and native soil to refill the hole, slowly increasing the proportion of compost as I approach the soil surface. For the final few inches, I mix the compost and native soil well, as seeds sprout better in fine-grained soils.

After I've turned the soil to this depth once, I don't bother going deeper than six to eight inches any year after that, if I choose to dig at all. That's because once you've introduced cracks in the subsoil, worms and roots will continue to erode this boundary over the years.

As an example, consider what happens below my tomato plants: By August, I've weaned my tomatoes off of the hose, training them to force their roots deep into the subsoil. The tomato's thick root mass fills every crack and fissure in the soil. When October ends the tomato season, I cut off the plants just below the soil surface. Immediately, that huge root mass underground starts to rot. Worms eat the rotting roots, follow the root paths into the subsoil, and line those paths with nutritious worm poop. Rainwater washes more topsoil nutrients down these tubes. These fertilizers pool down in the subsoil, forming buried treasure chests of nutrition. Fungi will send their fibrous transparent hyphae down these tubes.

In healthy soil, living things spend a lot of time and energy moving nutrients around, binding them together with spit and excrement into stable, porous crumbs, waiting for roots with whom they can strike a symbiotic deal, exchanging soil nutrients for starches and sugars created through photosynthesis. Next year, all that subsoil activity will give my plants plenty of reasons to send their roots down deeper than ever before. *(JM)*

• •

STEVE SOLOMON'S COMPLETE ORGANIC FERTILIZER RECIPE

While all soils have different requirements, you'll usually get away with applying a standardized organic fertilizer. You can use an expensive premixed fertilizer, or you can mix your own from inexpensive bulk ingredients from a feed store. Organic gardening expert Steve Solomon popularized the following recipe. I've adapted it slightly to fit ingredients we can find in the Pacific Northwest.

Mix uniformly, in parts by volume:
›   4 parts alfalfa seed meal or cottonseed meal*
›   ¼ part ordinary agricultural lime**
›   ¼ part gypsum
›   ½ part dolomitic lime**

Plus, for best results:
›   1 part bone meal, rock phosphate, or high-phosphate guano
›   ½ to 1 part kelp meal (or 1 part basalt dust)

To apply: Every spring before planting, spread a ½-inch-deep layer of steer manure or finished compost (if this is your garden's first year, you'll have applied much more). Spread 4 to 6 quarts of fertilizer for every 100 square feet of garden area.

*For a more sustainable and less expensive option, you can substitute chemical-free grass clippings for the seed meal, although clippings will not provoke the same strong growth response. Use about a ½-inch-thick layer of fresh clippings (six to seven 5-gallon bucketfuls per 100 square feet) chopped into the top 2 inches of your soil with a hoe. Then spread an additional 1-inch-thick layer as a surface mulch.
** If you apply biochar to your garden, you should omit lime and gypsum for one year.

For a list of places where you can buy organic fertilizer ingredients, see Resources, page 370. You can read more about Steve Solomon's gardening methods in his book *Gardening When It Counts*.

• •

mulching

While the subsoil maintains a constant level of moisture, the topsoil fluctuates through extreme changes in both moisture and temperature. The worst of these extremes occur at the frontier between topsoil and air. Here on the bleeding edge of the soil's surface, moisture can evaporate quickly, leaving a desert. Temperatures can swing dramatically as the sun rises overhead; in the winter, things will even freeze. Only the most resilient soil organisms can survive such an extreme environment. Those with legs (and a few without) can escape the dehydrating sun, the relentless soil-compacting rains, the swooping predators. They seek shelter in their holes, or under leaves.

You can make things much easier for these soil organisms by covering the soil surface with a course organic material such as fallen leaves, compost, or grass clippings. We call this layer a *mulch*.

- -

WHAT MATERIALS SHOULD I MULCH WITH?

The best mulches provide food for soil creatures and resist the compaction that occurs when you water your plants. Coarse mulches or mulches with a variety of particle sizes resist compaction better than mulches with a uniformly small particle size. For example, a mixture of leaves and grass clippings makes a better mulch than grass clippings alone, and rugged home compost makes a better mulch than fine-grained municipal compost.

Whenever you dig material into the soil, you want it to be fully composted. However, when you apply a material as a mulch, you have more freedom to use uncomposted or partially composted materials.

Recommended mulches for vegetable gardens:

Burlap	Home compost
Coffee chaff	Large leaves, shredded
Coffee grounds*	Composted steer manure
Composted chicken manure/bedding	Municipal compost*
Composted horse manure	Rabbit manure
Crushed eggshells	Reemay or another brand of row-cover fabric
Fine leaves, such as alder or willow	Shredded newspapers (ugly but functional)*
Goat manure	Straw
Grass clippings*	

*For best results, mix with coarser material

- -

When you cover the soil's surface with a mulch, the frontier becomes a gentler place, almost civilized. Worms lounge around, snacking on this or that, even as the killing frosts inch across the mulch surface. Slugs and snails peacefully lay their eggs . . .

Wait a minute! Slugs and snails? You don't want those in your garden, right?

Mulch is a double-edged sword. It protects the things you want in your soil, but it also protects the bad. In a healthy soil, beetles will help keep down slug populations by eating slug eggs. But they're unlikely to eat enough of them quickly enough to save your spring cabbage seedlings. For that reason, I like to use mulch carefully, at specific times of the year when slugs cannot threaten my seedlings.

These are the times I like to use mulch:

1. If I've waited too long to plant a cover crop, I apply a winter mulch of fallen leaves. This will partly protect my soil from winter rains, rains that would leach out nutrients and compact the soil. I always remove my winter mulch in early spring so the sun can warm up the soil. If you leave your mulch on too long, your soil will be too cold when you plant your garden. Cold soil microorganisms don't eat soil organic matter, so plants can't get the nutrients they need to grow.

2. After plants have grown tall enough to withstand slug attacks, I apply a summer mulch to help keep the soil moist. This helps protect plants and soil organisms from drought.

In a perennial garden dominated by woody shrubs and trees, you may actually welcome slugs as just another decomposer. That's why in perennial gardens you can use woodier mulches, mulches that take longer to break down.

I like to apply a thick carpet of arborist's chips throughout my perennial beds and permanent pathways. Arborists grind their tree trimmings and will gladly dump a truckful in your driveway. I like to sweeten the invitation by throwing in three or four microbrews, though recently word has gotten out and I may have to raise my tip to a whole six-pack. *(JM)*

growing cover crops

Cover crops protect the soil surface, much like a mulch. But because they're living plants, they benefit the soil much more directly than do mulches. Alive, their roots bind soil particles together; dead, their roots form veins of food for fungi and microorganisms.

Many garden centers carry bulk cover-crop seeds. I like to select a variety of them. First, I choose legumes like vetches, fava beans, and clover. These I mix with cereal crops like rye, buckwheat, and oats. Some cover crops perform better in cool weather, others in hot weather. By planting a variety of cover crops, I enjoy a successful cover crop no matter what the garden gods throw at me.

Once planted, cover crops create a little ecosystem of their own. The cereal crops grow tall and send their roots deep, while the legumes quickly build green biomass. Vetch uses the cereal crop to climb higher. Favas look beautiful and pull out easily for winter chicken food. Radish tops make great chicken food, and the taproots may be left to rot in place. In the summer, I add flowers like calendula to the mix. Although I dig my cover crops in before they blossom, I like to leave little patches of blossoming cover crop here and there as a thank-you gift for pollinating insects.

"any season" cover crop mix

This mix can be planted anytime from late winter through early fall. For every 100 square feet of garden area, plant:

›   ⅛ pound of cereal rye (you can experiment with other whole, unground grains from your pantry)
›   ⅛ pound of yellow blossom sweet clover (in case the weather gets hot)*
›   ⅛ pound of common vetch*
›   ¼ pound of fava beans*
›   a sprinkling of buckwheat seeds
›   a sprinkling of forage or fodder radish seeds (or substitute long daikon radish seeds)
›   a sprinkling of calendula seeds

*a nitrogen-fixing legume

For a longer list of cover crops appropriate for the Pacific Northwest, see page 369.

when to plant cover crops

›   After you've built a new garden bed. A cover crop, when dug in, will charge the soil with nitrogen, a requirement for plant growth.
›   In the early fall, for overwintering. Nitrogen is difficult to keep in the soil; it becomes water soluble too easily. Even with compost and biochar holding tightly on to some nitrogen, much of it will wash away in the winter rains. That means one of the safest places to store nitrogen and other nutrients for next year is in a plant's tissue. A cover crop acts as a nitrogen bank. In the spring, you'll cash in your account by digging in the cover crop.
›   Any time you want to give your soil a rest. A legume cover crop can recharge your soil

with new nitrogen, harvested from the air. Try to rest garden soils at least one season every second year.

when to dig in cover crops

To get the most nitrogen out of your cover crop, turn it under just as the first blossoms begin to emerge. If the soil isn't too muddy, you can chop it up into little bits with a sharp shovel. Make sure most of the crop is buried—anything lying on the surface will quickly give up its nitrogen to the atmosphere. *(JM)*

. . . .

LEGUMES: THE LIFE OF THE SOIL PARTY

If soil life is like a crazy frat party, then legumes are the guy who can drink beer while standing on his head. That's because legumes perform a clever party trick called "fixing nitrogen."

Most plants can't make their own nitrogen. They have to wait for soil microorganisms to mete out nitrogen slowly, as the little guys consume soil organic matter.

Legumes take a different route: They form symbiotic relationships with special bacteria that harvest nitrogen directly from the air. All that nitrogen fuels abundant green growth. This allows legumes such as clovers to flourish in poor soils even as other plants struggle. When you dig in your cover crop, much of that nitrogen returns to the soil, where soil microbes will release it for other plants.

The legumes like to keep things nice and comfy for their bacteria pets. They feed the bacteria a steady diet of carbohydrates, manufactured through photosynthesis. They provide free housing in the form of brittle, fleshy envelopes called "nodules," which line the legume roots. You can see them if you pull up a legume by the roots. Crack open a nodule with your fingernail. If you see red or pink inside, it's full of active bacteria. If you see only white, the nodule is vacant.

Each legume species coevolved with a slightly different bacterium. Although the bacteria reside naturally in the soil where the legumes grow wild, they may not yet exist in the soil of a young garden. That means that the first time you plant a new legume species in your garden, you need to introduce the appropriate bacteria to their new home. You can purchase these bacteria in powdered form, called "inoculants," at garden centers. They come in little plastic envelopes. On the back, you'll find a list of legumes served by that particular bacterium. After you've introduced a bacterium, you don't need to inoculate again, at least not for that specific legume.

To introduce an inoculant into a young garden bed, dampen your legume seeds with milk and roll them in the inoculant powder. Plant them right away. *(JM)*

. . . .

chapter 6
going to the source

As fulfilling as it is to grow your own food, you can make just as big
a difference if you seek out and buy from local farmers who grow
heirloom varieties in a way that stewards the land. That doesn't
mean simply switching from conventional big-company-grown
produce to organically grown produce. Those hermetically sealed
bags of prewashed baby spinach and spring greens you buy in January
may bear an organic label, but they are miles from having the same
nutritional punch, flavor, and low carbon impact as a bunch of local,
biodynamically grown Lacinato kale.

Seek out local farmers, or stores and markets that carry local, seasonal produce. Ask questions about where and how the produce is grown: Just because vendors are selling local produce at a farmers market doesn't mean they are doing the right thing by the land or by you. Take the time to visit local farms, to learn about their growing practices. If you buy direct from the farmer, you'll get better prices. In fact, the very best bargains come from farmers who are so small they don't even sell at farmers markets.

Farmers market scams are real and growing. Question the vendors. Find out where they farm, to make sure they work for the actual farm and are not just reselling produce from someplace else. If the market has an information table, ask about the vendors and the farms; you can even ask the farmers for information about one another. Whenever food co-ops and grocery stores display "grown locally" signs, take the time to find out which local farm grew the produce. This lets the store know that you care and makes them more accountable. *(AC)*

Harvesting produce at Marra Farm, a community garden.

CSA: community supported agriculture

Community Supported Agriculture began in Europe in the 1960s as a response to food safety issues (what a positive way of dealing with them!), and as a way for consumers to support farmers who follow less commercially viable but more ecologically sound farming methods. Under the CSA system, the consumer pledges to support a farm, usually for a full growing season, and shares the risks and benefits that the farmer may experience. Normally, the consumer receives a weekly box of produce, although some programs contain other types of foods, such as dairy products or meat, or even personal care products like soaps or lotions.

Some CSA programs are very flexible, letting you choose the items and the size of your box. Others are not as flexible. If you are a creative cook and open-minded about the types of foods you eat, CSAs can be wonderful ways to ensure that you always have a plethora of fresh produce around. If, however, you have a large and picky family, and your CSA box tends to contain small quantities of some things (think one lonely artichoke) and endless amounts of others (think months of spring radishes and kohlrabi), then perhaps a CSA—or the particular CSA you belong to—is not the right thing for you.

Here in Seattle, some CSA programs have become so commercialized that they buy mailing lists and send out advertisements to gain new customers. Any CSA large enough to support that kind of growth is not likely to grow all its own produce. They may be buying from other local farms, but more likely they buy produce grown outside the area and sometimes even outside the country, especially during the off season. I'm not sure that's much better than simply shopping at a food co-op.

If you join a CSA in order to support a local farmer, choose the farmer carefully. All local farmers are not created equal, nor are all CSAs. Go to the farm and see whether and how animals fit into the picture, and if they do, how the farmers house and manage their livestock. Observe how they manage their fields. Note the types of crops they grow. Ask about seed varieties and sources. Ask about brix measurements (plant sugar readings that help indicate the nutritional value of crops). Ask about soil amendments, livestock feed, and wildlife- and pest-management strategies. If animals are not incorporated into the farm, where do the soil amendments come from?

There is a lot more to farming than just growing crops, and being a good steward of the land is as important as producing a pretty heirloom apple or tomato.

Joining the CSA of a local farmer you want to support helps everyone. It helps smaller farmers predict future demand, providing them with much-needed seed and operational funds. And it helps you by providing you with a box of fresh produce delivered to you weekly at a fair price. It also commits you to local eating with little work on your part. *(AC)*

COA: community owned agriculture

Although I can do a lot on a small piece of land in the city, I can never do all the things I want to do here. Certainly, I can have chickens and ducks for eggs and a small amount of meat, or goats for dairy (provided my neighbors don't complain about the noise). But I can't grow all their food here. I'm also still buying sunflower oil, despite the fact that sunflowers are the one oil crop we can grow in our climate. When it comes to meat, I'm reliant on local farmers for most of it, and it doesn't always come the way I want it: My beef from the butchers doesn't come with the hide, my pig doesn't come with intestines for stuffing sausages, my meat birds don't come with feathers, and my lamb doesn't come with wool for knitting or weaving.

Instead, all those things are going into incinerators or landfills, and I'm buying new down pillows and belts and sausage casings and yarn. If the idea of making these things ourselves seems farfetched in this day and age, it may be because the work involved makes it undoable by a lone individual. In olden days it took a village (or a large family) to do these things; each member specialized in hog butchering or blacksmithing or curing hides or weaving.

Eggplant and a deep purple corn from Laos, at Marra Farm.

In the same way that I struggle to grow, preserve, and prepare enough of a variety of food for my family by myself, even the most determined back-to-the-lander would be hard pressed to accomplish all these things on her own. So, while I dream of having land outside the city where I can raise all my own meat animals, forage, grains, and produce, I know it's too big a burden for me to tackle alone. I'm not sure we could manage by ourselves even if the rest of my family shared these same ideals. While we've driven around all year looking for acreage outside the city, the reality of what that life would look like has prevented us from taking the plunge. The kids don't want to leave their friends or the city's many activities. My husband doesn't want the commute, or to have to deal with the amount of livestock that I would accumulate. I know there are intentional communities out there, but we aren't quite ready to give up our personal space and lifestyle choices to join one.

But what if there were a kind of hybrid of the two? A sort of timeshare farm, with co-owned land, where we shared chores, knowledge, and tools? If the land were close enough to the city, we wouldn't all need to live on site; if there were enough of us, we could afford—with the savings we'd enjoy on meat, eggs, and dairy—to pay one person to live there and tend the livestock.

The possibilities are endless: a cheese and charcuterie aging cave, space to pasture livestock, enough acreage to grow crops that take up more space than a city lot can offer (such as endless winter squashes, sunflowers, grains, and forage), orchards for fruits and nuts that don't come on dwarf-size trees, an aquaculture system for raising freshwater fish. In a sense it would be like an extension of our extremely popular communal gardens in the city.

I put out feelers for such a project, and I got an enormous response. As a result, a core group of us is now in the planning phase, drafting a legal framework and researching properties. The challenge is finding the right group of reliable people, as well as arranging the legal aspects so that if someone had a life-changing event and needed to leave the COA, they could get their investment back.

Because I don't know of any group that is already doing this, we are making it up as we go. You might try this too: If you are able to find some acreage not too far from the city to purchase communally or lease, recruit a group of friends and farm together. And watch my blog, www.SustainableEats.com, for further updates on this as my quest for communal farming continues. *Be the change you want to see.* —Mahatma Gandhi *(AC)*

yes, we have no bananas: the organic vs. local debate

During my monthly foray into the grocery store, my son Lander and I passed a display of organic bananas. Lander suddenly adopted the swagger of a chimp, singing, "Banana, banana, me want banana." His performance elicited smiles from passing shoppers, so he repeated it. Then he looked up at me expectantly. Instead of handing him a banana, I knelt down to have a quiet conversation with my monkey impersonator.

"Lander, bananas don't grow around here. How about a Washington apple instead?"

"I don't like those!" he insisted.

"Do you remember Diego?" I asked, referring to his favorite cartoon animal rescuer. "How he lived in a sunny and warm tropical rainforest?" Lander nodded. "That is the climate where bananas grow. Does it look like that around here?" Lander looked out the windows, where the sky hung cold and drizzly. He shook his head.

"In order to plant banana orchards, so little boys like you can eat bananas, people have to cut down the rainforests where the monkeys live. Now the monkeys that used to live in those rainforests have to leave their homes and find someplace else to live.

"But if we eat foods that grow around here, they won't have to cut down the rainforests and the monkeys won't lose their homes. Those monkeys want you to eat apples and leave their rainforest home alone. Don't you want to help the monkeys?"

Lander looked downcast but dropped his request for bananas. There's no arguing with the power of the monkey.

I could tell that the other shoppers thought I was crazy for not giving an adorable four-year-old monkey impersonator an organic banana. And I know they aren't alone. The choice between local and organic produce is confusing. Produce from China may be labeled as organic and be highly efficient to grow, but it is probably less nutritious than heirloom varieties grown in compost-rich soil. And getting that produce into our stores involves huge expenditures of fossil fuels.

On the other hand, that local apple may come from an orchard just outside the city, but perhaps it was grown using petroleum-based fertilizers and conventional insecticides and fungicides. Unless you buy produce directly from the farmer or grow it yourself, it is difficult to cut through the confusion. If you know your farmer and are comfortable with his growing practices, you won't need to decide between local and organic—you can have them both. *(AC)*

what's wrong with big agriculture, mono-crop farms, and big box organics?

What about the argument that small farms and backyard gardens are inefficient? They've even been called downright irresponsible. Why expend precious resources on small-scale farming when megafarms, with their state-of-the-art equipment and cutting-edge seed technology, can maximize yields and feed the world? There are even large farms gearing up to supply all the Walmarts and Costcos in this country with "organic" produce. Why not leave it to the experts and quit worrying about it?

Here's why: The argument for megafarms confuses efficiency with sustainability. Those yields per acre don't tell the whole story.

Conventional farms rely on chemical fertilizers, pollute nearby surface water and aquifers, and yield nutritionally inferior crops. Cutting-edge seed technology is efficiently farmed in large monocultures with few crop rotations to protect soil stability.

Without plant diversity and access to unpolluted water, native beneficial insects die off or take flight, leaving the crops open to a cycle of increasing pests and pesticides, further polluting and destroying surrounding wildlife. While this system may offer cheap food, we pay for the food in other ways, in the form of long-term environmental and health costs.

And though megafarms that are organic represent an improvement over those that use conventional techniques, they don't go far enough. Many organic fertilizers and amendments are mined from the earth, permanently altering the landscape, soil, and air supply or endangering fragile ecosystems like peat bogs, fishing grounds, and rainforests. Some large-scale organic farmers practice the same monoculture farming techniques, albeit with different fertilizers and pesticides, as the big conventional farms.

Organic certification organizations encourage farmers to use benign methods to control insects, but the farmers are allowed to resort to imperfect backup control methods when these fail. These include Bt *(Bacillus thuringiensis)*, a relatively harmless bacterium that nonetheless kills good caterpillars along with the bad when used indiscriminately, or sulfur sprays that kill beneficial fungi in the soil even as they kill harmful fungi on the plant. It's easy to understand why a farmer, overseeing a huge field of a single crop, would need to rely on blanket solutions like these to grow saleable crops.

Collins Orchards' peaches, fresh at the farmers market.

Smaller farms that raise a diverse assortment of crops can do better. On a smaller farm, or in a backyard garden or community garden plot, we can carefully steward the soil so as to take best advantage of precious resources like organic fertilizers. We can plant a variety of crops so as to create an environment friendly to beneficial insects that help control pests. Megafarms, whether organic or conventional, are just too big to steward with that degree of care.

So, yes, small-scale agriculture and gardens are inefficient, and maybe we locavores are a bit self-indulgent. But compared to conventional growing practices, with their genetically enhanced seeds and huge monocultures, small-scale agriculture has distinct advantages: It generates the least water, soil, and air contamination, the least loss of wildlife and degradation of ecosystems, the least energy use and greenhouse gas emissions, and the least landscape destruction. Choosing local, seasonal produce also eases the distribution and storage burden.

Now more than ever, it is imperative that we stop buying that conventional produce stacked up in grocery store displays. Luckily, this is one of the simplest things you can do in the Northwest. Even if you can't or don't want to garden, you have many choices, from CSA boxes to farmers markets to U-pick stands. Making any of these choices will have a tremendous impact on the future of farming, plant and wildlife diversity, and soil, water, and air quality.

Look at it this way: If everyone stopped buying conventional produce today, nonorganic amendment and pesticide companies and genetically modified seed companies would lose their market overnight. If that wouldn't change things, I don't know what would. *(AC)*

. . . .

PERMACULTURE AND BIODYNAMICS: THE NEW ORGANICS

Permaculture, a hybrid of the words *permanent* and *agriculture*, was introduced conceptually in the early 1900s as an agricultural method that could be sustained indefinitely. In the years that followed, permaculture pioneers expanded the concept to focus on design principles not only for agriculture, but for human establishments as well. Permaculture philosophy encourages mimicking natural eco-systems to create a state of harmony between humans and nature that minimizes effort, increases yields, utilizes waste products as resources, and restores natural balance.

The term "biodynamic farming" was coined by Rudolph Steiner and has been around nearly as long as the idea of permaculture. Steiner promoted some wacky ideas—for instance, he believed filling the skull of a domesticated animal with oak bark and burying it near a stream would imbue some kind of spiritual qualities to your compost. On the other hand, many of his better ideas, including his promotion of manure and compost, are backed by modern science. Followers of biodynamic methods focus first and foremost on feeding and protecting living organisms in the soil. They believe a farm should be independent of external inputs and that farmers should create their own soil amendments, rather than trucking them in. Biodynamic farmers work to create a self-sustaining system in which nothing is wasted.

Both permaculture and biodynamic systems strive to restore the natural balance and reduce human impacts. Because both systems focus on improving soil fertility, they provide the most nutritious and tastiest foods possible with the widest range of genetic diversity. Organic agriculture, on the other hand, is held accountable to a government standards board that votes on which specific practices must be followed and which chemical compounds are allowed. Think of permaculture and biodynamics as a set of morals to live by and organics as specific laws subject to cultural pressures and influenced by big business. Because permaculture and biodynamics aren't regulated, you have to ask questions about farmers' practices. What do these terms mean to them? Are they committed to feeding the soil? Or do they use these as a marketing term? In the end it all comes down to choosing your farmers carefully and supporting those growing practices that you agree with. You can't count on a governance board to do that for you.

. . . .

producer profile: Skeeter

To get to Skeeter's farm in the northeast corner of Washington State, we drove through apple country. Helicopters hovered overhead, emptying massive containers of pesticides over the conventionally managed orchards.

We turned off the interstate onto a winding dirt road. As we ascended into the brown hills, we left the imperfect world behind. From each bend in the road, sweeping views gave us a godlike perspective on the valley below, where conventional farmers struggled incessantly against their insect enemies. What fools these mortals be.

We parked beside a large, white tent—like those used for RVs. Skeeter hugged us both in greeting and offered to give us the grand tour. He started by leading us into the tent. "In the summer, I like to just open up the sides." He pulled aside a piece of plasticized canvas to show us the view. In the foreground was the tiny spring that irrigates his crops. Beyond that, we could see the deer fencing that surrounds one of his small farms. Deep in the valley below, we could just make out the town of Tonasket. Dusk was approaching and the town's faint display of lights made it seem very, very far away.

I looked around the tent, noticing a small stove and opened jars of food. "You live here?" I asked Skeeter.

"In the summer," he said. He showed us his bed, his dining room table, his desk. The furniture was jumbled together with the accoutrements of his livelihood—an herb dryer, giant bins of root crops, tables strewn with curing onions. I could see no separation between his personal life and his life as a farmer. The man is a monk.

Sometimes it seems as if all our farmers are either old hippies or high-tech dropouts.

It seems food, farmed in the way we prefer, must be cultivated by monks or millionaires. Either the farmers must be satisfied with a simple life in order to dedicate themselves to their craft, or they must subsidize their passions with dwindling fortunes, or at least day jobs at Blockbuster.

When you step back, you wonder about the sustainability of this system. Then you realize this isn't a permanent state, it's a system in transition: we're witnessing a passing of the torch. The old hippies bore that torch for years, pouring their lives into the development and demonstration of alternative farming methods. Just as they were getting ready to give up the ghost, in marched a new generation of farmers, inspired by financial success or economic crisis or simply life to leave their desk jobs as computer programmers and advertising executives and do something real, something of value.

Michael Pilarksi, a.k.a. Skeeter, in his permaculture garden.

Now, we consumers have finally caught up, and we're stepping into the marketplace in large groups, demanding food grown hippie-style. The new farmers have reached out to the old timers, looking for advice. René Featherstone, the man who lived for years in a tepee and grows our grains, recently spoke at a major regional agricultural conference. Skeeter's awards have been limited to permaculture enthusiasts, but the movement's fans are many and growing. When I pressed Skeeter to list any recognition he'd received, he joked "perhaps the plants point and whisper as I walk by." Whatever the form this recognition takes, we're glad to see these older farmers appreciated for their years of service. Like the ancient blues musicians who inspired a generation of musicians in the sixties, they're enjoying their first world tour, proud elders of an almost-lost tradition, bestowing credibility on new traditions.

It's an unlikely marriage, this coming together of outcasts, wannabes, and consumers with ridiculous demands. But like newlyweds, we are all proceeding optimistically, giving each other the benefit of the doubt, discovering each other's quirks—and loving them.

Skeeter took us into his garden, where there was just enough light for a tour. While he walked in front of me, I took a minute to check out Annette's favorite farmer. He's a spry seventy-six year old, with gray hair and a trim gray beard. He wears a practical and warm wool flannel shirt and a knit cap. At his belt, he carries a sharp, hooked knife in a holster. The knife functions as a sort of right hand for him. He pulls it out regularly to lop things off—roots, shoots, and leaves for us to taste, smell, or examine. "That there is teasel, it's for lyme disease. That's joe pye weed, it's for kidney stones." In his garden are hundreds and hundreds of species. Many of them are medicinal. He dries them and ships their leaves and seeds all over the world to wholesale suppliers of herbal remedies and teas. Finally, we got to the tomatoes. They formed a single, lengthy row amid a sea of blooming perennials.

Skeeter also grows celery, leeks, winter squashes, potatoes, and many other vegetable crops. Each of these tender, vulnerable crops he isolates, like islands, among his permaculture beds.

After Skeeter harvests once from his vegetable beds, he gradually begins to convert them to permaculture beds by interplanting perennials. As these mature, he phases out the annual plants and moves his vegetable garden to virgin ground. When he runs out of new space for vegetables, he simply digs up a perennial bed that's grown too tall and starts the process over again, this time in the rich, fertile soil created through permaculture's famous benign neglect. "Permaculture is about the ecosystem getting better and better while people are living in it," Skeeter explained. The vegetables that emerge from that system taste delicious and have never known a pesticide of any kind.

This is the polar opposite of conventional farming, where rows and rows of a single crop grow isolated from any sort of insect life. In Skeeter's garden, predatory insects quickly move in and attack any emerging pests. "Almost all farming in the world today is impoverishing ecosystems gradually, some faster than others," said Skeeter. "And permaculture is about turning that around. Reversing the trend from earth degradation to earth regeneration."

I crouch down, viewing the crazy-colored landscape of flowers and shrubs from an insect's perspective. You can almost imagine fairies living here. And indeed, Skeeter perceives this land as alive, home to tiny souls that flutter on the fringes of our perception. It fills him with a faith in the regenerative power of nature. As he digs down with his shovel to show us the life in the soil, I find his optimism contagious.

Most farmers can't do this sort of thing. The actions of tractors and fairies don't mix well. And speaking practically, the market for medicinal herbs that subsidizes Skeeter's vegetable operation isn't large or efficient enough to appeal to conventional farmers. That said, some of the principles demonstrated in Skeeter's garden scale up quite nicely.

Some farmers have been experimenting recently with leaving a row of native grasses and weeds at the edges of their fields. These wild places act as reservoirs for predators, much as did traditional English hedgerows. And hedgerows themselves have enjoyed growing interest. Seattle's King County Conservation District actively promotes their use, though few farmers have adopted the practice. Washington State University used to promote only the use of a chemical cocktail to fight insects. Today, the university also promotes integrated pest management, a method that involves bringing in insect predators to fight pests. These methods, once the domain of hippies, have become just another course at the land grant university.

At Skeeter's dinner table in Tonasket, we sat brainstorming the discussion points he wanted to bring up at a regional conference in Seattle on food security. "We need more community gardens, we need more farmers markets, we need to turn parking strips into vegetable gardens, we need to require low impact development that will contain stormwater runoff."

"Skeeter, that's not radical in Seattle anymore."

"It's not?"

"No, Seattle is embracing all those ideas. We've elected environmentalists. Those laws have already been changed."

Skeeter sat back in his chair, silent for a moment. Then, he broke out into a smile. After years of writing open letters to the President of the United States and anyone who would listen, Skeeter was no longer an outsider. Now, people like Annette and I drive to his door, seeking the best fresh produce. We want to learn how to make our gardens productive, how to rebuild the spent soils in our postage-stamp sized yards. We're growing into the army of backyard gardeners and small farmers Skeeter dreams could one day replace the modern system of agricultural production. But we'll never replace it entirely.

Buyers like us, and farmers like Skeeter, form a tiny part of the farming economy. Almost negligible. But it's a nurturing, sustainable economy. As Annette and I loaded up her car with crates of leeks, potatoes, Jerusalem artichokes, and parsnips, this movement didn't feel small. It's big enough for Skeeter, and it's big enough for us to feed our families, and the families of those in our buying clubs. And while Skeeter can't provide enough tomatoes for everyone in the city, he's not alone. There are plenty of other monk farmers and millionaire farmers out there, looking for their niche market. *(JM)*

Skeeter donates a percentage of his harvest to the local food bank.

Peaceful Valley

Farm & Garden Supply

Grow organic...for life!

Catalogna Chicory (Italian Da

GrowOrganic.com

Peaceful Valley

Farm & Garden Su

Grow organic...

Red Deer

UP
S

Territorial

P.O. Box 158, Cotta

100% Or

certified by W

Departmen

chapter 7
seeding your garden

In order to have a garden bursting with the most nutritious produce possible, you need to start with nutritious soil and nutritious seeds. Many of the fruits and vegetables you see in the supermarket today were hybridized or modified over the last fifty years to look attractive for as long as possible. You don't want those varieties: Numerous studies have shown that the nutritional quality of produce has decreased dramatically with hybridization.

In a 2004 study, Donald Davis, PhD, of the University of Texas at Austin Biochemical Institute, used USDA data to evaluate forty-three fruits and vegetables from 1950 to 1999. He found that over that time, broccoli had lost 63 percent of its calcium, 50 percent of its riboflavin, and 18 percent of its thiamine. Potatoes had lost 100 percent of their vitamin A, 57 percent of their vitamin C and iron, and 28 percent of their calcium. Other fruits and vegetables showed similar results.

By planting your own garden, you get the chance to choose heirloom, open-pollinated varieties that do well in your climate and have been historically selected for flavor and nutrition. Where do you find seeds like that? Here are some tips:

› Look for regional seed companies that operate trial gardens in climates similar to yours. It won't do any good to order heirloom muskmelon seeds if they require more sun hours to ripen than your garden is going to get. Read the descriptions carefully, including the number of days to ripen. Reputable growers will share information about how productive or early certain crops are, based on garden trials. Such information will give you a better idea of how those plants will do in your garden.

› Look for seed companies that disclose the results of germination tests.

› Look for seed companies that offer varieties that are part of the Ark of Taste—Slow Food's list of heritage foods in danger of extinction. To be listed in the Ark, foods must have outstanding taste and be of cultural or historical importance and at biological risk; they should also be sustainably produced in limited quantities.

› Look for seed companies that have taken the Safe Seed Pledge, created by organic seed growers in 1999 as a statement against genetically modified seeds. The pledge reads:

Agriculture and seeds provide the basis upon which our lives depend. We must protect this foundation as a safe and genetically stable source for future generations. For the benefit of all farmers, gardeners, and consumers who want an alternative, we pledge that we do not knowingly buy or sell genetically engineered seeds or plants. The mechanical transfer of genetic material outside of natural reproductive methods and between genera, families, or kingdoms poses great biological risks, as well as economic, political, and cultural threats. We feel that genetically engineered varieties have been insufficiently tested prior to public release. More research and testing is necessary to further assess the potential risks of genetically engineered seeds. Further, we wish to support agricultural progress that leads to healthier soils, genetically diverse agricultural ecosystems, and ultimately healthy people and communities.

(AC)

. . . .

OPPORTUNITIES FOR CHANGE
SEEDS

Buy seeds only from seed companies that have taken the Safe Seed Pledge.

Buy only organic or biodynamically grown seeds.

Buy only open-pollinated heirloom seeds.

Save your own seeds.

. . . .

sowing seeds

Now that you have good soil, it's time to put it to work growing food. Any seed can go directly into a garden bed (this is called "direct sowing"), but it won't actually germinate until the soil conditions are right. In the meantime, rains can wash the seed away, hungry birds may eat it, and slugs may devour emerging seedlings. You'll have better luck if you start some seeds indoors. This will give the tender seedlings a head start, protecting them until they are large enough to withstand real-world conditions.

starting seeds indoors

Seeds require moisture to germinate. Temperature is also crucial. While a few food plants, such as parsley and spinach, need cool temperatures to germinate, most of the plants you will start indoors need warm soil.

Usually, a house is warm enough for starting seeds. But if you have a particularly cool house, you may need to find a warm spot for your seed nursery—perhaps a utility room, near your oven, or on the counter above your dishwasher. Seed-starting trays with domed lids, called "nursery flats," help keep the soil moist with the least amount of effort on your part. You can also recycle your neighbor's takeout deli trays (the kind with the clear plastic lids).

Fill nursery flats or cell packs (plastic planting trays with dividers, much like egg cartons but for plants) with moistened seedling mix (see "Perfect Seedling Soil Mix," page 155), and plant your seeds according to the depths given on the packet. Wet the soil with lukewarm water so it's evenly moist, cover it with a lid to retain that moisture, and keep it in a warm location.

Seedlings benefit from vermicompost tea.

Check several times a day to see if the seeds have begun to sprout. Once they do, take measures to prevent "damping-off disease" (underground, soil line, or crown rot caused by a soilborne fungus). Remove the lid to provide good airflow, and don't overwater. Add diluted chamomile tea, a natural fungicide, and diluted vermicompost tea (see page 66) when you water your seedlings.

Depending on the particular plants' temperature requirements, you can take your seedlings outside or continue to grow them indoors under a grow light. If you grow them indoors, you can improve airflow around them with a small desk fan. They'll also need light from the sun or from a full-spectrum bulb positioned one to two inches from the plants for fourteen to sixteen hours a day. Insufficient light leads to spindly plants with long stems.

To set up a fairly inexpensive grow system under an upper kitchen cupboard, screw some hooks under the cupboard, and use thin chain to suspend "cool white" or "full spectrum" fluorescent tube lights from the hooks. The chain will let you raise the lights as your seedlings grow. If you can't spare the kitchen counter space, for about sixty dollars you can purchase a Jump Start Grow Light System (see Resources), which will provide even better light for your plants. It also allows you to move your seed-starting operation out of the kitchen entirely.

. . . .

GOOD PLANT CHOICES FOR STARTING INDOORS

Basil	Cucumbers	Melons
Broccoli	Heading lettuce	Peppers
Brussels sprouts	(lettuces that form tight	Sunflowers
Cabbages	heads versus loose leaf	Tomatoes
Cauliflower	varieties)	

. . . .

create a mobile seedling nursery

If you don't have space for seed flats, try this trick: Buy a mesh-bottomed wagon like those used in nurseries. Start the next season's plants in flats on the wagon, repotting them as they grow. The wagon's mesh bottom will allow for good drainage, and the wagon can easily be covered with a floating row cover (such as Reemay), to protect the tender seedlings from too much sun and pests. The wheels make it easy to move your mobile nursery into a partly shady spot on hot days, and slugs are less likely to venture up the cool metal of the wagon (the Reemay provides additional protection from these slimy pests or you can plant the wheels of the wagon in large cans full of water to keep slugs off).

Once your seedlings grow large enough to survive slug attacks, transfer them to the garden. One day your bed is filled with beets and greens, and the next, it's full of large cabbage starts—while the beets ferment in the pickle crock and the greens are blanched and frozen for winter gratins and lasagnas.

pricking and transplanting seedlings

"Pricking" is a gardening phrase used to describe the careful process of transplanting fragile seedlings. The first two leaves your seedling will grow are called the cotyledons. As your seedling continues to grow, it will produce "true" leaves that resemble those of the mature plant. Once your seedlings have two or three true leaves, prick them out of the flat carefully between two fingers, and move them into pots large enough to accommodate their growth until their move to permanent garden beds. Pricking seedlings works best in the evening, to give them sufficient time to recover overnight. Handle them gently by their leaves and never by the stem: Losing a leaf won't destroy the plant, but breaking its stem will. Water the soil from the bottom up by placing the seedling tray in a flat filled with water. Let them draw water up from the roots for about ten minutes at a time. Keep the soil evenly moist.

. . . .

PERFECT SEEDLING SOIL MIX

Developing seedlings require a finely textured soil medium. You can make your own by following this recipe:
› 1 part garden soil
› ½ part finely screened yard waste compost
› ½ part vermicompost (see instructions on page 66)
› 1 part leaf mold
› 2 parts builder's sand
› Blend into each 5 gallons of the above mix:
› 2 cups complete organic fertilizer (see instructions on page 131)

. . . .

direct sowing

To sow seeds directly into your garden, plant them at the depth recommended on the packet. In general, smaller seeds should be planted close to the soil surface and larger ones should be planted deeper. Cover them with soil and tamp the soil down lightly, then protect them from rains and marauding birds with a "floating" row cover, such as Reemay.

GOOD PLANT CHOICES FOR SOWING DIRECTLY INTO THE GARDEN

Baby green mix	Collards	Potatoes
Beans	Kohlrabi	Rutabagas
Beets	Leaf lettuce	Swiss chard
Broccoli raab	Mustards	Turnips
Carrots	Parsnips	Wild greens
Chervil	Peas	

. . . .

making sense of seed labels

"Heirloom," "open pollinated," "hybrid," "organic"—what does it all mean? It's confusing wading through a seed catalog trying to make sense of it all. The following definitions may help:

›   Organic seeds come from plants grown organically.

›   Heirloom and heritage seeds (the terms are used interchangeably) are seeds that are open pollinated (OP) by wind or insects. These varieties have been grown for centuries, adapting over time to specific climates. Many of these varieties have cultural significance and were the same ones your ancestors used. If you choose varieties suited to your environment, they will require less attention and fewer inputs to thrive in your garden.

›   Hybrid seeds are the first "child" of artificial pollination between two distinct "parents" of the same plant species. Such crossed plants are typically selected for commercial reasons: increased yields, longer shelf life, cosmetic appeal, suitability to mechanical harvesting. Seeds saved from hybrid plants typically don't produce true to type and may even be sterile.

›   Genetically engineered (or genetically modified) seeds come from plants with genetically altered DNA. Scientists splice plants' genes to create traits such as increased yield, resistance to specific herbicides, or even inability to reproduce after the first generation. At times, genetic engineering is used to introduce nonplant genes (from fish, for example) into plants.

Why the fuss about GE/GM seed? The Safe Seed Pledge does a good job of laying out the hazards and ethical issues. As a gardener, though, it's important to understand that

Last fall's onion, beginning to sprout.

genetically engineered seed can cross-pollinate with heirloom varieties, contaminating them. Furthermore, a growing body of research suggests that the use of genetically engineered seeds ultimately leads to greater fertilizer, herbicide, and pesticide use, and even lower crop yields.

EAT YOUR THINNINGS

I sow seeds much more densely than the planting directions call for, knowing full well that I'll need to thin them periodically. I use this opportunity to harvest thinnings for dinner—who doesn't love baby beets, turnips, and carrots? This strategy works especially well when our cool summers stunt plant growth. And by sowing older seeds thickly, I save myself the trouble of having to come back later and resow the same crop if germination rates are low.

buying starts

Many nurseries now offer heirloom variety vegetable starts, grown locally to ensure they'll be successful in this climate. This can greatly simplify starting a garden. But starts cost significantly more than seeds, and if you're not careful, you may end up spending as much for starts as you would to buy that same produce ready to eat at the farmers market!

join a "start csa"
Some farmers are offering a new kind of community-supported agriculture program, one that provides vegetable starts for your garden. This takes much of the guesswork out of starting a garden, since the CSA will provide you with starts seasonally, at just the right time for planting. This is a great option if you are a beginning gardener and want to try some new things.

host a seed or start barter
If you have friends who garden, consider hosting a spring seed or start barter. Perhaps you have too many carrot or kale seeds from last year, or want to try new varieties of tomatoes. Gather extra seeds, and then trade seeds or starts with other gardeners. This can save you a lot of money, and you may discover some new vegetables to grow.

saving seeds

Saving seeds is the ultimate in self-sufficient gardening.

It is easy to save relatively pure seeds from some plants, such as chicory, lettuce, kale, peas, beans, flowers, herbs, tomatoes, tomatillos, and groundcherries. However, seeds from other plants, such as beets, Swiss chard, broccoli raab, mustards, corn, cucumbers, summer and winter squashes, and melons, are easy to save but cross freely with other varieties in the same family, so the plants may not turn out true to type.

Because of this, I recommend planting a perpetual garden for herbs, perennial varieties, and plants that reseed easily, such as leafy greens. (See "Perpetual Gardening," page 172, to learn about this time-saving technique.) Concentrate your seed-saving efforts on those plants with easy-to-save seeds, while growing only one variety of plant from the types that cross freely. Form a gardening circle among your friends, with each member growing only one variety of the easily-crossing plants, and at harvest time you'll be able to share in one another's bounty while maintaining your own pure seed stock. If you apply these techniques, you will need to buy only a handful of seeds from year to year.

Different vegetables require different seed-saving methods, as described below. And don't forget to label your seeds before storing them!

Beans: Allow a few pods to mature on the vine, then let the vine dry out until the seedpods wilt. Bring the pods indoors to finish drying.

Peas: Allow a few vines to fully mature, then dry the vines in the garage.

Cucumbers, melons, squashes: Allow a few cucumbers to overmature and turn yellow. Scoop out the seeds and the pulp, and place them in a bowl of water on the kitchen counter (covered with a paper towel to keep the fruit flies out). Stir the stuff daily until it liquefies, pour off the liquid, rinse the seeds, and let them dry on a paper towel.

Corn: Leave a few ears of corn on the stalks until the husks have browned completely and the corn is dry and shriveled. (If the weather isn't sunny you may want to bring the husks in to a garage to finish drying.) Peel back the silks so the ear can dry completely.

Lander doesn't want to save these seeds yet!

Tomatoes, tomatillos, groundcherries: Select a few specimens of each variety. Scoop out the seeds and pulp, and place them in a cup of water covered with a paper towel on a warm windowsill or kitchen counter. In a few days, the liquid will mold. At that point, drain the liquid, rinse the seeds, and let them dry on a paper towel.

Beets or Swiss chard*: Leave a few beets or chard plants in the garden until they form flowering seed stalks. Once the stalks begin to dry, carefully collect them, place them on a plate indoors, and let them dry until brittle.

Mustard or broccoli raab*: Leave a few mustard or broccoli raab plants in the garden until they form flowering seed stalks. Once the stalks begin to dry, carefully collect them, place them on a plate indoors, and let them dry until brittle.

*In order to maintain seed purity, grow only one or the other of these two plants. Growing both beets and Swiss chard, or both mustard and broccoli raab, will lead to unstable seed types.

chapter 8
growing strategies to maximize space

My family lives on a one-fifth–acre city lot, with a large grassy play area, a play structure, a shed, a chicken and duck run, a roomy back patio, a house, and a driveway. Yet I still have room for twenty-two fruit and nut trees and enough vegetable plots to grow produce for us year-round. Intensive gardening is my secret.

Granted, I live in an off-the-beaten-path neighborhood, so I feel comfortable growing edible plants in the parking strip and next to the sidewalk. Also, my front yard is not surrounded by tall trees that block winter sunlight. But even if you lack those luxuries, I'm willing to bet that you can grow a lot more food than you ever thought possible. Walk around your yard and consider the possibilities. Could you take out at least some of the lawn and convert that area to food garden? Could you line your driveway with berry canes or espaliered fruit trees? Plant an intensive orchard in that narrow path between your house and your neighbor's? Tack an arbor onto the front of your house to grow grape or kiwi vines? Replace some shrubbery with blueberry bushes and some groundcover with strawberries? Or deepen your existing planting beds and add kale, lettuces, herbs, and tomatoes?

If deciduous trees shade potential garden areas, there still may be enough sunlight into the first part of summer for early apple trees, June-bearing strawberries, peas, and early potatoes to set fruit. The section of your yard that gets only part sun could provide you with mustards, arugula, lettuces, kale, parsley, and cilantro. They may take longer to harvest without full sun, but they'll be less likely to bolt and turn bitter. Even full-shade sections can be used for growing huckleberries and mushrooms, building compost piles, or even raising rabbits. If you have space for vegetable beds, there are many strategies to maximize your growing space. This chapter is all about strategies that work for us. I hope you will find something in here that will work for you. *(AC)*

Coffee bags create a flexible garden in a high traffic parking strip.

strategies

To an urban gardener, every wall represents a blank surface on which to grow something and every sunny kitchen counter offers a place to start seeds to plant out later. These strategies will help you make the most of your space, ensuring that your crops mature when and where you need them.

succession planting and staggering the harvest

"Succession planting" is the technique of staggering sowings to provide a constant supply of any particular food item, instead of planting or harvesting it all at once. Carrots and lettuces are perfect candidates for succession planting, providing you with fresh produce all spring, summer, and fall.

To succession plant, begin by sowing rows in the northern part of your bed, and work your way southward. This ensures that the tallest plants are at the north end of the bed, where they won't shade new seedlings. Sow at two- to four-week intervals until the bed is full. When you have finished harvesting the plants in the northernmost rows, plant winter vegetables there.

variety selection and interplanting

Another strategy for making the most of your garden space is to stagger your harvest by selecting varieties that ripen at different times. In February, I start brassicas such as broccoli, cabbage, Brussels sprouts, and cauliflower indoors. In early April, I plant the broccoli and Brussels sprouts in the same outdoor garden bed, spaced a foot apart. Between those, I interplant faster-growing brassicas from seed: broccoli raab, collards, and kohlrabi. These will shoot up quickly amid the slower-growing broccoli and Brussels sprouts.

By using a chessboard grid rather than a row pattern for planting, alternating early with late varieties, you can cram even more seeds into the garden bed. The early ripening ones will bush out and fill in the space quickly. Once those are gone, the later-ripening varieties will have room to grow.

By the time we finish harvesting the broccoli raab, collards, and kohlrabi in late spring, we can begin harvesting the sprouting broccolis for our summer plates. In late summer to early fall, after we have eaten all the sprouting broccolis, the heading broccolis mature. During this time, with so many gaps in the bed, I start a legume-based cover crop such as fava beans, which will come up around the slow-growing Brussels sprouts and help replace nitrogen in the bed that gave so much for so long. Finally, in late fall, the Brussels sprouts are ready, in plenty of time for Thanksgiving dinner.

In this way I can squeeze three seasons' worth of broccoli raab, kohlrabi, collard greens, broccoli, and Brussels sprouts into a four-by-eight-foot bed and still have time for one cycle of cover crop (that we or the chickens can eat in spring). You can do the same thing with carrots by choosing varieties with staggered harvest dates. By simply selecting varieties that will ripen at different times, you can enjoy a continual harvest from only one sowing.

vertical growing

Another strategy for packing more food plants into a tight urban lot is vertical growing. Think of your garden as a three-dimensional space, and look for opportunities to grow plants both up and over. Arbors along fences, attached to your house, or spanning your driveway can essentially double your border space. If you have a sitting area or a porch with full sun, building a structure over it will not only provide shade from summer sun but also extend your growing space.

Do you have an unsightly shed? Tack a trellis on it! Many vining edibles, such as kiwis, grapes, runner beans, hops, and squashes, need to grow on supports and are happy up in the air, as long as their roots have adequate soil. You can also espalier fruit trees (see page 174) and berry canes to form or replace fences, or to line walkways.

Annette's urban front yard.

This is a map of my front yard. Along the east side of the driveway is my intensive orchard, where I grow four kinds of apples, two kinds of cherries, a plum, a white table grape, asparagus, reseeding wild greens, a tea plant, a peppercorn bush, a yuzu, hardy ginger, three seaberry bushes, and raspberries.

On the west side of the driveway I have more raspberries, an early Concord grape, a columnar apple, three highbush blueberries, three rhubarbs, a large rosemary bush, and a raised bed. West of the walkway to the front, I have two long and two shorter raised beds, a seating area surrounded by potted fig trees and hop vines, and a spiraled herb garden.

Along the west fence I have fennel, a hardy kiwi vine, a fuzzy kiwi vine (the pollinating male is in the backyard in a mediocre spot, since it doesn't produce fruit), a crabapple, a quince tree, and reseeding greens. Along the front of the fence I grow onions, garlic, shallots, low-bush blueberries, cranberries, and lingonberries, and in the front planting strip I have an almond tree, a four-in-one pear tree, and two peach trees. There I also grow winter squash and potatoes in repurposed coffee bags, sunflowers for seeds, and medicinal flowers like echinacea. *(AC)*

Harvesting a nylon bootie-wrapped apple from an espalier apple tree.

With a vertical trellis at the back of your northernmost grow beds, you can squeeze in a crop of runner beans, peas or squashes. By trimming the lower leaves once the plant is vining and established, you won't use up a row of grow space. Use that row instead for shallow-rooted plants such as cress or lettuce, which won't compete with your vertical crop's roots. Those plants will thrive on the nitrogen that your runner beans fix in the soil.

Vertical growing has the bonus of providing shade that can extend the lifespan of cool-weather crops into the hot summer. For example, if your corn casts a shadow over part of your garden bed, try relocating established lettuces to that shady spot, where they're less likely to bolt than if they were in full sun. Once they're large enough, they can grow in near-full shade. I consider shady spots in my garden as ideal cold-storage locations for lettuces, where they'll wait patiently until I need them. Better that than to have them bolt and turn bitter in full sun, or rot in my refrigerator!

Vertical growing techniques can be used in permanently planted beds too. Underplant an area of tall edibles, such as fruit trees or bushes, with edible ground covers such as strawberries, cranberries, or lingonberries. Around my fruit trees, I grow potatoes in coffee bags. The bags serve as a slow-release watering system for the trees and help mulch the ground. You can also use that space for growing edibles in containers, or for your "perpetual garden" (see "Perpetual Gardening," page 172). *(AC)*

. . . .

INTENSIVE ROW CROPS—NOT FOR THE FAINT OF HEART!

When you plan your crop spacing, remember that you can squeeze plants close to the edges of the bed, providing room for more. Be bold: Start your first row right next to the border rather than deeper into your bed.

Another trick is to prune the large outer leaves of sprawling plants, decreasing their size and allowing room to plant more. (If you use this method, however, be sure to prune unnecessary leaves regularly, to allow proper airflow and prevent mildew.)

. . . .

optimizing light and extending the season

In the city, tall houses and trees can steal those few precious sun hours we get in the Pacific Northwest. To optimize production, determine which sections of your yard get the most sunlight and reserve those spaces for true sun hogs. I dedicate my sunniest spots to corn, squashes, tomatoes, the occasional eggplant, cucumbers, broccoli, cabbage, and Brussels sprouts. In shadier areas I plant peas, lettuces, kale, herbs, and radishes. I use part-sun areas for carrots, beans, beets, potatoes, turnips, and parsnips. (For plant-by-plant light requirements, see Edible Plants, in Plant Lists for the Pacific Northwest, page 356.)

Unfortunately, many of the foods we dream about having in our gardens—tomatoes, basil, and watermelons—are the most difficult to grow in the Pacific Northwest. These sun- and heat-hungry plants don't do well in our climate. We certainly can force them, but if you are a beginning gardener or trying to maximize your space, it may be better to buy those crops at the farmers market and focus instead on edible plants better suited to our environment.

If you do decide to grow sun-loving edibles, start them indoors in early spring using artificial light or a sunny window (assuming it's sunny in early spring). I start my tomato plants indoors in January, because I love tomatoes and want to extend their growing season as much as possible. Plus, every month that I have ripe tomatoes in my garden is one less month that I need to can tomatoes for.

Another option is to buy starts at spring plant sales. Plant the starts outside in late spring to early summer, and employ some magic to help them along (see "Dueling Tomatoes in Seattle," page 168). (AC)

early maturing varieties for cool summers

Cramming more plants into your garden isn't the only way to increase your garden's bounty. There are ways to simply make the plants you have more productive. For example, planting herbs and flowers throughout your garden will attract pollinating insects and birds. And of course building soil fertility will also dramatically increase yield per plant.

Another way to maximize plant output is by choosing varieties that produce reliably in your climate. In the Pacific Northwest, that can mean planting cherry tomatoes, bush squashes, or other edibles more likely to set and ripen fruit during our cool, short summers.

I always round out my plant selections with early-maturing selections such as the following (numbers in parentheses are days to maturity):

Aunt Molly's groundcherry (65–70)
Black Beauty zucchini (60)
Bush Delicata squash (80)
California Blackeye 46 shelling bean (60)
Carson yellow wax bean (58)
Derby Day cabbage (58)
Dragon Tongue bush bean (60)
Early cherry tomato (55)
Extra Early Golden Bantam corn (72)
Gold Nugget bush squash (85)
Helda Romano bean (60)
Koralik cherry tomato (61)
Legend extra early tomato* (68)
Manitoba heirloom tomato (66)
Marketmore 97 cucumber (55)
Maxibel French/filet bean (60)

Nickel French/filet bean (53)
Oregon cherry tomato (60)
Painted Mountain corn (70–90)
Purple Viking potato (79–90)
Red Thumb fingerling potato (79–90)
Siletz extra early tomato* (57–70)
Silvery Fir Tree heirloom tomato (58)
Soleil French/filet bean (60)
Stowell's Evergreen corn (80–100)
Stupice ultra early tomato (60–65)
Sunseed sunflower
Venture bush bean (55)
Wautoma cucumber (60)
Yellow Crookneck summer squash (60)
Yukon Gold potato (70–90)

Parthenocarpic (plants set fruit without pollination)

dueling tomatoes in seattle

Most of the time, Annette and I share gardening and kitchen tips in a friendly, cooperative way. But when it comes to tomatoes, our friendship turns competitive. Like Cold War scientists racing to land a man on the moon, we trumpet our successes to each other and brood over our failures.

During our first year of competition, Annette beat me to the first ripe tomato by six weeks, while I knocked her over the head with a much larger total yield. In truth, both our methods succeed in different ways. Below are the details of the two competing techniques. You decide which to use in your garden, and let us know your results. *(JM)*

annette's tomato growing technique
›　Mid-January: Start tomatoes indoors.
›　April 1: Prepare bed by laying out "T-tape" irrigation and covering soil with red plastic to increase soil temperature.

- Mid-April: Transplant tomato starts, one plant every 2-by-2-foot area.
- Immediately cover plants with cloche (small greenhouse) made from metal hoop frame and clear plastic.
- Place bricks or rocks and milk jugs full of water between the vines to absorb heat during the day and radiate it at night.
- Mid-May: When night lows exceed 50°F, remove cloche. Prune indeterminate plants to central stem and stake them. Remove suckers on determinate plants and cage them. (See "Determinate Vs. Indeterminate," on page 170.)
- Immediately surround bed on north and east sides with 24-inch-high walls made from reflective galvanized metal roofing. When plants fruit and begin to ripen, erect 24-inch-high corrugated metal panels on west and south sides to keep away rats. Light reflected off metal walls will bounce around as in a "solar tube" skylight, and metal will heat up the garden bed like a solar oven. (Annette's tomatoes ripen faster than anyone's in town!)
- Late May to early June: Harvest first perfect tomato.
- Early to mid-July: Harvest buckets full of large, ripe tomatoes. (Meanwhile, poor Joshua stares at the green tomatoes hanging off his tomato "trees.")
- July 1: Give indeterminate tomato plants a haircut: Cut off flowering branches just beyond the last fruits, to encourage the plant to focus its energy on ripening existing fruit and not making new fruit that will not ripen before fall.
- August 1: Stop watering. Compose haiku:

> *Tomatoes in Seattle . . .*
> *Whose will ripen first?*
> *Annette's will, that's whose.*

joshua's tomato growing technique

- Mid-April: Prepare bed: Dig in cover crop, apply complete organic fertilizer and compost, remove any leaf mulch.
- May 1: Purchase tall tomato starts at spring plant sale. Purchase one tomato plant for every 3-by-3-foot area.
- Immediately plant tomatoes in tepees made from short bamboo stakes. Protect plants with water-filled plastic sleeves (such as Wall O'Water brand).
- May through July: If it doesn't rain, water once a week.
- July 4: Lift water-filled plastic sleeves from sprawling tomato plants (takes two people). Alternatively, cut sleeve and apply Velcro along cut so you can reuse sleeve next year.

- › Immediately prune plants hard, to 6 to 9 branches per plant. Stake branches.
- › August 1: Cut off all water. Time to ripen.
- › Throughout August: Remove many young branches, thin flowers.
- › Late August through early October: Harvest a deluge of large, ripe tomatoes. Like a great zombie army, they will overwhelm the puny humans in your household.

. . . .

DETERMINATE VS. INDETERMINATE

Tomato plants come in determinate and indeterminate varieties, somewhat like bush and runner beans. Determinate varieties are bushier, more compact plants and stop growing once they begin to set fruit. The fruit ripens all at once and the plants begin to die. They require little to no pruning and minimal caging, unless the bushes are abnormally heavily laden with fruits. Indeterminate plants are vining and continue to grow and set fruit all summer long. Indeterminate plants require staking or trellising.

. . . .

ANNETTE'S FAVORITE TOMATO VARIETIES

- › Black Plum: OP (open pollinated), indeterminate, 72 days. Rich sweet/tangy flavor. This is my favorite drying tomato.
- › Cherokee Purple: OP, indeterminate, 72 days. Large, juicy late-summer fruit with full flavor. By far the rat's favorite tomato in my garden, followed by Green Zebra and Mortgage Lifter.
- › Legend: OP, determinate, 70 days. Blight-resistant plants are parthenocarpic* and require no staking. Large, round, red seedless fruit makes great canning or saucing tomatoes. Rich flavor.
- › San Marzano: OP, indeterminate, 80 days. Firm and meaty crack-resistant fruit with few seeds, perfect for sauces or canning.
- › Saucy: OP, determinate, 65 days. Meaty fruit with few seeds, great for saucing or drying. Keeps well on or off the vine—so long as you can keep the rats away.
- › Siletz: OP, determinate, 57 days. Full-flavored, seedless slicing tomatoes are Verticillium** resistant and parthenocarpic. These are my earliest tomatoes.
- › Stupice: OP, indeterminate, 60–65 days. Perfect on pizza.
- › Sungold: Hybrid cherry-type. Indeterminate, 62 days. Crack-resistant, sweet fruit with high sugar content and good tang; few seeds.

*Parthenocarpic means plants set fruit without pollination, a boon in cool summers when pollinators have not yet emerged.

**Verticillium is a fungus that harms the plant's ability to take in sufficient water, causing it to wilt, stunt and eventually die.

JOSHUA'S FAVORITE TOMATO VARIETIES

› Brandywine: OP, indeterminate, 85 days. We slice these a half-inch thick in a sandwich with little else.

› Mr. Stripey/Tigerella: OP, indeterminate, 65 days. Red and orange stripes (fun colors for kids), prolific.

› Polish Linguisa: OP, indeterminate, 73 days. For saucing. Huge, seems resistant to blossom end rot (a vulnerability with saucing tomatoes if you refuse to water them during droughts).

› Purple Calabash: OP, indeterminate, 80 days. Insanely deep lobes mean you have to pick immediately after it rains or they'll rot. But they're worth it for color and flavor. And I love an oddly shaped fruit.

› Stupice: OP, indeterminate, 60–65 days. Early tomato for fresh or salad eating.

· ·

crop rotation and polycultures

When we grow a single species of plants in the same garden location, such as planting a single bed with carrots, we practice small-scale mono-cropping. This makes it easier for pests to find their favorite foods, and leads to nutritional imbalances in the soil as certain nutrients favored by a particular crop are depleted. To avoid this, most organic gardening books include a large section on rotating crops. This helps somewhat less in the city than on a farm (since in the city the pests are only as far away as your neighbor's backyard), but crop rotation still helps, especially with smaller soilborne pests.

Another reason to rotate crops is that different plant types favor different kinds of soil nutrients. By rotating through different plant families, you'll use your garden's nutrients more evenly. You may still need to fertilize between crops, but by rotating, you'll avoid building up one nutrient while depleting another.

A good rule to plant by is "leaf to fruit to root to legume." Leaves (lettuces, kale, broccoli, arugula, cabbage) love nitrogen, fruits (squashes, tomatoes, cucumbers, melons, eggplants) love phosphorous, roots (carrots, parsnips, salsify, turnips, rutabagas) love potassium, and legumes (beans and peas) begin the cycle once more by fixing nitrogen in the soil for your next leaf crop.

Another method, taken from cues found in the natural world, is to plant groupings of several different crops together. This is called a polyculture, and it is the opposite of a mono-culture. The traditional South American "Three Sisters" planting is a great example of this. Native Americans planted corn, squash, and beans together (typically with native flowers that attracted insects). The beans fix nitrogen from the air for the squash and corn. The corn's roots emit sugars that feed the bean plants and provide a trellis for them to scramble up. The squash's sprawling and prickly leaves help retain soil moisture and created an environment uncomfortable to marauding critters. The native flowers help attract pollinators which the squash and beans need to set fruit. Researchers at Cornell University determined that corn set 20 percent more fruit when planted in this traditional polyculture, and the plants were able to utilize the nutrients in the soil in a more balanced manner.

Throw in some manure and compost each year, a duck slug patrol, and a few plants that naturally deter pests (like rue for instance) and you may eliminate your need for fertilizers and pesticides completely. *(AC)*

perpetual gardening

For years I would resow certain crops seasonally, only to struggle against them going to seed and resowing themselves in places I didn't want them. Finally it dawned on me to let the plants do the work for me. Now chicories, Catalogna dandelion, arugula, claytonia, purslane, chickweed, parsley, mâche, sorrel, orach, magentaspreen (a kind of lambs quarters), salad burnet, wild lettuces, Good King Henry, plantain, dock, and other hardy reseeding greens and perennials manage themselves with little to no effort on my part. Because these are wild greens, they hardily adapt to extreme changes in temperature, water, and sunlight, and reseed with abandon. A perpetual garden!

If you don't think you have the time or stick-with-it-ness to garden, try planting this sort of perpetual garden. Start by extending a current planting bed or part of your yard that is part sun/part shade. Follow our steps for readying the soil, then choose from any of the perennial or reseeding plants listed in the Perpetual Garden list in Plant Lists for the Pacific Northwest, page 361. Sprinkle some seeds around, then sit back and relax. And remember not to weed!

This won't be a neat, orderly garden with pretty maids all in a row, because seeds will find their perfect growing conditions and thrive where they root. (If you like the riotous look of a cottage-style garden, this is a great choice for you.) If things get too overgrown for your taste, just harvest them or let the chickens or ducks thin them for you. If the plants start growing in your walkways, tramp on them.

Once your perpetual garden is established, there will be no more seeds to buy or sow. These hardy, adaptable plants will require less watering, and if you continue to add mulch and manure, over time you should never have to rework the soil again. Once established,

Trellising peas and beans maximizes garden space in the small urban garden.

your perpetual garden will be virtually maintenance free. With it, you can enjoy the benefits of gardening without the effort! *(AC)*

dwarf fruit trees for the intensive orchard

If you can't figure out how to fit a full-sized fruit tree into your yard, don't worry. Create an intensive orchard of dwarf fruit trees instead; they'll provide you with many different varieties of fruit (a whole orchard's worth!) in one small space.

You can buy fruit trees grafted onto dwarfing rootstock that never reach more than ten to fifteen feet high, or you can espalier fruit trees (see below) into delightful patterns.

Smaller fruit trees offer many advantages over full-sized ones. With a smaller tree, you can actually reach and harvest all the fruit, instead of leaving half of it in the upper branches to fall to the ground and create both a mess and a pest problem. Smaller trees won't leave

Pruning an espalier pear tree.

you with a glut of fruit that you have to preserve immediately or give away. And smaller trees are easier to maintain, protect, and prune. Here are some dwarf fruit trees ideal for urban yards: apple, Asian pear, cherry, Cornelian cherry (*Cornus mas*), crabapple, jujubes (maintain size by pruning), medlar, mulberry, peach, pear, plum, quince.

espalier fruit trees: create a living fence

You can train some fruit trees to take on a flat form, called an *espalier*. On a small urban lot, this method lets you pack many fruit trees around the edges of your garden, without taking up much space. Apples and pears on severely dwarfing rootstock adapt well to this technique. Their roots constrain the growth of the tree, making the tree less rebellious against the aggressive pruning required to control an espalier. To espalier an apple or pear, first build the support structure. I drive heavy (¾ inch) 10-foot rebar poles about 3 feet into the ground, spacing them about 10 feet on center. Then I string metal cables between the poles at a height of 24 inches, then every 16 inches above that, until I reach about 7 feet tall. The 16-inch measurement is only a guideline; I usually decrease the vertical spacing slightly as I ascend, as the upper branches face less competition for sunlight. (Besides, this spacing creates pleasing proportions.)

Centered between the two rebar poles, I plant a bare root "whip," a young seedling with one or two flimsy lateral branches. I order these trees "bare root" in late winter or early spring through the mail from a regional fruit nursery.

Once I receive the trees, I shake the damp sawdust off the bare roots and place the roots in a bucket of water while I dig a hole. I may add a little compost to the soil, but this is less important with trees than with gardens. In fact, by improving the soil too much where you plant the tree, you may discourage the tree from sending its roots beyond the tiny patch of improved soil.

If it's not raining, I water the planting hole. Then I plant the tree, splaying the roots to direct them to where I think they'll find water and nutrients. I backfill the hole with dirt, making sure the tree's crown (where the roots begin) sits on a little raised mound of dirt about 3 inches taller than the surrounding grade. I compact the soil gently with my foot, and then I apply a mulch (such as arborist's wood chips) all around the root zone to help keep the soil moist on sunny days.

As the tree grows, I train the "lateral" or horizontal branches to grow along the horizontal metal cables. Because a tree will always put more energy into vertical branches than horizontal branches, you must fool it into growing horizontals. Let the laterals grow diagonally upwards for a while, then bend them down to the horizontal before they stiffen. Repeat the process: Grow and bend, grow and bend. It doesn't matter if the horizontal branch ends up looking a little zigzagged, because over the years it will increase in girth and smooth out a bit. Eventually your tree will have filled out its whole framework, and its "leader" or tip may be bent down to form the uppermost lateral.

Your tree may aspire to greater height despite its rootstock's discouraging influence, so you'll need to keep aggressive verticals trimmed to about 8 inches in the summer. Don't summer-prune too much at one time, or you'll encourage more vertical sprouts. In the winter you can trim your tree more aggressively back to its ideal form. A mature espalier will have a stiff main structure and a constantly evolving arrangement of smaller "spurs," the short budding branches that develop fruit. *(JM)*

. . . .

COLUMNAR APPLE TREES

If you don't have space for even dwarf trees, plant columnar apple varieties. These trees have been pruned and trained to fruit off of the central trunk of the plant, so they fit easily into a medium- to large-sized pot. The fruit sets directly along the main trunk in clusters. In the second year after planting my columnar apple tree, I harvested fifteen pounds of tasty apples. If you live in an apartment or condo but have a south- or west-facing balcony or patio, one or two of these in pots might be enough fruit to meet all your apple needs. *(AC)*

. . . .

chapter 9
garden pests and beneficial insects

As a new gardener, you may enjoy a year or two before pests discover your garden. But if you live in an urban area, insects eventually will find their way in. To combat insect pests, you have two options. You can go the conventional route and spray the heck out of them. But that is a dead-end street; you'll poison yourself and leave your garden vulnerable, in the long run, to insect plagues of biblical proportions. Or, you can just let nature take care of your pests.

I first discovered the latter method way back in college, when a beloved potted plant in my dorm room became completely covered with aphids. As the plant had been with me through final exams and a messy breakup, I couldn't bear to throw it in the Dumpster. So I abandoned it under a bush near some tall grass. "I set you free," I remember thinking.

I returned a few months later to find my plant not only alive, but thriving and completely aphid free. I picked up my revived plant and walked through the tall grass. Countless insects hopped and flew from my path. A light bulb clicked on: Tall, weedy grass = predator habitat. The insects in the grass had eaten my aphids.

Later, I learned how this system functions in a garden. In the community gardens where I learned to tend vegetables, I came to recognize weed flowers as nectar sources for predatory insects. Uncontrolled patches of borage, bachelor's buttons, Queen Anne's lace, calendula, dill, nicotiana, and grasses—these wild, forgotten corners of the garden sustained small populations of predatory insects. As soon as aphids colonized a broccoli plant on a nearby garden plot—*boom!*—in swooped the predators. Ladybugs would fly in and lay their tiny clusters of bright orange eggs. Soon the tiny, alligator-shaped larvae would emerge to find an all-you-can-eat buffet of stupid, succulent aphids. Soft-bodied caterpillars, munching on cabbage, would feel the telltale prick of a parasitic wasp laying an egg just under the skin. After a short gestation period, the wasp would hatch and consume the caterpillar from the inside out. I've even come to value yellow jackets, after seeing one eat the belly out of a green caterpillar.

If you provide habitat, food (nectar + prey), and water for predatory insects, and if you grow strong plants by building healthy soil, nature will take care of many of your pest problems. But you may experience boom-and-bust populations of insect pests for a few years. It takes that long for predator and prey populations to reach equilibrium. The first year I planted my current garden, I accidentally fertilized my second-year plum tree with organic nitrogen (you're not supposed to fertilize trees much, if at all). After a month of luxuriant but tender growth, the tree became covered with aphids. By the end of the summer, ladybugs had moved in by the thousands, along with small flocks of ecstatic birds. The next year, the ladybugs returned in droves (could they have remembered my tree?), and the aphid population didn't stand a chance. A month later, most of the ladybugs had flown away. Over the years, this cycle of boom and bust has evened out.

Scatter beautiful flowering weeds throughout your garden, or let plants such as mustard or kale go to seed and remain in your beds. The more inbred and domesticated the plant, the less likely it is to appeal to an insect as a food source or habitat. Choose plants with tiny flowers, as these tend to appeal to insects more than larger, highly cultivated flowers.

Choose plants with various shapes and sizes of foliage, and staggered bloom periods. Leave a pile of bamboo stakes rotting at the edge of the garden—you'd be surprised at what can overwinter there. Leave lichen and old spider webs for hummingbirds to build nests with. Maintain a birdbath with some small stones for butterflies and wasps to sit on. Do everything you can to make insects feel welcome. Then maybe the next time you spot a cabbage moth or an aphid, you won't see it as a threat. You'll see it as bait.

Organic pest control means adopting a number of complementary strategies. Grow strong plants in good soil while encouraging predators. Manually control those pests that beat the system by picking them off or creating mechanical barriers. Tolerate some insect damage. And as for those delicate plants you can't grow without pesticides, kick them out of your garden. You're too busy to pamper them all summer long. *(JM)*

• •

OPPORTUNITIES FOR CHANGE
PEST–FREE

🐝 Garden without insecticides.

🐞🐝 Incorporate plants that attract beneficial insects.

🐝🐞🐝 Raise mason bees.

• •

PLANTS THAT ATTRACT BENEFICIAL INSECTS

Below is a list of some ornamental and native plants that attract beneficial insects. When possible, choose simpler, wilder varieties over frilly cultivars.

Alyssum
Anise hyssop
Bachelor's buttons
Borage
Buckwheat
Calendula
Corn
Cup plant
Dandelions
Evening primrose
Fennel
Foxglove
Fuchsia
Golden marguerite
Goldenrod
Hairy vetch
Inside-out flower

Jacob's ladder (native variety)
Kinnikinnick
Lupine
Mullein
Mustards
Mints
Nettle
Oregon grape
Ornamental grasses
Pincushion flower
Rye
Sunflower
Tansy
Umbell family (including Queen Anne's Lace)
Vine maple
White clover
Yarrow
Zinnia

purchasing beneficial insects

Pests and diseases may travel freely between urban gardens, but so do beneficial insects. For this reason, urban gardeners don't need to go out and purchase ladybugs, lacewings, or parasitic wasps—these predators will find you. And if you haven't created good habitat, any predators you purchase will probably fly away anyway.

That said, it's difficult to resist that beautiful container of ladybugs at the garden store. If you succumb to the temptation, there are ways to combat these insect predators' urge to flee the moment you open the package:

›   Refrigerate them before opening (to slow them down).
›   Release them after dark (when they're sleepy).
›   Release them under an aphid-covered bush surrounded by pollen-bearing flowers and

recently sprayed with water (your predators will be thirsty and hungry).

› Sprinkle bee pollen under the plant (an easy-to-find food).

For best results, purchase lacewings or ladybugs as larvae or eggs. These you'll need to secure directly to the plant with a stapler, closer to the prey but hidden from birds. Larvae eat more aphids anyway; adults only really care about mating.

garden pests that beat the system

A few garden pests have carved out a niche for themselves by emerging at the first sign of spring, before predators have emerged. These pests fear no insect, for their predators still lie dormant in their eggs and cocoons. If they emerge at night, they need fear no bird.

twin terrors of spring: cutworms and slugs

Cutworms sleep during the day just under the soil surface at the base of my plants. Sometimes I'm lucky enough to disturb them with my garden spade as I work in the garden. I find them sleeping in a little "C" shape. "Good morning," I say, and toss them to the chickens.

But the cutworms outnumber me. A few hours after dark, the army of solitary munchers slowly climbs the stems of my plants to feast contentedly on the earliest spring growth. Left unmolested, they'll completely defoliate my blueberry plants.

And then there are slugs. Baby slugs hatch long before ground beetles start hunting down slug eggs. In the summer, slugs can't do much damage against my mature plants; I can tolerate a few slug holes in my lettuce. But in the spring, tiny slugs can wipe out a whole crop of pea seedlings in a couple of nights.

You can surround your garden plants with copper tape, but the tape costs a lot, oxidizes quickly, and is difficult to apply effectively. You can make beer traps, but baby slugs don't like to travel very far between traps. You can spread various things on the soil surface to deter them, from crushed eggshells and biochar to hot chili powder and diatomaceous earth. None of these things work very well, as most of them stop working in the rain. And in the spring it rains a lot.

Sometimes a gardener has to take matters into his own hands. After putting the kids to bed at night, I arm myself with a flashlight and an empty wine bottle. Perhaps a little tipsy from finishing off the wine, I carefully inspect the leaves of my growing plants. I pick off cutworms one by one and drop them in the bottle. I scoop slugs off the ground, though they leave an almost unwashable slime on my fingers. Sometimes the neighbors walk by, eyeing me with curiosity. What—have they never witnessed vigilante justice before?

Sometimes when I'm out there in the cold, I wonder what it would be like to just spray the problem away with pesticides. But it's worth the entertainment my chickens provide as they scramble to snatch up the pests when I dump them out in the coop the next morning. And as the insect predators slowly emerge later in the season, I know I've made the right decision. *(JM)*

coddling moths and apple maggots

There's nothing more discouraging than finding your whole crop of apples infested with maggots. In the city, that nightmare will happen to you unless you protect your apples.

Infested trees are everywhere. The culprits are two different pests: coddling moths and apple maggots. These two pests share a similar life cycle. The adult moths or flies mate, then look for an apple on which to lay their eggs. After hatching, the maggots of both species tunnel to the apple's core, eat the seeds, and tunnel out again.

Home gardeners can prevent mature moths and flies from laying their eggs on apples by bagging the fruit with nylon booties available from your local tree fruit society. You can also buy Japanese paper apple bags.

Unfortunately, coddling moths lay some eggs before the fruits are large enough to bag, so even if you bag, you're likely to have some coddling moth damage. On my own trees, it appears that a small number of coddling moths succeed in penetrating the nylon barrier. Some gardeners have reported success by soaking their booties in a liquefied kaolin clay often sold under the brand name Surround. When a moth lands on an apple, pieces of the clay break off, and suddenly the moth forgets all about laying eggs and starts grooming itself. Who knew coddling moths were so vain!

Even if you can't keep out coddling moths, you may consider their damage tolerable, as I do. They burrow through the apple in a direct line, and while you couldn't sell those apples, you can enjoy them at home if you cut out the insect damage. The apple maggot is a different story. It takes its sweet time burrowing around and around the apple. Apple maggots destroy apples; fortunately, they're the easier of the two pests to control with bags and booties.

After the apple maggot and coddling moth larvae emerge from the apple, they drop to the ground or find a crack in the bark. There they pupate for a while, maturing in cocoons until they emerge as adults, ready to start the cycle all over again. Several generations can emerge in one summer. As a backyard gardener, you can do these pests some damage by allowing your chickens to root around in the mulch beneath apple and pear trees. Throw down some scratch to make it worth their while to dig. Confine them under the trees for several days from early March to late April, then again periodically through the summer.

DUCKS LOVE SLUGS

Tired of midnight forages with a headlamp, Annette has enlisted the ultimate slug patrol: a small flock of ducks. When they're not providing eggs or entertaining you with their antics in the abandoned kiddie pool, ducks aggressively hunt down slugs.

Many gardeners purchase chickens to eat their slugs, but most come to realize that chickens cause more problems than they solve when allowed to roam the garden. While a hen may be trained to eat slugs, she'd rather eat worms. And if she's an heirloom breed, she'll dig aggressively, uprooting your garden seedlings. I let my chickens roam the garden in late summer, but by this time the slugs don't threaten my plants anyway. *(JM)*

· ·

bees

Another reason to attract beneficial insects is to pollinate your fruits. One of the best pollinators is the "orchard mason bee." Many gardeners purchase these by mail, ordering them in early winter before suppliers run out. The bees arrive in small cardboard tubes. Keep them dormant in the produce drawer of your fridge until early spring.

When you see blossoms in need of pollination, warm up your bees indoors for a few hours, then secure them to a "mason bee house" (see illustration, opposite).

When the solitary bees emerge in spring (males first, then females), they'll mate. Then the female will look for holes nearby in which to lay her eggs. She'll stock the eggs with pollen and wall them off with mud from your garden. She'll continue to lay eggs and gather pollen, stopping only at night, until she dies.

The eggs will hatch in the summer. The larvae will eat their pollen, then pupate in a cocoon until warmed by the following spring.

Of course, if you *really* want to get the most out of your pollinators, you can't do better than honeybees. Honeybees help pollinate fruit trees, but unlike mason bees they also produce honey. Beekeepers can get up to a hundred pounds of honey from a single hive in the hive's second year. And most people choose to keep at least three hives. That's a lot of honey.

To keep bees in the city, you'll need a flat sunny spot with easy access at least eight feet above the ground. In Seattle, you can keep them lower if you build a solid fence to protect the neighbors. Honeybees don't tend to bother people, but you don't want their flight paths to directly intersect human paths. Interestingly, if you point them at the inside corner of a solid fence, their flight path will lead them straight up into the air and over people's heads. *(JM)*

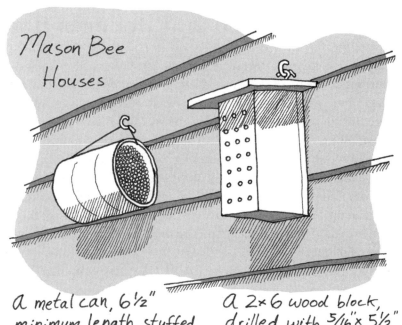

Mason Bee Houses

A metal can, 6½"
minimum length, stuffed
with mail order bee-tubes
or large plastic straws.
Protect from weather.

A 2×6 wood block,
drilled with 5/16" x 5½"
holes, 1×6 on back to
seal holes.
Add houses annually.

· ·

OPPORTUNITIES FOR CHANGE
BEES

🐝 Buy organic honey.

🐝🐝 Buy local organic honey.

🐝🐝🐝 Have a beekeeper install a hive on yours or a neighboring property.

🐝🐝🐝🐝 Raise your own honeybees.

· ·

producer profile: Ken and Rebecca Reid

From the moment Ken and Rebecca Reid received their first beehive, they knew they were in love. Every morning at breakfast, Ken would eat his cereal by the window and watch the bees. When their four-year-old daughter, Evelyn, wanted to participate, Rebecca made her a makeshift bee suit out of snow boots, an old sun hat, and a mesh laundry bag. Evelyn climbed out the window onto the flat garage roof and sat down right in front of the hive's entrance. She sat there a long time, letting the bees fly harmlessly around her.

These were conventional Italian honeybees, the same kind you can order in a box through the mail from California. They have evolved in symbiosis with modern beekeeping practices, living out their lives in standardized hive designs that discourage their natural instincts in favor of increased honey production. And they are reliant on chemicals to keep down harmful mites and fungi.

By the next spring, Ken and Rebecca's bees were dead. Like those of so many beekeepers, their hive had been hit by "colony collapse disorder," the mysterious cocktail of diseases that has hit commercial beekeepers so hard.

Ken and Rebecca's unusual backyard beekeeping methods keep hives free of toxic chemicals.

Conventional beekeepers have responded to the crisis by applying more miticides and fungicides. But Ken suspected those chemicals could create more problems than they resolved, further stressing out the chemical-saturated honeybees. As he and Rebecca were also organic gardeners, they suspected that nature, rather than chemistry, could provide a better solution.

The question was, How do honeybees operate in nature? Though honeybees have evolved closely with humans, they do revert to certain behaviors when allowed to escape into the woods and form wild hives. In a feral beehive, bees build cells of all different sizes. Bigger worker bees emerge from big cells, smaller worker bees from smaller cells.

When it comes to domesticated hives, beekeepers assume bigger bees are better; after all, shouldn't they be able to haul more nectar? Too many small cells encourages the hive to produce males, and since males don't produce honey—they think only about sex—modern beekeepers fool bees into creating cells of a uniformly large size by stamping the desired cell shape into a wax sheet called a "foundation." What emerges from these prescribed cell layouts are supersized, mostly female bees.

But bigger bees take longer to mature, and during their prolonged adolescence they're more vulnerable to mites. So most beekeepers spray their hives with nasty pesticides. Beeswax absorbs these chemicals. Commercial beekeepers melt down this polluted wax and resell it in the form of new foundations. Bees interact intimately with wax foundations, chewing on them, walking all over them, so even a beehive managed without chemicals can soon grow toxic from this legacy wax.

Ken and Rebecca decided to experiment with a progressive approach called "foundationless" beekeeping. Under this system, bees can choose whatever cell sizes they wish within the confines of a traditional honeycomb frame, controlling the makeup of their populations. They create smaller bees with fewer mites, and more males. More males means more opportunities to swap genes with other hives, increasing evolutionary adaptability. And while males also tend to attract mites, they take those mites with them when the females kick them out of the hive at the end of the year.

But Ken and Rebecca wanted to go further than just treating their domesticated bees like feral bees; they wanted to find a feral hive. Through a bee club, Ken located a hive in the Kent Valley, a heavily paved suburb of Seattle.

The bees had made their home in an ancient telephone pole, two-and-a-half feet in diameter at the base and over sixty feet tall. Years of decay had rotted out the core, which now buzzed with life. In an ordinary hive, Ken would have expected to see a slow trickle of bees coming and going from the entrance. But from this hive the bees flowed in a rushing stream.

As Ken eyed the hive, pondering how he'd extract the bees from it, he spotted the swarm.

On the other side of a chain link fence, a basketball-size mass of bees had clustered on a branch, weighting it to the ground.

A healthy bee colony will throw off swarms when its population climbs beyond a certain number. But this was the largest swarm Ken had ever seen. He walked around the fence to take a look. That's when he spotted a second swarm, even bigger than the first.

These bees, thought Ken, had thrived even as colonies across the country died off. They weren't pampered Italian honeybees, sent through the mail from sunny California. These bees had adapted over generations to the cool, wet springs of the Pacific Northwest. Their colors varied dramatically, indicating a deep gene pool. Yet despite their wildness, they didn't seem to mind Ken's presence a bit. These were the gentlest bees he'd ever seen.

Ken wanted these bees. He captured the swarms carefully in a couple of large boxes, working to make sure he collected the queen at the center of the swarm.

He drove them home to fill his empty hives, and today, feral bees form the cornerstone of Ken and Rebecca's beekeeping operation. They keep some Italian colonies, and some Northern European colonies too, for comparison. But it's the hives collected from wild swarms that perform the best.

The formerly feral bees emerge when the temperature hits 41°F, even on cloudy or rainy days. This is much colder and wetter than tolerated by heavily domesticated bees. That means the wilder bees collect pollen and nectar all spring, whereas other bees sleep in. When winter rolls around, these bees have more honey to survive the winter with, and more honey to give their beekeepers.

Today, Ken and Rebecca have expanded their operation to twenty-one hives on many urban properties. They maintain the hives for friends and acquaintances, one of whom lives next door to Annette. In exchange for allowing the bees on their property, host families get some of the honey.

Ken says his ideas about beekeeping have made him a bit of an outsider in the beekeeping club. But colony collapse disorder has really shaken things up. The new president of the club recently asked him about foundationless beekeeping. As backyard beekeeping gains popularity, the idea of raising bees with fewer chemicals seems to be gaining followers.

Many people think you can't have truly organic honey, because bees will visit organic and pesticide-laden flowers without distinction. But if you keep a foundationless beehive or three in your backyard, you can enjoy gallons and gallons of honey each year, as close to organic as you can get. *(JM)*

BEEKEEPING EQUIPMENT FOR "FOUNDATIONLESS" METHOD

Personal Equipment
› Beekeeper's suit (coveralls, veil, gloves)
› Smoker (and fuel), hive tool, bee brush (or a stiff feather)

Woodenware
› Standard "Langstroth" hive boxes, hive stand, other associated parts
› Foundationless frames
› Feeder

Honey Processing Equipment
› Knife, potato masher, fine strainer/mesh bag, or purchase, rent, or borrow centrifugal extractor

SUMMER

Summertime and the living is anything but easy. During my first year off the industrialized food grid, I preserved everything in sight, lest we want for anything in the winter. My thirty tomato plants meant constant harvest and a continually simmering saucepot and canner. I ordered eighty pounds of peaches and forty pounds of apricots from the organic orchards of Rama Farm, in Eastern Washington, to can and jam. I canned applesauce from eighty pounds of Early Gold apples from Tonnemaker Farms (another organic farm east of the Cascades). I pickled cases of beets.

With a monkey on my back, I daily picked beans, cucumbers, zucchini, and corn, then pickled or canned them. I fermented carrots, beets, radishes, cucumbers, and beans. I dehydrated apples, peaches, cherries, apricots, plums, and plum tomatoes. I froze strawberries, blueberries, and raspberries. I ground basil, arugula, and sorrel into pesto, then froze it. I made chutney and salsa and finally, when fall arrived, I canned green tomato enchilada sauce and chow-chow.

Then summer was over and I realized with remorse that I had missed the whole thing. And I was exhausted. This is how it feels, I rationalized, to create enough food for one family to eat all winter. My husband constantly reminded me that preserving so much food was unnecessary—there were stores and markets to fall back on—but I rejected that idea. After all, I had ripped out the front lawn. There was no going back.

That fall, a man I'd never met posted a message on the Seattle Farm Co-Op message board. He had been gifted a huge supply of plums from a backyard tree and had made cases of plum jam. Would anyone be interested in trading some of their home-canned goods for his jam? I jumped at the chance and we organized a bartering event at his house. That man turned out to be Joshua, my co-author. And it was the beginning of a wonderful friendship between our two families.

Statistics show that we have less leisure time today than people had in the early to mid 1900s—back when most people performed their own gardening, canning, knitting, sewing, and other homemaking tasks. My grandmother, born in 1916 to a poor family in rural South Dakota, learned of necessity how to grow and make just about anything a family could need. Yet she still had more leisure time than I. How had she done that? Joshua helped me realize that she hadn't done it alone.

My grandmother had community. When the apples in her small orchard were ripe, she invited other families to help her process the fruit and take some home for themselves. When those families had a bounty of another food, such as honey or salmon, they gifted it to my grandmother in exchange for the apples. Even if my grandmother could have done everything herself, she knew that building a community and fostering friendships were more important. And certainly easier! So, I stopped trying to do everything myself and started exploring ways to work with friends and neighbors to produce food for my family. And like my grandmother, I discovered community.

There are two other ways to provide enough food for your family year-round, without spending the summer in perpetual harvest and preserve mode. One way is to eat only what is in season. In the Pacific Northwest, eating seasonally is a viable option (especially if you don't mind eating months of colcannon—a traditional Irish dish of mashed potatoes mixed with cooked cabbage). Those summer potatoes, parsnips, carrots, and salsify can remain in the ground and be dug up as needed, and kale, mâche, chicory, claytonia, turnips, rutabagas, and collard greens will keep just fine in a maritime garden with minimal to no protection all winter. Or lacking a garden, you can find many of these "over wintered" foods at year-round farmers markets or through local CSA programs. Another way to spend less time preserving food is to store it. And you can do this without the root cellar my grandmother used. Maritime Northwest garages provide ideal storage conditions for foods such as winter squashes, cabbages, and apples. Even though nearly everything we eat during winter was really grown in summer or fall, we still consider it seasonal winter fare.

If preserving the harvest like a busy ant is one way to avoid shopping at the store, then eating seasonally and cellaring your produce are other, far more sustainable options. So before you plunge blindly into mad canning sessions, come up with a strategy for your time, find friends to barter with, and make sure you don't lose sight of how short, sweet, and important summer really is. *(AC)*

recipes for a summer meal

Nothing quite says summer like the first run of Chinook salmon in the Pacific Northwest. Here we treat them simply with fresh-from-the-garden horseradish, pan-roasted new potatoes, and summer's first cucumbers with chive and dill crème fraîche. While the adults are busy chatting and chopping, the children collect flowers and leaves from the garden for a dinner salad bursting with summer colors. What they really want, though, is the mixed berry cobbler with lemon verbena ice cream that will end the meal.

Horseradish Crusted Salmon
Makes 6–8 servings

> 1 egg, beaten
> 1 cup flour
> ½ teaspoon salt
> ¼ teaspoon freshly ground black pepper
> ¼ cup butter or olive oil
> 2 fillets sustainably harvested salmon, cut into 8 portions
> ⅓ cup finely minced horseradish*

1. Break egg into a pie pan, and whisk thoroughly. Combine flour, salt, and pepper on a plate.
2. Heat a large, heavy-bottomed skillet over medium-high heat. When a drop of water sizzles on pan, add butter or olive oil.

Chickens beg for scraps from a summer meal.

3. Working with one piece of salmon at a time, spread one side with horseradish, then dip that side in egg and then flour. Place in pan flour-side down. Repeat quickly with remaining salmon pieces, then reduce heat to medium-low.

4. As pieces cook, spread top of each one with horseradish. Cook for about three minutes, and then, with a pair of tongs, lift each piece out of pan, dip its uncooked side in egg and then flour, and return to pan with newly coated side down. Cook for another 2 minutes, and serve immediately.

*To finely mince horseradish, grate it with a ginger grater or microplane then finely mince with a chef's knife or in a mini food processor.

Pan Roasted New Potatoes
Makes 4–6 servings

> 2 tablespoons lard, bacon grease, or olive oil
> 2 pounds baby potatoes, jackets scrubbed
> 1 pound baby carrots, scrubbed

1. Preheat the oven to 375°F.
2. Place lard, bacon grease, or olive oil in a heat-proof casserole dish, and if using lard

or bacon grease, place dish in oven until it melts. Add potatoes, carrots, and salt and pepper to taste, and combine thoroughly. Roast for about 45 minutes, stirring halfway through cooking.

Cucumbers with Dill and Chive Crème Fraîche

Makes about 3 cups

> 2 cucumbers, peeled
> 1 teaspoon salt, or more to taste
> ½ pint crème fraîche (recipe page 88)
> ¼ cup chopped chives
> ¼ cup chopped fernleaf dill

1. Halve cucumbers lengthwise, and scoop out seeds. Slice into thin crescents, salt, and drain in a colander for 15 to 30 minutes.
2. In a bowl, combine crème fraîche, chives, and dill. Add cucumbers and mix well. Chill.

Flower and Herb Salad with Verjus Mustard Vinaigrette

Yield varies with ingredients

One of the joys of having a garden is creating amazing salads that change with the seasons. Like your garden, these salads are artful arrangements of many colors, shapes, and textures.

> ¼ cup verjus (recipe page 328) or sherry vinegar
> 1 tablespoon young balsamic vinegar, like Rockridge Orchard's
> 2 teaspoons prepared mustard (recipe page 244)
> ½ teaspoon salt
> Freshly ground black pepper
> ¾ cup sunflower or olive oil
> Any combination of large, medium, and small, variously colored leafy vegetables from the garden, plus herbs and flowers of your choosing

1. Combine verjus, vinegar, mustard, salt, and pepper in a mixing bowl. Slowly whisk in oil in a thin stream.
2. Just before serving, toss greens with vinaigrette, evenly coating leaves. Arrange leaves on the plate, herbs next, and flowers on top, making sure colors are well balanced.

When greens are less sweet, or anytime you are serving small children, you may prefer to add a tablespoon or two of local organic honey to your dressing. Add it with the first round of ingredients, before whisking in the oil.

. . . .

THE KITCHEN GARDEN SALAD

When building a salad, strive for a large number of ingredients. Here are some of our favorites:

Anise hyssop	Echinacea petals	Purslane
Arugula	Fennel	Radicchio
Baby chard or beet greens	Lemon balm	Rose geranium petals
Baby kale	Lemon thyme	Rose petals
Basil	Lemon verbena	Salad burnet
Borage flowers	Lettuces	Sorrel
Calendula petals	Magentaspreen	Spinach
Chamomile petals	Mustards	Stevia
Claytonia	Nasturtium flowers	Strawberry spinach
Cress	Orach	Tarragon
Dandelion	Parsley	Violet flowers
Dill	Pea blossoms	Violet leaves

. . . .

Mixed Berry Cobbler with Lemon Verbena Ice Cream
Makes 8 servings

For the filling
> 2 quarts (8 cups) fresh or frozen berries, in any combination (raspberries, blueberries, blackberries)
> ¾ to 1 cup sugar, depending on how sweet the berries are
> 1 tablespoon organic cornstarch, all-purpose flour, or potato flour
> Juice from ½ lemon or yuzu (optional)

For the topping
> ½ cup organic sugar combined with 1 teaspoon molasses*
> ½ cup ground spelt or soft wheat
> ½ teaspoon salt

½ teaspoon ground nutmeg or mace
½ teaspoon ground cinnamon
4 tablespoons chilled butter, cut into small pieces
½ cup rolled spelt or oats
¼ cup coarsely chopped hazelnuts or almonds

1. Preheat the oven to 375°F.
2. In a flameproof casserole dish, mix filling ingredients (or mix in a bowl and transfer to single-serving ramekins or ovenproof bowls or coffee mugs). Set aside while making topping.
3. In a food processor or mixing bowl, combine sugar and molasses and blend well. Add flour, salt, and spices, mixing until combined. Add butter pieces, and blend or cut in with a fork just until mixture resembles coarse meal. Add oats and nuts, mixing just to combine.
4. Sprinkle topping mixture evenly over filling, and place casserole or ramekins on a jelly roll pan to catch any drips.
5. Bake for about 40 minutes, or until filling begins to bubble around edges. Let cool until just warm, then serve with lemon verbena ice cream (see the recipe "Master Recipe for Pudding and for Custard-Based Ice Cream," page 69).

You can also substitute brown sugar for white sugar and molasses. I don't bother buying brown sugar because it is literally white sugar with molasses added—and I can do that myself.

chapter 10
eating seasonally

For those of us who raise our own food, eating seasonally is a joy during summer harvest time. The gardens on my in-city lot produce more vegetables, fruits, and herbs than my family of four can begin to consume. We feast on deliciously sweet carrots, succulent beets, crisp cucumbers, and tender broccoli; pack our salads with Swiss chard, mustard, and ten types of lettuces; pick handfuls of peas that remain sweet to the end, never woody or flavorless. Thick slices of meaty tomatoes, oozing with flavor, adorn our grilled burgers or get converted into summer salsa.

We have zucchini muffins for breakfast and basil pesto for dinner. Fresh fruit accompanies every meal: rhubarb, strawberries, blueberries, huckleberries and jostaberries, currants, figs, peaches, plums, sweet and sour cherries, pears and apples. The raspberries are so luscious and succulent—the perfect balance of sweet and acid—that every July I am tempted to tear out the back lawn and plant nothing but more of them.

But what about the rest of the year? At my house, we are slowly transitioning to eating only what is in season, every season. Although I still can or freeze a few batches of fruits, and store some apples and pears in the garage to convert into applesauce and fruit leather, their numbers decrease each year.

Part of eating seasonally is consuming as much as possible of everything that is currently ripe. Once you've eaten it all, you won't miss it again for another year! Eating seasonally can also include tactics such as urban foraging and trading with your neighbors, to supplement the produce in your garden. *(AC)*

Highbush cranberries from an urban park.

urban foraging

If you don't have the room or desire to grow fruits, consider urban foraging. Make a mental note about fruiting trees in your neighborhood or ones you pass during your errands or daily commute. Leave a note on the homeowner's door introducing yourself and telling them that you would be happy to help them harvest the fruit in exchange for keeping a portion of it. Many in-city fruiting trees are owned by elderly people who can't harvest the produce themselves, or by new homeowners who aren't as excited about the fruit tree they inherited as you are.

City parks often have edible plants ideal for foraging. Fruits from plants and trees such as Oregon grape, elderberry, salal, and crabapple make wonderful jellies and syrups and are there for the taking. Look for urban foraging tours to learn what is safe and available. And don't forget plants we consider "weeds," such as nettles, dandelions and chickweed. Many of them are edible and were highly prized by Native Americans.

The best part about this is you can find enough for yourself and many others who might not have access to fresh grown fruit. Consider teaming up with a local organization that counts on volunteers to harvest and distribute free fruits to those in need, such as the Portland Fruit Tree Project and Seattle's City Fruit Program (see Resources, page 370). *(AC)*

. . . .

OPPORTUNITIES FOR CHANGE
FORAGING AND TRADING
Find an abandoned fruit tree and can its treasures.

Trade your surplus fruits with others.

Register your fruit tree with an organization that harvests fruit for low-income families.

. . . .

northwest berries in the kitchen

What better way to experience a region's terroir than to incorporate its native foods into your diet? Exploring native berries can make you feel rooted here. *(JM)*

berries to eat fresh

Evergreen huckleberries. Our kids will hang out for an hour eating these delicious little berries off the bush. Also good in jams and pies, though time-consuming to harvest. Natives harvested them with fishbone combs. Try a hair pick.

Red huckleberries. I know of nothing so lovely as a red huckleberry bush on its mossy stump pedestal, illuminated by a shaft of sunlight. For kids, it looks like a pot of gold at the end of the rainbow. It would take all day to harvest enough for jam, so we enjoy these tart little berries fresh off the bush. The Northwest has many other delicious native huckleberries, but sadly, those varieties don't seem to thrive in urban parks at low elevations.

Salal berries. Great for eating fresh; wonderful in pies and jams (they develop a subtle cinnamon flavor when baked). Later in the summer, some will become infested with a little worm (just like blackberries do) and must be run through a food mill and used for jams.

Saskatoon berries (a.k.a. serviceberries). Wonderful fresh, though sometimes musky in flavor. I have not baked with these yet; my kids and I eat them too quickly. Some people find them seedy. Often planted as a street tree. Annette's chickens have been spotted making impressive vertical leaps to acquire these berries.

Thimbleberries. Delicious fresh, can taste a little "jammy" or overpowering in pies.

berries and fruits for jams and pies

Salmonberries. A little sour fresh, though my kids don't seem to mind. Some mature berries have a musky flavor that makes them an interesting addition to jams.

Oregon grape. Too sour to eat fresh, but fine in jams and jellies. Natural source of pectin.

Highbush cranberries. Brilliantly colored. Use as you would tart pie cherries.

berries and fruits for jellies or herbal teas

Red elderberries. Make a fantastic jelly, though you must cook them to break down a mild toxin. I recommend running them through a food mill to remove seeds and skins.

Blue elderberries. More common east of the Cascades, this plant thrives in the urban heat island of Seattle. Prepare as you would red elderberries to remove toxins.

Rosehips. Make lovely floral-scented jelly, tea, and syrup.

Haws. Our native hawthorn fruit is like a tiny apple with huge seeds. Distinguishable from the European hawthorn by its huge thorns and lack of aphids. We harvest haws for the chickens, though you could try them in a jelly.

Wild currants (from the widely planted red-flowering currant). We harvest these for the chickens.

Joshua's Forager Jam

Makes 4–6 half-pint jars. The quantity depends on how much sugar you use and whether you screen out seeds.

Since we eat whole-wheat pancakes and waffles almost every morning for breakfast, we prefer runny jams and jellies that can be used more like syrup. This means we're free to add sugar to taste, rather than the amount required to achieve a solid set. If you want a solid set, include some unripe berries in your fruit, as these provide pectin.

> 8 cups foraged wild berries (10 if your berries contain large seeds)
> 4 cups sugar plus up to 4 more cups

1. Prepare water bath, jars, and lids.
2. Stir together berries and 4 cups sugar in a cold stainless steel pot. Let sit for 10 minutes, to draw out some of the juice.
3. Bring berries to a boil over medium heat, stirring frequently. Once berries are soft, you have the option of running the heated mixture through a food mill to remove large seeds and skins. If you do that, return seeded and skinned mixture to pot and return to a boil.
4. Taste mixture for sweetness, adding up to 4 more cups sugar according to taste. Boil for 10 minutes. If you want a solid set (and included unripe berries for pectin), you could check for gel now, boiling longer if required.

5. Ladle into jars, leaving ¼ inch headspace. Wipe rims, screw lids on tight, and process in a water bath for 10 minutes.

stealing fruit

One of my greatest pleasures is taking "fruit walks" with my kids. I have several routes near our house, along which I know of a vast, weedy serviceberry tree, a sidewalk-staining mulberry tree, and a park with a climbable plum tree. On one our first walks, I unclipped my daughter from her stroller and used the curved handles to reach a persimmon hanging far above the sidewalk. As I was stretching onto my tiptoes, my son asked, "Are we stealing?"

"No," I said. I pulled on the stroller handle and the bright orange fruit dropped neatly into my open hand. "If the fruit hangs over the sidewalk, it's okay to take it." Just to make things clear, I pointed to a pear tree well within someone's yard. "See that tree over there—we'd never take that fruit. Not without asking. After all, we're not thieves."

Sally Anne harvests Oregon grape from a roadside shrub.

"Oh," said my son. So nice when things are so black and white.

A few weeks after that fruit walk, I was working in the planting bed along the sidewalk in front of my house. Earlier that year, I'd planted fodder radishes to break up the subsoil. One of the plants had grown to several feet tall. As I prepared to harvest one for my chickens, an elderly woman addressed me from the sidewalk. "Oh, I loved that plant," she said in a thick Eastern European accent "What was it?" I wondered why she referred to the plant in the past tense, though we were both staring at it.

"It's a fodder radish," I said.

"It was delicious. I took the leaves and cooked them. My husband loved them."

She never thanked me for the leaves she'd taken. She didn't seem to feel any explanation was required. Neither did I. I left the fodder radish in the ground an extra month before I pulled it out, just in case her husband wanted seconds. *(JM)*

A strongly flavored Karmijn de Sonnaville apple catches Luella off guard.

trading with neighbors

During the height of the economic crisis, Emily and I questioned whether we could afford good food. Buying clubs were still okay, we decided; purchasing produce as a group had actually saved us money. But the farmers market was out. Even organic fertilizers for our garden seemed out of the question. We looked into food stamps, but it seemed every few months we'd earn just enough to disqualify us.

During this time, our friend Sally Anne revealed to us how much free fruit the city has to offer. Every week or so, she'd show up with a huge bag of fruit, gleaned from a friend's underutilized grape arbor or another friend's forgotten plum tree. If she saw a tree full of ripe fruit, she'd walk up to a stranger's door, knock and ask, "Are you going to eat that?" Many of the homeowners were glad to have someone harvest their fruit—they didn't want it themselves, but hated to see it go unused. Sally Anne helped ease their consciences.

So we began looking for fruit ourselves. Drawing on family, friends, and neighbors, we gleaned enough fruit to can dozens of pints of jam, many of which we later bartered for other homemade products.

The beauty of this system is that not everyone has to have the perfect, sunny garden to participate. In the city, few of us have room to grow everything we need anyway. Try to specialize in something to trade with your neighbors. Some of the people with whom we trade produce only honey or homebrew. One of my neighbors gives me lawn clippings and fallen leaves for my compost and bamboo stakes for my garden. I give him tomatoes. From another neighbor, I borrow greenhouse space. I bring her a few eggs now and then.

On a farm in the countryside, you can probably find a space for all of your agricultural and culinary hobbies. But viewed through the right lens, my urban neighborhood is a farm. *(JM)*

. . . .

WHERE ELSE CAN YOU GET FRESH PRODUCE?

Assuming you don't have a huge garden and orchard, and aren't able to buy entire crops, where can you find nutritiously grown and affordable produce for preserving?

› Check with farmers at your local farmers markets to see if anyone offers case pricing.
› Search online for U-pick farms in your area where you can pick your own produce.
› Ask community kitchens that offer canning classes where they buy their produce.
› Drive out of town and look for roadside signs advertising produce for sale.
› See Resources, page 370, for more ways to locate farms in your area.

. . . .

chapter 11
winter gardening:
it starts in summer!

It may sound odd to talk about winter gardening in the same sentence as seasonal eating and summer but in truth they are connected. Here we are so far north and our skies are so cloudy that crops don't grow during the winter so all the local produce you get in the winter is really grown during the late summer and fall, then stored in the garden or cellar until needed. As a rule of thumb, you should start most of your winter crops around mid-summer.

It's no small feat finding room to start fall, winter, and spring produce at a time when your summer garden is just hitting its stride. The easiest way I've found is to start long-maturing crops in seedling trays that live on a two-tiered nursery cart with metal mesh bottom for good drainage. (You could also use an old child's wagon if you drill some drainage holes in it.) In the early spring, it doubles as a roving farm stand that my son pulls around the neighborhood, selling fresh salad greens, peas, and strawberries. With a wheeled cart, you can easily move the seedlings in and out of sunlight. Another bonus of using a cart is that you can place copper banding around the edges to keep the slugs at bay.

You can also use a stationary outdoor shelving unit for your trays of seedlings, wrapping copper banding around the legs to ward off the slugs. Continue repotting your seedlings as they grow until you ultimately have room in the garden for them. *(AC)*

OPPORTUNITIES FOR CHANGE
WINTER PRODUCE

Join a winter CSA that delivers only local produce.

Sprout indoors and shop at winter farmers markets.

Plant a winter garden.

. . . .

selecting winter varieties

Selecting cold hardy varieties is the key to winter gardening success. I've selected the following varieties because they grow quickly in fall then overwinter in our maritime climate with little or no protection. This is by no means an exhaustive list of winter-hardy varieties, but these work well for me and are reliable year after year, so I can whole-heartedly recommend them.

Some of these plants, such as turnips, parsnips, carrots, kale, dandelions, mâche, and claytonia, will be ready to eat by late fall yet be content to remain in the garden all winter until you need them. Others, like broccoli and Brussels sprouts, will need the growing days of late summer, fall, and early spring in order to mature, so they won't be ready to eat until mid-spring.

Plant	Variety	Sow Date	Harvest Date	Notes
Broccoli	Thompson, De Cicco, Belstar	August	April	
Brussels sprouts	Roodnerf	July	October through January	Wait until the first frosts to begin harvesting for sweetest flavor
Cabbage	Tundra, January King	April	October	
Collards	Champion	July, August	October through late spring	
Kale	Nero di Toscana, Fizz, Dwarf Siberian, Red Russian, White	August	October through late spring	
Kohlrabi	Kohlribi, Superschmeltz	August	October	
Carrots	Red Dragon, Scarlet Nantaise, Merida	July, August	October through spring	Plan to eat these by early spring as they degrade in quality with warmer weather.
Parsnips	Cobham, Improved Marrow	July, August	April	

An overwintered Purple Dragon carrot.

Plant	Variety	Sow Date	Harvest Date	Notes
Turnips	Purple Top White	August, September	October/November through winter	Plant densely and thin by pinching off the greens and steaming them throughout the fall and winter. Remove any roots so you don't attract sow bugs and centipedes once the leafless roots begin to decompose.
Rutabagas (Swedes)	Joan	July, August	November through winter	
Lettuce	Outredgeous, Continuity, Drunken Woman Frizzy Head, Winter Density, Italienischer,	July, August, September	September through spring	
Spinach	Bloomsdale Savoy, Giant Winter	August, September	March, April	
Arugula	Roquette, Sylvetta Wild	July, August	September through hard freeze	
Mâche (Vit)		July, August	November through early spring	
Claytonia	Miner's Lettuce	August, September	November forevermore	
Cress	Belle Isle	July, August	November through spring	
Pac choi	Ching-Chiang	August, September	November through spring	
Peas	Cascadia, Oregon Sugar Pod II	September	April	
Beans	Broad Windsor Fava	September	May	
Hardneck garlic	Spanish Roja, Purple Italian Easy, Siberian, Chesnok Red	October	September	Plant in October
Softneck garlic	Polish Softneck, Inchelium Red, Susanville	October	September	Plant in October
Shallots	French	October	September	These can be stored for 6 months in dry, cool conditions. Plant in early October.
Cover crops	Crimson Clover, Austrian Field Peas, Common or Hairy Vetch, Annual Rye Grass	Anytime	Anytime	
Forage crops	Austrian Field Peas, Common or Hairy Vetch, Annual Rye Grass	Anytime	Anytime	

protecting the winter garden

For years, I've dreamed of a greenhouse but I've never found an affordable one large enough to be useful, sturdy enough to last, and small enough to fit in my yard. Instead, I carefully select the hardiest winter varieties I can. I group the more tender ones, such as Beira Trochunda cabbage, Lacinato kale, or chard, together and cover them using a low plastic tunnel. This low tunnel is constructed of pieces of bent metal tubing with a clear plastic cover clipped on using standard office-variety plastic and metal binder clips. I found the binder clips actually work better than the expensive PVC clamps you can buy for this purpose. In the spring, this grow tunnel, or "hoop house," becomes the greenhouse for my tender tomato, pepper, basil, eggplant, and melon starts. If the summer is cool or particularly wet, I may leave the hoop house on right through to fall, raising up the sides to allow in beneficial pollinators. Through careful planning, I isolate those few things I grow that need special protection so that I don't need more than one hoop house. A small hoop house like this can also serve as a seedling nursery. *(AC)*

An inexpensive hoop house.

chapter 12
preserving the harvest

There are many ways to preserve the harvest, depending on your time, energy, and how many freezers you want to have. Before deciding what to preserve, review the "Sample Produce Eating Plan" you developed last spring. Think about what fruits and vegetables your family likes to eat and how much of each item you'll need to preserve to get your family through the lean months of late winter and early spring.

And remember that freezing and canning aren't the only ways to preserve food. Cellaring, drying, and fermenting are equally effective methods and sometimes nutritionally superior.

So if you have no desire to build up an arsenal of canning jars or install a new freezer in your basement, take heart! In the following pages, you'll learn many other methods of preserving enough harvest to complement a steady diet of seasonal produce all year long. *(AC)*

PRESERVING

annette's grocery list

ORIGINAL LIST

Applesauce
Barbecue sauce
Canned tomatoes
Dried fruit
Fruit leather
Hot sauce
Jam
Jelly
Ketchup
Mustard
Pasta sauce
Pickles
Relish
Salsa
Sauerkraut
Sugar

REVISED LIST

First year: Canning jars, funnel, magnetic wand, jar lifter, fermentation airlocks, rubber gaskets
Canning jar lids
Handful of lemons or vinegar
Sugar
Local peaches or apricots (since they are hard to grow here)

🥫 Can or freeze foods to eat out of season.

🥫🥫 Ferment, cellar, or dry foods you eat out of season.

🥫🥫🥫 Eat only what is in season (no need to preserve anything!)

. . . .

freezing

Freezing locks in nutrients and texture—two things that are dramatically compromised by canning. Freezing is my preferred method for preserving pesto, berries, green beans, and peas. I also freeze jars of pre-dried apples to add to breakfast sausage, muffins, or oatmeal. You certainly can freeze other foods, but I have limited freezer space so I stick with this short list.

One of the keys to successful freezing is to minimize the food's contact with air. I use a vacuum-type sealer. Unfortunately, the bags are made of plastic and are not re-useable—another reason I try to limit how much food I freeze.

To keep frozen vegetables fresh you must first blanch them. This brief heat treatment will slow the enzyme activity that causes vegetables to continue growing (and getting woodier and more bitter) even once frozen. To blanch vegetables, lower them into boiling water, using about one gallon of water per pound of vegetables. Immerse the vegetables briefly, according to the times listed below, and then transfer them to a container of ice water to stop the blanching process. A skimmer or handled sieve will help you quickly scoop the vegetables from the boiling water and into the ice bath. Remove the vegetables from the ice water, drain them completely, and then package and freeze them. *(AC)*

timelines for blanching vegetables

Green beans: 2 minutes
Shelled peas: 1½ minutes
Snow peas: 2½ minutes
Corn: 4 minutes, then cut kernels from cob
Sliced carrots: 2 minutes
Greens (kale, spinach, etc.): 2 minutes
Broccoli florets: 3 minutes

cellaring

For several years, I dreamed of having my own root cellar. I read books about them and researched how to build one. Meanwhile, I stored my winter squashes, potatoes, and apples in the garage. I finally realized they were keeping just fine that way. Who needs a root cellar?

In the Pacific Northwest, the temperatures and levels of humidity in a winter garage are about the same as in an underground root cellar. Also, our climate is well suited to leaving root crops and hardy greens in the garden right through the winter, harvesting them only as needed. I leave my fall kale, collards, cabbages, carrots, parsnips, salsify, and turnips in the ground till spring and I know many farmers who do the same with their potatoes.

There are a few rules to help preserve the quality of your "winter keepers" as long as possible:

›   Potatoes need absolute darkness. I store mine in a covered cardboard box that completely blocks out the light. There is some evidence that storing potatoes with an apple or two will help prevent them from sprouting early. This will, however, shorten the life of the apples. Check the box occasionally and replace the apples as necessary, removing any potatoes that have gone bad.

›   Carrots and beets need a high level of humidity and cool temperatures. Either store them in closed plastic bags in a refrigerator or put them into a closed plastic container full of damp, clean sand or sawdust and store the container in the garage. The carrots and beets should keep for two to three months, depending on the variety. (Alternatively, you can lacto-ferment root vegetables; see "Fermenting," page 217.)

›   Storing onions and shallots should be left in the ground until the tops die down. After that, dig them up and let them cure for a week in a dry location, then store them in a dry, warm area with good airflow. You can hang them in wire baskets or nets, or tie the tops together and suspend them with string from the rafters. If any onions sprout, plant the sprouts in the garden for next year's seed. (You can also make onion or shallot marmalade to can or freeze; see the recipe "Caramelized Onion Jam," on page 241.)

›   Garlic should be left in the ground until the tops die down. After that, dig them up and let them cure for a week in a dry location. Hardneck varieties can be stored in a hanging wire basket or mesh bag; they will typically last four to six months. Roast any remaining heads by New Year's, divide the roasted heads into cloves, and freeze them. Softneck varieties can be braided partway through the curing process while the tops are still supple and easy to work with. They will last six to nine months. Plant any sprouting cloves in the garden for next year's harvest or seed.

›   Cabbages can be nestled in clean, dry straw in a box or ice chest and kept in the garage.

A subterranean garage makes the perfect root cellar and cheese cave in the city.

Stored this way, they will usually last until early spring. (Alternatively, you can convert cabbage into sauerkraut (See "Fermenting," page 217) or kimchi, which will last much longer.

› Winter squashes should be left on the vine until just before the first frosts. After that, bring them in and place them on shelves with good airflow in the garage or house.

› Corn that was left on the stalk too long, either by accident or by design, can be used all winter to make polenta (see page 19), masa harina, or cornmeal for pickled pepper cornbread (see recipe, page 264), or be fed to chickens or goats. Leave the cobs on the stalks until they begin to dry, then remove them from the plant, peel back the husks to improve airflow, tie them with a rope, and hang them in a warm, dry location for a few weeks longer until they dry completely. You can leave the cobs hanging all winter or, once dried, pick the kernels off and store them in a Mason jar in the pantry.

› Shelling beans can be left on the vine when they die down in late summer. If the forecast calls for endless rain, uproot the vines and hang them upside down in a utility room or near a heat source to dry. Be sure there is good airflow around the plants so they don't mold. Alternatively, you can remove the pods from the plant and dry them on Low in a dehydrator. Once the pods are dried, shell them and store the beans in Mason jars in your pantry. (AC)

dehydrating

Dehydrating is a great way to preserve fruit for winter meals. It is also a quick and easy way to create snacks for outings or school lunches.

I love having a good supply of dried apples on hand. I dry pears, apricots, peaches, cherries, strawberries, and tomatoes. I sometimes whizz up dried apples and pears in an old coffee grinder until they become powdery, then use this natural sugar for sweetening pancakes or muffins. You can do the same with tomatoes, then add that powder to stews and soups in place of tomato paste.

Tomatoes are great either totally or partially dehydrated. Partially drying tomatoes reduces the volume and concentrates the sugars while retaining some of the tomato's original freshness and juice. Store any partially dried tomatoes in the freezer since the remaining moisture will cause them to mold.

It is possible to dry fruit on screened trays in the sun, but in the Pacific Northwest, the odds of getting enough sunny days in a row are so slim that it makes sense to use an electric dehydrator. My dehydrator is well loved. I use it heavily in the summer to dry fruit and then all winter to make fruit leather from applesauce or old apples, beef jerky, and even yogurt fruit leather treats. You can often find electric dehydrators at thrift stores or on craigslist, or if you belong to a local gardening forum, you may be able to borrow one. *(AC)*

guidelines for drying fruit

Some fruits, such as apples, pears, peaches, and apricots, need a quick dip in an acidic medium before dehydrating, in order to stop them from turning dark. You can make an acidic dip by combining ¼ cup lemon juice or 2 tablespoons of good-quality apple cider vinegar with a few cups of filtered water. Dry all fruit until no moisture comes out when squeezed. Once it is dried, I store my fruit in Mason jars in a dark pantry. For longer keeping you can also freeze them, but they will never be as good as they were before freezing.

Dried apple slices: Peel apples, then either core them using a coring tool to create rings, or quarter and remove cores with a knife. Cut into ¼-inch slices and dip for a few minutes in acidified water. Spread out on dehydrator trays so there is good airflow around each slice, and dry for 6 to 10 hours on Low, depending on your particular dehydrator. Alternatively, you can slice apples into rings, string them with a needle and thread, and hang them in a utility room or near a radiator or fireplace to dry. Once they are dry, you can keep them in a jar with things like cinnamon sticks and cloves, dried rose petals, elderflowers, or lavender to flavor them. For a really sweet treat, try sprinkling them with a little bit of mixed sugar and ground cinnamon before drying.

Dried pear slices: Peel pears, then quarter, and remove cores with a knife. Dry using the same method as apples.

Dried peach slices: Slip off skins and remove pits, then slice into ¼-inch slices. Dip for a few minutes in acidified water. Spread out on dehydrator trays so there is good airflow around each slice, and dry for 6 to 10 hours on Low, depending on your particular dehydrator.

Dried apricots: Slice in half, remove pits, and lay each half skin-side up on dehydrator trays, allowing for good airflow around each slice. Dry for 10 hours or more on Low, depending on your particular dehydrator. Dried apricots are wonderful added to scones and rehydrated into sauce. You can even dry them now and then make jam from them in the winter, but they taste pretty amazing eaten plain as well. This is one fruit that is improved many times over by dehydrating. If you don't like fresh apricots you really should try them dried.

Dried strawberries: Remove stems, slice small strawberries in half, and cut larger strawberries into slices. Spread out on dehydrator trays so there is good air flow around each slice, and dry for 4 to 8 hours on Low, depending on your particular dehydrator.

Dried cherries: Pit cherries, slice in half, spread out on dehydrator trays so there is good air flow around each slice, and dry for 4 to 8 hours on Low, depending on your particular dehydrator. Dried cherries are excellent in baked goods, or rehydrated in brandy or scotch for Christmas trifle.

Dried tomatoes: Because tomatoes have such a high liquid content, you end up with a small bit of fruit for your effort. For this reason, I dry only plum or pasting tomatoes and save the heirloom varieties for fresh eating. If you are using heirloom tomatoes, slip off skins and slice them. This step is not necessary for plum or paste tomatoes, though: Simply cut them in half, gently squeeze out most of the seeds, spread them out on dehydrator trays cut-side down so there is good air flow around each slice, and dry for 6 to 10 hours on Low, depending on your particular dehydrator. You can rehydrate them later for fresh eating, or simply throw them dried into pots of soup or stews, where they will rehydrate nicely. Try whizzing them up in an old coffee grinder and adding them to dishes in place of tomato paste.

Kale chips: Wash kale leaves and remove central ribs. Blanch in boiling water for 2 minutes, then dip in soy or teriyaki sauce. Spread out on dehydrator trays so there is good airflow around each piece, and dry for 3 to 6 hours on Low, depending on your particular dehydrator. *(AC)*

MAKING FRUIT LEATHER

I always have fruit leather on hand to throw into school lunches. To make fruit leather, start with pureed fruit (or vegetables). I sauce my oldest apples or pears first, since they have already begun to dry out. You can add purees of other fruits or vegetables (like rhubarb or pumpkin or mashed carrots) up to about 50 percent of your total mixture. The pectin in the apple will keep the final fruit leather soft and pliable rather than hard and brittle. Feel free to add a smidgen of sugar or spice to taste.

Apple pie fruit leather? Just add some brown sugar and cinnamon. Pumpkin pie fruit leather? Add pureed pumpkin, cinnamon, ginger, and cloves. Curried carrot fruit leather? Add curry spices to your applesauce and pureed carrots. Part of the fun of making things from scratch is that you can use your imagination!

To make, combine your chosen purees and mix well. Pour them onto fruit leather sheets and place them in your dehydrator according to the manufacturer's directions. Dry until they are no longer sticky to the touch. I roll mine tight and store them in quart canning jars. *(AC)*

fermenting

Fermentation is one of the simplest methods of preserving fresh foods and has been around for thousands of years. Sauerkraut and sauerruben, kimchi, miso, poi, fermented fish, beet kvass, sour pickles, cheese, yogurt, wine, and sourdough—fermented foods such as these have been mainstays in the diets of people across the globe and across the centuries. Fermentation makes the enzymes and vitamin C found in produce available during those winter months when fruits are scarce. Ancient Romans, invading Mongols, and seafaring sailors carried fermented cabbage on their travels to protect against digestive problems and scurvy (two life-threatening conditions). Fermented vegetables are so nutritious, in fact, that during Captain James Cook's twenty-seven month-long voyage round the world, sauerkraut completely protected his crew from scurvy.

The fermentation process breaks down the foods, making them easier to digest. It also changes the sugars in milk and the carbohydrates in vegetables into lactic acid, which helps regulate the acidity of stomach acids, improves movement in the intestines, and promotes a beneficial pH in the body. Fermentation not only preserves food with vitamins and enzymes intact, it creates new nutrients such as vitamin B complex, digestive enzymes, and omega-3 fatty acids that were not present originally. It also mitigates the effects of certain harmful acids such as phytic acid in grains, and prussic acids, oxalic acids, and nitrates in leafy green vegetables. *(AC)*

∙∙

ADDING WHEY TO THE PROCESS

Lactic acid comes from various sources, including the produce itself. But the longer it takes for the lactobacillus bacteria to overcome other bacteria, the more the food degrades before the fermentation process begins. Because of that, I use supplemental lactobacillus from whey. You can get whey from raw milk (see "Curds and Whey," page 84), from homemade cheese if the milk is never heated above 115°F, or by skimming the clear liquid off your yogurt, buttermilk, or kefir (see "A Simple Way to Make Whey," page 50). Do not use freeze-dried whey from health food stores! Whey typically sold as a nutritional supplement no longer contains live cultures. Even if you are dairy intolerant, you may be able to eat fermented foods kick-started with whey. *(AC)*

∙∙

fermentation recipes

Start the fermentation process with scrupulously clean equipment and hands, well-rinsed organic vegetables, filtered water, and sea or kosher salt. Salt helps slow the natural process of decay until the lactic acid can begin the fermentation process. If you prefer to use less salt, increase the amount of whey; if you don't want to use whey at all, increase the amount of salt. Alternatively, you can replace the whey with an equal amount of liquid from the last batch of whatever it is you are making.

For the first few days, your ferment should be at around 70°F to encourage the lactic fermentation to begin quickly, while the food is still fresh. After two days, move your ferments to cooler temps—more in line with a subterranean basement (around 55° to 60°F). After two weeks, the food should be completely fermented (although the flavor will continue to change with age). Once the fermentation is complete, transfer your food to clean canning jars, cap them tightly, and store them in the refrigerator or cold cellar (around 45° to 50°F). The faster the fermentation process happens, the less sour your finished product will taste.

You can ferment foods in a nonreactive pot, a crock, or a large canning jar. It's critical that you completely submerge the food in the brine. If you use an open crock or pot, keep the vegetables submerged with a plate or wooden round. Skim any mold that develops on the surface of the brine every few days during the first two weeks. If you use glass jars, keep them in a dark environment by placing them inside a cardboard box or wrapping a towel around them. You can also use a special fermenting crock like a Harsch or TSM, both available on Amazon. The benefit of these crocks is the weighted stone that keeps the vegetables submerged and the external moat around the lid that keeps the mold completely out of the container. These make fermenting virtually foolproof and fuss free, but they are not cheap.

I use a Harsch fermenting crock and traditional open crocks, but I also use half-gallon canning jars. I buy plastic screw top lids for them, drill a hole into each lid, and insert a rubber gasket and airlock, which you can buy at any homebrew store. Be sure to drill the hole slightly smaller than the rubber gasket so air can't get into the jar. If you use canning jars, be sure there is at least an inch of headroom at the top because the mixture will bubble up as the fermentation process begins. *(AC)*

Fermenting hot sauce.

Sauerkraut

Makes approximately 4 quarts

>6 pounds cleaned cabbage, outer leaves removed and set aside and the remainder
>   finely shredded
>1 teaspoon caraway seed (optional)
>3 juniper berries (optional)
>¾ tablespoon kosher salt*
>1 pint whey*

1. Combine shredded cabbage, spices, salt, and whey in a large bowl and mix thoroughly. Fill crock or jars with cabbage, tamping firmly with a potato masher after each layer. Fill to within a few inches of top of jar or crock, then cover final layer of shredded cabbage with clean outer cabbage leaves. It may take some tamping before the salt draws out enough liquid to fully submerge the cabbage.
2. If using a lid with an airlock: Pour whey over cabbage leaves to no higher than 1 inch from top of container. Cap tightly and add water to airlock. Place container in a warm place, and wrap with towels to keep interior dark. After two days, replace airlock lid with a regular lid. Store in refrigerator or a cold cellar.

If you are using an open crock: Place a plate or board over cabbage leaves, and be sure cabbage is completely covered by liquid. *If you are using a Harsch-style crock*: Place weights over outer leaves and be sure they are submerged in brine. Keep in a warm place for 2 days, then move into a cold cellar. After 2 weeks, transfer sauerkraut to glass storage containers, cap tightly, and store in a refrigerator or cold cellar.

As an alternative, use 2 tablespoons salt and 3 tablespoons whey, or 4 tablespoons salt and no whey.

Variation: Sauerruben. Follow the sauerkraut recipe, but replace the shredded cabbage with grated turnip or rutabaga.

Fermented Dilly Beans

Makes approximately 1 quart

>1 quart green beans, strings removed
>2 tablespoons kosher or sea salt

1 quart filtered water
2 tablespoons whey
1 teaspoon mustard seed
1 peeled garlic clove
Pinch red pepper flakes
1 head of dill (the flowering stalk containing
the seeds)

Fermented Sour Dill Cucumbers

1. Place beans, salt, and water in a heavy-bottomed stockpot. Boil beans until crisp-tender, 5 to 10 minutes. Drain beans and reserve water, letting cool. When water is lukewarm, combine with whey.
2. Pack beans tightly in a quart canning jar, along with mustard seed, garlic clove, red pepper, and dill head. Be sure to leave about 2 inches headspace above beans, and take care that they are packed tightly enough that they will not float freely when you pour in liquid.
3. Pour whey/water over beans, making sure they are completely covered and there is at least 1 inch headspace above brine. If you like, you can lay grape or oak leaves over beans; this is thought to help keep them crisp.
4. If you are using a jar with an airlock or a regular lid: Cap jar tightly and add water to airlock, or screw a regular canning lid on tight. Place jar in a warm place, and wrap with towels to keep interior dark. After two days, replace airlock lid with a regular lid. Store in refrigerator or a cold cellar.

If you are using an open crock: Place a plate or board over vegetables and make sure liquid completely covers it. *If you are using a Harsch-style crock:* Place weights over beans (or leaves) and make sure all vegetables are submerged in brine. Keep in a warm place for 2 days, then move to a cold cellar. After 2 weeks, transfer beans to glass storage containers, cap tightly, and store in a refrigerator or a cold cellar.

Variation: Sour Dill Cucumbers. Substitute cucumbers for green beans. Trim and discard blossom ends. Do not cook them as you did the beans. Decrease total salt by ½ tablespoon, and warm the water to make sure salt totally dissolves in it. (Let water cool to lukewarm before proceeding with recipe.)

Fermented Salsa
Makes about 1 quart

> 3 pounds organic tomatoes, peeled, seeded, and chopped*
> 1 medium onion, finely chopped
> 5 cloves garlic, minced
> Hot peppers to taste, finely chopped
> 1 bunch cilantro, chopped
> 1 tablespoon fresh oregano leaves
> 1 tablespoon kosher or sea salt
> 4 tablespoons whey
> ¼ cup lime or yuzu juice, or verjus (recipe page 328)

1. Thoroughly combine all ingredients, and place in a quart jar. Press down with clean fingers, making sure all solids are submerged, and taking care to leave at least 1 inch headspace. If necessary add filtered water to cover.
2. Cap jar tightly and add water to airlock, or screw a regular canning lid on tight. Place in a warm place, wrapping with towels to keep interior dark. After two days, replace airlock lid with a regular lid, then store in refrigerator or a cold cellar.

See tip on peeling in "Additional Canning Tips," page 235.

Fermented Root Vegetables
Makes about 1 quart

> 1 quart cleaned, peeled, and chopped or grated root vegetables such as carrots, parsnips, beets, turnips, or celeriac
> 1 small onion, peeled and chopped
> 1 tablespoon freshly grated horseradish
> 1 bay leaf
> 10 black peppercorns
> 1 tablespoon kosher or sea salt
> 1 pint filtered water
> 2 tablespoons whey

1. Combine vegetables with spices, mixing well. Pack tightly in a quart canning jar, being careful not to mash vegetables.
2. In a saucepan over low heat, dissolve salt in water, and set aside to cool. When water is lukewarm, add whey and mix well.
3. Cover vegetables with brine, making sure there is at least 1 inch of liquid over the top of them and at least 1 inch headspace. Cap tightly, and add water to airlock, or screw a regular canning lid on tightly. Place in a warm place and wrap with towels to keep interior dark. After two days, replace airlock lid with a regular lid, then store in refrigerator or a cold cellar.

Variation: Omit onion, and replace spices with 1 tablespoon grated fresh ginger.

Beet Kvass
Makes 2 quarts
Because beets are such an important liver cleanser, we drink this the morning after imbibing. Think of it as beet-flavored Gatorade with health benefits! I make this by the gallon, and we try to drink a small glass of it each day.

2 large organic beets, peeled and cubed
¼ cup whey
1 tablespoon kosher or sea salt
Filtered water

1. Place beets in a half-gallon canning jar, or divide between two quart jars. Add whey and salt, then top jars with filtered water.
2. Cap tightly and add water to airlock, or screw a regular canning lid on tight. Place jars in a warm place, and wrap with towels to keep interior dark. After two days, replace airlock lid with a regular lid, then store in refrigerator or a cold cellar.

Fermented Chili Sauce
Makes about 4 pints (depending on how fine the sieve is)
This is a ringer for Sriracha hot sauce, and it takes just minutes of active time to make enough to last a whole year.

6 pounds hot peppers of your choosing (I prefer Scotch bonnet or habañero)
Up to 1 whole, small head of garlic, peeled and chopped (optional)

¼ cup kosher or sea salt

¼ cup whey

1. Rinse peppers well, and remove stems. Place peppers and garlic (if using) in a food processor or blender with just enough water to let them circulate, and puree.
2. Pour puree into a half-gallon jar or crock, and add salt and whey. Cover jar with a towel to keep out fruit flies, and let jar sit on counter for 5 to 7 days, until bubbling subsides.
3. Filter sauce through a fine sieve, transfer to 1-pint canning jars, and screw lids on tight. Reserve some of the seeds to add when making either red pepper jelly (see variations for "Apple or Quince Jelly," page 232) or red pepper apricot preserves (see variations for "Apricot, Peach, or Plum Preserves," page 233). The seeds help identify and add visual interest to an otherwise clear jelly. Store jars in refrigerator. As you open and use them you may notice mold on top. Simply scrape it off.

producer profile: Firefly Kitchens

Chop cabbage. Mix in salt. Leave it be.

That's Julie O'Brien's recipe for sauerkraut. Sometimes she gets fancy and adds onions, carrots, or a few spices. When I signed up to volunteer at her fermented foods company, Firefly Kitchens, I'd expected something much more complicated. But good sauerkraut isn't about complicated recipes. Good sauerkraut is about what you don't do. You don't pasteurize it. In fact, you don't apply any heat at all. "It's raw," explained Julie. "It's alive." She dipped a gloved hand into the container of kraut. "Want to try some?"

The sauerkraut tasted crunchy and zingy. Nothing like the sauerkraut I knew from cheap hot dog stands. I had actually liked the taste of the cheap stuff. But this stuff, you could write a book about it. Traditional sauerkraut isn't cooked, it's fermented.

Julie learned about fermented foods in a class she took about nutrition. Partway through the class, she began to suspect she was being primed to sell vitamin supplements. "I had this underlying problem with just pushing another pill." She understood the reasons behind taking supplements. "Our food supply sucks." But she felt she could come up with a better solution. If people ate more nutritious food, they wouldn't have to take pills. She shared her frustration with her friend Richard Climenhage, who felt the same way. Together, they started Firefly Kitchens.

A couple times a week, the pair are joined by a small cadre of dedicated volunteers in their small commercial kitchen. They chop vegetables, or scoop sauerkraut, kimchi, or any number of other fermented foods from large stainless steel vats and put them in jars. They call across the kitchen to each other like old friends. They tease each other, sometimes crack dirty jokes. Some of the volunteers hope to be hired when the business takes off. But others help out simply because they want to learn about traditional fermented foods. Julie says sometimes people help out a little bit, take home a jar for themselves, then become loyal customers.

Julie's foods seem to fill an unmet need. "We don't have enough sour in our diet," she told me. "As a culture we tend to eat salty and sweet. Most cultures around the world serve some little morsel of sour on the side." Once you get past the unexpected shock of eating something sour, it can become addicting.

Julie and Richard make Ruby Red Sauerkraut at Firefly Kitchens.

When I next saw Julie, she was sitting in her stall at the farmers market. She gave me a jar of kimchi, a spicy Korean medley of fermented vegetables. That night, I mixed some kimchi into a plate of scrambled eggs. The next night I added it to my taco meat at the last minute. By the fourth night, I was drinking the last drops of brine from an empty jar. Immediately I started craving more.

I drove to the only two stores where you can buy Firefly kimchi other than at farmers markets. Both were fresh out of the stuff. Desperate, I turned to YouTube and browsed countless videos of Korean housewives making kimchi in the kitchen sink. They wielded large heads of uncut cabbages slathered in a spicy red paste. It all looked very confusing.

I made a mental note to call Julie again. Next time I volunteer at Firefly Kitchens, I'm showing up on kimchi night. *(JM)*

canning

There is nothing quite so satisfying as a shelf lined with a wide array of home-canned garden bounty. The very sight of it feeds the soul and on bleak winter days, the contents of those jars feeds the stomach with the flavors of summer. Home canning has been popular since the late 1800s when the price of both canning jars and sugar dropped enough to make it affordable for most Americans. It experienced a huge resurgence during the Great Depression as a means to preserve vegetables grown in kitchen gardens. Patriotic housewives during World War II did their part as well, growing 40 percent of the nation's produce and canning as much of it as possible.

If you aren't prepared to try your hand at canning, you can skip it altogether by freezing any of these fruit recipes in plastic containers, or storing any of these pickle recipes in the refrigerator for up to two months. *(AC)*

. . . .

WHY MAKE YOUR OWN PECTIN?

I taught myself how to can during college in the late eighties—a period that was fairly devoid of homemaking skills. My recipes came from pectin companies and I had no clue there was any other way to can fruit. Then I discovered marmalades, fruit preserves, and apple jelly, and never looked back.

Commercial pectin speeds up the jam-making process, but I view it as yet another unnecessary synthetic additive. Many of us believe that commercial pectin imparts an off taste to the finished product and that ultimately it can mask delicate flavors like rose petals, lemon verbena, and anise hyssop.

Instead of using commercial pectin, I prefer to can with high-pectin fruits, or to use a high-pectin fruit in combination with a low-pectin fruit to ensure the final product will set up, or thicken of its own accord. Their flavor is crystal clear, unmuddied by anything other than fruit and sugar. Even so, my apricot preserves do not come out like those thickly gelled ones made with commercial pectin. Instead they consist of chunks of fruits swimming in a delectable sauce, perfect for filling the nooks and crannies of homemade crumpets. *(AC)*

Apple or Quince Pectin Stock
Makes 4 cups

Old-fashioned jelly begins with juice that you can make ahead of time. One pound of apples will make about one cup of juice.

4 pounds organic quinces*, crabapples, or green apples*, stemmed and quartered but not cored
4 cups filtered water

› Place apple quarters and water in a large, heavy-bottomed stockpot. Bring to a boil while stirring, then reduce heat and simmer gently until just tender.
› Mash apples in liquid, using a potato masher or food mill. Line a colander with a dampened tea towel, and place over a deep bowl. Pour applesauce into tea towel, and let drain for about 10 minutes.
› Gently take up all four corners of towel, and tie into a hobo sack. Suspend sack from a wooden spoon stretched across a deep bowl, or tie to kitchen faucet and place bowl underneath in sink. Let apple stock drain, undisturbed, overnight.

*If using green apples or quinces, add the juice of one small lemon to prevent discoloration. The pigment in red apple skins will usually give the juice a rosy hue, making the lemon unnecessary.

. . . .

basic canning how-to

Canning can be a steamy affair, but in the Pacific Northwest, it's fairly easy to schedule your canning on a cool and rainy day. To make it even more pleasant, invite some friends to share the work and the booty. You'll remember that camaraderie all winter as you cherish those jars of home-canned goods.

Equipment: All of the recipes below can be made using a water bath canner, or any deep stockpot lined with an insert to keep the jars off the bottom of the pot. The insert can be as simple as a round metal cake rack or metal canning jar rings laid down to make a solid layer. You'll also need glass canning jars with two-part lids. These are simple to use, inexpensive, and easy to find. Once you've eaten their contents, canning jars make great plastic-free storage containers for grains, beans, or leftovers. They are by far the most-used item in my kitchen and well worth the initial investment. I also recommend getting a large canning funnel, magnetic wand for removing the metal lids from hot water, and a jar lifter—but you can certainly get by without these additional pieces of equipment.

Prepare jars and lids: Place your cake rack or canning insert inside your pot. Fill the canning jars two-thirds of the way full of water and fill the pot with water a quarter of

A bookcase provides additional pantry space.

the way up the sides of the canning jars. Put the pot on the stove and bring the water up to a simmer. Turn off the burner until you need the jars. Since all of the following recipes include a ten-minute processing time, you don't need to sterilize anything.

Place the metal jar lids into a smaller pan of water and bring the water just up to a simmer; then turn off the burner.

Fill the jars: Your jars and lids should be warmed and ready by the time your recipe is done. Fill and cap the jars one by one so the contents stay as warm as possible until time to process. As you pull each jar from the pot, empty the water from the jar into the canner. Fill the jar according to the directions, then cap and place each jar back into the pot before proceeding with the next one.

Remove any air bubbles: Air bubbles can cause spoilage, so be sure and remove them by gently tapping the jar on the counter and then carefully viewing the jar from all sides for more bubbles. If there are any, insert a clean butter knife into the jar and gently dislodge the bubbles.

Adjust headspace: The headspace is the amount of space between the top of the food in the jar and the lid of the jar. Too much headspace, or not enough headspace, can cause spoilage and improper seals. The amount of headspace is a function of the amount of processing time. Foods with longer processing times have greater headspace than foods with shorter processing times.

Close the jars: Use a clean, wet finger and rub it around the rim of the jar to remove any food residue. Place the jar lid inside the ring and screw it on the jar as tightly as you can using just your fingertips. Then loosen about a quarter-inch turn. As your jar contents heat, they expand and push the oxygen in the jar out. By screwing your jar lid tightly and then loosening it, you ensure that oxygen is able to escape.

Process in water bath: When you have filled all the jars, add more water to the pot so that there is at least an inch of water over the top of the tallest jar. Place the pot lid on and bring the water up to a full rolling boil. Set the timer according to the recipe and ensure that the water is at a continuous boil for the entire processing time.

When the time is up, take the pot off the burner, remove the lid, and let it cool for five minutes before removing the jars. Be careful not to tip the jars as you lift them out of the pot since the seals are not yet set. Once the contents cool enough that the air pressure outside the jars is greater than the pressure inside them, the seals will set. Place the jars on a towel-lined counter to cool overnight.

Check jar seals: In the morning, check the seals by removing the rings and pushing down on the center of each lid with one finger. If the jar is not sealed, the lid will compress and make a little "pop" sound. Set those jars aside and perform an additional check on the jars that passed the first test. Place your hand over the top of each jar and with your fingertips, clutch the lid. Carefully lift the jar off the counter. If you can suspend the jar by just its lid, you have a good seal.

Reprocess any poorly sealed jars: You can reprocess any jars that did not seal properly within twenty-four hours, but because color, texture, and flavor degrade with longer processing times, you may not want to do this. I prefer instead to freeze the contents in plastic containers or refrigerate and use the contents up quickly.

producer profile: Sarah Elmore

Don't tell Sarah Elmore you don't have space for canning. When students in her canning class whine about canning in tiny apartments, Sarah tells them she canned five hundred pints this year on the leaking sailboat where she lives. With a one-burner stove. That shuts them up pretty quick.

It's not as though Sarah can't afford a bigger place. She's employed as a research assistant, studying neurobiology. But she chooses to live simply, because it gives her freedom to change the course of her life at regular intervals—in order to stay happy.

"I watched my mother, for years, struggle with having so many things. She had a suburban house, a garage full of stuff. She was basically working to pay for her mortgage. I didn't want to do that, I like to travel, to go sailing, to write." And to can. Sarah does a lot of canning.

Sarah invited our photographer, Harley, and me over to watch her make Ginger Vanilla Asian Pear Jam. As the water bath heated on the stove, she chopped up the pears. Then came the first of several pot switches. The water bath moved from the burner to a spot under the table. The fruit moved onto the burner. Sarah's moves are carefully choreographed, refined over the years to conserve propane and make the most of her burner.

Compared to my kitchen, where multiple burners process jars, fruit, and lids at the same time—where the forgotten water bath boils on and on—Sarah's kitchen is a model of efficiency. You might call Sarah's method "slow canning." She has only one thing heating at a time. While she waits for the water to boil, or for the fruit to cook down, she sits at her tiny table an arm's reach from the stove and calmly reads a book. For Sarah, canning is relaxing, a great way to unwind after a difficult day at work.

I asked Sarah if she ever felt constrained canning on a boat. "Well," she admitted, "I have learned not to can huge batches." One time, her friend brought her forty pounds of peaches

Sarah Elmore cans in small batches on a one-burner stove, on a leaky sailboat.

from Eastern Washington. The two of them didn't leave the sailboat for two days. Steam saturated the boat's tiny cabin. As the pints of peach jam piled up, Sarah found she had no room to store the cooling jam. She and her friend extended every additional table leaf, unfolded every secret folding shelf. Every conceivable horizontal surface had a cooling pint of peach jam.

That experience changed the way Sarah thinks about canning. She started focusing on smaller batches, only a few pints at time. She's found it's quicker, and allows her to can a greater variety of things. That may explain why canning isn't a chore for Sarah—it's a quest, driven by her urge to experiment, to perfect her recipe for quince pickles, to incorporate spices she's accumulated sailing the world's great trade routes. "I try to use local ingredients whenever I can. But some things—certain spices, for example—I just can't live without.

"This vanilla bean here. You just can't beat a real vanilla bean. Most people don't realize, all the flavor's in the seeds." She removed the softened bean from the boiling fruit, scraped out the seeds with a spoon, and dropped them back into the fruit. "I'll use the empty bean pod to flavor my sugar," she said. Waste not, want not.

Because she doesn't have a garden, Sarah's come to see the world around her as a garden. As she walks through Seattle's Ballard neighborhood, she sees fruit on the side of the road—Oregon grape to use for pectin, blackberries to mix with some exotic spice. She buys lots of fruits and veggies at the farmers market. They're more expensive there, but she says the quality's much better. And she doesn't have to pour her income into a mortgage.

So what does one person do with five hundred pints of preserves?

"Well, a hundred pints of pickles went to my friend's wedding. She loves a good Bloody Mary, so I prepared a huge spread of pickles for her Bloody-Mary-themed reception." Still, that leaves her with a jar to consume every day. Who eats that many pickles? Who eats that much jam? "Honestly," she admits, "I give away seventy-five percent of what I make."

Still, Sarah hopes someday she might turn her canning quest into a business. She wants to preserve fruit and vegetables over on the Olympic Peninsula, then sail them into Seattle to sell. "I'll be making carbon-neutral preserves. Well, except for the jars and a few of the spices."

This sounds a little dreamy to me. Especially since Sarah expects to be laid off in a few months. But without a mortgage, Sarah can afford to dream. Sarah teaches canning through the Seattle organization Community Kitchens Northwest. *(JM)*

canning recipes

Apple or Quince Jelly

Makes about 3 half pints, but because pectin levels can vary greatly in apples depending on variety, ripeness, and growing conditions, yields may vary.

> 4 cups apple pectin stock (see recipe on page 226)
> 4 cups organic sugar (using unbleached sugar will make for a darker jelly)

1. Prepare water bath, jars, and lids.
2. Combine pectin stock and sugar in a large, heavy-bottomed saucepan. Bring to a boil over medium-high heat, stirring frequently. When jelly begins to sheet off spoon, check for gel set.
3. Fill jars, leaving ¼ inch headspace. Remove any air bubbles, wipe rims, screw lids on tight, and process in a water bath for 10 minutes.

Jelly Variations:

Rose Petal Jelly: Before making jelly, add 3 cups clean, organic rose petals to pectin stock in a heavy-bottomed saucepan. Bring to a simmer, then turn off burner and let sit for 1 hour to infuse. Strain juice through a wet tea towel, then proceed with jelly recipe. Add a handful of rose petals to each jar before filling.

Lemon Verbena or Mint Jelly: Before making jelly, add 10 sprigs lemon verbena or one small bunch chocolate mint to pectin stock in a heavy-bottomed saucepan. Bring to a simmer, then turn off burner and let sit for 1 hour to infuse. Strain through a wet tea towel, then proceed with jelly recipe.

Rosemary or Lavender Jelly: Add a sprig of fresh rosemary or lavender to each jar before filling. In a week or so, jelly will take on rosemary flavor. Tie dried lavender flowers or a rosemary sprig to the neck of the jar before gifting.

Spicy Pepper Jelly: When jelly begins to sheet off spoon, add Fermented Chili Sauce (recipe on page 223) and crushed pepper or finely chopped hot peppers to taste. Proceed with jelly recipe. Tie a dried pepper to the neck of the jar before gifting.

Rhubarb Jam

Makes about 8 half pints

This method for making rhubarb jam leaves you with a sparkling, crimson-red jam much like raspberry.

2¼ pounds diced rhubarb
3¾ cups organic sugar

1. Prepare water bath, jars, and lids.
2. Combine rhubarb and sugar in a nonreactive bowl, cover with a plate, and refrigerate overnight or up to 24 hours.
3. Strain juice through a sieve, and pour into a heavy-bottomed stockpot. Over high heat, bring to a temperature of 200°F (juice will be bubbling). Add diced rhubarb, return to a boil, and cook for 5 minutes, stirring frequently. Check set.
4. Pour into jars, leaving ¼ inch headspace. Wipe rims, screw lids on tight, and process in a water bath for 10 minutes.

Apricot, Peach, or Plum Preserves
Makes about 8 half pints

6 pounds peeled, pitted, and diced apricots*, peaches, or plums
6 cups organic sugar
¾ cup lemon or yuzu juice

1. Prepare water bath, jars, and lids.
2. Combine fruit, sugar, and citrus juice in a nonreactive bowl, cover with a plate, and refrigerate for at least 1 and up to 8 hours.
3. Pour into a heavy-bottomed stockpot and bring to a simmer over medium-high heat. Remove from heat, strain through a sieve, reserving strained fruit, and return juice to stockpot. Cook over high heat until it reaches 220°F or gel set. Add strained fruit, and return mixture to a boil.
4. Immediately fill jars, leaving ¼ inch headspace. Remove any air bubbles, wipe rims, screw lids tight, and process in a water bath for 10 minutes.

Apricots may require extra sugar. Taste the mixture in step 2 and adjust if necessary.

Variation: Add some chili sauce to apricot preserves for a flavor bomb that makes the perfect accompaniment to chèvre (see recipe on page 90) and "Crisp Whole Grain Crackers" (page 49).

Groundcherry (a.k.a. Husk Tomato) Preserves
Makes about 6 half pints

> 3 pints groundcherries, husks removed and rinsed
> 3 cups apple juice
> 1½ cups organic sugar
> Juice of 1 small lemon or yuzu*

1. Prepare water bath, jars, and lids.
2. Combine apple juice, sugar, and citrus juice in a heavy-bottomed stockpot, and bring to a boil over medium-high heat. Add groundcherries, and boil until translucent but still whole. Pour mixture into a nonreactive bowl, cover with a plate, and refrigerate overnight or up to 24 hours.
3. Strain through a sieve, reserving fruit, and return juice to a boil over high heat. Check for gel set, and gently stir in strained fruit.
4. Fill jars, leaving ¼ inch headspace. Remove any air bubbles, wipe rims, screw lids on tight, and process in a water bath for 10 minutes.

Many jam and jelly recipes call for a small amount of lemon juice, but lemons don't grow in the Pacific Northwest. There is one citrus fruit, however, that does: the yuzu. Wade Bennett of Rockridge Orchards (see his profile on page 324) grows it commercially for restaurants in the Seattle area, but you can grow it in a sunny, well-drained spot in your yard.

Peaches in Syrup
Makes about 8 pints
Although you can preserve peach sections using water or apple juice, they won't retain their shape, color, texture, or flavor as well as with medium sugar syrup.

> 10 pounds peaches, peeled, halved, pitted, and briefly dipped in a mixture of ¼ cup lemon or yuzu juice and 4 cups water
> 5 cups water
> 3 cups organic sugar

1. Prepare water bath, jars, and lids.
2. Combine water and sugar in a heavy-bottomed saucepan. Bring to boil over medium-high heat, stirring occasionally until sugar is dissolved. Reduce heat to low, and keep

syrup warm while preparing jars of fruit.

3. Pack peach halves tightly into each jar. Insert a vanilla bean or cinnamon stick in jar if you like. Cover peaches completely with warm syrup, leaving ½ inch headspace. Carefully remove any air bubbles, wipe rims, screw lids on tight, and process in a water bath for 25 minutes.

• •

ADDITIONAL CANNING TIPS

Removing peach and tomato skins: Submerge each fruit in boiling water for twenty to sixty seconds, until the skin begins to split. Immediately place the fruit in ice water to stop the cooking process. The skins should slip right off.

Adjusting for elevation: The cooking times in the recipes below are based on being at sea level. If you are canning at a different altitude, check with your state's extension program (www.csrees.usda.gov/Extension/) for appropriate canning times.

Testing for gel stage in fruit preserves: In the jam, jelly, preserves, and marmalade recipes that follow, you will see the words "cook to gel stage." That means that you cook the fruit long enough to sufficiently evaporate the liquid, and to cause the natural pectin in the fruit to create a gelled product once cooled. Because the pectin won't gel until completely cooled, however, gel stage is not obvious while you are cooking. And if you cook too long, you may end up with a tough, rubbery product.

How do you check for gel stage? Your fruit is at gel stage when:
› It has reached 220°F on a thermometer.
› A teaspoon of it frozen on a plate for one minute forms surface wrinkles when nudged with your finger.
› A spoonful held horizontally does not drip or pour from the spoon, but lazily oozes off it in a sheet like a waterfall. This last method requires the most practice, so you may want to use a thermometer first, and then perform the other two tests so you can see exactly what 220°F looks like. The next time, you can skip the thermometer with confidence. *(AC)*

• •

Tomatoes in Their Juice

Tomatoes are technically a fruit, but they have such a low pH that adding citric acid or lemon juice is the only way to guarantee a safe product when canning at home. These recipes call for citric acid, which you can find at most grocery and homebrew stores. Bottled "lemon juice" will also give you consistent and safe results, but since it is highly processed, contains preservatives, and imparts an off flavor, I prefer to use citric acid.

Per pint

> 1½ pounds tomatoes, peeled
> ¼ teaspoon citric acid, or ½ teaspoon bottled lemon juice

Per quart

> 3 pounds tomatoes, peeled
> ½ teaspoon citric acid, or 2 tablespoons bottled lemon juice

1. Prepare water bath, jars, and lids.
2. Add citric acid or lemon juice to each jar. Pack tomatoes tightly into each jar, pushing down on them to release their juices and making sure there is enough juice to cover.
3. Fill each jar, leaving ½ inch headspace. Carefully remove any air bubbles, wipe rims, screw lids on tight, and process in a water bath for 85 minutes.

Variation: Raw pack method. Bring water to a boil and keep hot. Add lemon juice or citric acid to each jar. Pack tomatoes into jars, leaving a little more than ½ inch headspace. Pour hot water into each jar to cover tomatoes, leaving ½ inch headspace. Remove air bubbles, then make sure headspace is still ½ inch. Wipe rims, screw lids on tight, and process in a water bath for 40 minutes.

Applesauce
Makes about 8 pints

> 12 pounds apples, peeled, cored, and quartered*
> 4 tablespoons lemon or yuzu juice
> Sugar to taste

1. Prepare water bath, jars, and lids.
2. Combine apples with just enough water to cover in a heavy-bottomed stockpot. Bring to a boil over medium-high heat, then reduce heat and simmer gently until tender.
3. Strain apples, reserving liquid for juice for jelly, cooking, or drinking. Working in batches, sauce using a food mill or potato masher. Add sugar (or not) to taste.
4. Pour into sterilized pint jars, leaving ½ inch headspace. Wipe rims, screw lids on tight, and process in a water bath for 20 minutes.

*If using a Roma food mill you only need to quarter the apples, since it will remove the skins and cores for you. The Roma food mill is unlike other food mills in that it actually separates larger particles like seeds and skins and pushes them into a discard pile while forcing your sauced apples into a different bowl.

Variation: Add cinnamon or cloves to taste.

Bread and Butter Cucumber Slices

Makes about 6 pints

> 3 quarts pickling cucumbers, sliced
> 1½ cups onions, thinly sliced
> 2 red bell peppers, seeded and chopped (optional)
> ⅓ cup kosher salt
> 3 cups good-quality apple cider vinegar (at least 5 percent acidity)
> 2⅓ cups organic sugar
> 2 teaspoons celery seed
> 2 teaspoons mustard seed
> 2 teaspoons turmeric
> 1 teaspoon dried mustard
> 1 teaspoon dried ginger

Older, soft apples are ideal for saucing and making fruit leather.

1. Prepare water bath, jars, and lids.
2. Combine cucumbers, onions, and peppers (if using) in a large, nonreactive pot. Sprinkle with the salt, mix well and pour cold, filtered water over them just to cover. Let soak for 3 hours, then drain in a colander, and rinse well.
3. Combine remaining ingredients in the empty pot, and simmer for 10 minutes. Add vegetables and bring to a boil.
4. Immediately fill pint or quart jars, leaving a little more than ½ inch headspace. Ladle enough pickling liquid from pot to cover vegetables in jar, leaving ½ inch headspace.

Remove air bubbles, then make sure headspace is still ½ inch. Wipe rims, screw lids on tight, and process in a water bath for 10 minutes.

Variation: Use chopped cabbage, small cauliflower florets, green tomatoes, sliced celery, sliced carrots, chopped red or green peppers, and chopped onions instead of the cucumbers to make a Southern relish called chow-chow.

Dill Pickle Spears or Slices
Makes about 5 pints

> 3 quarts freshly picked cucumbers, ends trimmed and quartered (or sliced lengthwise)
> 4 cups good-quality apple cider vinegar (at least 5 percent acidity)
> 4 cups filtered water
> ½ cup kosher salt
> Fresh dill flower heads
> Bay leaves
> Fresh or brined grape leaves (optional, for crisping)
> Garlic cloves, peeled
> Mustard seed
> Black peppercorns
> Whole coriander
> Red pepper flakes

1. Prepare water bath, jars, and lids.
2. Combine vinegar, water, and salt in a large, heavy-bottomed stockpot, and simmer for 10 minutes, stirring until salt is dissolved.
3. In the meantime place one dill head, one or two cloves garlic, one bay leaf, and one grape leaf in each jar, along with ¼ teaspoon each (or more, depending on how strong you want the spices to be) mustard seed, black pepper, coriander, and red pepper.
4. Pack cucumber spears or slices vertically into jars, leaving a little more than ½ inch headspace. If using grape leaves, place one on top of each batch of cucumbers, to help keep them submerged in brine.
5. Once the brine is ready, immediately add to jars, leaving ½ inch headspace. Remove air bubbles, then make sure headspace is still ½ inch. Wipe rims, screw lids on tight, and process jars in a water bath for 10 minutes.

Pickled Beets
Makes about 8 pints

3 quarts beets, boiled till tender, peeled, and sliced crosswise
3¼ cups good-quality apple cider vinegar (at least 5 percent acidity)
1¼ cups filtered water
¾ cup packed brown sugar (or ⅔ cup organic sugar plus 2 teaspoons molasses)
½ teaspoon dried ginger
Mustard seed

1. Prepare water bath, jars, and lids.
2. Combine vinegar, water, and sugar in a large, heavy-bottomed stockpot and simmer for 10 minutes, stirring until sugar is dissolved.
3. In the meantime place ¼ teaspoon mustard seed in each jar. Pack sliced beets into jars, leaving a little more than ½ inch headspace.
4. Once the brine is ready, immediately add to jars. leaving ½ inch headspace. Remove air bubbles, then make sure headspace is still ½ inch. Wipe rims, screw lids on tight, and process in a water bath for 30 minutes.

Pickled Asparagus
Makes about 4 pints

4 cups good-quality apple cider vinegar (at least 5 percent acidity)
2 cups filtered water
¼ cup organic sugar
2 teaspoons salt
Garlic cloves, peeled
Mustard seed
Black peppercorns
Whole coriander
Red pepper flakes
2 quarts asparagus spears, woody ends removed, trimmed to leave a little more than ½ inch headspace in jars

1. Prepare water bath, jars, and lids.
2. Combine vinegar, water, sugar, and salt in a large, heavy-bottomed stockpot. Stir until salt and sugar are dissolved.

3. Into each jar place one or two cloves garlic followed by ¼ teaspoon each (or more, depending on how strong you want the spices to be) mustard seed, black pepper, coriander, and red pepper.

4. Pack asparagus spears vertically into jars, leaving a little more than ½ inch head-space. Pour in brine, leaving ½ headspace. Remove air bubbles, then make sure headspace is still ½ inch. Wipe rims, screw lids on tight, and process in a water bath for 20 minutes.

Variation: Replace asparagus with cleaned, trimmed pea pods, blanched green beans with strings removed, carrot sticks, and/or seeded and sliced or whole hot peppers.

Zucchini Relish
Makes about 6 pints

> 2 quarts zucchini, peeled and grated or finely chopped
> 1 onion, peeled and finely chopped
> 1 green pepper, seeded and finely chopped
> 1 red bell pepper, seeded and finely chopped
> ⅓ cup kosher salt
> 4 cups good-quality apple cider vinegar (at least 5 percent acidity)
> 1½ cups packed brown sugar (or 1¼ cup organic sugar plus 1½ tablespoon molasses)
> 1 teaspoon celery seed
> 2 teaspoons mustard seed
> 1 teaspoons turmeric
> 1 teaspoon dried mustard
> ½ teaspoon dried ginger
> 1 pint apple jelly (optional, for thickening)

1. Prepare water bath, jars, and lids.

2. Combine zucchini, onions, and peppers in a large, nonreactive bowl. Sprinkle with the salt, mix well, and let sit overnight. Drain in a colander and rinse well.

3. Combine vinegar, brown sugar, celery seeds, mustard seed, turmeric, dried mustard, and ginger in a heavy-bottomed stockpot. Simmer for 10 minutes. Add vegetables and apple jelly (if using), and bring to a boil.

4. Fill pint or quart jars with vegetables, leaving a little more than ½ inch headspace. Add pickling liquid from pot to cover vegetables, leaving ½ inch headspace. Remove

air bubbles, then make sure headspace is still ½ inch. Wipe rims, screw lids on tight, and process in a water bath for 10 minutes.

Caramelized Onion Jam
Makes about 2 pints

2 large onions, peeled and sliced into very thin rings or crescents
¼ cup packed brown sugar
1 cup dry red wine
3 tablespoons good-quality apple cider vinegar (at least 5 percent acidity)
¼ teaspoon salt

1. Prepare water bath, jars, and lids.
2. Combine onions and brown sugar in a nonreactive, heavy-bottomed stockpot. Cook, uncovered, over medium heat, stirring occasionally. If onions begin to stick, add a splash of wine and scrape bottom of pot with a wooden spoon to deglaze. Continue cooking until onions are brown and soft.
3. Add wine, vinegar, and salt. Simmer while stirring frequently, until most of the liquid has evaporated, 5 to 10 minutes.
4. Fill half-pint or pint jars, leaving ½ inch headspace. Remove air bubbles, then make sure headspace is still ½ inch. If not, add as much vinegar as needed. Wipe rims, screw lids on tight, and process in a water bath for 10 minutes.

Pasta Sauce
Makes about 6 pints or 3 quarts

4 quarts (about 9 pounds) plum or paste tomatoes, peeled
2 cups chopped onions
3 cloves garlic, finely chopped or sliced
1 teaspoon salt
1 teaspoon dried oregano
1 teaspoon dried basil
Red pepper flakes to taste
Lemon juice (2 tablespoons per quart or 1 tablespoon per pint) or citric acid
    (½ teaspoon per quart or ¼ teaspoon per pint)

A Roma Mill makes quick work of tomato and apple sauces.

1. Prepare water bath, jars, and lids.
2. Puree tomatoes in a food mill or blender. (If using a Roma mill, simply run washed tomatoes through the mill and it will remove the skin and seeds for you.)
3. In a nonreactive, heavy-bottomed stockpot, cook onions over medium heat, stirring frequently until they begin to soften. If they begin to stick to pan, add a small amount of water. Add garlic and cook for another 2 minutes.
4. Add tomato puree, salt, oregano, basil, and red pepper flakes to pot. Cook at a simmer, stirring occasionally, until sauce is smooth and thick. This can take 6 to 8 hours, depending on how much liquid was in tomatoes. To shorten cooking time, strain tomato puree through a fine sieve before cooking, to remove some of the liquid. Reserve liquid for drinking as tomato juice or Bloody Marys, or for making gazpacho.
5. Add lemon juice or citric acid to pint or quart jars. Fill jars, leaving ½ inch headspace. Carefully remove any air bubbles, wipe rims, screw lids on tight, and process in a water bath for 35 minutes.

Summer in a Jar Salsa

Makes about 4 pints

    10 cups tomatoes, peeled and chopped
    2 cups green bell or sweet peppers, seeded and chopped
    2 cups chopped onions
    6 hot peppers, seeded and chopped*
    1¼ cups good-quality apple cider vinegar (at least 5 percent acidity)
    15 cloves garlic, finely chopped
    6 tablespoons chopped cilantro
    6 teaspoons dried oregano
    1 tablespoon salt
    2 to 3 teaspoons ground cumin

1. Prepare water bath, jars, and lids.
2. Combine all ingredients in a large, nonreactive, heavy-bottomed stockpot and bring to a boil. Reduce heat to medium, and stir until slightly reduced and vegetables begin to soften.
3. Fill pint jars, leaving ½ inch headspace. Carefully remove any air bubbles, wipe rims, screw lids on tight, and process in a water bath for 15 minutes.

Because there is so much vinegar in this recipe, you can safely vary the amount of hot peppers to suit your taste.

Tomato Ketchup

Makes about 5 pints
Note: Unless you use the apple jelly, this will not be as thick as commercial ketchup.

    16 pounds organic paste tomatoes such as Roma, San Marzano, or Amish Paste, peeled and seeded
    2 large onions, peeled and chopped
    1 clove garlic, minced, or 1 teaspoon garlic powder
    2 cups organic sugar
    2 cups good-quality apple cider vinegar (at least 5 percent acidity)
    1 tablespoon sea salt
    ½ teaspoon freshly ground black pepper

1 teaspoon dry mustard
Generous pinch of red pepper flakes
Pinch of celery seed
1 pint apple jelly (optional, for thickening)

1. Prepare water bath, jars, and lids.
2. Combine all ingredients except apple jelly in a heavy-bottomed stockpot, and simmer for 2 to 4 hours, until thick. Turn off burner. At this point you can strain ketchup through a fine sieve and reserve juice for making Bloody Marys or gazpacho.
3. Return paste to stockpot. If you have an immersion blender, you can give it a good whiz to make sure onions are broken down and texture is nice and smooth. I don't recommend doing this in a blender or food processor because it's too easy to splash scalding tomato paste on yourself. Add apple jelly, if using, and stir until melted and distributed throughout.
4. Fill pint jars, leaving ½ inch headspace. Carefully remove any air bubbles, wipe rims, screw lids on tight, and process in a water bath for 15 minutes.

Mustard
Makes about 3 half-pint jars

¾ cup beer or wine
¾ cup mustard seed
1 cup mild vinegar, such as rice, white wine, or sherry or ½ cup good-quality apple
    cider vinegar plus ½ cup water
½ cup honey
¼ teaspoon kosher salt

1. Combine beer or wine and mustard seed in a nonreactive bowl, and let sit overnight until completely absorbed by seeds.
2. Prepare water bath, jars, and lids.
3. Combine hydrated seeds, vinegar, and water in a food processor or blender, and process until seeds are pureed.
4. Transfer mixture to a nonreactive saucepan. Add honey and salt and simmer, stirring frequently, until mustard thickens to your liking.
5. Fill half- or quarter-pint jars, leaving ¼ inch headspace. Carefully remove any air bubbles, wipe rims, screw lids on tight, and process in a water bath for 10 minutes.

Alternative method: Instead of canning you can ferment the mustard. Let thickened mustard cool, and mix in 4 tablespoons whey (see "A Simple Way to Make Whey," page 50). Divide between 2 jars, ensuring there is at least 1 inch headspace, cap tightly, and leave on the counter for 2 days to ferment. Transfer to refrigerator. If surface grows white mold, simply scrape off and transfer mixture to a clean jar.

chapter 13
building food community

There's a grocery store just a few blocks from my house. It's an independent local chain, with a small but growing focus on local food. There's a checker there I really like, a young man with big hoops in his ears. Even when he's glum, he seems cheerful, whether he's working early in the morning or late at night. But as much as I like him and the other checkers, these grocery store acquaintances are no substitute for a real food community.

It's not as though there's anything evil about grocery stores. It's just that right now, I want to connect with my community in a way more centered around food and less centered around commerce. Every bag of cherries I buy from the grocery store is one time I can't visit my neighbor Kate, with her massive cherry tree that she invites us to pick from every time we walk past. Every time I scoop spelt flour from the bulk bins is one less time I get to meet René at the back of his truck, where he'll chat my ear off about the new heirloom grain he's trying this year. For each item I no longer buy at the store, I now have one more friend.

In this chapter, we'll show you how to expand your food community by bartering with one another and by forming buying clubs to purchase large quantities of food directly from farmers.

The word "community" gets a lot of buzz these days. But the real thing isn't something you can buy off the shelf. It's something you build. So let's start. *(JM)*

bartering with friends

Long ago, I had a weakness for unnecessary kitchen equipment. I acquired fondue pots, encapsulated vegetable choppers, strawberry de-stemmers. I wanted to be at home in the

Bartering jam, pickles, homebrew, honey, and much more at the harvest fair.

kitchen, and imagined I could accomplish that by having every conceivable kitchen device. In time, I learned that these tools aren't necessary. I was trying to buy into the dream of good food, without really understanding what good food is.

This tendency to see life through a lens of commerce also colored my idea of community. So many of the things I enjoyed about the city were purchased experiences. We joined friends at a bar or restaurant, paying our admission by purchasing items from the menu. We met other parents at our children's sports events, we paid for our toddlers to play together at Gymboree. But when the economy took a nosedive and we had to scrutinize every receipt, every credit card bill, when unnecessary purchases could lead to anger or tears, we found ourselves shut out of many of the city's day-to-day social experiences.

We had little money, but we found ourselves rich in fruits and vegetables—from our garden, from our foraging trips, from the cases of cucumbers and tomatoes we purchased directly from farmers. So we arranged a barter event to coincide with a harvest fair at the Seattle Farm Co-op, an organization that sells chicken feed and other garden supplies to people in the city.

We spent much of the next month canning the summer's excess produce. We didn't even mind canning twenty-four jars of the same plum jam, for we knew that each of these could be traded for something unique.

Finally, the day of the harvest fair arrived. We arrived at the giant warehouse temporarily housing the co-op, and set the kids loose, confident there were enough watchful adults around to let them do their own thing. They ran wild and knocked each other over while the grown-ups traded jars of pickles, jams, and homebrew. All around us, the air was alive with enthusiasm for urban farms, for the collective effort we felt, for the faith we had that the messy, inefficient, and eccentric business of urban farming leads to something worthwhile. We encouraged each other to try bees, rabbits, goats. We traded goods together. The trading activity took us much longer than it should have, as we all took the opportunity to meet new friends and catch up with the old ones.

The fair ended with a big square dance, but my family couldn't stay. Though it was only eight o'clock, my kids were exhausted. We scooped them up and carried them to the car, their heads resting on our shoulders. As we drove away, we could see the square dancers illuminated in the warehouse door.

The barter gave us a nice break from the world of money. Money makes the world go round, it's true. It allows us to specialize in our chosen careers, to delegate the business of food production to the farmers. It allows our food to pass through convenient intermediaries like grocery stores. It allows investors to think abstractly about our food, to buy and sell it on the commodities market. Most of these advancements make our lives better, more convenient.

Sometimes, it's useful to step outside that world of convenience, to put aside money and engage in less efficient interactions, interactions that require us to meet face to face, to engage in shared work. It's inconvenient to prepare our own preserves for barter, when we could just pick them up instead at the grocery store. It's inconvenient to tear out our lawns and plant gardens. It's enormously inconvenient to verify the morality and gentleness of our animals' deaths. But when we undertake these inconveniences, we regain control over our food, we rebuild our diets in ways that improve our health. When we undergo these inconveniences together with friends and neighbors, we rebuild community. *(JM)*

. . . .

WAYS TO BUILD FOOD COMMUNITIES

› Find a garden buddy. Split the list of things to grow.
› Find a canning buddy. Split the list of things to can.
› Start a local online food forum—this can cover backyard livestock to shared garden spaces, trading supplies, and buying in bulk. Invite any and all local small farmers and ranchers to join, thereby connecting them directly with consumers.
› Trade knowledge, equipment, books, and labor.
› Organize group buys and encourage others to do the same.
› Host periodic events to make online connections real—a fall preserved foods/garden surplus barter, a spring seeds and seedling barter, a holiday craft barter.

. . . .

what are bulk buying clubs?

I entered the world of bulk buying accidentally, having no idea how much it would change my life. While trying to find sources for local milk, I discovered it was legal to buy raw milk in Washington State. The prices, however, were astronomical. But then I learned that many local farmers would sell raw milk directly to the public for a reduced price. That got me wondering—if I could get reduced pricing from these dairy farmers, maybe I could get it from other kinds of farmers as well. And when I asked around at farmers markets, I learned that most of the farmers did have bulk-buying discounts.

That's right—discounts on local, organic food. You know, the best kind of food you can eat, the right thing to do, and usually, the highest priced items.

Bulk pricing benefits not only the consumer but also the producer, allowing him or her to sell more products with fewer transactions. To qualify for a bulk-buying discount, you must meet a minimum order, which can be challenging. For example, you might have to

Hot peppers from a bulk buy, ready to be converted into Fermented Chili Sauce.

find enough people to buy a hundred and fifty dollars worth of grains or a thousand dollars worth of tuna. But it's worth the effort. Here are a few of the items I've found bulk pricing for:

›   Produce by the box
›   Grains by the twenty-five- or fifty-pound bag
›   Honey by the gallon
›   Wild-caught tuna and salmon by the case of fillets or in cans
›   Coconut oil by the gallon. (Actually so many of us participated in this purchase, we bought it by the pallet.)
›   Natural laundry soap by the pound
›   Natural candles by the case
›   Weck canning jars by the case
›   Garden seeds in sizes usually purchased only by farmers
›   Cabbages, apples, squashes, potatoes, tomatoes, garlic, carrots, beets, cucumbers
›   Artisan cheeses

At farmers markets, ask farmers if they offer discounts for buying clubs. The worst they could say is, "No," but likely they will say, "Oh, yes. I'll email you the wholesale price list." And there you go—down the path to saving money and doing the right thing for the farmer and for your family. Below are two more great bulk-buying sources:

›   Bob's Red Mill sells all their items on their website, with significant savings if you purchase by the case or if you purchase bulk grains. Shipping is pretty nominal, they have many organic items and no genetically modified ones, and they will gladly tell you where each item is sourced. All their wheat is from Washington or Montana, and their lentils are from Washington. Their oats are from British Columbia.
›   Azure Standard is like a traveling healthy food co-op. Most of the items that carry the Azure Standard label are grown organically in Durham, Oregon. Getting set up with a delivery point is tricky because the items are delivered by a full-size semi-truck, and the driver doesn't like to leave the freeway to negotiate city streets. You can have Azure ship your order via UPS, but then you pay the shipping fee.

So—remember—ask your farmers, cheese makers, fishmongers, and ranchers about buying clubs. *(AC)*

. . . .

OPPORTUNITIES FOR CHANGE
FOOD ACTIVISM

Buy directly from a local farmer.

Buy entire crops from a local farmer and sell them for him.

Convince a farmer to grow specialty crops for you and your buying club.

. . . .

bulk produce buys: flex your activist might!

Now that box chain stores are flooded with a plethora of "sustainable," "certified organic" produce, it's time to take the movement to the next stage. Seek out local farmers or CSA programs. Tell them you want them to go "beyond organic" in their farming practices. Promise them that if they adopt permaculture or biodynamic methods, you will sell their crops for them, at a fair price.

A good scale and a willing helper—two essentials for a group produce buy.

This may sound daunting. It may sound impossible. But if you want access to nutritional food raised with sustainable methods, you need to create the market.

Selling a farmer's entire crop helps the farmer: providing him seed money up front, ensuring demand for his crops, mitigating his risk in the event of natural disasters, and most importantly, removing a large degree of emotional stress caused by market uncertainty. In many ways, organizing a bulk buy is like joining a CSA. The difference is that you are the farmer's sole customer, which enables you to control more elements. You can avoid getting one artichoke per box or weeks of radishes and kohlrabi. You can request that he grow only the foods you find difficult to grow in your city garden, such as large cabbages, corn, or tomatoes.

Perhaps you want only a few crops, but you want them all at once so you can preserve them over the course of a weekend. One summer I did this with tomatoes. I contacted an Eastern Washington farmer who practices permaculture methods and promised to sell his entire tomato crop. Then I posted a message on some local chat groups, explaining that I was helping a farmer sell his crop of heritage tomatoes. I set up a shared Google document and gave everyone who emailed me the link. I was nervous that night, afraid I would end up on some busy street corner trying to sell a truckload of tomatoes.

When I opened the shared Google document the next morning, I discovered that I had sold the farmer's tomato crop many times over. I scrambled to find more biodynamic farmers to round out the order, and coming up short, contracted with a larger organic farm to make up the shortfall. Over the course of the season, I helped sell nearly five thousand pounds of produce in two separate bulk buys. In the process, I gave my original permaculture farmer the confidence in his new-found market to increase his plantings dramatically.

Bakeries that buy entire crops of organic wheat are responsible for converting acres of conventional wheat to organic each year. In the same way, people who participate in bulk buys can create markets for farmers who are willing to go beyond organic standards. Farmers will plant only what they believe the market will support. Until we demand sustainably grown produce at fair prices, in sufficient quantities to support farmers, that type of produce will not exist. It begins with us. *(AC)*

test case: the big tomato buy of 2010

The spring of 2010 progressed into summer without much change in the weather. The days were cool and cloudy, and tomatoes refused to set fruit or ripen. I had organized a bulk buy of tomatoes from Eastern Washington: 1,500 pounds from Skeeter (my permaculture farmer) and another 1,000 pounds from the organic fields of Tonnemaker Farm. We had planned on two deliveries, but the tomatoes were taking so long to ripen that Skeeter and his friends decided to harvest the whole crop at once, before early fall rains could ruin their entire crop. So there I was on September 16, scrambling to find a community center kitchen where we could take delivery of 2,500 pounds of tomatoes and can them on the same day.

I phoned every community center and church I could think of, imagining a roomful of people picking up their boxes and participating in one large communal can-fest. But by the day before the scheduled delivery, I had heard back from only one place, a church that would allow us to use their meeting room until 5:00 PM. My dream of community canning crumbled like burnt toast.

The next morning I headed to the church with my ordering information and my cell phone. The delivery from Tonnemaker Farms arrived first, and the driver was not happy to discover that she would have to carry 1,000 pounds of boxed tomatoes up a flight of stairs. I instructed her to unload the van while I schlepped the boxes up myself. Just as I was feeling the first pangs of back spasms, my tomato army began to trickle in and helped me carry the last boxes up the steps. During our short wait for the next delivery truck, a food service worker pulled up to stock the church kitchen with processed foods. "Is he the farmer?" someone asked. "No," I whispered, "he's the enemy."

Finally a large truck pulling a trailer loaded to the gills with tomatoes arrived. These were the tomatoes from my permaculture farmers. Compared to the romas from Tonnemakers, these new arrivals were a dizzying kaleidoscope of reds and greens and yellows and oranges. There were Cherokee Purples and Green Zebras, Brandywines and Old Germans, San Marzanos and Amish Paste, and boxes of juicy red Legends just waiting to be canned. The mood of the tomato army was euphoric as folks eagerly weighed their tomatoes, wrote out checks, and hurried home with their booty. Among these strangers, there was a feeling of brotherly love normally reserved for holidays.

At quarter to five, I shooed the last of the tomato army out the door, loaded boxes of unclaimed tomatoes into my car, collapsed tables, and frantically vacuumed the rug. As I climbed into my car, the full realization of how much food had transferred hands hit me. On paper 2,500 pounds of tomatoes didn't sound like that much, but in real life it had filled a chapel. And the distribution of the bulk buy had gone off virtually without a hitch.

Over the next few days, I became better acquainted with my tomato army. I invited several to my house, where we spent the next three days canning tomatoes: in juice, in salsa, in pasta and pizza sauces.

I learned what a beautiful singing voice Rebecca has, heard stories about growing up on a farm from Linda, of Carolyn's life in the Peace Corps, and what amazingly fast and willing workers Kate and Katie are. I had always canned alone, and I discovered what a joy it was to can with other people. The whole experience made me think about how women in times

A large produce buy requires plenty of space for distribution.

past had gathered to make dreary or monotonous work enjoyable. It's true that when we lost our community we gained individual privacy and some emotional freedom, but we've lost joy and kinship. What better way to restore unity and peace among strangers than with a box of sun-ripened tomatoes? *(AC)*

how to coordinate a bulk produce buy

Find a farmer who doesn't already sell at farmers markets but who is committed to growing food in a way that protects the environment and nourishes the soil. To find such a farmer, email the extension program at your agricultural university, talk to farms with existing CSA programs, or contact the Biodynamic Gardening and Farming Association (located in Junction City, Oregon) or your local Permaculture Guild. Post your request on local urban farming message boards or shared email sites.

Promise to sell a set amount of that farmer's upcoming crop (or the entire thing). Unless you have a large group of buyers, stick with foods that are easy to sell in bulk, such as tomatoes, peaches, and apples, or long-storing items such as winter squash, cabbage, and potatoes.

pricing

Help the farmer determine a fair market price. This buy eliminates time the farmer would spend packing produce, selling at a market, and bringing unsold produce home. The price should reflect those time savings but should be higher than what he would receive by selling directly to a store or distributor. In this way, you and the farmer split the amount that would have gone to a middle man and you both come out ahead. The farmer will need payment at the time of delivery.

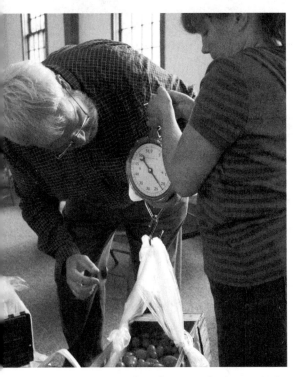

A customer weighs out his own produce to report to the event organizer.

Check with your county food and health departments to see if you need a business license to sell unprocessed foods at cost. If you do, then all buyers need to make their checks out directly to the farmer so you aren't legally the one selling the food. If not, it might be simpler to pay the farmer with one check and have everyone make their checks out to you.

finding the buyers

Advertise and find interested buyers. You can do this by posting notices on urban farming message boards, local mommy chat groups, bulletin boards at healthy food coops or coffeehouses, Weston Price message sites, community kitchens, daycare centers, small restaurants, or with local canning instructors.

Communicate to your potential buyers what distinguishes this produce from what they could buy at a farmers market or grocery store. Introduce your farmer and his growing methods and explain why this is important activism. Also let everyone know where and when to pick up their produce. You don't want to be stuck at the end of the day with unclaimed boxes of produce.

Create a shared spreadsheet (using a program such as Google docs) with a list of crops, total available quantities (so you don't oversell), and price per pound or per piece. If there is an additional delivery fee or room rental, factor in that cost. You could split the extra fee based on number of pounds purchased or per head. The shared spreadsheet will make it easy for you to prorate any extra charges.

Ask buyers to enter their own orders directly into the shared document. This will allow you and the farmer to monitor the order and close it when you've sold the entire crop.

delivery

Discuss delivery with the farmer. He may charge extra for delivery, or you may have to hire a driver or rent a truck.

Find a delivery location. Look for plenty of parking, delivery access, a ramp, and a hand cart. Many churches and most community centers and park picnic areas will allow you to use space for a token donation or a nominal fee. If your produce is not perishable or is packed in cardboard boxes, you could even use a not-so-busy Park and Ride lot; if the buy is small enough, you could use someone's home or garage (be sure and check local rules for group buys).

Allow for a large window of time for pickup to accommodate people with day jobs. There should be someone present at all times to take checks, answer questions, and oversee the process, so if you can't be there the entire time, ask volunteers to help.

Remind people where and when to pick up their produce and whether or not they need to bring bags or boxes. Have as many hanging or floor scales as possible to speed up the weighing process. Bring several printouts of the spreadsheet displaying names and quantities ordered, along with several calculators. Large items such as squash are sold by the pound, so weights won't come out exactly as estimated and there may be a balance due.

At the end of the pickup window, clean up your area and get any final checks off to the farmer. Thank everyone for participating (including the farmer!) and remind them what a difference they are making. *(AC)*

buying clubs and the law

If you're just buying cases of fruit or vegetables to share with friends, it's easy to stay under the radar of the law. But once you expand your buying club to include much larger buys, the state and federal goverments would like you to follow certain rules. They care about the safety of the food supply and that neither you nor the farmer are victimized. The following guidelines should help you keep you and your government regulators on friendly terms.

Whatever the size of your buying club, keep good business practices.
›   Keep a ledger of transactions. Someday, a government agency may ask you to "open the books."

›   Collect invoices from the farmer. Keep a record of the farmer's address.
›   Create a receipt and keep a copy when being reimbursed by buying club participants.
›   Anticipate cash flow problems. Do you have enough cash to pay the farmer on delivery, before reimbursement from members? Banks will not help you, as you must demonstrate consistent profits to qualify for a bank loan. Buying clubs earn zero profit—that's the whole point, to share savings among your friends and neighbors.

Consider carefully where you distribute your produce.
›   Financial transactions conducted in church basements and community centers can threaten those institutions' property tax exemption. Take financial transactions to the public sidewalk.
›   Better yet, partner with a business to use their space for your distribution center.
›   Run small group buys out of your home. This way you can allow members to schedule pickups over two or three days.

Consider government regulations.
Typically, there are two state and one federal government agencies interested in your activities: your state's departments of agriculture and revenue, and the U.S. Department of Agriculture. As an example, below are the regulations in the states of Washington and Oregon, a sales tax state and an income tax state respectively. Your state's regulations will likely bear some resemblance to one of these. Check with your own state regulators to determine how things work. For our purposes, we assume the buying club and its organizers receive no compensation, just reimbursement of produce and license costs.

In Washington State:
›   Under $12,000 in revenue: no requirement to register business.
› $12,000 to $50,000 in revenue: must register business with the state department of revenue and file a "Combined Excise Tax Return." However, no taxes will be collected since you are under the $50K threshold.
› $50,000 and above: Pay B&O tax on revenue above $50K (less than ½ percent).
›   As long as you deal only with food, there is no sales tax.
›   The Washington State Department of Agriculture requires a reseller's license. Of the available licenses, a "Cash Buyer" license costs the least at $125 a year, but requires you to pay the farmer with cash, cashier's check, or bank draft and to use a special transferrable license plate when transporting produce from the farm. You can't use the license to purchase livestock, hay, grain, or straw. Group buys under this permit should aim not

to exceed more than about sixty people per buy. Beyond this, your purchases represent too large a financial risk for the farmer (imagine if you rejected a farmer's delivery). If the state perceives your group as a financial risk to farmers, it may require a more expensive license that also carries a sizeable bond requirement.

›   Grains are excluded from the Cash Buyer license. To purchase grains as a group, you must collect individual checks ahead of time, so that the farmer is paid directly by the end consumer. This then is not a buying club. Discuss the arrangement ahead of time with the farmer.

In Oregon:

›   Oregon taxes income, not revenue, so buying clubs do not have to open an account with the state's department of revenue.

›   If your buying club name includes your full legal name (John Q. Smith Buying Club), you don't have to register your business name. The state strongly advises you to register your business with Oregon's secretary of state, at a cost of fifty dollars every two years.

›   The Oregon Department of Agriculture requires a $100 Cash Buyer license almost identical to the one required in Washington.

Federal Government:

The U.S. Department of Agriculture requires a Perishable Agricultural Commodities Act (PACA) license for some produce distributors. Thankfully for buying clubs, this $995 license is *not* required if you keep your purchases small and don't cross state lines. Technically, you may not buy or sell more than 2,000 pounds of produce on any given day. If you're planning a larger buy, you will need to spread payment and reimbursement out over multiple days, mailing the farmer a down payment ahead of time if required and reselling the produce over several days.

For links to Washington, Oregon, and federal licensing agencies, see Resources, page 370.

FALL

Just as we preserve some of summer's flavors in canning jars, our animals preserve summer in their bodies. The healthy grasses, the vitamin-rich fruits and vegetables—all these contribute to the flavor and texture of our meats. And when we eat these animals during the dark days of fall and winter, we rediscover summer on our plates.

While there are good environmental arguments against eating too much meat, we believe healthy meat, produced in as responsible a manner as possible, can be part of the solution rather than part of the problem. We seek large animals raised on sustainable feed. We raise our own backyard animals, supplementing their feed with table scraps and garden weeds, incorporating their manure into the soil as compost. We stew old laying hens and roosters and celebrate the rabbit, the most efficient backyard animal ever. We use whole animals, not just the choicest cuts. We teach our children how to honor what these animals have given us.

While you and your farmer may not be able to do everything in this chapter—few farmers can afford both high-quality grains and the land costs to keep animals in lush

what we are eating now

Apples
Arugula
Beets
Cabbage
Carrots
Collards
Corn
Fall raspberries
Figs
Garlic
Grapes
Hazelnuts
Hops
Kale
Kiwis
Late tomatoes
Medlars
Mushrooms
Mustard greens
Onions
Parsnips
Pears
Persimmons
Rosehips
Winter squash

pasture through the fall—we hope to give you the tools to evaluate the quality and sustainability of your meat with more confidence.

Freezing much of the year's meat is only one of the ways that we extend the harvest's reach. We also smoke our bacon and hams, we make fresh cider and verjus, we make household supplies like lotions, soaps, and cleaning supplies. These homemade products liberate us from the culture of chemistry that finds expression in our store-bought toothpastes and window cleaners. Why do we need these chemicals, with their unknown long-term consequences? We simply don't. A shelf of these homemade products can help snip the final thread binding you to the grocery store and its pharmaceutical approach to food. *(JM)*

recipes for a fall meal

Hog-slaughtering time means smoking to us. We kick off fall with pulled pork, Carolina style. That means mopped with vinegar rub and topped with whiskey barbecue sauce, plus baked beans, long-simmered greens, and pickled-pepper cornbread on the side. We finish the meal with an heirloom apple pie.

Smoked Pork Shoulder, Ribs, or Loin
Makes 5 pounds
The rub for this pork is adapted from Steven Raichlen's Memphis Rub, a great all-around spice mixture for pork, beef, or chicken. It is so versatile that we make up an extra-large batch and store it in an old Lawry's shaker jar. See the notes on smoking without a smoker under "Maple Cured Smoked Bacon," page 286.

> 3 tablespoons paprika
> 1 tablespoon freshly ground black pepper
> 1 to 2 tablespoons brown sugar
> 1 tablespoon sea salt (smoked if you have it)
> ½ teaspoon celery seed
> 1 teaspoon cayenne
> 2 teaspoons garlic powder
> 1 teaspoon dry mustard
> 2 teaspoons cumin
> 5 pounds any combination of 1 pork shoulder butt, 2 racks of pork ribs, or 2 pork loins

1. Combine all ingredients except pork. Set aside 3 tablespoons of mixture, and coat pork with remainder. Refrigerate, uncovered, overnight.
2. Hot-smoke between 200° and 300°F, until meat registers an internal temperature of 190°F (about 3 hours for ribs, 6 hours for shoulder).
3. If using shoulder butt, shred or slice it, and pour "North Carolina Vinegar Sauce" (see below) over it to season and moisten. Serve on buns with "Whiskey Barbecue Sauce" (see below).

North Carolina Vinegar Sauce

Makes 1 cup
This also makes a fine dressing for shredded cabbage, to serve alongside the pork sammies.

1 cup apple cider vinegar
3 tablespoons Memphis rub from the above recipe
Combine well.

Whiskey Barbecue Sauce

Makes about 3 pints

1 medium onion, minced
1 glug of olive oil
4 cups thin tomato sauce, or 2 cups homemade ketchup (recipe page 243) plus
    2 cups water
⅓ cup good-quality apple cider vinegar (at least 5 percent acidity)
1 cup packed brown sugar (or ¾ cup organic sugar plus scant 1 tablespoon molasses)
2 tablespoons Worcestershire sauce or Asian-style fish sauce (optional)
2 teaspoons sea salt
2 teaspoons liquid smoke (optional, unnecessary if you will be smoking your meat)
3 tablespoons whiskey or bourbon
½ teaspoon freshly ground black pepper
½ teaspoon garlic powder
¼ teaspoon paprika

1. Sauté onion in a glug of olive oil until it begins to soften and caramelize.
2. Add remaining ingredients and bring to a low simmer, uncovered, for about 1½ hours, until it thickens to your liking.

This will keep in the refrigerator for a month or two. For longer keeping, add 4 tablespoons whey (see "A Simple Way to Make Whey," page 50) after the sauce cools. Divide between 2 jars, ensuring there is at least 1 inch headspace in each jar, cap tightly, and leave out for 2 days to ferment. Transfer to refrigerator. If surface grows white mold, simply scrape off and transfer mixture to a clean jar.

Pickled Pepper Cornbread
Makes 6–8 servings

> 1 cup freshly ground cornmeal
> 1 cup freshly ground soft white wheat or whole wheat pastry flour
> ½ teaspoon salt
> 4 teaspoons baking powder
> 1 backyard egg
> 1 cup buttermilk (recipe page 87)
> ¼ cup butter (recipe page 86), melted

A load of gleaned apples destined for cider.

½ to 1 cup drained, chopped pickled peppers (see variation of Pickled Asparagus
   recipe on page 239), depending on pepper heat
1 teaspoon butter (to grease the pan)

1. Preheat the oven to 425°F.
2. Put 1 teaspoon butter in an 8-inch cast-iron skillet, and place in oven.
3. In a bowl, combine cornmeal, flour, salt, and baking powder, and stir well.
4. Make a depression in middle of dry ingredients, and pour in egg, buttermilk, and
    melted butter. With a wooden spoon, blend liquid ingredients first, then slowly in-
    corporate into dry ingredients. Do not overmix. Gently fold in pickled peppers.
5. Spoon batter into preheated pan, and bake for 20 to 25 minutes, until top begins to
    brown and edges pull away from pan.

Greens, Roots, and Hock
Makes 6 servings

3 quarts water
1 smoked ham hock
2 pounds winter greens such as collards or mustard, central stems removed
½ onion
3 carrots, peeled
1 turnip, peeled
¼ cup Rockridge Orchard apple cider vinegar

Combine all ingredients in a nonreactive stockpot. Cover, bring to a boil, and then
turn down and simmer for about 1 hour, until vegetables are soft and flavors meld.
Remove vegetables from cooking liquid. Reserve liquid for soup the next day.

Pickled Green Beans
See variation of Pickled Asparagus recipe on page 239.

Better than Canned Baked Beans
Makes 6–8 servings

1 pound dried small white or kidney beans
3 tablespoons good-quality apple cider vinegar such as Rockridge Orchards

2 quarts water

1 large onion cut into large wedges

½ pound bacon ends and trimmings, cut into bite-size pieces (recipe page 286)

¾ cup maple syrup

½ cup organic sugar

1 tablespoon molasses

½ cup tomato sauce or ketchup (recipe page 243)

1 teaspoon dried mustard or ⅛ cup prepared mustard (recipe page 244)

1 teaspoon salt

½ teaspoon freshly ground black pepper

¼ teaspoon red pepper flakes

Pinch of dried ginger

1. Soak beans overnight in vinegar mixed with enough water to cover by at least 1 inch. In the morning, drain and rinse beans. (This removes the phytic acid that causes gastric distress.)

2. Preheat the oven to 225°F.

3. Place beans, onion, and 2 quarts water in a heavy-bottomed stockpot. Gradually bring to a simmer, and cook until skins crack when blown on (the Ma Ingalls test), about 45 minutes.

4. Add remaining ingredients and mix well. Cover and bake for 8 to 12 hours or until the liquid is thick and velvety. Check after 6 hours to make sure all liquid hasn't evaporated. If beans are getting too dry, add some water, apple cider, or pork stock.

• •

FAVORITE HEIRLOOM BAKING APPLES

Akane

Belle de Boskoop

Bramley's Seedling

Esopus Spitzenburg

Lodi

Newtown Pippin

Northern Spy

Winesap

• •

Heirloom Apple Pie with Whipped Cream
Makes 6–8 servings

There are a million apple pie recipes, many with unique twists. We believe what makes an apple pie special is the apple, and we choose not to mess with this very basic pie. Supermarkets sell only a handful of apple varieties, but orchard stalls at Pacific Northwest farmers markets offer a cornucopia of heirloom apples. These can turn a run-of-the-mill apple pie into an extraordinary one.

This recipe uses half as much sugar as most others, making it slightly tart. It can also be adapted to virtually any fruit, such as blackberries or even salal berries.

Serve with a dollop of whipped cream, crème fraîche (recipe page 88) or vanilla ice cream (recipe page 69).

> 2 chilled Easy as Pie Crusts (recipe page 101)
> 4 pounds apples (about 6 large), peeled, cored, and thinly sliced
> 3/4 cup sugar
> 3 tablespoons all-purpose or soft whole wheat flour, or organic cornstarch
> ½teaspoon cinnamon

1. Preheat the oven to 425°F.
2. Following instructions in Easy as Pie Crust recipe roll and cut dough for a top crust, and chill until needed. Roll out dough for bottom crust. Fit dough into pie plate, fold edges under, and flute them. Refrigerate pie crust for an hour before baking, to prevent shrinking.
3. Mix apples with sugar, flour or cornstarch, and cinnamon. Pour mixture into pie pan, mounding apples slightly in the center.
4. Apply chilled top crust, either making a lattice or leaving it plain and slitting it with a knife. Crimp edges to pie plate with tines of a fork; this will help keep crust from shrinking.
5. Place the pie on a cookie sheet to catch any drips. Bake at 425°F for 15 minutes, protecting crust edges as necessary with foil or pie crust protector.
6. Reduce heat to 375°F, and continue to bake until top is golden brown and apples are soft, 40 to 45 minutes. Let pie cool before serving, to solidify juices and make slicing easier. You can always rewarm it later if you like. Serve with apple brandy–spiked whipped cream.

chapter 14
going whole hog

To market, to market,
To buy a fat pig.

After watching the movie *Food, Inc.*, I found I could no longer eat meat unless I understood everything about the source—the breed of animal, the quality of its life, how it was killed and butchered. I could no longer buy meat even at the farmers market or from a local healthy food store. I wanted to visit the farm, see how the animals lived, and be present at the moment of death.

My meat-purchasing habits took on an ethical element in addition to the nutritional and environmental ones. I started looking for farmers and ranchers I could trust and who would sell me the whole animal, not just choice pieces wrapped in plastic. The great thing about finding a personal farmer is that it gives you the chance not only to support a

MEAT

annette's grocery list

ORIGINAL LIST

Bacon

Chicken nuggets

Ham

Jerky

Lunch meat

Meats from unknown ranchers

Rabbit meat

Sausages

REVISED LIST

Alfalfa (for rabbits)

Oats (for rabbits)

Half pig, from a local farmer

Quarter cow, from a local farmer

Chickens, from a local farmer (or eat your rooster or old hens)

Sausage casings

local small farm but also to find someone whose ethics are in line with yours, someone who pastures animals in a sustainable fashion and slaughters them on the farm (which is the most humane and least traumatic method). It gives you access to beef cattle that are 100 percent grass fed, rather than being fed grains that are not a part of their natural diet.

A direct connection to the animal raiser means you can visit the ranch to see conditions firsthand. You can see whether the fields are close to industrial sites or are sprayed with pesticides, whether the animals are pastured on grass or in mud. (Pastured animals play an integral part in land management by naturally fertilizing the land, whereas animals raised in pens or feedlots contribute to greenhouse gasses and pollute local groundwater and streams.)

Buying your meat directly also usually means you can purchase a whole animal. This saves you money, lets you choose the cuts you want from the butcher, means you can stop watching the news for meat recalls, and provides the benefits of bones for broth, tallow and lard for frying and soap, raw food for pets, and nutrient-dense organ meats. In short, it turns a lot of problems into solutions. *(AC)*

· ·

OPPORTUNITIES FOR CHANGE
MEAT FROM LOCAL ANIMALS

Buy sustainably raised meat.

Buy local, sustainably raised meat.

Buy whole, sustainably raised animals direct from local farmers.

· ·

U-slaughter on the farm

Luke Conyac was a lawyer with a very long knife. He drove an ancient Chevy van with pheasant and wild turkey feathers tucked behind the visors. Where the back seats should have been, there were none. Instead, there were blankets, as if for hiding a body. Before the day was done, they would do just that: Luke, his brother Jeremy, Annette, and I—we were going to kill a couple of hogs.

I wondered about the man driving the van, his bird dog sitting obediently at his side. Was he some sort of weekend cowboy, unfulfilled by his desk job? Over time, I would discover he was not. Luke is one of the most thoughtful men I've met, a man committed to doing what he feels is right. This commitment outweighs the enormous inconvenience of spending a day slaughtering a hog and breaking down its carcass.

Simply put, Luke feels that if he's going to eat meat, he must first look it in the eye. This conviction moves him to help initiate others into the art of slaughter as well, so one day he invited Annette and me to accompany him. Luke and Jeremy would kill and butcher one pig, and Annette and I would butcher the second, under Luke's guidance.

Annette combed the internet and found a hog farmer named Bruce King, whose operation, Ebey Farm, looked nothing like the feedlots where most supermarket hogs are raised. Bruce did a lot of things right. Whereas feedlot operations separated piglets from their parents at six weeks, Bruce let his hogs grow up with their parents and grandparents. He told me, "My herd has its own rituals and society, which the pigs consider very important. They sleep in giant pig piles with the pigs that they choose to consort with. I will find the same pigs sleeping together in groups for years at a time. They naturally mate and they have the experience of seeing their progeny mature."

While this warmed our hearts, it was the way Bruce fed his pigs that really enchanted us. Feedlot pigs receive little food other than genetically modified corn and soy; Bruce's pigs had a diverse diet that contained plenty of fresh fruits and vegetables. How could he afford that? The answer came in the form of a large dump truck that deposited a mountain of squashes in the muddy pigyard.

Bruce had worked out a deal with Walmart, allowing them to dump their expired produce in his field. It wasn't organic, and it wasn't nutritionally calibrated by scientists to produce the fastest-growing pig, but these vegetables represented a huge improvement over the fare given to most pigs. The hogs ran greedily towards the heap of squashes, happily smashing open the fruits to get to the sweet, golden flesh inside.

Not everything Bruce feeds his hogs is food we would eat ourselves. From a local cold-storage facility he receives expired foods like sweetened condensed milk and seven-layer bean dip. Were this to represent his hogs' entire diet, we'd look elsewhere for our meat. But no single ingredient dominates these animals' diet, and we're comfortable with that.

Our favorite meat farmers pasture their animals, making sure they have fresh grass all year long. Access to grass gives all meats a more healthy balance of fatty acids than that of animals fed only grains. And while it would be hard to call Bruce's hogs pastured—since their pasture is already trampled into mud partway through the summer—their diverse diet goes a long way toward easing our health concerns. Because Bruce achieves this diet by relying partly on grocery store waste, he can provide this healthy meat quite affordably, even as he eases the environmental cost of meat production. Farmers who raise their pigs on pasture for the whole season, supplementing it with the highest-quality grain-based feeds, those farmers must charge twice as much for their meat as Bruce does. And because he is willing to let people slaughter their own animal or hire a butcher to perform a "farm kill" on his land, the price comes down even further.

Bruce reviewed the killing process with Luke and Jeremy, as Jeremy quietly checked the pistol. "Imagine an X that connects the eyes and the ears. That's where you want to shoot. Then you'll have ten seconds to stick it before it starts twitching."

Jeremy's shot hit the pig a little low, and the twitching began too early. He jumped on the 300-pound animal, trying to hold it down so Luke could plunge the knife under its chin. The hog flailed violently in the mud, but somehow Luke's knife drove home, severing the jugular and scoring the back of the spine in the proper manner. As I watched them hobble away from the battle, Jeremy's bare sock soaked in mud (he had lost one of his boots in the struggle) and Luke's arm covered in blood, I knew I could not kill a pig myself. I felt prepared mentally, but physically the act looked as dangerous as anything I'd ever seen anyone do. This was like hand-to-hand combat with a walrus.

Mercifully, Bruce shot our pig for us, and Luke stuck it with the knife. This time, the pig did not struggle.

After the pigs had bled out, we inserted hooks into their ankles and attached the hooks to a great wooden bar that Bruce hoisted into the air with a bucket loader. We hosed them down, watching the mud and blood disappearing into the huge bed of wood chips beneath us.

We began to dress the hogs one by one. First we cut off the head, sparing the jowls for salt preservation. Then, preserving as much of the fat as possible on the body, we began cutting off the skin. We slit down the belly of the pig, careful not to pierce the intestines or stomach, as that can spoil the meat. We excised the anus, and the digestive tract, released from its tether, fell into a waiting bucket.

After saving a few choice organs in recycled plastic grocery bags, we donated the lungs, intestines, and stomach to Bruce's dogs (intestines can also be saved to stuff sausages). Now, only the meaty parts of the pig were left, hanging by hooks in the air. Using a large saw, we sliced through the spine, cutting the hog into two sides. These we lowered into plastic garbage bags, which Bruce took to the butcher for us. Luke and Jeremy broke down their hog further still, before wrapping it in a clean sheet and putting it in the back of their van.

Later, we helped Luke carve up his hog at home. He taught us his system for cutting, wrapping, and labeling the meat, breaking it down into meal-sized chunks to go in the freezer or the smoker. When all that was done, we sat back with glasses of Luke and Jeremy's homebrew and reflected on the day's work.

Luke Conyac (right) and a friend skin their hog.

I admired Luke for his moral consistency. But I didn't share the same sense of obligation to kill my own animal. I'm happy to have had the experience, though, which allowed me to understand the cuts of meat in a fundamentally new way. Today, when I think of pork loin roast, I think of the long muscle that runs along the animal's back. I know bacon hangs from the belly and a ham comes from the muscular back leg.

But when it comes to wielding the gun and the knife, I'm happy to yield this service to a professional butcher. He'll come out to the farm to do a "farm kill" for sixty dollars. He'll break down the hog in minutes, whereas it took us hours. He'll salvage more of the lard and bacon than we ever could.

For me, it's enough to know my farmer, and perhaps to visit the farm and pick out a healthy, happy animal. I want to know what my hogs have eaten, and I want to take every step possible to ensure they've had a gentle death.

Over time, we've come to know (and taste) many of Bruce's hogs, including such memorable beasts as Baby Killer and The Mean One That Almost Ate Andrea. But as grandparents secretly favor their first grandchild, so we will always remember that first year's pig, Chubby. Chubby taught my family to cook meat. We savored her slow-roasted hams and her smoky

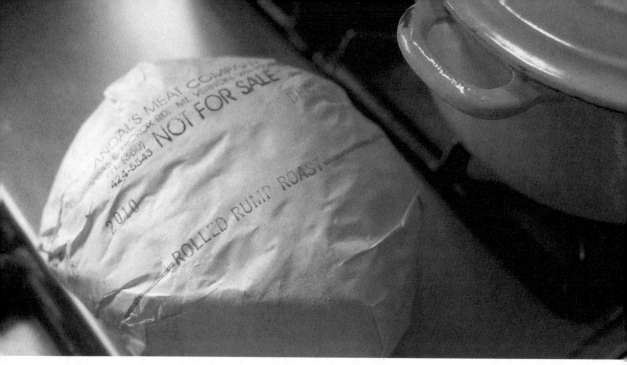

Grass-fed beef from the freezer—part of a whole cow split with friends.

bacon, and came to know every part of that animal from bone to loin. When her name was invoked at the dinner table, I could speak about her with pride.

Chubby was a happy pig. She enjoyed sunlight, the companionship of her peers, and the protection of a kind farmer. And she sure tasted good. *(JM)*

the ethics of eating meat

I've always loved animals and struggled with the idea of eating meat. At one point in high school I gave up eating pork, because pigs were so cute. I angrily lashed out at a schoolmate who mentioned he was going hunting that weekend. "If you're so tough, why don't you hunt with your bare hands?" I chided. "Then you'd even the playing field! Picking on a poor, defenseless deer . . ."

When the classmate asked if I ate meat, I replied yes, but only from animals raised in happy confinement and slaughtered humanely. Much better, I thought, than terrorizing wild creatures.

Many of us believed that same thing, lured into a false sense of reality by images of contented domesticated farm animals. The illusion is that domestic animals prefer confine-ment, receive excellent care, and have a dignified death. If that's not true, how can we eat meat with a clear conscience?

Once I learned the truth about feedlots, however, I could no longer justify eating meat, and I became a vegetarian.

The problem was, this was a time in my life when I was extremely active playing soccer, training for marathons, and climbing mountains. After a few months on my new, kinder diet, my muscles started to hang differently when not in use, my skin and hair became dull, and I would tire quickly.

I grudgingly began to eat meat once more. Still, I stayed on the periphery of the meat-eating world, eating just enough to stay healthy. After all, didn't eating meat make me unethical, as well as contribute to greenhouse gases?

It was only after I began my locavore journey that I realized I could source meat from happy domesticated animals that had been treated well in life and in death. And in the Northwest, where we can grow grass year round, often without irrigation, grass-fed meat may be one of the most sustainable crops we can raise, certainly in comparison with high-irrigation monoculture farming. I was prepared to embrace meat eating again, as long as the animals were 100 percent grass (or otherwise appropriately) fed, and as long as I could see their life and death conditions firsthand.

So, one Saturday morning, Joshua and I journeyed to Ebey Farm to meet our future bacon. We had arranged to buy a live pig and slaughter it ourselves with the help of our friend Luke, but I was already beginning to have serious doubts. Pigs are highly intelligent creatures; when Luke scratched one pig's back, it glanced up at him with the same expression my dog gives me, a combination of aware gratitude and satisfaction. Chubby, it turned out, enjoyed the same things in life as my dog does. That made me wonder: If I could eat pork, could I also eat dog? Is a cow that awfully different from a horse?

What makes it okay to eat one living creature and not another? Is it that we can form an emotional bond with some creatures and not with others? There are plenty of backyard chicken owners who consider their birds family—you can even buy chicken diapers, so your fowl can watch TV with you. And why are many vegetarians not averse to eating fish, anyway? Does a fish not have the same natural instinct to survive that a pig, chicken, or cow does? As a gardener, I have no problem unleashing rabid ladybugs on my aphids and attracting parasite-eating wasps to my yard. I got ducks specifically hoping they would eat the snails and slugs that devastate my garden. Are those too not living things with an instinct to survive, like the rest? If my broccoli could scream, would I still be excited about harvesting it?

In exploring the ethics of eating meat, I looked to Buddhism. To my surprise, I found that not all Buddhists are vegetarians. The Dalai Lama himself, having spent a life reflecting on ethics, eats meat. Chagdud Tulku Rinpoche, in the book *Change of Heart*, explains how a Buddhist could reach such a decision:

"It's a hopeless situation, because if we don't eat we die. Since we have to eat, how can we minimize the harm involved? . . . To Buddhists, every life is of equal value. Most Tibetans don't eat fish because usually several have to be consumed to satisfy a single person's hunger. Highlanders prefer to eat yak because twenty people can live on the meat of a single animal for twenty days. They often think of lowlanders as non-virtuous because they kill so many beings when they plow the land—beings living in the ground, by exposing them to the elements and the birds; beings living above the ground, by burying or squashing them; and even more beings during the cultivation and watering of crops. . . . None of these people want to create non-virtue, but they can't avoid it." *(AC)*

. . . .

THE FINANCES OF SLAUGHTER

By taking control of the animal's slaughter, you'll save money. Below is the cost breakdown for a hog slaughtered in the year 2011.

Luke Conyac Method
› $300 to the farmer for a 300-pound living hog.
› Kill, skin, and halve it on the farm yourself.
› Break it down further at home.
› Brine and smoke various cuts at home.
› Final yield: 168 pounds (56.25 percent of live weight; excludes lard and stew bones)
› Final cost per pound: $1.79

Honorable Coward Method
› $300 to farmer for a 300-pound living hog.
› $60 to a "farm kill guy" to kill your hog and prepare it for the butcher. (In our case, Bruce the farmer is willing to perform this service but would tack another $200 onto the original price of the hog.)
› $120 to butcher for cut and wrap of 225-pound hanging weight hog, at 53 cents a pound (figure hanging weight at 75 percent of live weight). To find a butcher, search the internet for "custom meat" in your area.
› $2.50 butcher's "disposal fee."
› Brine and smoke various cuts at home.
› Final yield: 168 pounds (56.25 percent of live weight; excludes lard and stew bones)
› Final cost per pound: $2.87–$4.06 if Bruce takes care of all the details.

Additional Services Available from the Butcher
› Smoking: 59 cents per pound
› Seasoning: 25 cents per pound (as for sausages, loose or stuffed)
› Sausage stuffing: 75 cents per pound (using natural casings)

. . . .

how to buy a whole animal

Most ranchers slaughter in the fall in order to avoid overwintering their animals. The most sought-after ranchers may have sold all their meat animals by early spring (or sooner), so start early in the year.

Step 1: Find a rancher. Check www.eatwild.com or www.craigslist.com, or ask around. Phone butchers outside the city and ask for names of local ranchers they respect and routinely deal with. Once you find a likely farmer, do your research. Check www.googlemaps.com for any heavy industry in the area that may contaminate the soil and air. Ask the farmer how the animals are housed, what they are fed, whether he breeds his own stock, and whether the animals are killed off site (a gentle death on the farm is far less traumatic). Ask if pastures are adjacent to conventional fields, where there may be overspray of pesticides.

If you are buying a cow, ask if it is 100 percent grass fed. If not, find out how much grain or hay it is fed and for how long, and whether the grain is organic (too much grain in the diet can alter the pH of the animal's stomach and encourage *E. coli*). If you are buying a pig, ask what it was fed, if its diet was varied, and how much access it had to pasture.

Part of finding a rancher is knowing what butcher that rancher uses. Is the beef wet packed or dry hung? If it's dry hung, how long is it aged? Dry hanging and aging will decrease your overall meat yield but dramatically improve flavor and texture. Any losses from dry hanging are merely moisture and are not really food anyway. Hanging for seven to fourteen days before butchering is the norm, although some butchers can be persuaded to age the meat for twenty-one days.

Step 2: Pre-sell the entire animal if necessary. How much meat will your family eat in a year? Keep in mind that a whole cow may be 400 pounds or more once processed and require thirteen to fourteen cubic feet of freezer space. A whole pig may be 120 pounds or more and require four cubic feet (average upright fridge/freezer size).

Some ranchers will sell part of a cow or pig, and others will sell only the whole animal. If you don't want a whole animal, find others to split it with. Check with friends and neighbors or members of your buying group.

Step 3: Find out when the kill date will be. Let the rancher know if you want to be present when the animal is killed. Your presence may be necessary if you want blood, organs, entrails for pets, or the head. Many cultures prize these organ meats and innards, and learning to make blood sausage or head cheese is a great way to honor the death of this creature, ensuring you use as much of it as possible.

Step 4: Communicate with the butcher about cuts. The butcher will ask you a series of questions: long or short ribs, hamburger or stew meat, thickness of steaks, how many steaks/

A customer purchases a freshly slaughtered Thanksgiving turkey directly from Pastured Sensations Farm.

chops per package, size of roasts, etc. This is the time to request the brisket or skirt steak, for example; otherwise, it may be made into hamburger. Ask what other cuts might be turned into hamburger or stew meat, just to be safe. Let the butcher know if you want cuts such as tongue, heart, kidneys, liver, tail, fat for tallow, or lard. If you want fat, ask that it and scraps be bagged in manageable sizes, so you can easily divide them among your buying group.

Some butchers will only divide cows into halves; others will split them into quarters. If more than four people are splitting a cow, form teams by quarters and let those buyers work out how best to split up each quarter. Everyone sharing a quarter cow will need to agree on the cuts.

Decide ahead of time who gets the tail, tongue, heart, liver, and kidneys. Also ask how long the butcher will hold your animal once butchered; he may have limited freezer space and need you to pick it up the day it is butchered.

Step 5: Organize the pickup. Most large animals are raised and butchered well outside the city, so one or more people from your group will have to drive out to the butcher to pick up the meat. You'll need a large vehicle (or more than one vehicle), since a whole cow can be too large to fit into a small sedan or even an SUV. If you are picking up for others, have them provide ice chests for transporting their meat. Agree on a meeting place and time for distributing the meat. Consider asking for gas money.

Step 6: Ready your freezer. Simple pieces of cardboard placed strategically in your freezer will help make meat easy to find.

Step 7: Bring gloves! The butcher will wheel out a cart stacked with bins. You will be transferring packages of frozen meat from the cart into ice chests or boxes. In addition to staving off painfully cold hands, rubber gloves can speed things up by giving you a better grip on those packages.

Step 8: Use up scraps. Render lard or tallow, make bone broth, dry out and burn remaining bones in a biochar oven (see page 128) for the garden (some dry bamboo will help it burn).

small-farm slaughter and the law

Your state probably cares about how and where your meat is slaugthered. In Washington State, for example, the law offers some guidance, but many activities fall into a legal gray area subject to interpretation by state agricultural inspectors. Usually these inspectors want to help small farmers succeed, but if they perceive a safety risk, they will respond. Following is a summary of Washington State's animal slaughter guidelines. Use them as a starting point for exploring your own state's laws.

beef, hogs, sheep, and goats

These larger animals may be slaughtered and distributed according to the following methods:

Slaughter by the farmer. Farmers may slaughter an animal on their own farm for personal consumption at any time, within certain limits. They must have an approved plan for dealing with waste. They can't sell or give away a carcass, or any individually wrapped portions of these animals.

Slaughter by "kill truck." A farmer can sell you a live animal. In this scenario, you are responsible for the animal's slaughter. Most people pay a state-certified "kill truck" (mobile abattoir), to kill, skin, and halve the animal for them. The operator of the truck is responsible for inspecting the meat, then taking it to your WSDA-licensed "custom butcher" for further cutting and wrapping. We refer to this activity as a "farm kill," and it is our preferred method for dispatching large animals.

MEAT WEIGHT—DEFINITIONS

›   Live weight: The weight of a living animal.
›   Hanging weight: The weight of the prepared carcass upon arrival at the butcher, usually 75 percent of live weight.
›   Finished weight: The final weight of your wrapped packages. This is usually about 75 percent of hanging weight, meaning about 56 percent of live weight (excluding lard and stew bones). Farmers figure that if your finished weight falls below 50 percent of the live weight, you can suspect your butcher of skimming pork chops!

Pork Primal Cuts

1. Ham
2. Ribs, loin, tenderloin, chops
3. Belly
4. Butt (shoulder butt, Boston butt)

5. Picnic ham
6. Hocks and trotters
7. Jowls

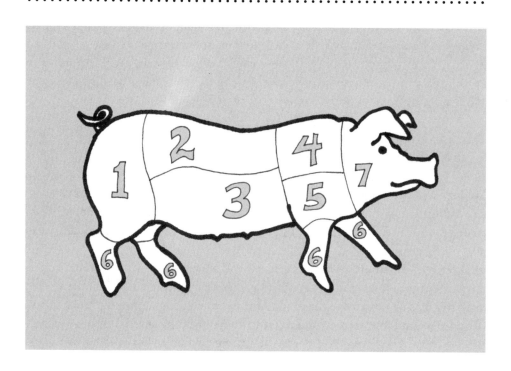

Beef Primal Cuts and Common Fabricated Cuts

(Note: Because cows are bigger than pigs, the list of cuts is longer and more complex.)

1. Neck, chuck, and blade
a. Shoulder clod roast
b. Blade steak
c. Chuck roast
d. Chuck arm roast
e. Country-style chuck ribs
f. Short ribs
g. Cross rib roast
h. English roast

2. Brisket

3. Rib
a. Prime rib
b. Ribeye roast
c. Ribeye steak (Delmonico)
d. Rib steak
e. Short ribs
f. Back ribs

4. Short plate
a. Short ribs
b. Skirt steak

5. Short loin
a. Strip steak
b. Filet of strip
c. Strip roast
d. Tenderloin roast
e. T-bone steak
f. Porterhouse steak
g. Filet mignon tenderloin steak
h. Hanger steak, hanging tender

6. Flank

7. Sirloin
a. Sirloin steak

b. Filet of sirloin
c. Tri-tip steak
d. Tri-tip roast

8. Round
a. Rump roast
b. London broil
c. Top round roast, top round steak
d. Bottom round roast, bottom round steak
e. Eye of round roast, eye of round steak
f. Sirloin tip roast, sirloin tip steak

9. Shank

10. Cheeks

Nick Johnson eviscerates a turkey at Pastured Sensations Farm.

U-slaughter on the farm. While a purchased live animal is technically yours to slaughter, you're in a legal gray area if you choose to slaughter the animal yourself on the farmer's land. Inspectors generally tolerate this activity as long as the processing area is clean and properly equipped, and as long as the neighbors don't complain. The practice of U-slaughter represents a liability risk to the farmer, so be careful.

Hog, sheep, or goat slaughter classes. Legally identical to the U-slaughter option above.

Slaughter for sale through resellers. If a farmer wants to sell meat through a reseller such as a grocery store or restaurant, the Federal Meat Inspection Act requires that the meat be slaughtered and processed in a USDA-licensed facility. Inspectors check the animal both before and after slaughter. After all, when you buy meat through a reseller, you don't know the farmer; you can't know the health of the animals or the conditions in which they lived.

While a couple of mobile USDA slaughter units serve limited areas in Washington State, most small farmers must ship their live animals off site to be slaughtered at these larger facilities. This stresses the animals.

Backyard slaughter. As urban milk goats become increasingly popular, residents will likely begin slaughtering five- and six-month-old bucks in the backyard for meat. Technically, most cities have zoning laws that prohibit this activity. Whether the practice will end up being tolerated anyway, as backyard chicken and rabbit slaughter is frequently tolerated, depends in part on whether the neighbors complain.

Sharing a large animal with friends—restrictions on payment. Many people who choose the U-slaughter or kill-truck method intend to divide the animal among friends. Washington State law allows this, but only if each party pays the farmer directly for their portion of the animal; if all money passes through one person who writes a single check to the farmer, that person has just become a reseller and has violated the law. (Privately, some officials admit that this law is difficult to enforce.)

"Not for sale" stamp—restrictions on further distribution. All large animals processed outside a USDA-inspected facility must bear a "Not for Sale" stamp on each package. This has nothing to do with the quality of the meat, but rather indicates that the end user has purchased the live animal directly from the farmer.

. . . .

SUSTAINABLE SCORECARD FOR MEAT

To ensure that you are buying a sustainably raised animal that has been ethically treated, you have to talk to your farmer. Keep in mind, though, that few farmers will meet every one of your expectations. Choose the issues most important to you. Here are some key questions to ask your farmer:

› Are animals birthed, raised, and slaughtered on the same farm? Animals raised this way aren't subject to the stresses of transportation or slaughterhouses.
› Are the cows 100 percent grass fed? If not, they may start or end their lives on feedlots.
› Are the pigs provided a varied diet and not just predominantly soy and grains? Pigs need a varied diet for their health and to minimize their impact on the environment.
› Are the animals pastured, as opposed to being kept indoors? For animals to be healthiest, they need access to sunlight and fresh air.
› Are the facilities clean?
› Are antibiotics or hormones used, and if so, under what circumstances?
› Are the animals' tails docked? This practice is typical in facilities where animals are over-crowded and stressed.
› Do the pigs have nose rings? This is meant to prevent them from rooting in the dirt, but rooting is a natural instinct that gives pigs access to nutrients found in soil and roots.
› Are the animals bred naturally, or through artificial insemination?
› Are the animals treated with respect, in a stress-free environment?

- › Is the manure composted for use in agriculture, or is it stored in lagoons? Animal manure lagoons poison local watersheds and contribute to greenhouse gases.
- › Are the animals stunned before slaughter?
- › What is the policy toward "downer" animals (weak, sick, or crippled animals that are down and cannot get up)?

Rabbits over worm bins inside a chicken run make efficient use of a small backyard.

rabbits, chickens, geese, turkeys, emus, and ostriches

The laws concerning these "smaller" animals are less restrictive.

Slaughter by the farmer. A farmer may slaughter an animal on the farm for personal consumption at any time, within certain limits.

Selling fresh animals to consumers. Farmers can sell up to 1,000 fowl directly to end consumers as long as they obtain a Special Poultry Permit, and as long as consumers pick up the whole birds, fresh (not frozen), within forty-eight hours of slaughter.

Selling processed animals to consumers and resellers. An inexpensive WSDA Food Processor License permits a farmer to sell up to 20,000 birds annually, as well as an unlimited number of rabbits in processed form (cut up, frozen, or ground into sausages). They can sell directly to you or through retail such as restaurants, stores, and farmers markets.

Farm slaughter classes. Some farmers offer small-animal slaughter classes for chickens and rabbits on their farm. Legally speaking, this activity falls into a gray area. Most inspectors allow this sort of slaughter, as long as the class takes place in a clean and correctly equipped processing area (for chickens, this can be outdoors). Again, this represents a potential liability risk for the farmer, so be sensitive.

Backyard slaughter. In city backyards, zoning regulations may forbid animal slaughter. However, backyard slaughter of chickens and rabbits is frequently tolerated, as long as the neighbors don't complain.

· ·

WHAT'S WITH ALL THE SATURATED FATS?

There's a scene in the movie *City Slickers*, after the old cowboy Curly dies of a heart attack. A character named Phil says, "The man ate bacon at every meal . . . you just can't do that!" This is the stance of the medical establishment: Saturated fats lead to death and despair.

Today, I'm not so certain. Some scientists believe that saturated fats have been unfairly scapegoated for our nation's obesity epidemic. They suggest that many broadly accepted studies fail to control for other recent changes in the American diet, changes that may bear equal or greater responsibility for heart disease and obesity. They point to trans-fats, highly refined and processed foods, and even polyunsaturated fats as more likely culprits.

Most doctors are far from embracing saturated fats. But some people have nonetheless begun to reintroduce these fats into their lives.

The jury is still out as to whether saturated fats should play a major role in our diets. But knowing what we know, we can say a few things for certain:

› If you eliminate fast foods and highly processed foods from your diet, you'll have much more room to enjoy saturated fats.
› Fats from animals that consume plenty of greens are healthier than fats from animals fed only grains. This is also true of eggs.
› All fats become unhealthy once they're heated past the smoke point. *(JM)*

· ·

whole animal recipes

A tempting slice of Maple Cured Smoked Bacon.

Maple Cured Smoked Bacon
Makes 5 pounds

Once you taste smoked bacon made without artificial ingredients, you'll have a hard time eating it any other way! It's simple to make and well worth the effort. I don't just cure the belly according to this recipe; I also cure the loin and jowls, in order to maximize the amount of breakfast meat we get from each pig.

If you don't have a smoker you can use a barbecue or an oven. Make a foil pouch, fill it with wood chips that have been soaked in water for 30 minutes, and poke holes in the top with a fork. Place the pouch in *the hottest part of the barbecue or oven, and check every 45 minutes to see if you need to replace it.*

¼ cup kosher salt
¼ cup maple or brown sugar
¼ cup maple syrup
1 5-pound pork belly, preferably with skin on and cut in pieces to fit into gallon Ziploc bags

1. Combine salt, sugar, and syrup, and rub mixture on pork pieces. Place pieces in bags, and refrigerate for 7 days, turning daily to distribute cure, until meat is firm to the touch. Brine will form inside bags.
2. Remove pork from bags, pat dry, and place on a rack over a plate in refrigerator for 24 hours.
3. Smoke at 180°F to an internal temperature of 150°F. Refrigerate bacon overnight to firm it up before slicing as thinly as possible.

Canadian Bacon
Makes 3 pounds

1 gallon water
1½ cups kosher salt

1 cup sugar
1 bunch fresh sage or 2 tablespoons dried sage
1 bunch fresh thyme or 2 tablespoons dried thyme
2 cloves garlic, smashed
1 3-pound pork loin

1. Combine all ingredients except pork loin in a large pot, and bring to a simmer, stirring until sugar and salt are dissolved. Cool brine completely, place pork loin in it, and use an overturned plate to keep it submerged. Refrigerate for 48 hours.
2. Remove loin from brine, pat dry, and place on a rack over a plate in refrigerator for 24 hours. Hot-smoke at 180°F until it reaches an internal temperature of 150°F.

Apricot Glazed Ham

Yield depends on size of ham

For the ham
1 gallon water
1½ cups kosher salt
2 cups packed dark brown sugar (or 1¾ cups white sugar mixed with 5 teaspoons molasses)
1 ham, aitch bone removed

For the glaze
1 cup apricot preserves (recipe page 233)
1 tablespoon mustard (recipe page 244)

1. Combine all ingredients except ham in a container large enough to hold ham. Stir until sugar and salt are dissolved. Add ham, and use a plate to keep it completely submerged. Refrigerate half a day per pound.
2. Remove ham from brine, rinse, and pat dry. Place on a rack in refrigerator, uncovered, for 24 hours.
3. Hot-smoke ham at 200°F until it reaches an internal temperature of 155°F. Allow to cool then refrigerate or freeze. See cooking instructions below.

To bake a thawed ham
1. Cover ham tightly with aluminum foil, and bake at 250°F for 10 minutes per pound.

2. Make glaze by thoroughly combining apricot preserves with mustard.
3. Remove from oven, increase oven temperature to 350°, remove foil, and brush ham with one-half the glaze.
4. Return ham to oven and bake, uncovered, until glaze begins to caramelize, about 10 minutes. Remove from oven, and brush with remaining glaze. Let rest 10 minutes under foil before carving.

Bulk Italian Sausage
Makes 4 pounds

4 pounds pastured pork, ground
½ cup red wine
4 garlic cloves, minced
1 tablespoon black peppercorns, freshly ground
4 teaspoons sea salt
1 tablespoon dried or 3 tablespoons freshly minced oregano
1 tablespoon dried or 3 tablespoons freshly minced basil
1 tablespoon dried fennel

1. Combine all ingredients, mixing thoroughly.
2. Divide into 4 portions and freeze until needed.

Apple Breakfast Sausage
Makes 4 pounds

4 pounds pastured pork, ground
4 tablespoons finely chopped dried apple (see page 215)
½ teaspoon dried ginger
½ teaspoon ground cinnamon
1 tablespoon plus 1 teaspoon salt
2 tablespoons plus 2 teaspoons ground dried sage

1. Combine all ingredients, mixing thoroughly.
2. Divide into 4 portions and freeze until needed.

Previous page: Flower and Herb Salad (recipe p. 193)
Opposite page, top: Harvesting wild edibles from parking strip.
Opposite page, bottom: Sucking nectar from a nasturtium.
This page: Horseradish Crusted Salmon with Cucumber Dill Sauce (recipe p. 191).

This page: Mixed Berry Cobbler with Lemon Verbena Ice Cream (recipe p. 194).
Opposite page, top: Wild berries for Joshua's Forager Jam (recipe p. 200).
Opposite page, bottom: Aunt Molly's groundcherries—tropical fruit from the parking strip.

This page: Dried heirloom tomatoes.
Opposite page, top: Fermenting sauerkrauts and kimchee.
Opposite page, bottom: A few items from the pantry.

Lavender Jelly

Honey

RYE

Bulk produce buy: eggplants (top), unloading winter squashes (bottom).

Peppers (top) and garlic (bottom left) at a bulk produce buy.
Bottom right: Pickled peppers (recipe p. 239)

Top: Smoked Pork Shoulder and fixin's (recipe p. 262).
Bottom: Grass-fed hogs at Pastured Sensations Farm.
Opposite page: Heirloom Apple Pie (recipe p. 267).

Opposite page: Luke washes his hog at Ebey Farm.
Top: Turkey at Pastured Sensations Farm.
Bottom: Humane rooster slaughter in the backyard.

DUTCH MIGNONNE

Origin: Holland to USA in 1800s
Size: Medium
Color: Lackluster yellow
Use: Dessert
Harvest: Early October
Notes: Keeps well. Usually bennial bearing

Top: Piper's Orchard in Seattle.
Bottom: Local citrus flavor—sorrel,
lemon verbena, and lemon balm.

This page: Thawing Black Elderberry Syrup (recipe p. 330).
Next page: Winter squashes from Skeeter's farm.

HOW NOT TO CURE SAUSAGE

I once stayed up until two in the morning stuffing pepperoni sausages from our grass-fed cow. Finished at last, I hung the sausages in my utility room to cure for two weeks. Two days later, the utility room door was left open and our dog ate every last sausage.

If you don't have a secure area for curing sausages, you can keep them as loose sausage or stuff them in casings and eat them fresh.

Beef Jerky
Makes 1 pound
The flavor of jerky can be customized by altering the marinade ingredients. When you make up your own flavors, feel free to use more liquid than this recipe calls for, but if you use any less, the mixture may not penetrate and flavor the meat in a short marination time. If you choose to use less liquid, marinate the meat overnight. Choose lean cuts of meat and remove any large pockets of fat, which will mold.

 ½ cup soy sauce
 1 teaspoon onion powder
 1 teaspoon garlic powder
 1 pound lean beef, trimmed of fat and sliced into ¼-inch-thick pieces

1. Combine soy sauce, onion powder, and garlic powder. Thoroughly coat beef with mixture, and marinate in the refrigerator for 2 to 4 hours.
2. Place beef on dehydrator trays on the Meat setting (165°F), and dry for 4 to 8 hours, depending on your dehydrator. Store in Mason jars in refrigerator for several months, or freeze for longer storage.

Variation: Pepperoni Beef Jerky. Pepperoni seasonings also make a great jerky marinade. Follow recipe for Bulk Pepperoni Sausage (below).

Bulk Pepperoni Sausage
Makes 5 pounds
This sausage tastes like pepperoni and works great in pasta and on pizzas—without the trouble of stuffing or of using nitrates required for curing.

5 pounds lean, grass-fed beef, ground
3 tablespoons kosher or sea salt
⅓ cup dry red wine
3 teaspoons cayenne pepper, or to taste
½ teaspoon ground allspice
1 teaspoon fennel seed
4 tablespoons organic sugar
2 tablespoons paprika

1. Combine all ingredients, and mix well.
2. Use in bulk on pizza or pasta. Store in freezer.

Variation: Stuffed, Uncured Pepperoni Sausage. For about ten dollars, you can purchase a sausage stuffing attachment for a KitchenAid. You can insert that attachment into a cloth pastry bag or plastic bag with a corner cut out and then apply pressure to the bag to fill sausage casings. Freeze until cooking.

Corned Beef

Makes 5 pounds
What would St. Patrick's Day be without this?

1 gallon water
1 cup kosher salt
¼ cup sugar
1 tablespoon cracked black pepper
1 tablespoon mustard seed
½ tablespoon ground allspice, or 1 tablespoon cracked allspice berries
1 tablespoon dried thyme
2 bay leaves
1 5-pound beef brisket

1. Combine all ingredients except brisket in a large pot and bring to a simmer, stirring until sugar and salt are dissolved. Cool brine thoroughly and place brisket in it, using an overturned plate to keep it submerged. Refrigerate for 5 days.
2. Drain brine, add just enough water to cover brisket by 1 inch, and bring to a boil,

removing any scum that forms on surface. Reduce heat, cover, and simmer gently for 3 hours, until fork tender.

3. Bring the mixture to a boil. Add sliced carrots or small potatoes and boil for 10 minutes. Add cabbage wedges and boil 10 more minutes. Serve with Black and Tans.

Easy Liver Pâté
Makes 1 pound

1 small onion or shallot, minced
Bacon drippings or lard
1 pound good, pastured pork or chicken liver, cut into pieces
1 cup cream
3 tablespoons brandy
1 tablespoon salt
1 teaspoon freshly ground white pepper

1. In a pan, fry onion or shallot in bacon drippings or lard until soft. Add pork or chicken liver and cook, covered, until internal temperature reaches 155°F. Refrigerate until completely chilled.
2. Place all ingredients in a food processor, and blend until you achieve a smooth paste. Serve on slices of bread with mustard, pickles, or sliced hard-boiled eggs.

Bone Broth
Yield varies with type of meat

Bone broth can be made from bones from roasts, steaks, and birds you have already cooked, or uncooked bones from animals you have had slaughtered. When we get our cow, pig, and goat in the fall, I make large batches of broth and can it to save on freezer space. I freeze any roast chicken carcasses or back sections until I have a full pot's worth.

Some people roast the raw bones first to caramelize them and deepen the flavor. It's delicious either way. I generally simmer my bone broth for 48 hours—the longer you simmer it the more nutrients you draw out of the bones. You can do this using a slow cooker or if you have a reliable stove, by turning your stove down to a gentle simmer overnight. You can, of course, cook it for less time but I find it fairly easy to make over the weekend.

Having ready broth in your pantry allows you to make nourishing last-minute soups for dinner when you are running short on time.

4 pounds organic soup bones

¼ cup good-quality apple cider vinegar (at least 5 percent acidity)

3 medium onions, each cut into 8 wedges

3 carrots, cut into 1-inch pieces

3 celery stalks, cut into 1-inch pieces

1 teaspoon whole black peppercorns

1. If making beef you can first roast them by placing bones in a 350°F oven and roasting until all traces of meat are browned.
2. Place bones in a nonreactive stockpot, and add vinegar and enough filtered water to cover. Let sit for 1 hour before cooking. (Letting bones soak in acidic liquid for an hour helps leach minerals from them, fortifying the broth.)
3. Add vegetables and peppercorns to the pot and gradually bring it to a simmer. Simmer for 24 to 72 hours, adding more water as needed. The longer you simmer, the more minerals the broth will have. To keep stock clear, always keep it uncovered and never let it boil.
4. Strain broth and let cool. Refrigerate overnight, and in the morning remove any fat that has floated to the top. (You don't have to throw this away: Beef tallow makes tasty fried potatoes and also great soap.)
5. Can broth with a pressure canner, freeze it, or turn it into bouillon. Making bouillon is a great way to save on freezer space. To make it, instead of cooling strained broth, return it to pot and continue cooking down to a syrupy consistency. Freeze in ice cube trays. One ice cube is approximately 1 ounce, or equivalent to one commercial bouillon cube. Add a cube to 1 cup water to reconstitute broth, or add directly to gravy or soup to improve the flavor.

Rendering Lard or Tallow

Yield varies with type of meat

If you have ever fried bacon, then you have rendered lard. Lard is rendered pork fat and tallow is rendered beef fat. Both are excellent for frying things like french fries or doughnuts, and lard makes amazing pie crusts. They also make excellent soaps—and I promise they won't smell like a barnyard.

You can buy pork and beef fat from a farmers market vendor or butcher, but if you buy a whole animal, you should have plenty for free. If you aren't quite ready to render your own lard, try saving your bacon grease for frying eggs and potatoes. That just might make a believer out of you.

You can render fat on the stovetop, in the oven, or in a slow cooker. It will come out the same regardless of your method, but the slow cooker is the simplest since you can set it and forget it. Plan on an hour or two for each pound of lard. Grinding it beforehand shortens the rendering time.

Rendering method
1. Cut up pork or beef fat, or run through a meat grinder. Put in a heavy-bottomed stock-pot on low heat, a roasting pan in a 200°F oven, or a slow cooker at its lowest setting.
2. Cook, stirring occasionally, until fat begins to liquefy (much like when you fry bacon). Either remove liquefied fat with a turkey baster during cooking process, or simply wait until all fat has rendered.
3. Strain through a cheesecloth-lined sieve, and store in Mason jars. If completely rendered and strained well, lard or tallow will cool to a beautiful creamy white and keep in a cool, dark larder for several months. They should also keep in the refrigerator for 6 months, or freeze even longer.

Any crispy cracklings left over from the rendering can be eaten as is, served on top of beans, or added to cornbread as Ma Ingalls did.

chapter 15
raising small animals for meat

While I didn't pull the trigger on Chubby, the hog that Joshua and I
shared, or plunge the knife that ended her life, I did help break down
her carcass and willingly cured and smoked the meat. Did that make me
a killer? I felt much better about eating Chubby than about any meat I
could buy in a Styrofoam package. But one can't live on bacon alone, and
after talking to Bruce (the farmer who raised Chubby) about how much
food it takes to bring a hog to market weight, I began to seriously doubt
that a pig could ever be a truly sustainable meat source.

So I started researching backyard rabbits. They are easily raised in small spaces, are highly
efficient converters of food to meat, and multiply, well, like rabbits.

For a time my father had raised meat rabbits. One day when I asked how they were,
he confided that he had stopped. Pressed for a reason, he responded, "It's not easy hitting
something so cute and fluffy over the head. I just didn't have the stomach for it." When the
time came, would I?

I decided that, before setting up a backyard rabbit operation, I should learn to butcher
one, lest I not be able to go through with it and end up with yet another unintended pet
(or ten). I arranged for a private session with Brad of Abundant Acres Farm and recruited
a group of others to join me. The night before our lesson, I did a YouTube search for
"process rabbits" and was terrified by what I saw. Camouflage-wearing men gleefully
killed and gutted rabbits without remorse or concern. I felt like retching and dreaded the
morning.

The next day I met my fellow students. We were a small group of mostly middle-aged
women. We wanted to connect with our food, to take responsibility for our meal choices,
and to gain life skills that we city dwellers were sorely lacking. We embraced our fears and
summoned our resolve.

But as we entered the yard, I saw each face fall and heard a collective sigh of defeat. "I can't do this," mumbled one woman; "I don't think I can either," said another. The rabbits sat in holding cages, each one a perfect, fluffy bunny with quivering nose and downy fur. I hadn't exactly expected to be gleeful, but I was completely unprepared for how adorable and trusting these creatures were. They didn't look like food, they looked like slippers.

Was I this hungry? I had a freezer full of Chubby the Hog at home. Was I this sadistic? Nope: I dreaded inflicting suffering and had nightmares about being responsible for the death of other living creatures. What was I doing here?

But Brad carried on matter-of-factly. He grabbed a broomstick and a cage and reached in unhesitatingly for a victim. He picked up the rabbit and held it like a pet: the rabbit instantly relaxed and nestled into the crook of his arm. As he stroked, Brad explained the process to us. Put down the rabbit, lay a broomstick across the back of its neck, step onto both ends of the broomstick to hold the rabbit in place, then quickly and firmly grab the back legs and pull them up to snap the neck.

After explaining the process, he demonstrated. We watched as he put the rabbit down on the ground, gave it a small pile of kibbles for distraction, and placed the broomstick across the back of the neck while reassuringly stroking the rabbit. In a second it was over; the animal's eyes had gone from shiny to dull in a split-second. Its back legs began to kick, but Brad assured us that was a muscular reflex. There was no apparent awareness, obvious pain, or distress.

Brad showed us how to cut off the head and feet with kitchen shears, hold the rabbit upside down to bleed out into a bowl, and remove the skin with a simple snip and tug. The skin came off as easily as a wet sock. The whole rabbit was fully processed in less time than it takes me to find a particular cut of meat in my freezer, and all without a firearm or large mess to clean up.

Compare that with the huge event of slaughtering a cow or pig, either of which is grown outside the city and requires transportation to the butcher and then to your freezer. Beef and pork fill the better part of a large freezer and use a lot of plastic-lined wrapping paper. Live rabbits, on the other hand, require housing and feed, and that's about it. In terms of sustainability rabbits win, paws down. And the neighborhood kids who love to visit the chickens would adore the rabbits.

Until, perhaps, they realized that their favorite rabbits kept disappearing. What would my neighbors think of me? The garden and the chickens had already changed the nature of our relationship, and finding out that I killed pet rabbits for food would more than likely be the last straw for some. They might not even want their kids at my house anymore.

I also wondered if it would change me. Chickens had been the gateway drug to farming—would rabbits be the gateway to hunting? Would I buy a rifle and start wearing orange fleece?

I stole a look at my companions. They were solemn and focused, offering each other support and advice as they learned this new life skill. For a moment I felt as if I were at one of those team-building events that bosses use to cover up the fact that they've lost touch with their employees. It also struck me just then that there was only one male class participant. It's interesting that the only two people I knew who had raised meat rabbits were men (my father and one other farming mentor), and they had both given it up because it was emotionally too hard on them!

Yet here were women hopping at the chance to kill rabbits on a regular basis. And not just any women: These were mothers, the most nurturing and saintly bunch of all, slaughtering rabbits without blinking an eye. By now everyone had completed their first bunny and had begun processing seconds. After all, a single rabbit makes a pretty meager meal for a family.

Just then I had a fleeting memory of visiting my grandmother and her hobby farm when I was around three years old. "What shall we have for Sunday night supper?" she asked me. "Fried chicken!" I replied resoundingly. My grandmother made the world's best fried chicken as far as I was concerned.

"Should we go for a walk?" she asked, smoothing her apron. We went past the pail of clams we had just dug out on the peninsula and meandered through the garden. She threw some scratch into the hen yard and they came running over, greedily gobbling it down.

Then suddenly she reached down, grabbed a hen, and swung it over her head like the blades of a helicopter. I heard a sickening crack and the chicken went limp. It might have been my imagination, but her fried chicken just didn't taste very good after that. I wonder if my grandmother's neighbors thought any less of her for killing her pets and eating them. Probably not; this issue of eating meat is complicated nowadays.

My son Max understands full well where his food comes from. He has finally learned to trust that when I tell him we are having pot pie for dinner I mean pot pie the dinner and not Pot Pie his pet chicken. His brother, Lander, on the other hand, quit eating meat when we went to pick up a "pig" at the butcher's and it turned out to be in neatly wrapped frozen blocks. Max knows that someday we will eat some of our laying hens, and he knows that part of the deal with getting rabbits is that we will eat the offspring. He has expressed an interest in seeing his food slaughtered, and yet I still feel the need to shelter him. But maybe I shouldn't: When we become so disconnected from the natural order of things, it ceases to feel natural.

Many vegetarians believe they cause less pain and suffering in the animal kingdom by not eating meat. What they may not realize is that millions of deer and elk are killed each year to protect those vegetable crops. Countless ecosystems, untold amounts of bird and insect life, are destroyed by monoculture farming of soy and legume crops to supply those meatless breakfast patties. So are they not killers too?

I'm not sure what the answer is, but I do know that we all affect the lives of other creatures every time we eat. I am at peace with that, because I know exactly what lives I have affected with my food choices. This particular rabbit and that specific pig. It's my fault they are dead, but my guilt stops with them. And I would not be able to say that if I didn't know everything about their lives and deaths. *(AC)*

· ·

OPPORTUNITIES FOR CHANGE
BACKYARD MEAT

Order chicks "straight run" (you'll receive both males and females), and eat the roosters.
Raise rabbits for meat.
Eat the offspring of your dairy goats.

· ·

rabbit

After exploring my inner butcher, I came to terms with the idea of killing my dinner. And I have to admit that being able to do that while the pan warmed was appealing in a French countryside sort of way. Forget to take meat out to thaw? Well then, how about rabbit tonight, dear?

The ancient Romans raised rabbits to eat, and you can too. Raising rabbits in a shady spot in your yard is a great way to optimize your growing space. Their feces provides valuable fertilizer and needs less time to age before you can use it in the garden. They are silent and easy to keep under the radar. Rabbits breed in minutes, and their gestation period is thirty days. You can breed the doe again sixty days after birthing, although frequent breeding will shorten her lifespan. If you breed continuously, you can have a new litter every three months, or about thirty-six offspring per doe per year. In seven to eight weeks you get small, tender rabbits best prepared by frying or broiling; in nine to thirteen weeks, you get larger ones for braising or stewing.

When selecting a backyard rabbit breed, strive for high meat-to-bone and feed-to-meat ratios, high milk production, and large litter size. New Zealand white and Californian rabbits, Silver Fox, Creme d'Argent, and Champagne d'Argent are great choices.

A raised rabbit hutch can work well inside a chicken run, since foraging chickens will benefit from the pre-digested alfalfa in rabbit droppings, and help eliminate any insect eggs or larvae. *(AC)*

what rabbits need

›   A predator-proof hutch, ideally with room for the rabbits to move about. As an alternative to the hutch, you can use hanging or stacking cages.
›   Protection from sun, wind, and rain. Clear fiberglass sheets or wood over the cages will help keep them dry. Rabbits overheat easily, so keep them out of afternoon sunlight.

Rabbit Hutch

You will require two such hutches.
(1 cage for buck, 2 cages for does & their litters,
 1 cage for everybody you haven't eaten yet)
Area below makes a great chicken run.

- A separate cage for the buck and another for each birthing doe.
- Plentiful, clean drinking water, covered to protect it from bird droppings. Large, hanging drip water bottles like those used in hamster cages work well.
- Organic alfalfa hay or pellets, along with fresh greens and a variety of rolled or cracked grains.
- A salt block for licking, if you are not feeding pellets that already contain salt.
- When kitting, a 12-by-18-by-12-inch nest box with a door cutout 4 to 6 inches off the bottom of the box, to prevent the babies from hopping out until they are big enough.
- The company of other rabbits. Rabbits don't need to share cages, but the cages should touch or be in close proximity to other rabbit cages.

producer profile: the unlikely rabbit farmer

In the wealthy Seattle suburb of Clyde Hill, you don't see many farmers. You'd have better luck finding local celebrities, like retired Mariners first baseman John Olerud. To all outward appearances, Brad Andonian fits right in. His wife, Karen, says that when she married him she saw him as a cashmere-wearing wine connoisseur.

But Brad's not your average owner of a luxury carpet store. Just listen in while his seven-year-old daughter, Caroline, does math homework at the kitchen counter: "We had six rabbits. And Daddy chopped off one rabbit's head, and now we have five rabbits."

When Caroline's friends come to visit, she takes them to see the bunnies. "Yes, they're very cute," she tells them. "And later, we're going to eat them."

Brad bought his first rabbits to cook for his wine group. The dinner went over so well, he started looking for more online. He found a used double hutch and twelve rabbits for eighty dollars. To keep the animals safe, he set the hutch in his garage. Rabbits are food for many predators, and so fear strangers; they can literally die of fright. A panicked doe can stomp her babies to death, thinking she's hiding them.

Brad worked to earn the rabbits' trust, handling them gently, slowing his movements, keeping visitors quiet. And one evening, as he sat silently in his garage watching the rabbits, he heard something unexpected: A tiny, repetitive squeak, almost inaudible. Brad was hearing the rabbit version of a cat's purr—the secret sound of happy rabbits.

Brad expanded his herd. He stacked cages in an old chain-link dog kennel behind his garage. The does gave birth to litters in old wine boxes they lined with straw. He learned to assess their diet by examining their droppings. He learned to find undernourished kits by touch, to help them find a nipple. He came to care deeply for his rabbits. At dinner parties, everyone wanted to hear all about them. "It sure is a lot more interesting than talking about carpets," he told me.

One night, Brad had a raging party at his house. People had a lot to drink. At one point in the evening, the party seemed strangely quiet. Brad had just begun wondering where his guests had gone when his neighbor staggered through the back door, leaned up against Brad, and slurred, "They're so-o-o-o-o *furry*".

You know how at most parties everyone ends up in the kitchen? At this party, they all ended up at the rabbit cages, petting the furry bunnies. Brad ran to the cages and cleared out the oblivious party guests, but it was too late: Five of his best does had died of fright.

After 9/11, Brad's mom wanted the family to purchase rural acreage as a sort of family retreat, just in case the world went to hell in a handbasket. Brad helped steer the family toward good farmland. He hoped to raise pastured beef there, to help pay for the land, but the rabbits changed all that. After getting some initial interest from gourmet restaurants for locally raised rabbits, Brad rewrote his business plan. He decided to raise only animals he

Brad and one of his rabbits.

could process himself on the farm. Although it limited him to bunnies and poultry, it meant less stress for the animals, as they wouldn't need to be trucked off to slaughterhouses. It also meant less stress on Brad, since it saved him from butcher's fees and complicated schedules. Scheduling was important, as he hoped to balance being both a luxury carpet salesman and farmer.

To learn more about farming, Brad took a course in small-farm management from Washington State University's agricultural extension. The instructors told him he'd need to go to all the farmers markets, he'd need to make sure he never ran out of product, he'd need to keep his table plump with inventory. That's when Brad raised his hand.

"I asked, 'So what do you do with all the food you don't sell?' And they said, 'Oh, you just give it to the food bank.' And I thought, 'What kind of a moronic business plan is that?' My idea is I show up at eight in the morning, I'm sold out at ten-thirty, and I'm home by noon. Why do I want to spend eight hours on my feet and go home with two-thirds of my product?"

Ignoring his instuctors' advice, Brad focused on selling directly to restaurants. "I want to make something they'll sell regularly. It's totally different from everybody else. I deliver fresh, I don't freeze. There's nobody else in my space doing this. That's my competitive advantage. So I get to name my price."

Brad has another business strategy: He doesn't invest in expensive farm machinery. His biggest investments have been a scalder and a plucker for processing chickens. Compare that approach with that of the grain farmer down the road from Brad's farm. "Eric probably has a quarter-million dollars in grain equipment. He has eleven tractors!"

Brad says that large debts for equipment limit a farmer's ability to try unusual things such as raising rabbits. So instead of buying tractors, he paid Eric to cultivate and seed his pasture. Today Brad's Abundant Acres Farm has expanded dramatically to include thousands of small animals, from rabbits to geese to chickens. By its second year of operation, he says, the farm will have paid off its startup costs. The income will pay the salary of an on-site caretaker, plus the monthly mortgage on the land. And all this at the end of only two years of farming—during a recession! The only thing his operation won't cover is the down payment on the land.

To achieve this sort of profitability, Brad must charge full price for his product. I told him sometimes it's tough to afford the best food. I get that Europeans spend a larger percentage of their money on food, but they don't pay such a high price for health care, either.

Brad makes no apologies for the price of good food. He believes you either pay for good food up front, or you pay for it later with your health. Still, he understands how such things can seem out of reach, so, where many farmers might tell us to leave the farming to professionals, Brad teaches city dwellers how to raise and butcher rabbits in their own backyards. "I think that people are crazy for not eating more like this. They should raise their own vegetables, they should raise some of their own meat. It's not just the fact that it's good for you as food, it's good for you as a person. You can have a sense of connection to where you come from, and a sense of fulfillment of creating something. And that's something that few people have in their life anymore."

A week after I heard these words from Brad, I met him in his South Lake Union carpet store, Pande Cameron. He led me past beautiful rugs to a small white Styrofoam cooler near the back door. He made quite a picture, standing there in his fine suit, holding a bag full of freshly butchered rabbits.

Every one of us faces barriers, impediments to good food. Sometimes it's money, sometimes it's social pressure. In recent decades, rabbits have been construed as low-class, as an indicator of financial desperation. Sometimes we need a luxury carpet salesman to remind us that quality is worth paying for. *(JM)*

cooking with rabbit

As with all grass-eating animals, rabbits have very little fat. To avoid drying them out, you need to cook them low and slow, with a little added moisture.

Brad's favorite rabbit recipe is adapted from the out-of-print *The Northwest Kitchen: A Seasonal Cookbook* by Judy Geise. He keeps a first edition in his kitchen, complete with beautiful *sumi* illustrations by George Tsutakawa.

Alsatian Rabbit

Makes 4 servings

> 1 savoy cabbage (about 3 pounds) cut into 1-inch shreds
> 5 tablespoons butter
> ½ cup diced bacon
> 1 fryer rabbit cut into pieces: 2 loins, 2 forelegs, 2 hind legs
> ½ cup flour heavily seasoned with salt, pepper, and paprika
> 2 onions, diced
> Salt
> Pepper
> 2 tablespoons plain flour
> 1 cup vermouth or white wine

1½ cups milk
2 tablespoons prepared mustard (preferably grainy)
Nutmeg to taste

1. Preheat the oven to 350°F.
2. Blanch cabbage by boiling in salted water for 5 minutes. Drain in colander and refresh under cold running water. Allow to drain well, and set aside.
3. In a heavy 12-inch skillet, melt 3 tablespoons of the butter over medium heat. Add bacon, and allow to brown and render completely. Remove solids with a slotted spoon and reserve. Leave fat in skillet.
4. Wash rabbit pieces quickly in cold water, and dry well. Dredge heavily with seasoned flour, shaking off any excess. Heat skillet over high heat, and put in only enough rabbit pieces to cover bottom. Brown well, turning only once. Continue until all pieces are browned. Remove and set aside, leaving fat in skillet.
5. Place one-half the onions and one-half the cabbage in skillet, and sprinkle with salt and pepper. Sauté over medium heat for about 10 minutes. Remove to a bowl

Eviscerating a rabbit.

and repeat with remaining onions and cabbage. Mix bacon pieces with cooked vegetables, and set aside.

6. In skillet, prepare a roux: Melt remaining 2 tablespoons butter, whisk in plain flour, and cook over low heat for 5 minutes, stirring well; do not brown. Add vermouth, and whisk in until there are no lumps. Stir in milk, and blend well. Stir in mustard, and season with nutmeg and salt.

7. Place one-half of cabbage mixture in a 4- to 6-quart Dutch oven. Mix in one-third of mustard sauce. Lay rabbit on top of cabbage, and spoon one-half of remaining sauce over it. Top with remaining cabbage and sauce. Casserole should be tightly packed.

8. Cover and bake for 1½ to 1¾ hours. Serve directly from casserole.

chicken

Raising chicken for meat can be as simple as buying your chicks "straight run," meaning not sexed. The industry often employs inhumane methods to destroy male chicks, knowing they are not allowed in cities, and by ordering them straight run you prevent that. Buy twice as many chicks as you plan to keep, assuming at least half, if not more, will turn out to be roosters. As they begin crowing, you can cull them as necessary. In six to fourteen weeks (depending on breed) you get small, tender fryers; in up to twenty-four weeks you get "roasters." As the roosters age, their meat will become tougher, but they can still be stewed low and slow until the meat falls from the bone. Older hens may also be cooked this way. *(AC)*

case study: cornish crosses vs. heritage birds
Kari and Beau Holsberry started raising chickens during the recent recession. Their family had been hit hard, and Kari found she couldn't afford organic chicken at the grocery store anymore. But she couldn't bring herself to buy the cheap chicken offered at door-buster prices: She knew too much about how that chicken was raised. So she decided to raise chickens, calculating that she could raise her own meat birds on quality organic feed for much less than she'd pay for good chicken at the grocery store.

When deciding which breed of chicken to grow, Kari chose the most popular meat bird in the country, a breed respected by the poultry industry for its unparalleled efficiency in converting feed into meat, the famous Cornish Cross. But soon Kari and Beau learned that the bird undermined the lessons they wished to teach their children. The Cornish Cross challenged the notion that all living things deserve respect.

Kari had ordered a few "heritage" birds too, birds that came from an older gene pool. At first, the Cornish Cross and heritage breeds appeared similarly cute and fuzzy. But when Kari gave them food, the differences became obvious. The Cornish Crosses went crazy, like sharks in a tank full of blood. "It was a feeding frenzy," says Beau. Three days later, Beau says, they were "orders of magnitude bigger" than the heritage chick. "I understand breeding something to bring out the best in the breed. We want bigger, fatter chickens. But these things are not bred to be healthy, they're bred to be big."

Kari and Beau concluded that the Cornish Cross chicks would have eaten all day and all night if they'd let them. Soon, Kari began to fear for the safety of the heritage chicks. "They were getting hurt and trampled by the Cornish Cross. We couldn't keep them together." Furthermore, as the Cornish Crosses grew, they became dirty. Their undersides became crusted with excrement. They didn't seem to understand the concept of a dust bath.

As the heritage birds grew, they learned to supplement their diet with bugs and leaves from the yard. The Cornish Crosses, in contrast, stayed huddled together when released from the coop. They moved only rarely, and when they did, they hobbled around on tiny legs barely strong enough to support their ballooning frames.

After they had slaughtered their first batch of chickens for meat, Kari and Beau repopulated their yard with heritage chickens. Unlike Cornish Crosses, heritage birds have good instincts. They know how to forage and bathe. They have a complex social structure. And they're full of personality.

Kari and Beau invited me into their backyard, where hens chase each other under hedges and roost on the children's play equipment. Kari scoops up an ornery hen. "We call her Bitchy Bonita," she says. "She goes around and just bitches at everybody." True to form, Bitchy proceeds to cluck aggressively in another hen's face when she's set down. Beau points out Roosty, the rooster grandfathered in before Seattle's rooster ban. "When we let him out in the morning, he comes flying out to see his girls. He puts his wing down, like a flamenco dancer, and dances around them in a circle. Usually the girls are like, 'Uh-uh, I'm outa here.'"

I wonder out loud what it would be like to put down birds with so much personality. Wouldn't that make the slaughter more difficult? Beau thinks for a moment. "Even though it'd be more difficult to put them down," he says, "I'd rather get chickens that I could respect."

When Kari first turned her backyard into a henhouse, Beau felt a little awkward in his new role as a farmer. He admired Kari for plowing ahead, but he did endure some teasing at work. Coworkers would say, "Here comes Farmer Beau," and he'd say, "Oh, yeah, whatever." But now he's kind of proud. "I say, 'Yeah, we raise chickens. And they're fun and they're

The Holsberrys with a few of their respectable birds.

funny.' And I've told them some stories. And I've had one or two people who have gone off to different areas. And they'll call me up and say, 'Hey, you know what I really miss? I miss us talking about the chickens. Do you have any good chicken stories?'"

Thanks to his heritage birds, now he can answer yes. *(JM)*

. . . .

CHOOSING A MEAT BIRD

Cornish Crosses were bred by the modern poultry industry to achieve the highest profitability within factory farm conditions. Before the rise of the Cornish Cross, all chickens were heritage birds, and most meat birds were culled roosters or old laying hens. Because heritage birds were expected to peck out much of their own sustenance on the farm, they retained many of their instincts for survival (which we humans see as "personality").

Many farmers will tell you they can't make a profit raising heritage birds. And while that may be true for large-scale commercial meat producers, whose chickens live in crowded warehouses, it's less true for small farmers whose small flocks can freely select much of their diet by wandering through the pasture, usually protected from hawks by mobile tentlike structures. In your backyard, you can supplement your chickens' diet with bugs, weeds, and (healthy) leftovers. The table below compares some of the Cornish Cross's traits with those of heritage birds.

Cornish Cross	Heritage Birds
Fastest growers (5–9 weeks)	Slower growers (16–18 weeks)
No foraging instinct	Strong foraging instinct
High feed-conversion ratio means less money spent on grain	Lower feed-conversion ratio, but can supplement diet by foraging if pastured
Limited nutrient value derived from grain feed	Diverse diet can produce meat that is more nutritious
Tender meat, but without much flavor	More flavorful meat
Poor hygiene	Strong grooming instinct
Health problems: weak legs, ruptured gall bladders, disease-prone	Generally healthier
Stupid: Basically just eat, drink, and sleep	Intelligent: More personality and social structure

. . . .

producer profile: Pasturized Sensations Farm

On a foggy Saturday one week before Thanksgiving, Paul Johnson and his three boys had set up an efficient production line. Austin (the youngest) stuffed turkeys into a metal cone with their heads poking out a hole in the bottom. They'd look around with curiosity at this new position—until Paul came over and sliced open their necks.

After they bled out, Ryan dunked them in the scalding tank and plucked them. He then handed them to Nick, who stood waiting with a very sharp knife. "We've never timed Nick on a turkey," said Paul. "But he eviscerated a chicken in forty-four seconds last week." As if on cue, Nick spun around and gently dropped a finished turkey carcass into a tub of ice water.

Paul took one of the turkeys that hadn't been slaughtered yet and set it on the grass, so I could watch it eat. Its breed was Broad Breasted White, the same kind used by factory farms.

"Why don't you grow heritage turkeys?" I asked.

"Most people buy a heritage turkey once. Heritage turkeys look different, you have to cook them different, there's less meat on them. After people try one heritage bird they go back to a regular turkey."

When it comes to meat farmers, there are many paths to perfection. Although Paul's farm doesn't grow the breeds I like, his birds enjoy unusually healthy diets.

First, there's the pasture. Paul estimates his Cornish Cross chickens get 15 percent of their food from the pasture, turkeys a little bit more because they're smarter. And while a heritage bird could find much more of its own food, for these birds, that little bit of green makes a huge difference in taste and presumably nutrition too.

That means, of course, that 85 percent of the birds' diets comes from grains. But this is where Paul rises from extraordinary to unique: He pays closer attention to grains than anyone else. To understand why, you need to know a little bit about how animal feed is formulated.

Chicken feed has two main components: grains and "premix." Premix is a powder containing the minerals, vitamins, and enzymes chickens need for a well-rounded diet. Most farmers buy chicken feed made from corn and soy, with the premix already added. But Paul's customers don't want genetically modified products (almost a certainty with corn and soy), so he sources his own grains locally, mostly wheat and barley from the Puget Sound region and field peas from the Palouse region of Eastern Washington. (A small bit of sunflower meal comes in from North Dakota.)

Most premixes are designed to complement corn and soy. Paul could do what most people do, that is, simply use the standard premix, knowing in his heart it's not the correct complement for his grains. But that's not good enough for him. He sends a sample of the season's grains down to a lab, which analyzes them to determine which minerals they're missing. Based on those results, Paul orders a custom premix to complement the grains he finds.

When it comes to sourcing ingredients for his chicken feed, Paul is a small fish in a sea full of whales. The agribusiness companies that supply big chicken farms don't have much interest in responding to his tiny orders. In fact, sometimes, when Paul is ready to close a deal, the supplier will finally realize Paul needs only a pickup truck's worth of grains rather than several train cars full, and will back out of the deal. So Paul has had to find larger buyers and piggyback onto their purchases. "Finding people to work with you is *hard*. And when you find the people, you pay them on time, you show up when you said you're gonna show up, because if you tick them off once, you can't replace them. They don't need you."

When Paul finds the product he needs, he has to act fast. "Because that's another thing that will tick them off. If you find a supplier, but you're not in a position to buy it when you ask for it, then all you are is a nuisance. You've got to be willing to pull the trigger on the deal. Which is hard, because sometimes I can only make this deal if I find the other things that need to go with it."

Paul Johnson prepares a turkey for plucking.

Juggling all those balls can be difficult, even for someone who comes from a marketing and logistics background like Paul. And so he's had to make some difficult business decisions, including the decision not to pursue "organic" certification. Paul doesn't raise organic chickens because he can't get organic field peas in this part of the country. And field peas are the only practical non-GMO alternative to corn and soy. Although he could find organic wheat and barley, Paul holds back on those, choosing conventionally grown grains instead. It doesn't pay, he explains, to be only half-organic. But he looks forward to the day when he'll be able to add "organic" to his labels too.

By selling his custom feed to backyard chicken owners, Paul has increased his clout as a grain buyer. Soon, he predicts, he'll be able to put together an order for thirty tons of peas a year. That's enough to persuade a farmer to grow organic field peas just for him.

Farmers like Paul walk a difficult road. They must balance the desire to run a profitable business with the impossible demands of consumers like me who want it all: heritage, organic, pastured, *and* affordable. They troll local online forums, doing damage control when consumers grow concerned over some rumor or another. They pick up odd jobs when the money gets tight. The year 2010 was a very hard one for Paul, and he had to take a job managing a Blockbuster video store. Luckily, the successful turkey harvest I was watching had allowed him to quit and return full time to farming.

"Retail sucks, doesn't it?" I confided.

He shook his head, visibly disgusted by the memory. "Never again," he said.

Meanwhile, Paul's son Austin was hard at work. "Dad, I've got another turkey for you," he said. A turkey's head looked up at Paul quizzically from the killing cone. He reached for the knife, and with one quick motion sliced through the bird's neck.

Paul had found his right place in the world. I looked over at his sons, each working a station in the slaughter operation, and I wondered if they felt constrained by this work, anxious to move into other lives, far away from the farm. I wandered over to the eldest, Nick, who seemed to be almost dancing as he eviscerated turkeys. He pulled out one of his earbuds so he could talk to me.

"I'm excited," he explained, "because my band just finished recording." They had cut an album, and Nick's band was starting to get gigs. Okay, I thought, he must be happy because he'll never have to touch another turkey or chicken carcass again.

"So is that your dream," I asked, "to take your band as far as it can go?"

"Well, the band is awesome and the band is fun. And if it goes anywhere, that would be great. But what I actually want to do is I want to cook. I've already taken two years of the culinary program at my high school and just fell in love with every second of it."

For fun, Nick brings his friends in the culinary program down to the farm. He says for many of them, it's a life-changing experience. Before they visit the farm, they may know how to cook a chicken or a turkey, but they have no idea what it takes to raise one. He pointed to the slippery carcass on the counter in front of him and spoke to it. "I know exactly where you were your entire life, I know exactly how you were treated, I know exactly what you ate. I can go and eat what you ate your whole life." He turned back to me. "And by the way, it doesn't taste bad. The chicken feed."

"Oh, you've eaten the chicken feed?"

"Yeah, the peas especially. You get some moisture up in them, let them soften up, and they're sweet."

After a moment, Nick admitted, "I guess part of the reason I'm out here is I get paid. But I take pride in everything that I work on. When I'm playing drums and I play something I couldn't have played six months ago, I feel really good about that. Or when I cook something great, it's the same feeling." He described with excitement a ravioli dish he'd made from scratch, rolling out the dough with a rolling pin. "I mean, nobody does that! And you know what else makes me feel good? I can butcher a chicken in forty-four seconds!"

That seemed too good to pass up. "Wait a minute," I said. "Did I just hear you compare the feeling you get playing a sweet drum solo to the feeling you get eviscerating a chicken in forty-four seconds?"

"Yeah," he answered, smiling. "I guess so."

Many farmers seek to achieve sustainability, to build something that will last beyond their years. But few farmers' dreams can survive the eviscerating scrutiny of a teenager. I caught Nick smiling many times during my visit, infecting those around him with optimism. He broke character only briefly—when he dropped his iPod into the icy water full of floating turkey carcasses. *(JM)*

YOU ARE WHAT YOUR ANIMALS EAT

Owners of backyard chickens tend to spend more money per bird on good feed than would a factory farm. And as the backyard chicken movement has grown, so has the number of small mills. These mills supply feeds of a quality agribusiness cannot match.

In the Northwest, one of the most prominent feed suppliers is Scratch and Peck. Diana Ambauen-Meade began her business in the backyard, using a borrowed cement mixer. Since then, she's expanded into her own mill in Bellingham, Washington. Today she sells fifty tons of feed every month.

Diana sells mostly organic feed and offers corn-free and soy-free versions for those concerned about contamination of organic crops by genetically modified crops. Of her ingredients, only the camelina seed is not certified as organic, and she's working on changing that.

At a recent workshop on growing grains in the Puget Sound region, Diana's son Bryon sat in the audience. After the workshop, many of the farmers in attendance gathered round him, anxious to meet the new buyer in the neighborhood. At that moment, I understood just how much of an impact backyard chicken owners can have on the agricultural community. We're just big enough to help organic grain farming establish a foothold.

Pastured Sensations Farm (see the profile on page 308) also offers locally sourced feed. As this operation grows, its owner hopes to achieve organic certification.

children, backyard chickens, and slaughter

At four years of age, my son Gavin's moral compass spun wildly. One day he accidentally smashed a spider on the sidewalk and burst into tears; another day, I found him in the garden squashing spiders with his fist.

How could I communicate to him that this was wrong, even as insects kill each other every day? "Gavin, it's okay for you to feed a spider to a chicken," I said. "But if you just squish the spider for no reason, it will have lived its life in vain." I struggled to put my feelings in words my son could understand. After a few curious questions, Gavin began to cry.

When he turned five, I felt Gavin could benefit from further clarification. I invited him to Kari and Beau Holsberry's house for a class in humane chicken slaughter. He accepted with enthusiasm. In the car, he asked many questions about the process. I described what I'd seen in cartoons, scenes involving a stump, an axe, and a chicken trying to escape a murderous farmer. I spoke of chickens running around with their heads cut off, and of Mike, the famous rooster who survived two years after losing his head to a poorly aimed axe. So much for drawing a bold line between life and death.

Kari brought out coffee and hot cocoa for her guests. She had raised twenty-eight Cornish Cross chickens from chicks, but now that they had reached slaughter age, she lacked the confidence to kill them herself. Her husband, Beau, wasn't any more enthusiastic and had refused to participate in the killing. "I was a real brat about it," he told me later.

So Kari turned the slaughter into a community event. She hoped the rest of us would give her the strength, or at least the willing hands, to dispatch her birds.

The guests chatted nervously until our instructor, Charmaine Slaven, appeared. With a gentle, confident tone, Charmaine described how to hold the birds tenderly, how to slice the jugular with a sharp knife, letting the birds bleed out so they might relax into death as into sleep.

A happy Lander with his chicken pal, Drumstick.

Gavin watched the first bird die, then said, "I don't want to see this." He retreated into Kari and Beau's basement to play video games with the other children.

An hour later the backyard had become a killing field. In one corner, the reluctant Beau had somehow been elected prime executioner. A small group scalded and de-feathered the birds. A third team disemboweled the carcasses, distributing organs and feet into aluminum pie pans. A light breeze spread the small white feathers across the yard.

While Charmaine had given us excellent instructions, she couldn't be everywhere at the same time. A number of us, convinced the knives were too dull, had foolishly opted to try a utility knife instead. The knife failed to cut cleanly through the skin, and the bird bled slowly. Beau shook visibly as he tried to cut deeper into the jugular.

At that moment, Gavin came out, along with Beau's ten-year-old son, Rees. He sidled up to me and stared into the open eye of the bird in Beau's shaking hands. "Is it dead?" he asked.

"Yes," I said, "the chicken keeps its eye open after it's dead."

The bird blinked, revealing the lie. Did Gavin see it?

"Dad," started Gavin, "can I play video games? They're playing Star Wars downstairs."

"Can you choose another game? That one's too violent," I said. You could cut the irony with a knife.

Beau's seven-year-old, Morgan, popped her head out the window, took one look, and disappeared for the rest of the day. Later, she told me the sight of chickens dying had made her feel "very bad." But our sons shared an interest in how things work, and over the next hour, Gavin and Rees increased the length of their visits to the yard. By the time I was ready to leave, Gavin didn't want to go home. I took him around the yard to peer into the different pie pans. I showed him a muscular gizzard full of grain, a tiny heart, intestines. I picked up a foot and pulled the tendon, drawing the yellow claws into a fist.

On the ride home, I asked Gavin questions, trying to divine his emotions. I had wanted to show Gavin something black-and-white, to illustrate clearly the difference between needless violence and violence with a purpose. Instead, he had seen our concern, our discomfort.

I shared this memory later with Kari and Beau over coffee. Beau told me that the day after the slaughter, Rees had asked him whether his role as executioner had been easy, or hard. "And I told him it was very hard. I told him it was emotionally draining on me to have to do that." Somehow, showing that vulnerability to Rees gave Beau the critical tools he needed to teach his son about violence.

"We weren't just killing these chickens because it was a cool part of a game," Beau told him. "Or because we just wanted to kill them to see what would happen. This has a reason behind it. It's not okay to raise your fist in violence for any reason other than taking care of yourself and your family. Protecting yourself or feeding yourselves."

Now, when Rees asks him whether he can play an especially violent video game, Beau confidently tells him no. And until Rees shows Beau he has the right perspective on violence and can discuss what's right and what's wrong, the answer will remain no. Surprisingly, Rees accepts this explanation.

"I'm sure it's different for every parent," said Beau. "And every relationship is going to have a different dynamic. But for me and Rees, it helped us to come to an understanding." He said he wouldn't have been able to express his point clearly had he not gone through with the slaughter. Nor did he think Rees would have understood, had Rees not been his witness. "This was basically a life changer."

I'm not certain I did the right thing by bringing my son to a chicken slaughter. But for all the moral ambiguity I revealed to him, in the conversations that followed I believe he's heard one consistent message: Violence wounds us all, no matter which end of the knife you face. And so we wield that knife carefully. *(JM)*

how to slaughter a rooster or old hen

Slaughter doesn't have to be a traumatic experience. I like to hold the bird tightly and speak gently throughout the process, as this comforts the bird. I keep my knife sharp, so the bird feels little pain. Slaughtering it upside down allows it to bleed out quickly and slip almost immediately into unconsciousness.

If you don't feed your bird for 24 hours before slaughter (water is fine), you'll have an easier time removing the crop and intestines. In backyard flocks, such confinement isn't always possible.

slaughter

1. Add ½ teaspoon of dishwashing soap to a large pot of water. Heat the water to about 150°F, then turn the burner to its lowest setting. Prepare a very sharp kitchen knife or #12 surgical blade (this blade has a hook shape). From a nail on a fence, hang a short piece of string with a slipknot on the end. This lasso will secure the bird's feet. (As an alternate method, you can span a bamboo stick between two chairs and hang the rooster by the feet from the stick using zip-ties).
2. Once you have the bird's feet secured, let the bird hang upside down. With one hand, hold down the head by placing your thumb under the beak, exposing the neck just below the jaw. You may use your body or arms to restrain the wings and hug the bird. Alternately, you can restrain the bird's wings by tying a rag around its body.
3. With your free hand, pick up the knife and slice the neck in a deep, diagonal slash just below the jaw. If you've sliced deep enough, the bird will immediately begin to bleed freely and will begin to black out from lack of blood to the brain. A second symmetrical cut on the other side of the jaw will help speed the blackout. Keep the head held down and the wings restrained until the bird is still. Don't be surprised if the dead bird flaps a couple times; this is a natural convulsion.
4. Take the temperature of your water. It should be 150°–155°F. If it's too hot, add tap water and stir until it hits 150.
5. Scald the bird to loosen the feathers. Hold it by the legs under the soapy water for 30 seconds, swishing it around to help the liquid penetrate the feathers and reach the skin. After this, pull the bird out and test to see how easily the feathers pull out. If you can't

pull them out, return the bird to the water for another 30 seconds, this time ruffling the feathers underwater with a wooden spoon to help the water get through.

6. Pull off the feathers in handfuls, reserving them for the compost pile. Plucking a chicken can take up to 15 minutes per bird, sometimes longer if your bird has many pinfeathers. Dunk again in the water as required.

7. If you're doing more than one bird, you may need to reheat the water every two birds or so.

evisceration

1. Prepare two or three bowls next to a cutting board, one for the waste parts and one or more for any secondary parts you wish to keep.

2. Cut off the head with a large knife and place it in the waste bowl.

3. Cut off some of the bird's neck skin until you can fish out the crop, a grain-filled sack between the skin and upper breast where the bird stores food before passing it to the gizzard. Sometimes you can pull this free by pulling on the esophagus, which formerly connected the crop to the mouth. At other times you must get your fingers around it and work it free. (It's okay to tear or sever the tube that connects the crop

Slaughtering a pair of roosters.

to the gizzard.) You can pull the gizzard out from the top of the bird now, or pull it out from the bottom later—it doesn't matter.

4. Cut off the legs at the joint, working the knife between the bones in the "knee." Chicken legs make excellent stock, so you may wish to keep them.

5. Cut off the small visible gland on the top of the bird's tail.

6. Place the bird on its back. Squeeze the tail and anus between your thumb and finger (you will be gripping to the left and right of the anus), so that the bird's skin bulges just above this area. Make a deep horizontal cut just above your hand. This should get you into the body cavity without cutting through the intestines, something you must work hard to avoid. If you do cut the intestines, just clean things up as best you can—it's not the end of the world, just messy and somewhat unsanitary.

7. Make vertical cuts to either side of the anus, looking through the hole you've already made to verify that the knife stays clear of the intestines.

8. Make a horizontal cut between the anus and the tail. Carefully work around the anus until you can remove it completely. As you carefully pull it away from the bird's body, the intestines will trail with it. Carefully place all the guts in the waste bowl.

9. Reach inside the body cavity and pull out everything you find in there. You'll have to scrape the lungs off the back near the spine. But don't throw everything away: You can fry and eat the liver and heart, and you can stew the muscular gizzard after halving it, emptying it, and removing the tough inner lining. The waste can be buried 12 inches deep in the garden or fed back to your other hens (creepy but okay).

10. Wash the bird inside and out, and dry it well with a towel. It should relax in the fridge for 24 hours before you freeze or cook it. *(JM)*

Cock 'n' Beer

Makes 4 servings

When my wife and kids leave town for the weekend, I pull a rooster from the freezer and cook up a batch of "Cock 'n' Beer." I came up with this recipe one night while staring at Greg Atkinson's excellent *coq au vin* recipe. I couldn't bear to pour all that wine on the bird. This hot and spicy variation appeals to my manly side and brings back memories of Mexican mole. *(JM)*

> 1 rooster, skin on
> 4 slices smoked bacon, chopped coarsely
> 1 tablespoon plus 1 tablespoon butter
> ½ teaspoon salt, plus more to taste

Roosters ready for cooking.

1 onion, halved and cut in thick slices

1 whole head garlic, cloves mashed with a cleaver or other heavy knife, and peels removed

1 tablespoon finely chopped chipotle peppers, or more to taste

1 tablespoon unsweetened cocoa powder

1 bottle beer (stout, porter, or even IPA)

2 to 4 cups low-salt or unsalted beef, pork, chicken, or other type of stock

½ cup heavy cream (optional)

Fistful of flat-leaf (Italian) parsley, chopped

1. Preheat oven to 250°F.

2. Pluck and gut rooster, and let meat relax and dry out in refrigerator for one or two days under a dish towel. For a frozen bird, allow at least 24 hours under a towel to thaw and dry out.

3. Cut off legs and wings. Rub them and rest of bird with coarse salt. Make sure entire bird will fit into your Dutch oven or cast-iron pan. If body is too big to fit, cut in half alongside spine. Set rooster pieces aside.

4. In the heavy pan, brown bacon in 1 tablespoon of the butter. When bacon has rendered about halfway and is still chewy, remove with a slotted spoon and set aside.

5. Brown rooster pieces in bacon fat and butter mixture, skin side down, a piece or two at a time. Set browned meat aside.

6. Add other tablespoon butter, and sauté chopped onions over medium-high heat. Cook until nearly browned, or until translucent if you prefer a French onion soup sweetness. Add garlic, then chipotles, and finally cocoa powder, stirring for about 1 minute.

7. Add beer to deglaze pan, then add about 2 cups of stock and cream (if using). As mixture warms, taste for salt. It should be mildly salty; if not, add salt sparingly, as liquid will concentrate during cooking.

8. Place rooster pieces in pot, skin side up. Add stock as necessary until meat is about three-quarters submerged. Scatter cooked bacon over exposed pieces, cover pot, and bake for about 4 hours. To serve, scatter chopped parsley liberally across open pot. Serve as you would a stew: in a bowl, with rustic bread, or over rice.

• •

CLOSING THE CIRCLE ON GOATS

In order to produce milk, a female goat must kid every year or so. While any resulting baby female goats (called doelings) can often find homes with new backyard goat keepers, males (called bucklings) are much less popular. A few lucky males find homes with brush-clearing companies, and others end up on distant farms. But sooner or later, supply is bound to outstrip demand. We're going to have to start eating them.

Like all lean meats, goat makes an outstanding meal if cooked low and slow in a slightly acidic liquid. Some parts of five- or six-month-old goats are tender enough to be cooked at higher temperatures. Many people claim goat burgers beat beef hamburgers any day of the week. The bones can be used for stock. You can even tan the hides and make rugs, blankets, or belts.

• •

ducks and more

Raising ducks for meat can be just as simple as raising chickens. In fact, since male ducks (called drakes) don't crow, you can keep one for breeding stock and skip mail ordering, hatching your own instead.

While chickens tend to go broody and remain on the nest for twenty-eight days to hatch eggs, ducks make notoriously bad mothers. They rarely stay on the nest long enough to

Ducks patrolling a lawn for slugs and worms.

incubate the eggs themselves, so you will most likely need to buy or borrow an incubator or broody hen to hatch any ducklings. Hatching eggs is a delightfully fun project for kids (and adults) and eliminates the travel-induced stress that mail-order chicks can have.

Ducks are like cattle dogs—they need a job to do or they soon get into trouble. If your yard is big enough and full of slugs and caterpillars, then ducks may work out for you. I have learned the hard way that ducks can be treacherous to lawn areas and, to that end, your marriage. My delight with backyard ducks was quickly eclipsed upon discovering that in the span of just a few short, unsupervised hours, my small flock managed to turn a 45-square-foot area of sodden, patchy grass into one gigantic squelching puddle of mud. My husband, who had spent hours cultivating grass in that high-foot-traffic area with poor drainage, was not at all happy. So even though ducks contribute far more whimsy and entertainment value than chickens, I plan to focus my future meat-raising efforts on chickens and rabbits. *(AC)*

pigeons and doves (squab)

The pigeon family includes both pigeons and doves. Their offspring are known as squab and can be processed for meat at around four to six weeks. Colonizing Romans built dovecotes (special structures for raising pigeons) throughout Europe and the Middle East. Pigeons and doves provided a major source of protein in times of famine as recently as the Great Depression in the United States and in wartime England. Pigeons grow quickly and are easily domesticated, striking out to find their own food during the day but returning home each night.

But because you can't control the diet of a free-ranging pigeon, you may want to build a predator-proof aviary or get large cages for them. Pigeons and doves mate for life, so you will need one male for each female. The incubation period is about eighteen days, and they continue to lay a new batch of eggs every three to six weeks. Because squab are so small, you should plan on either having several pairs of laying birds or processing the squabs and freezing them until you have enough to make a full meal. *(AC)*

backyard fish and aquaponics

Here's another radical idea: backyard fish. You don't need a full-sized pool to raise your own fish. You can use a decommissioned hot tub, a rigid plastic swimming pool, or even a fifty-five-gallon drum to grow tilapia, trout, freshwater mussels, freshwater prawns, or crayfish.

Tilapia can survive at water temperatures of 60°F but grow fastest when it is above 80°. They need a good source of oxygen, so you will need an aquarium pump or a garden water fountain and a tank filter. An outside greenhouse or three-season sun porch with a downward pointing floor lamp and grow bulb can provide elevated temperatures as well as plenty of lighting to grow algae and duckweed for the fish, in addition to giving you a great place to grow your tomatoes, peppers, and basil. Beyond algae and duckweed, goat and rabbit droppings (rich in protein, fat, and carbohydrates) can supply the rest of the tilapia's nutrients. Tilapia, like rabbits, are coprophagous, meaning they eat feces but because of the acidity of their stomachs are in no danger from bacteria or parasites. Keeping a well-aerated compost pile or large rocks inside the greenhouse, or painting the tilapia tanks black will help trap and retain the sun's heat into the evening hours.

Aquaponics combines both aquaculture (the farming of aquatic organisms, such as fish) and hydroponics (growing plants in water without soil) to create a fully integrated system. Plant beds are suspended above the fish tank. Water from the fish tank is carried up into the plant beds, where nutrients from the fish waste are removed (filtered by gravel, used by plants) before the water is returned to the fish tank. With enough fussing you can grow just about any kind of plant this way, but the simplest systems grow plants that naturally prefer wet roots, such as watercress. *(AC)*

• •

LIST OF EDIBLE WATER PLANTS

Cranberries	Spatterdock	Water chestnuts
Duckweed (to feed the	Sweetflag	Water lettuce
tilapia)	Vietnamese cilantro	Watercress
Perennial or wild rice	Water celery	Water spinach

• •

chapter 16
beverages and syrups

Thinking back on how many boxes of juice, bags of cough drops, and bottles of vitamin C I used to buy each winter is embarrassing now. The packaging, the sugar, the chemicals, all so unnecessary.

Most of these I now make from honey and foraged fruit. I've found the syrups in particular are excellent substitutes for cough drops, with rosehips providing vitamin C and elderberries providing immunity-boosting qualities. So if you are looking for a nudge to swap your soda habit for juice, or want to incorporate more natural remedies into your medicine cabinet, I hope this chapter will provide it. *(AC)*

BEVERAGES

annette's grocery list

ORIGINAL LIST

Apple juice
Elderberry syrup
Grape juice
Tea
Vitamin C

REVISED LIST

Elderberries*
Local apples*
Local grapes*
Local organic honey*

*If you grew or foraged these items, there would be no revised list!

OPPORTUNITIES FOR CHANGE
JUICES

◌ Buy local fruit juices, ciders, and wines.

◌◌ Make your own cider, fruit juices, and wines using fruits from local farms.

◌◌◌ Make your own cider, fruit juices, and wines from fruits you forage or
grow yourself.

. . . .

producer profile: Wade Bennett

If you buy your apple cider from the grocery store, it may taste just fine. But if you buy it from the farmers market you may run into a farmer like Wade Bennett, and if you're a gardener or a foodie, he can teach you things you'd never learn at the grocery store.

The farmers market is more than a place to get fresh, local food. It's also a motor for agricultural innovation, a great exposition of the region's terroir.

Farmers must constantly innovate to stay ahead of the competition. The most profitable crop is the crop that no one else is growing, but that everybody wants. Many farmers become experts in crops that conventional wisdom says cannot be grown here. And while conventional wisdom can sometimes save us the heartache of failure, at other times it is just plain wrong.

Farmer Wade grows apples and makes apple vinegars and ciders. But like many small farmers, he experiments regularly with new crops and techniques in order to reach new customers. This makes him a fantastic resource for horticultural knowledge. Think figs won't ripen here? Wade harvests bushels every year and sells them to restaurants. Want to know which varieties of bamboo shoots you can eat? Wade will gladly tell you, as he maintains a small forest of edible bamboo on his farm.

Wade figures every small farmer needs one big idea every three to four years; that's about how long it takes other farmers to figure out what you're doing and saturate the market with competition. At any moment, Wade has several irons in the fire, any of which could become his next big idea. For example, he grows local tea; it's expensive, but he suspects people are finally willing to pay for it. On trees with three-inch-long thorns, he grows the hardy citrus called yuzu. "It's sour as hell," he explains, "but great for juicing and zesting."

A small farmer's innovations can't stop with the crops. Farmers like Wade also make political change. On any given day, Wade is as likely to be testifying before a city council or state legislative body as he is to be harvesting his crops. He wants to be allowed to sell hard liquors such as apple brandy directly to consumers. He wants tasting rooms in farmers markets where he can offer samples of hard cider and fruit wines.

One day, Annette approached this affable farmer at the market. She had recently embarked on a quest to grow her own food, and asked about what she might realistically grow. On that winter day, the weather was bad and the customers were few. Not the kind of day that might inspire you to plant a garden. But the ebullient Wade Bennett filled Annette's head with visions of local tea leaves, peppercorns, hardy ginger, and local citrus. In short, he transformed her understanding of this climate from one of limitation to one of great possibility.

It's true that local farmers can provide us with great local food. But they can also provide us with a deeper connection to the land by expanding our understanding of what we can grow. *(JM)*

Wade sends apples to the cider press at Rockridge Orchards.

beverage and syrup recipes

Apple or Pear Cider

In the fall, you frequently can find apple and pear trees loaded with ripe fruit for the taking. Cider is a great way to use up less-than-perfect fruit. Cider is juice's unfiltered, unsweetened counterpart, with a purer fruit flavor.

Making apple cider.

Although you can make cider by straining mashed apples through cheesecloth, a cider press allows you to make large batches. Small presses cost a few hundred dollars, or you can make your own. My friend Wally uses a refurbished garbage disposal to mash the pulp, and he made his own press out of laminated plywood and screws.

To prepare the fruit, simply clean it well and remove any bad spots; the cheesecloth should filter out hidden bugs. Cut the fruit into slices and use a potato masher, food processor, or refurbished garbage disposal to sauce them. Line the press with fine cheesecloth, and press until cider runs out.

To can the cider, heat it to 190°F over medium-high heat—don't let it boil—and maintain that temperature for 5 minutes. Following the directions for water bath canning on page 227, give it ¼ inch headspace and process for 10 minutes.

· ·

OLD ORCHARDS MAKE GOOD CIDER

Annette and I decided we'd bring canned cider to our annual barter fair, so we took our two families to an old pioneer orchard, now part of a city park. A few decades ago, the trees languished under a mountain of blackberry brambles. Today, each tree bears a small sign identifying the heirloom apple variety. The volunteer organization that maintains the trees lets you harvest these apples, so long as you wait until after the group's annual cider-making festival.

"I found a dessert apple over here," I called out from the top of a tree. The kids came running to the base of the tree, holding up their cardboard boxes to catch apples as I threw them down. Annette's husband, Jared, lifted their youngest son high into the air so he could pick apples "all by himself."

Back at home, we made cider in the backyard. Our kids took turns cranking the handle on Annette's cider press, watching with fascination as the giant screw drive pressed sweet juice from the mash. They held their cups beneath the spout and drank with obvious pleasure. To them, this was much more than juice. It was something they had made. *(JM)*

· ·

Unsweetened Grape Saft

All over Sweden in the summer, you can see people hunting elderflowers and wild berries to make saft, a concentrated syrup that is added to water to make a beverage. Typically, Swedes use a large amount of sugar, which helps keep the syrup shelf-stable without canning. I prefer instead to use fruit whose syrup can be drunk unsweetened if diluted in enough water. Instead of canning the saft, you can freeze it in ice cube trays, to add later to water or smoothies.

1. Clean grapes, berries, plums, or rhubarb.
2. Place fruit in a large, nonreactive stockpot and add just enough water to cover. Bring to a boil while crushing with a potato masher. Reduce heat, and simmer for about 30 minutes, until juice has been fully extracted.
3. Layer a colander with cheesecloth, and place over a deep bowl. Pour fruit into colander. Let drain for about 10 minutes, then tie four corners of cloth over a wooden spoon or a faucet. Suspend cheesecloth bag over bowl to drain, undisturbed, overnight.
4. To can saft, heat to 190°F over medium-high heat—don't let it boil—and maintain that temperature for 5 minutes. Following directions for water bath canning on page 227, give it ¼ inch headspace and process for 15 minutes.

Variation: Sweetened Saft. Weigh the strained liquid, add an equal weight of sugar after straining, and cook until sugar is dissolved.

Verjus

Makes 2 cups

Verjus was widely used in the Middle Ages and has a sour flavor that is a perfect stand-in for lemon juice in most recipes. It's a great use for those grapes that don't ripen in our cool maritime summers.

While you can use any kind of distilled alcohol to make it, I love the fruity taste that apple brandy imparts. And someday, when Wade Bennett is able to sell his apple brandy, I will make this with all local ingredients. You can omit the alcohol and vinegar, but the mixture will last only a few weeks refrigerated if you do.

½ cup whole unripe grapes
1 cup juice from unripe grapes, filtered through cheesecloth
½ cup distilled alcohol
½ cup good-quality apple cider vinegar (at least 5 percent acidity)

1. Prick grapes with a fork, and place in a quart Mason jar. Add grape juice, alcohol of choice, and vinegar.
2. Cover with a homemade fermentation lid as described in the fermentation section of Chapter 12, or fasten cheesecloth over mouth of jar with a rubber band. Let sit

in a dark spot until all solids and impurities have settled on the bottom. Strain out sediment, and store in an airtight jar in a dark cupboard.

Dandelion Coffee
Makes none, and you'll be glad about that. Trust me.
Last year I was determined to kick the coffee habit. I knew it was the right thing for the planet: Demand for coffee is speeding up the destruction of rainforests, increasing the use of synthetic fertilizers and pesticides, and, thanks to both the poisons and the destruction of habitat, endangering wildlife populations. Tremendous amounts of resources go into curing and drying the beans, and then of course there is the packaging and the shipping.

Dandelions are plentiful and local, and I knew that they had traditionally served as coffee substitutes during times of war. So in the spring I dug up some dandelion roots, scrubbed them carefully, and roasted them in the oven to caramelize and develop their nutty flavor. Then I ground them up in the coffee grinder and made my brew. My husband watched with a knowing smile, declining a cup when it was ready.

I took that first sip and spat out the mouthful. So. Not. Worth. Drinking! I vowed instead to drink more tea. *(AC)*

Tea
In addition to growing your own tea bush *(Camellia sinensis)*, you can make your own tea from all manner of garden plants.

Spend some time scanning ingredients in the herbal tea section of the grocery store, and you'll get an idea of what combinations may be worth trying. For example, a blend of chamomile flowers, mint, and lemon balm produces a near exact replica of Sleepytime tea. Other common ingredients are rosehips, raspberry or blackberry leaves, elderberry flowers, hyssop, lemon verbena, jasmine flowers, currants, and rose petals.

The tea plant, *Camellia sinensis,* grows up to Zone 8, which means it's well suited to our maritime climate. It's an evergreen shrub that makes an attractive landscaping plant. It wants well-drained, slightly acidic soil.

To make white tea: Steam the fresh leaves for about 30 minutes, then dry them. You can do the steaming in a rice cooker or pan with steamer basket, and the drying either in a dehydrator or on a cookie sheet in the oven. (Preheat to 250°F, place the cookie sheet with steamed leaves in the oven, then turn off for a few hours. Repeat the process, stirring the leaves, about 4 times.)

To make green tea: Skip the steaming and follow the drying instructions.

Homegrown tea.

To make black tea: Black tea is fermented before drying. Put fresh tea leaves in a casserole dish or jelly roll pan, and add water to cover. Leave on the counter overnight. In the morning check for signs of bubbles. Your goal is to lightly ferment the tea, which can happen in 8 to 12 hours, depending on your house temperature. Once the tea begins smelling like black tea, strain the leaves through a sieve, pat them as dry as you can get them with a dish towel, and dry them according to the above instructions. *(AC)*

Black Elderberry Syrup
Makes 3 cups
Black elderberries are one of those "wild" foods that pharmaceutical companies are scrambling to market, in light of evidence supporting its effectiveness at boosting the immune system. You can grow your own black elderberries *(Sambucus nigra canadensis)*, or you can order them dried. If you are picking berries from your own bushes, be careful to collect only the berries, as the stems and bark are poisonous.

1 cup fresh black elderberries, or ½ cup dried
2 cups water
1 cup honey

1. Place berries and water in a heavy-bottomed saucepan, crushing berries with a potato masher or large wooden spoon. Bring gradually to a simmer and continue simmering for 30 to 45 minutes.
2. Strain with a sieve or cheesecloth-lined colander. Combine strained liquid with honey, and bottle. Store in refrigerator for 2 months, or in freezer indefinitely. During cold and flu season take 1 teaspoon twice a day.

Rosehip Syrup

Rosehips are purported to have 60 percent more vitamin C than citrus fruits. They also grow well in our climate and come from beautiful plants. Because vitamin C is destroyed by heating, I prefer to make a simple rosehip syrup that isn't cooked and doesn't contain processed sugar.

The biggest rosehips come from the plant *Rosa rugosa*, which is frequently used in landscaping, making them easy to forage. They make delicious jams and teas. Pick them after the first frosts, when they have begun to soften just a bit. The fruits are full of seeds, so don't expect a large yield of juice.

To make the syrup, grind the fruit in a food mill until you have extracted most of the juice. Mix the juice with equal parts honey, if desired, and freeze it in ice cube trays. During the winter, add one cube to a mug of warm water for a soothing, vitamin C–filled drink.

chapter 17
soaps and other sundries

After finally whittling down my grocery list, I realized that the only things left on it were not groceries at all. They all fit into the inedible category: dish and laundry soap, cleanser, bar soap, lotion, lip balm. It frustrated me to have to make a special trip to the grocery store to buy these things, so I set about figuring out how to make them myself.

It turned out not only that they were easy to make, but I already had most of the ingredients in my pantry. Soon I knew exactly what substances my skin was drinking up in the form of lotions and soaps, and what made up the residue I was sending down the sewer. Instead of my bathroom smelling of bleach after cleaning, it smelled of lavender. And I noticed that our garbage and recycling had all but disappeared. *(AC)*

SUNDRIES

annette's grocery list

ORIGINAL LIST

Bar soap
Bleach
Dish soap
Lip balm
Lotion
Mouthwash
Scrubbing cleanser
Toothpaste
Underarm deodorant
Window cleaner

REVISED LIST

Baking soda
Beeswax (unless you have hives!)
Coconut oil
Essential oils
Hydrogen peroxide
Lye
Olive oil
Salt
Vinegar

. . . .

OPPORTUNITIES FOR CHANGE
REDUCE WASTE

🗑 Make your own household cleaning supplies.
🗑🗑 Make your own cleaners and bar soap.
🗑🗑🗑 Make your own cleaners, bar soap, and personal care products.

. . . .

making soaps

Making your own soap is both fun and frugal—and homemade soaps make great gifts. It's also another way to use any animal fat that you may have. I promise your soap will not feel or smell porky at all! I've even made soap from bacon grease (after first cleaning it), and it came out lovely and fresh.

In the following recipes, you can use any combination of oils in place of part or all of the animal fat. Coconut oil, palm oil, almond oil, olive oil, and cocoa butter all make great bar soap. Replacing a few ounces of the oil with beeswax in place of some of the oil will make your bar of soap harder, so it lasts longer. Use oil infused with fresh herbs, flowers from your garden, or dried flowers to add natural scent or healing properties to your soaps (see "Infused Oils," below).

When making soap, always add the lye (sodium hydroxide) to the liquid. If you add the liquid to the lye, it may erupt and splash on you. Lye is caustic and can cause burns, so wear gloves, goggles, and long sleeves, and be sure there is good ventilation. The process of cooling the lye can take as long as an hour. Once the lye has sufficiently bonded with the fats and liquid (through a process called saponification), it is completely consumed, leaving a soap bar free of lye and gentle on the skin.

I have carefully proportioned the following recipes so that the fat-to-lye ratio ensures that no lye remains in the mixture. However, some lye could remain on your immersion blender or in your bowl, so make sure both blender and mixing container are exclusively dedicated to soap making. Stick blenders are inexpensive to buy new (although you may be able to find one at a thrift store), and the money you save making soap will offset the expense.

Soap molds can be as simple as clean milk cartons or yogurt containers, or rectangular glass casserole dishes lined with wax paper. Soap needs to cure for several weeks in order to complete the saponification process.

Save any scraps or trimmings for making liquid soap or soap jelly. You can use this soap jelly to clean just about anything, including dishes and laundry. Because it's chemical free, it is suitable for greywater that can be used in the garden. *(AC)*

Goat Milk Soap

A combination of goat's milk and oatmeal makes a wonderfully gentle and soothing soap, perfect for the most sensitive skin. Partially freezing the goat's milk will help keep the temperature low and ultimately make a lighter-colored bar of soap.

Equipment

> Gloves and safety goggles
> Immersion blender (one used exclusively for soap making)
> Large nonreactive bowl or pot (also dedicated to soap making)
> Grain or coffee grinder for grinding the oat groats or oatmeal
> Mold to shape your bars. This can be clean milk cartons or small yogurt containers
> Wax or parchment paper
> Knife for cutting the bars

Ingredients

> 14.5 ounces lye (sodium hydroxide)
> 30 ounces partially frozen goat's milk (do not substitute cow's milk, since it will turn orange)
> 48 ounces animal fat (lard or tallow; see recipe on page 292)
> 48 ounces coconut or olive oil*
> ¼ cup honey
> 2 ounces beeswax
> ½ cup oat groats or oatmeal, ground to a fine powder

1. Wearing goggles and gloves, combine lye and goat's milk. (I prefer to do this outside.) The mixture will immediately heat up and may sputter so stir slowly and carefully. Allow mixture to cool to 115°F.
2. While lye and milk are cooling, gently heat fat, oil, honey, and beeswax until no lumps remain. Allow oil to cool to 115°F.
3. Combine lye and milk with melted fat, oil, and wax, being careful not to splash. With immersion blender, mix until you achieve "trace." This means soap resembles thick cake batter and, when drizzled on surface of mixture, leaves a trail that does

not immediately sink in. If you don't achieve trace within 15 minutes, let mixture rest for 15 minutes and then blend another 5 minutes. Repeat process as many times as necessary.

4. In the meantime, prepare your molds. You can use yogurt containers (your soap will get sliced into rounds when done), cardboard milk cartons with the tops cut off, or small rectangular cardboard boxes or drawer storage trays lined with wax or parchment paper.

5. Add ground oatmeal and stir gently until thoroughly incorporated and distributed.

6. Pour soap mixture into prepared molds. In 2 to 5 days, it should be firm to the touch and ready to cut. Remove from molds, slice off thin layer of powdery white soda ash that formed on surface, and trim any uneven edges. Cut into bars, and stand bars up with some space in between to complete curing process, about two weeks.

Use 100 percent animal fat for a lower-sudsing soap.
Variation: Substitute distilled water for the goat's milk, eliminate the honey and oatmeal, and add 40 grams store-bought essential oil, or substitute infused herbal or floral oils for part of the oil in the recipe.

Soap Jelly
Soap jelly is a liquid soap you can use for washing hands or for hand-washing dishes and clothes. You can make soap jelly from the trimmings and scraps of your homemade soap. And because it's homemade soap rather than commercial soap, you can safely recycle your bathwater or dishwater for use in your garden. To make soap jelly, combine one part soap trimmings or scraps with one part hot water and stir until the soap pieces are completely dissolved.

infused oils

Making your own infused oils requires nearly no active time, but it lifts your soaps, lotions, and salves to the next level. Infused oils also make for a luxurious bath or can be used directly on the body after bathing to keep skin moist.

To infuse oil, simply fill a jar with dried leaves, roots, or flowers, cover them with oil, and let them sit on the counter for a few weeks, gently swirling the jar once a day to speed up the process. Once infused, strain out the plant matter with a cheesecloth-lined sieve, and store the oil in a sealed jar in a dark cupboard until you are ready to use it.

Lavender, rose geranium, rose, lemon verbena, lemon balm, rosemary, magnolia blossom, jasmine, and mint add wonderful scents, while chamomile, comfrey, calendula, borage, and plantain are all soothing to the skin.

. . . .

PLANTS TO GROW OR FORAGE FOR INFUSING OILS

Borage	Dandelion	Mint
Calendula	Lemon verbena	Plantain
Chamomile	Lavender	Rose
Comfrey	Mallow	Rosehips

. . . .

lotions, salves, and balms

Making your own lotions and salves is fun and rewarding. They make thoughtful gifts and can be infused with flowers or healing herbs from your own garden.

Either make your own infused oils (see above) or purchase essential oils to add at the end of the mixing process. They are all lovely: Citrus and mint scents are uplifting, whereas lavender and geranium are calming. My favorite plants for infusing are chamomile, comfrey, and calendula, with their soothing, anti-inflammatory properties. At the height of the gardening and canning season, I soothe my hands with chamomile and comfrey lotion and apply peppermint lotion to cool my hot, aching feet.

While it is possible to mix your lotion with a regular blender or food processor, an immersion blender makes it a cinch. I use a recycled quart yogurt container for both mixing and storing, eliminating a lot of clean-up work.

Making lotion is essentially the same process as making mayonnaise: suspending tiny particles of oil in water. The beeswax or emulsifying wax helps stabilize the mixture and prevent separation. You can use any kind of oil, or combine various types. Distilled water will give you the longest shelf life; plain filtered or tap water work too, but your cream or lotion will develop surface mold sooner. Keeping it refrigerated also helps extend shelf life.

Basic Lotion Recipe

Here's a basic formula for a nice, thick lotion. The choice of individual ingredients is up to you, but stick with these ratios and you'll get good results. This makes great handmade

Chamomile flowers for tea and lotion.

gifts when poured into half-pint jelly jars. Decorate them with raffia and flowers or sprigs of greenery from your garden.

Equipment

> A double boiler of some kind (this can consist of a large glass measuring cup sitting in a water bath, or a smaller saucepan that fits into a larger one)
> Scale
> Immersion blender
> 3 ounces solid oil (coconut oil, cocoa butter, or shea butter)
> 6 ounces liquid oil (olive oil, almond oil, jojoba oil, sunflower oil, including infused oils)
> 1½ ounce beeswax, shaved or grated, or emulsifying wax pellets, or a combination of the two*
> 8 ounces distilled water
> essential oil (optional)

1. Combine solid oil, liquid oil, and beeswax in top of double boiler. Over medium heat, stir until oils and wax are melted and thoroughly blended.
2. Remove top saucepan or cup, and let cool to body temperature, stirring occasionally to keep oil and wax mixture smooth.
3. When oils have cooled, warm distilled water to body temperature. Pour water into a tall container, and, with immersion blender set to Low, slowly add oil to water in a thin stream. After a few minutes of mixing, a cream will begin to form. Initially it will look like milk curdling, but a little more mixing will produce a nice, smooth lotion.
4. Add essential oil, if using, a few drops at a time until it's scented as much as you like. Feel free to divide lotion into a few bowls and scent each one differently.

Substituting emulsifying wax for some of the beeswax helps make the lotion more stable.

salves and lip balms

Salves and lip balms are even simpler than lotions and creams, because you don't add water. Simply melt wax and liquid oils together in a water bath, add essential oil if you like, and pour the mixture into a convenient container—recycled breath mint tins work perfectly.

Adjust the hardness of your salve to suit you:
› 4 parts oil to 1 part wax = medium soft (my favorite consistency)
› 3 parts oil to 1 part wax = medium hard
› 2 parts oil to 1 part wax = very hard

Salves make wonderful additions to your medicine chest. Menthol and eucalyptus (the active ingredients in Vicks VapoRub) are great for breaking through foggy congestion, while plantain makes a soothing balm for bug bites and rashes.

For lip balm, recycle your lip balm tubes, and choose good-tasting oils or extracts like peppermint or vanilla. To recycle lip balm tubes, simply wash empty tubes in warm, soapy water and let dry completely, then pour the melted salve solution in. Mixture will harden as it cools.

personal care and household cleaners

By equipping yourself with a small arsenal of essential oils and a few specialty items, you can turn the contents of your pantry into the kinds of products that take up multiple aisles at the drugstore or grocery. For containers, recycle your food or lotion bottles, and repurpose a spray bottle.

Little if any of the planet's resources go into manufacturing, distributing, marketing, or developing (which may include animal testing) these homemade products, and there are no bottles to recycle when you use them up. It really doesn't get much more sustainable than that—and you can't beat the price.

If stored properly, essential oils will last for years. You can buy them at almost any health food store, but I've found the quality of oils from Mountain Rose Herbs to be amazing, and they don't have those NOT FOR HUMAN CONSUMPTION warnings on them. That's nice if I plan to use them in a toothpaste or mouthwash.

personal care products

All-Purpose Facial Oil

This is especially great for skin that is dry or rosacea prone.

> 2 tablespoons sweet almond, olive, or apricot oil
> 1 teaspoon jojoba, borage seed, or carrot oil, or any combination
> 10 drops evening primrose oil
> 15 drops German chamomile essential oil
> 5 drops lavender or geranium essential oil
> 5 drops palma rosa oil

Mix all ingredients well. To use, spray clean face with a lavender or rosewater spritzer (a little essential oil with distilled water in a spray bottle), then gently massage in oil. Blot any excess with tissue after a few minutes (but it seems to soak right in for me).

Toothpaste

> 2 tablespoons baking soda
> ½ teaspoon salt
> 10 to 20 drops essential oil such as clove, cinnamon, or mint
> Liquid stevia to taste

Combine all ingredients, and brush with zeal!

Tooth Powder

> 2 tablespoons baking soda
> ½ teaspoon salt

Combine all ingredients, and sprinkle on toothbrush as needed.

Mouth Rinse

Shot glass (about 1 fluid ounce) water

1 to 2 drops clove or mint essential oil

Combine, gargle, and spit.

Spray Deodorant

¼ cup vodka or witch hazel

¼ cup water

10 drops tea tree oil

20 to 40 drops essential oil of your choice. (Lavender, rose geranium, clary sage, vanilla, clove and citrus are all nice. Juniper, fir, sage, and bay laurel are more masculine.)

Mix all ingredients well. Apply as needed with a small spray bottle.

Cream Deodorant

Coconut oil

Baking soda

Blend equal parts coconut oil and baking soda into a paste. Apply lightly as needed.

household cleaning products

Disinfectant/Cleaning Spray

Dash soap jelly (recipe page 336) or dish soap

2 tablespoons vodka

5 ml lavender essential oil

5 ml niaouli essential oil

5 ml lemon myrtle essential oil

3 ml oregano essential oil. (You can use pine if you like, but I abhor that pine smell!)

32 ounces filtered water

Combine all ingredients well. Apply with a spray bottle.

Note: Because essential oils are so concentrated they are nearly always measured in milliliters and most bottles contain 15 ml. There is no need for exact measurements in this recipe—simply eyeball ⅓ of the bottle.

Air Fresheners

Add drops of essential oil to water to get the strength and scent you love, and spray with abandon (avoiding eyes!). You can also place the liquid in a shallow bowl of pebbles with a bamboo skewer to act as a wick to scent the room. Essential oils can be applied to scent pine cones or dried flowers and placed in a bowl, potpourri-style. Or, some stores sell plug-in air fresheners with blank filters—try applying your own essential oils.

Kitchen Counter and Sink Disinfectant

According to a study at Virginia Tech, spraying hydrogen peroxide followed by vinegar is just as effective at killing germs as chlorine bleach.

Scratch-Free Scrubbing Cleanser (Baking Soda)

Pour baking soda into an old spice shaker and use with abandon. I once used a "bleach stick" to clean the grout between my bathroom floor tiles. When it didn't work I tried baking soda. The baking soda actually did a better job!

Window and Glass Cleaner (Vinegar)

Pour into a spray bottle. Vinegar does a great job of cleaning windows without streaking or leaving buildup. The smell disappears in minutes.

where did all the garbage go?

And Man created the plastic bag and the tin and aluminum can and the cellophane wrapper and the paper plate, and this was good because Man could then take his automobile and buy all his food in one place and He could save that which was good to eat in the refrigerator and throw away that which had no further use. And soon the earth was covered with plastic bags and aluminum cans and paper plates and disposable bottles and there was nowhere to sit down or walk, and Man shook his head and cried: "Look at this Godawful mess." —Art Buchwald, 1970

According to EPA figures, the average American generated 2.7 pounds of municipal solid waste per day in 1970. In 2005 that number was 4.7 pounds. While we can point to increases in recycling and diversion of food waste into composts, the truth is that those processes are powered by huge amounts of petroleum and coal: petroleum to run the garbage and recycling trucks to cart those items to the recycling plant, petroleum, and coal- or nuclear-generated electricity to convert them into usable mediums.

Meanwhile, things that are not recyclable go into landfills or incinerators, polluting the soil, water, and air. And that's not even taking account of the energy that went into mining and manufacturing the packaging or additives in the first place.

As you begin making the items in this book, you will notice your garbage and recycling dwindle rapidly. Many cities have options for smaller-sized garbage cans, while more rural areas allow you to cancel your garbage service altogether. In addition to saving the planet, you can save on garbage service as well.

10 SIMPLE WAYS TO REDUCE WASTE

1. Make food from scratch, choosing seasonal produce from local farms. Bring your produce home in reusable cloth bags or baskets instead of plastic.
2. Buy bulk grains and beans. Bring your own reusable containers.
3. Store leftovers in reusable glass canning jars or bowls.
4. Plant a garden or a container. Even the smallest, partly shaded area can support lettuce and herbs that you would normally buy packaged.
5. Get a green cone, a worm bin, or chickens for disposing of table scraps.
6. Start a compost pile for yard waste.
7. Make some of your own personal-care products. Put them in recycled containers.
8. Buy only natural fiber clothing. Learn to mend it, and then compost it at the end of its life.
9. For gifts, try giving services or homemade food or personal-care items, rather than conventional consumables.
10. When shopping for new items, first check thrift stores or Craigslist.

annette's grocery list

Apple juice

Applesauce

Bacon

Baking powder

Baking soda

Bar soap

Barbecue sauce

Bleach

Bread

Breakfast cereal

Butter

Canned tomatoes

Cheese

Chicken nuggets

Crackers

Croutons

Dish soap

Dried fruit

Eggs

Elderberry syrup

Flour

Fresh and dried herbs

Fresh, canned and frozen fruit

Frozen pizza

Frozen waffles

Fruit leather

Grape juice

Ham

Herbal extracts and essential oils

Honey

Hot dog buns

Hot sauce

Ice cream

Jam

Jelly

Jerky

Lip balm

Lotion

Lunchmeat

Kefir

Ketchup

Meats from unknown ranchers

Milk

Mouthwash

Mustard

Oatmeal

Pancake mix

Pasta sauce

Pepper

Pickles

Rabbit meat

Relish

Salsa

Salt

Sauerkraut

Sausages

Scrubbing cleanser

Sour cream

Sugar

Tea

Toothpaste

Underarm deodorant

Vitamin C

Window cleaner

Yeast

Yogurt

annette's grocery list

Alfalfa for goats and rabbits

Baking powder

Baking soda

Black sunflower seeds for goats and rabbits

Chicken feed

COB (corn, oats, barley) for goats

Coconut or olive oil

Elderberries (unless you grow or forage your own)

Essential oils

Half pig, from a local farmer

Hydrogen peroxide

Lemons

Local grains

Local peaches and apricots (since they are hard to grow here)

Lye

Meat chickens, from a local farmer (unless you eat your roosters)

One-time purchase of canning, drying, and fermentation equipment

One-time purchase of yogurt and buttermilk cultures

One-time purchase or gifting of kefir grains

One-time purchase of Flora Danica and mesophilic cultures

One-time purchase of fruits and berry root stock, seeds, peppercorn, and tea plants, and beehives

Quarter cow, from a local farmer

Rennet

Salt

Sausage casings (unless you save your pig or lamb intestines)

Sugar

Vegetable seeds

Vinegar

Yeast

annette's calendar
WINTER

JANUARY

Preserve lemons

Make lemon, orange, and lime
marmalade and freeze cubes of
juice for summer jams

Start seed lists

Order seeds!

Start tomatoes and onions indoors

FEBRUARY

Start cole crops indoors

Start new cover crops, chicken
forage, peas, and wild greens
outdoors

Make onion jam

MARCH

Take inventory of canned and frozen
goods

Host spring barter

Make IPA

Get new chicks and ducklings

Start potatoes, carrots, and beets
outside

Celebrate equinox!

annette's calendar
SPRING

APRIL

Pickle or ferment asparagus

Make rhubarb jam

Freeze rhubarb juice for summer soda

Move tomato starts outside under protection

Start carrots, parsnips, radishes, dill, and cilantro outside

Fertilize strawberries, raspberries, and blueberries

Hill potatoes

MAY

Start squashes, beans, and corn

Dehydrate spring herbs and tea leaves

Make herbal tinctures

Order lamb, pig, and cow

Forage for mushrooms and nettles

Hill potatoes

JUNE

Harvest early potatoes

Make strawberry jam and dehydrate strawberries

Pickle hardy ginger shoots

Pickle or freeze peas

Make raspberry jam and freeze berries

Celebrate solstice!

Start winter crops in trays

Pickle and ferment beets

Hill remaining potatoes

annette's calendar
SUMMER

JULY

Take out pea vines and feed to goats

Dry mustard seeds

Pickle and ferment remaining spring carrots, drench beds with beneficial nematodes, and start winter carrots

Make crab apple pectin

Make applesauce from early apples (ginger gold, king or lodi)

Dehydrate and can cherries

Can peaches and peach salsa, dehydrate apricots, and make preserves

Direct sow remaining winter crops

Braid garlic, dry onions

Dry mint, lemon verbena, lemon balm, chamomile, echinacea, jasmine flowers, and elderberry flowers and raspberry leaves for winter teas

AUGUST

Forage for elderberries and sumac, make syrup

Make zucchini relish, bread and butter pickles, and kosher dills

Can, ferment, or freeze eating beans, dry shelling beans

Freeze or dehydrate blueberries

Harvest late potatoes and peppercorns

Can or dehydrate tomatoes; make tomato sauce and ketchup; ferment salsa

Go blackberry picking and make blackberry jelly or syrup

Make plum jam and dehydrate plums

Plant turnips, rutabagas, and cover crops or chicken forage

Pick up frozen chickens from farmer

Pick up lamb from butcher

SEPTEMBER

Ferment or can pickled or roasted peppers, red chile sauce, hot sauce, and fermented green tomato enchilada sauce

Make beet and carrot kvass, sauerkraut, and kimchi

Take out zucchini, beans, and tomato vines; feed to goats and rabbits

Store winter squash, potatoes, onions, and garlic in garage

Amend strawberry bed and cut down fruited raspberry canes; compost both

Make apple cider

Can grape juice and dehydrate grapes

Make kiwi jam and dehydrate kiwis

Dry and store almonds and hazelnuts

Press sunflower oil or dry flower heads to save seeds

Celebrate equinox!

Pick up pig and cow from butcher

Make and can bone broth

Stuff sausages

Cure bacon, ham, and prosciutto

Smoke butt and other cuts

Render lard and tallow

Harvest hops

Make cheese!

Smoke feta and chipotles

annette's calendar
FALL

OCTOBER

Make winter soap and lotion

Make beeswax candles

Forage for rosehips; make rosehip jam and honey

Mulch strawberries

Plant new fruit trees and vines

Store apples and pears in garage

Start Christmas beer

Make chow chow

Make mustard

Plant crocus for saffron, garlic, shallots, and onions

Make apple butter

Attend fall barter fair

Move red wiggler worms inside

Start indoor mealworms for winter chicken feed

NOVEMBER

St. Martin's Day—eat goose!

Make pumpkin butter

Make gingerbread houses

Host Jul gift barter

Forage for medlar, make paste or jam

Prepare Thanksgiving Feast

DECEMBER

Make applesauce and apple jelly with any apples starting to dry out

Bake Lucia Bullar and celebrate Santa Lucia

Prepare Jul foods ahead of time; pickle salmon, make meatballs, prepare Johanson's frestelse, make crackers and bread

Celebrate solstice!

one front yard and one pantry at a time

Annette

During the past year, I made more than sixteen hundred pancakes, a hundred loaves of bread, and eighty pizzas. I milked Mona the goat and slaughtered Chubby the pig, as well as various chickens and rabbits. I grew over four hundred and sixty pounds of produce; collected more than a thousand backyard eggs; stuffed twenty-five pounds of sausages; cured eighteen pounds of bacon; put up two hundred and fifty jars of preserves; pressed twelve wheels of cheese; scooped thirty pints of chèvre; cultured twenty-six gallons of yogurt, buttermilk, or kefir; mixed one and a half gallons of herbal tinctures or medicinal syrups; and made sixty bars of soap and twelve jars of lotion. I transformed my urban house into a pre-industrial farm.

It hasn't been easy.

The sheer number of hours I spend preparing food for my family has, at times, seemed absurd even to me, and has definitely shocked others. But what I've found is that with experience, I've become efficient and organized. I remember as a child watching my grandmother effortlessly glide through her tiny kitchen, preparing food, hand-washing dishes, and cleaning up in a few swift and graceful movements. I thought she was magic (I still think that).

But I've discovered in the same way that tying a shoe feels impossible to a preschooler but is second nature to an adult, coordinating kitchen experiments, preparing meals, and managing a kitchen garden and livestock have become second nature to me. I can't imagine not having chickens, a garden, orchards, ducks, and bees. Why would I want to? They take such little effort once established and provide so much pleasure and flavor. It's hard to be stressed out when a parade of ducks waddles past my window. That cackle from the backyard means there are fresh eggs waiting to be collected whenever I need some fresh air. And someday, when I get dairy goats, that bleating will mean it's milking time.

It is possible to farm in the city, on a scale that is manageable. You can have it all without significantly changing your lifestyle. But after tasting the farming life that I've revered since early childhood and visits with Grandma, I decided that I actually want to change my lifestyle. I can grow enough produce and eggs and dairy on my city lot to support my family, but I want to do more than that. I want to support other families making this same journey. And to do that, I feel I need more than my one-fifth acre to help others successfully farm on their one-fifth acre…

In the past, we had to choose between city and country, or split the difference and live in the suburbs. But by connecting with farmers, I've learned that a food community can span the divide between city and country. I now consider many of my farmers my friends. And I have learned that leaving the city doesn't have to mean leaving my community behind.

While looking for land to support a COA (Community Owned Agriculture) project I was planning with some fellow urbanites, I stumbled across a log home on 5 mostly wooded acres outside the city. It's not at all ideal farmland. The elevation is 400 feet. It's shady. There will be early fall frosts and late spring ones. There will be snow. There will be deer and bears and moles. Yet those challenges are not dissimilar to city ones: I'm trading marauding dogs and raccoons for bears, crows and slugs for deer and moles, a yard shaded by neighboring buildings for deep forest.

I'm leaving the security and community of my city, which scares me a little. But inviting other families to come farm with me makes the change seem less intimidating. These families—my urban farming community—will provide me a lifeline back to the city, while I will be giving them the opportunity to raise their own meat and dairy animals without drastically changing their urban lifestyles. I'm looking forward to expanding my experiments with intense orchards, early and ultra early varieties of vegetables, and most of all, my perpetual garden. I'm excited to work out the kinks in the COA model so that it can become something truly replicable anywhere. So even though I am moving to the country, my central goal remains the same—to do as much as I can to strengthen food communities and food security in the city, one front yard and one pantry at a time.

We need community, not only to change the world, but for support: support in finding small farmers, support while learning new skills, support for changing existing food paradigms, both for ourselves and our extended families. It's through the support of community that we learn to make the most of our space in the city, no matter how small (or how large) it may be. It's through the support of community that we learn to change our eating habits.

According to Joel Salatin, the fastest way to change the current food system is to opt out of it completely. It's not easy. But with community, it can be cheap and fulfilling and tasty. And you can be the one who changes things.

a question answered

Joshua

When I tell people that we're grinding our own wheat, slaughtering our own chickens, and buying directly from farmers instead of shopping at grocery stores, they often ask, Is it worth it?

That is a tricky question to answer because the answer isn't something you can lay out in a clear, cost-benefit analysis. My family now eats better food for less money, but we also work harder to get that food. If this were just about the food, I'd burn out. But it's not just about the food.

Throughout the writing of this book, I've found inspiration in the stories of others, in the experiences we've shared together. I've met people who've taught me how to feel passion for my food. I've met farmers visionary enough to grow food answerable to their consciences. I've met friends and neighbors who've found ways to get that food despite significant obstacles. When all these people gather together, it feels like a movement. That's significant because movements are fueled by optimism. And in an age when environmental disaster looms over the horizon, when we still bear bruises from the economic recession, optimism is a precious thing.

One of the most optimistic people I met was Patricia Stambor, a woman who chose to grow a teeny tiny field of spelt farro (a grain) in her urban backyard. We didn't include a profile of her in this book because the reward for growing a backyard full of grains (a few loaves of bread, a few pilaf dinners) didn't seem worth the labor or the garden space. On the surface, growing grains would appear to be *not worth it*.

But somehow, I can't stop thinking about Patricia. For Patricia, it's not just about food. Though she first grew backyard grains on a whim, she soon found it stirred up strong memories from her childhood in the fertile rolling hills of southeastern Washington's Palouse region. She recalled the smell of a freshly shorn wheat field spiked with the faint scent of chamomile (a garden escapee). She could distinguish between the feel of wheat stubble and soft field peas under bare feet. She now associates these sensations, burned into her brain, with a period in her life of complete freedom. During those summers, she wandered fields alone, or sometimes accompanied by a horse or a good friend. She discovered abandoned apricot trees and ate their delicious fruit until reaching her fill. She encountered coyotes and feared for her safety. From those independent explorations, she emerged a woman.

Now, she has children of her own, whom she hopes to imbue with a similar sense of freedom and optimism. Her son, Alex, and daughter, Olivia, watched the grains grow in her backyard and developed an interest in plants. Olivia went on to an internship with Bluebird Grain Farms, a local grower of heritage grains. Though Olivia now explores her environs by city bus rather than by horse, and though she now pursues a career unrelated to food, the explorations she shared with her mother created a common language between the two, a language in which the smell of grain and the smell of freedom are intermingled. In short, it brought them closer together.

As human beings, we have an obligation to share what we love with the people we love. If we love food, we can show our children, our spouse, our friends and relatives, our neighbors and our community that food can be a wonderful thing. It needn't be something sterilized and frozen in a supermarket freezer; it needn't be endlessly refined and pasteurized, powdered and reconstituted, pickled by preservatives, or marketed by charismatic cartoon characters. Food doesn't have to be that bad. When finely raised and finely wrought, food achieves a higher value. It is alive, not only biologically, but semantically, as each meal carries with it a story—a story steeped in our values, a story that communicates who we are and where we fit in the larger world. These stories have allowed me to feel at home in the city.

For me, this was a big change. I finally recognized its significance when Annette decided to give up her place in the city and move to rural Carnation, Washington. When Annette told me the news, I expected to feel torn up inside—torn up by my competing desires to live both in the country and in the city. But instead, I felt strangely at peace. "You know what's weird?" asked Emily, when I told her about Annette. "I don't feel the least bit jealous."

When I think back to the days Emily and I used to spend searching the internet for rural real estate, zooming high over the farmland from the comfort of our web browser, that period seems so long ago. Since then, all these stories, all these labors and layers of meaning piled on top of our food—they've complicated but also enriched our lives.

With each story, we send down a root. Grow enough roots and you will find yourself at home, where you stand.

plant lists for the pacific northwest

edible plants

☼ Full Sun   ◐ Part Sun   ● Shade   P=Perennial   R=Reseeds

Common Name	Scientific Name	Light	Life	Edible Parts / Use
Agretti (land seaweed)	Salsola komarovi	☼		Leaf
Akebia (chocolate vine)	Akebia quinata	☼/◐	P	Fruit
Alexander's seeds (black lovage)	Smyrnium olusatrum	☼/◐	P	Leaf, seed
All field berries	Rubus arcticus x stellarcticus	☼		Fruit
Amaranth	Amaranth Opopeo	☼		Flower, leaf, seed pod
Anise hyssop	Agastache foeniculum	☼		Flower, leaf, tea
Apple	Malus spp.	☼/◐	P	Fruit
Aronia	Aronia melanocarpa	☼/◐	P	Fruit
Artichoke, globe	Cynara scolymus	☼	P	Flower
Arugula	Eruca sativa	☼/◐/●	R	Flower, leaf
Asparagus	Asparagus officinalis	☼	P	Shoots
Bamboo	Phyllostachys	☼	P	Shoots
Barberry	Berberis vulgaris	☼/◐	P	Fruit, tea
Barley	Hordeum vulgare	☼		Seed
Basil	Ocimum basilicum	☼		Leaf, flower
Bay laurel	Laurus nobilis	☼	P	Leaf
Beans, fava	Vicia faba	☼		Fruit
Beans, pole and bush	Phaseolus spp.	☼/◐		Fruit
Beans, yard long (asparagus)	Vigna unguiculata	☼/◐		Fruit
Beebalm	Monarda didyma	☼/◐	P	Flower, leaf, tea
Beetberry (aka strawberry spinach)	Chenopodium capitatum	☼/◐/●	R	Leaf, fruit
Beets	Beta vulgaris	☼		Leaf, root
Bittercress	Cardamine hirsuta			Leaf
Black hawthorn	Crataegus douglasii	☼	P	Fruit
Blackberries	Rubus spp.	☼/◐/●	P	Fruit
Blueberries	Vaccinium spp.	☼/◐	P	Fruit
Borage	Borago offinalis	☼	R	Flower, leaf
Broccoli	Brassica oleracea, botrytis	☼		Flower, leaf
Broccoli raab	Brassica rapa var. cymosa	☼/◐		Flower, leaf
Broccoli, perennial	Brassica oleracea botrytis aparagoides	☼/◐	P	Flower, leaf
Brussels sprouts	Brassica oleracea, gemmifera	☼		Flower, leaf
Buckwheat, perennial	Fagopyrum dibotrys	☼/◐	P	Leaf, seed
Burdock (Gobo)	Arctium spp.	☼/◐	P	Flower, leaf, root
Cabbage	Brassica oleracea, capitata	☼		Leaf
Calendula	Calenula officinalis	☼	R	Flower
Camas	Camassia quamash	☼/◐	P	Root
Cardoon	Cynara cardunculus	☼	P	Leaf
Carrots	Daucus carota var. sativus	☼/◐		Root
Catsear	Hypochoeris radicata			Flower, leaf
Cattail	Typha angustifolia	☼/◐	P	Root
Cauliflower	Brassica oleracea, botrytis	☼		Leaf, flower
Celeriac	Apium graveolens var. rapaceum	☼		Leaf, flower, seed, stalk
Celery	Apium graveolens var. secalinum	☼/◐		Leaf, flower, seed, stalk
Chamomile	Matricaria recutita	☼/◐	R	Tea
Cherry	Prunus spp.	☼	P	Fruit
Chervil	Anthriscus cerefolium	☼/◐	R	Leaf
Chestnut	Castanea	☼	P	Nut

Common Name	Scientific Name	Light	Life	Edible Parts / Use
Chickweed	Stellaria spp.	☼/◐/●	R	Leaf
Chicory	Cichorium intybus	☼/◐	R	Leaf, root
Chinese dogwood	Cornus kousa	☼/◐	P	Fruit
Chives	Allium schoenoprasum	☼/◐	P	Bulb, flower, seed, Stem
Chives, garlic	Allium tuberosum	☼/◐	P	Bulb, flower, seed, Stem
Cilantro/coriander	Coriandrum sativum	☼/◐	R	Leaf, seed
Claytonia	Claytonia perfoliata	☼/◐/●	R	Leaf
Clover	Trifolium	☼/◐/●	R	Flower, tea
Collards	Brassica oleracea, acephala	☼/◐		Leaf
Corn	Zea mays	☼		Fruit
Cornelian cherry	Cornus mas	☼	P	Fruit
Cranberry	Vaccinium (trilobum, macocarpon)	☼/◐	P	Fruit
Cranberry, highbush	Elaeagnus multiflora	☼	P	Fruit
Cress, garden	Lepidium sativum	☼/◐	R	Flower, leaf
Cress, garlic	Peltaria alliacea	☼/◐		Flower, leaf
Cress, land	Barbarea verna	☼/◐		Flower, leaf
Cucumber	Cucumis sativas	☼		Fruit
Cumin	Cuminum cyminum	☼		Flower, leaf, seed
Currant, black	Ribes nigrum	☼/◐/●	P	Fruit
Currant, red	Ribes rubrum	☼/◐/●	P	Fruit
Dandelion, common	Taraxacum officinale	☼/◐/●	R	Leaf, root, flower, tea
Dandelion, garden	Cichorium intybus	☼/◐/●	R	Leaf, root, flower
Daylily	Hemerocallis fulva	☼/◐	P	Root, leaf, flower, pollinator
Dill	Anethum graveolens	☼	R	Leaf, flower
Echinacea	Echinacea purpurea	☼	R	Flower, medicinal
Edamame	Glycine max	☼		Fruit
Eggplant	Solanum melongena	☼		Fruit
Elderberry, black	Sambucus nigra	☼/◐	P	Flower, fruit
Elderberry, blue	Sambucus caerulea	☼/◐	P	Flower, fruit
Endive	Cichorium endivia	☼		Leaf
Fennel	Foeniculum vulgare	☼/◐	R	Bulb, seed, stem
Fig	Ficus carica	☼	P	Fruit
Flying dragon	Poncirus trifoliata monstrosa	☼	P	Fruit
Garlic	Allium sativum	☼		Bulb, seed, stem
Ginger, hardy	Hedychium	●	P	Flavoring, shoot
Goji berry	Lycium barbarum	☼/◐	P	Fruit
Good King Henry	Chenopodium bonushenricus	☼	R	Flower, leaf
Gooseberry	Ribes uva-crispa	☼/◐	P	Fruit
Goumi berry	Elaeagnus multiflora	☼	P	Fruit
Grape	Vitis vinifera	☼	P	Fruit, leaf
Groundcherry	Physalis heterophylla	☼	P	Fruit
Hazelnut (a.k.a. filbert)	Corylus spp.	☼/◐	P	Nut
Honeysuckle	Lonicera caerula edulis	☼	P	Flower, fruit
Horseradish	Armoracia rusticana	☼	P	Flavoring
Huauzontle	Chenopodium nuttalliae	☼		Leaf
Huckleberry	Vaccinium (ovatum, parvifolium, ovalifolium, membranaceum)	☼/◐/●	P	Fruit
Jasmine	Jasminum officinale	☼/◐	P	Flower, tea
Jeruselem artichoke	Helianthus tuberosus	☼/◐	P	Root
Jostaberry	Ribes spp.	☼/◐	P	Fruit

Common Name	Scientific Name	Light	Life	Edible Parts / Use
Jujube	Ziziphus zizyphus	☼	P	Fruit
Kale	Brassica oleracea, acephala	☼/◐/●	R	Flower, leaf
Kale, tree	Brassica oleracea ramosa	☼/◐	P	Flower, leaf
King's spear	Asphodeline lutea	☼/◐	R	Flower, leaf
Kinnickinnick (bearberry)	Arctostaphylos uva-ursi	☼	P	Fruit
Kiwi, fuzzy	Actinidia deliciosa	☼	P	Fruit
Kiwi, hardy	Actinidia arguta	☼	P	Fruit
Kohlrabi	Brassica oleracea, gongylodes	☼		Leaf, root
Lambs quarters	Chenopodium album	☼/◐/●	R	Leaf, seed
Lavender	Lavandula spp.	☼	P	Flower, leaf
Leeks	Allium ampeloprasum	☼		Bulb, leaf
Lemon balm	Melissa officinalis	☼/◐	R	Leaf, flower, oil, pollinator
Lemon verbena	Aloysia triphylla	☼		Leaf, flower, flavoring, oil
Lettuce	Lactuca sativa	☼/◐	R	Leaf
Lingonberry	Vaccinium vitis-idaea	☼/◐	P	Fruit
Lovage	Levisticum officinale	☼/◐	P	Leaf, stalk
Mâche	Valerianella locusta	☼/◐	R	Leaf
Magentespreen	Chenopodium giganteum	☼/◐	R	Leaf
Malabar spinach	Basella alba	☼/◐	P	Leaf
Mallow	Hibiscus syriacus	☼	P	Tea
Marjoram	Origanum majorana	☼/◐	P	Flower, leaf
Maypop	Passiflora incarnate	☼	P	Flower, fruit
Medlar	Mespilus germanica	☼	P	Fruit
Melon	Cucumis melo	☼		Fruit, seed
Mint	Mentha spp.	◐	P	Leaf, tea
Mitsuba	Crytotaenia japonica	☼	P	Leaf
Mulberry	Morus alba or nigra	☼	P	Fruit
Mullein	Verbascum thapsus	☼/◐	R	Tea
Mushrooms		●	P	
Mustard	Brassica spp.	☼/◐	R	Leaf, seed
Nasturtium	Trapaeolum minus	☼	R	Flower, leaf, seedpod
Nigella (black cumin)	Nigella Sativa	☼		Seed
Oats	Hulless Oats - Terra	☼		Seed
Oca	Oxalis tuberose	☼/◐	P	Flower, leaf, root
Onion	Allium cepa	☼		Bulb, leaf, seed
Onion, Egyptian perennial	Allium cepa proliferium	☼	P	Bulb, leaf, seed
Onion, multiplier	Allium cepa aggregatum	☼	P	Bulb, leaf, seed
Orach	Atriplex hortensis	☼/◐	R	Leaf
Oregano	Origanum spp.	☼/◐	P	Flower, leaf
Oregon grape	Mahonia	◐	P	Fruit
Ostrich fern (fiddlehead)	Matteuccia struthiopteris	◐	P	New shoots only
Pac choi	Brassica rapa, chinensis	☼/◐		Leaf
Parsley	Petroselinum crispum	☼/◐	R	Leaf
Parsnips	Pastinaca sativa	☼		Root
Passion flower	Passiflora caerulea	☼	P	Flower, fruit
Paw paw	Asimina Trilobata	☼/◐/●	P	Fruit if in full sun
Pea	Pisum sativum	☼/◐		Flower, fruit, young vines
Pea, perennial	Lathyrus latifolius	☼/◐	P	Leaf
Pear, Asian	Pyrus serotina	☼	P	Fruit
Pear, European	Pyrus communis	☼	P	Fruit

Common Name	Scientific Name	Light	Life	Edible Parts / Use
Peppercorns, Sancho	Xanthoxylum piperitum	☀	P	Fruit, leaf, flavoring
Peppermint	Mentha x piperita vulgaris	◐	P	Flavoring, tea
Peppers	Capsicum annuum	☀		Fruit
Persimmon	Diospyros spp.	☀/◐	P	Fruit
Plantain	Plantago major	☀/◐/●	P	Leaf, root
Plum	Prunus spp.	☀	P	Fruit
Poppy	Papaver spp.	☀	R	Flower, seed
Potato	Solanum tuberosum	☀/◐		Root if part sun choose early varieties
Purslane	Portulaca oleracea	☀/◐/●	R	Leaf
Pumpkins	Cucurbita spp.	☀		Fruit, seed
Quince	Chaenomeles speciosaor Cydonia oblonga	☀	P	Fruit, flower
Radish	Raphanus sativus	☀	R	Root
Ramps	Allium triccocum	●	P	Bulb, leaf
Raspberry, black	Rubus occidentalis	☀/◐/●	P	Fruit
Raspberry, red	Rubus idaeus	☀/◐	P	Fruit
Rhubarb	Rheum rhabarbarum	☀/◐	P	Stem
Rose	Rosa spp.	☀/◐	P	Flower
Rosehips	Rosa rugosa	☀	P	Flower, fruit, tea
Rosemary	Rosemarinus officinalis	☀	P	Flower, leaf
Rutabagas	Brassica napus	☀/◐		Leaf, root
Saffron crocus	Crocus sativus	☀	P	Flavoring
Sage	Salvia spp.	☀	P	Flower, flavoring, leaf
Salad burnet	Sanguisorba minor	☀/◐	R	Flower, leaf
Salal	Gaultheria shallon	☀/◐/●	P	Fruit
Salsify	Tragopogon porrifolius	☀		Root
Salt bush	Atriplex halimus	☀/◐		Leaf
Saskatoon, serviceberry	Amelanchier alnifolia	☀/◐	P	Fruit
Savory, summer and winter	Satureja montana	☀	R	Flavoring
Sea buckthorn	Hippophae rhamnoides	☀	P	Fruit
Seakale	Crambe maritima	☀/◐	P	Flower, leaf
Shallots	Allium cepa, aggregatum	☀		Bulb
Shephard's purse	Capsella bursa-pastoris	☀/◐	R	Leaf, seedpods
Shiso	Perilla frutescens	☀		Leaf
Sorrel, French	Rumex scutatus	☀/◐/●	P	Leaf
Sorrel, wood	Oxalis acetosella	◐	P	Leaf
Spearmint	Mentha spicata	◐	R	Flavoring, tea
Spinach	Spinacia oleracea	☀/◐		Leaf
Squash	Cucurbita spp.	☀		Flower, fruit
Stevia	Stevia rebaudiana	☀		Flavoring
Stinging nettle	Urtica dioica	☀/◐/●	P	Leaf
Strawberry	Fragaria spp.	☀/◐	P	Fruit
Strawberry tree	Arbutus unedo	☀	P	Fruit
Strawberry, alpine	Fragaria vesca	◐	P	Fruit
Sugar maple	Acer saccharum	☀/◐	P	Syrup
Staghorn sumac	Rhus typhina	☀	P	Fruit
Sunflowers	Helianthus annuus	☀		Seed
Sweet cicely	Myrrhis odorata	◐	R	Leaf, seed
Sweet flag	Acorus calamus	☀/◐	P	Leaf, root
Swiss chard	Beta vulgaris, cicla	☀/◐		Leaf
Swiss chard, perpetual	Beta vulgaris, cicla	☀/◐	P	Leaf
Tarragon	Artemisia dracunculus	☀/◐/●	P	Leaf
Tea	Camellia sinensis	☀/◐	P	Tea

Common Name	Scientific Name	Light	Life	Edible Parts / Use
Thistle	Sonchus oleraceus		R	Flower, leaf
Thyme	Thymus spp.	☼/◐	P	Flower, leaf
Tomatoes	Lycopersicon lycopersicum	☼		Fruit
Turkish rocket	Brassica unias orientalis	☼/◐	P	Flower, leaf
Turnips	Brassica rapa	☼/◐		Leaf, root
Violet	Viola	☼/◐	R	Flower
Walnut, black	Juglans nigra	☼	P	Nut
Walnut, English	Juglans regia	☼	P	Nut
Wapato	Sagittaria latifolia	☼/◐	P	Root
Watercress	Nasturtium officinale	☼/◐/●		Leaf
Wild carrot, Queen Anne's lace	Daucus carota	☼/◐	R	Root, seed, pollinator
Wood violet	Viola sororia	◐	R	Leaf, flower
Yacon	Polymnia edulis	☼	P	Root
Yampah	Perideridia gairdneri	☼	P	Root
Yuzu	Yuzu ichandrin	☼	P	Fruit

plants, nonedible uses

Common Name	Scientific Name	Light	Life	Use
Bamboo, clumping	Fargesia spp.	☼/◐/●	P	Fiber, garden stakes
Barley	Hordeum vulgare	●		Hay, straw
Bayberry	Myrica spp.	☼	P	Candle wax
Beets	Beta vulgaris	☼		Dye
Black hawthorn	Crataegus douglasii	☼	P	Dye
Blackberries	Rubus spp.	☼/◐/●	P	Dye
Blueberries	Vaccinium spp.	☼/◐	P	Dye
Borage	Borago offinalis	☼	R	Oil for lotion
Calendula	Calenula officinalis	☼	R	Dye
Carrots	Daucus carota var. sativus	☼/◐		Dye
Cattail	Typha angustifolia	☼/◐	P	Dye
Chamomile	Matricaria recutita	☼/◐	R	Dye
Cherry	Prunus spp.	☼	P	Dye
Comfrey	Symphytum officinale	☼/◐	P	Oil for lotion
Cornelian cherry	Cornus mas	☼	P	Dye
Cranberry	Vaccinium trilobum	☼/◐	P	Dye
Cranberry	Vaccinium macocarpon	☼	P	Dye
Cranberry, highbush	Elaeagnus multiflora	☼	P	Dye
Currant, black	Ribes nigrum	☼/◐/●	P	Dye
Currant, red	Ribes rubrum	☼/◐/●	P	Dye
Dandelion, common	Taraxacum officinale	☼/◐/●	R	Dye
Elderberry, black	Sambucus nigra	☼/◐	P	Dye, medicinal
Elderberry, blue	Sambucus caerulea	☼/◐	P	Dye
Evening primrose	Oenothera spp.	☼		Oil
Feverfew	Tanacetum parthenium	☼	R	Medicinal
Grape	Vitis vinifera	☼	P	Dye
Hops	Humulus lupulus	☼	P	Dye, preservative

Common Name	Scientific Name	Light	Life	Use
Horehound	Marrubium vulgare	☼	R	Medicinal
Huckleberry	Vaccinium (ovatum, parvifolium, ovalifolium, membranaceum)	☼/◐/●	P	Dye
Kale	Brassica oleracea, acephala	☼/◐/●	R	Dye
Kinnickinnick (bearberry)	Arctostaphylos uva-ursi	☼	P	Dye
Lavender	Lavandula spp.	☼	P	Flower, oil
Lingonberry	Vaccinium vitis-idaea	☼/◐	P	Dye
Malabar spinach	Basella alba	☼/◐	P	Dye
Mallow	Hibiscus syriacus	☼	P	Dye, medicinal, soap
Marigold	Tagetes			Dye, nematodicidal
Mulberry	Morus alba or nigra	☼	P	Fruit, dye
Mullein	Verbascum thapsus	☼/◐	R	Medicinal
Mushrooms		●		Dye
Mustard	Brassica spp.	☼/◐	R	Dye
Nasturtium	Trapaeolum minus	☼	R	Dye, trap crop
Oats	Hulless Oats - Terra	☼		Fiber, hay, straw
Onion	Allium cepa	☼		Dye
Oregon grape	Mahonia	◐	P	Dye
Parsley	Petroselinum crispum	☼/◐	R	Dye
Raspberry, black	Rubus occidentalis	☼/◐/●	P	Dye
Raspberry, red	Rubus idaeus	☼/◐	P	Dye
Rhubarb	Rheum rhabarbarum			Dye
Rosehips	Rosa rugosa	☼	P	Medicinal, oil for lotion
Saskatoon, serviceberry	Amelanchier alnifolia	☼/◐	P	Dye
Sea buckthorn	Hippophae rhamnoides	☼	P	Dye, medicinal, oil for lotion
Siberian pea shrub	Caragana arborescens	☼	P	Dye
Soapwort	Saponoria officinalis	☼		Soap
Sorrel, French	Rumex scutatus	☼/◐/●	P	Dye
Spinach	Spinacia oleracea	☼/◐		Dye
Stinging nettle	Urtica dioica	☼/◐/●	P	Dye
Black Sunflower Seeds	Helianthus annuus			Dye
Tea	Camellia sinensis	☼/◐	P	Dye
Thyme	Thymus spp.	☼/◐	P	Dye
Violet	Viola	☼/◐	R	Dye
Walnut, black	Juglans nigra	☼	P	Dye, medicinal

the perpetual garden

Common Name	Scientific Name	Light	Life	Edible Use
Akebia (chocolate vine)	Akebia quinata	☼/◐	P	Fruit
Alexander's seeds (black lovage)	Smyrnium olusatrum	☼/◐	P	Leaf, seed
Apple	Malus spp.	☼/◐	P	Fruit
Aronia	Aronia melanocarpa	☼/◐	P	Fruit
Artichoke, globe	Cynara scolymus	☼	P	Flower

Common Name	Scientific Name	Light	Life	Edible Use
Arugula	Eruca sativa	☼/◐/●	R	Flower, leaf
Asparagus	Asparagus officinalis	☼	P	Shoots
Bamboo	Phyllostachys	☼	P	Shoots
Barberry	Berberis vulgaris	☼/◐	P	Fruit, tea
Bay laurel	Laurus nobilis	☼	P	Leaf
Beebalm	Monarda didyma	☼/◐	P	Flower, leaf, tea
Beetberry (strawberry spinach)	Chenopodium capitatum	☼/◐/●	R	Leaf, fruit
Black hawthorn	Crataegus douglasii	☼	P	Fruit
Blackberries	Rubus spp.	☼/◐/●	P	Fruit
Blueberries	Vaccinium spp.	☼/◐	P	Fruit
Borage	Borago offinalis	☼	R	Flower, leaf
Broccoli, perennial	Brassica oleracea botrytis aparagoides	☼/◐	P	Flower, leaf
Buckwheat, perennial	Fagopyrum dibotrys	☼/◐	P	Leaf, seed
Burdock (gobo)	Arctium spp.	☼/◐	P	Flower, leaf, root
Calendula	Calenula officinalis	☼	R	Flower
Camas	Camassia quamash	☼/◐	P	Root
Cardoon	Cynara cardunculus	☼	P	Leaf
Cattail	Typha angustifolia	☼/◐	P	Root
Chamomile	Matricaria recutita	☼/◐	R	Tea
Cherry	Prunus spp.	☼	P	Fruit
Chervil	Anthriscus cerefolium	☼/◐	R	Leaf
Chestnut	Castanea	☼	P	Nut
Chickweed	Stellaria spp.	☼/◐/●	R	Leaf
Chicory	Cichorium intybus	☼/◐	R	Leaf, root
Chinese dogwood	Cornus kousa	☼/◐	P	Fruit
Chives	Allium schoenoprasum	☼/◐	P	Bulb, flower, seed, stem
Chives, garlic	Allium tuberosum	☼/◐	P	Bulb, flower, seed, stem
Cilantro/coriander	Coriandrum sativum	☼/◐	R	Leaf, seed
Claytonia	Claytonia perfoliata	☼/◐/●	R	Leaf
Clover	Trifolium	☼/◐/●	R	Flower, tea
Cornelian cherry	Cornus mas	☼	P	Fruit
Cranberry	Vaccinium (trilobum, macocarpon)	☼/◐	P	Fruit
Cranberry, highbush	Elaeagnus multiflora	☼	P	Fruit
Cress, garden	Lepidium sativum	☼/◐	R	Flower, leaf
Currant, black	Ribes nigrum	☼/◐/●	P	Fruit
Currant, red	Ribes rubrum	☼/◐/●	P	Fruit
Dandelion, common	Taraxacum officinale	☼/◐/●	R	Leaf, root, flower, tea
Dandelion, garden	Cichorium intybus	☼/◐/●	R	Leaf, root, flower
Daylily	Hemerocallis fulva	☼/◐	P	Root, leaf, flower, pollinator
Dill	Anethum graveolens	☼	R	Leaf, flower
Echinacea	Echinacea purpurea	☼	R	Flower, medicinal
Elderberry, black	Sambucus nigra	☼/◐	P	Flower, fruit
Elderberry, blue	Sambucus caerulea	☼/◐	P	Flower, fruit
Fennel	Foeniculum vulgare	☼/◐	R	Bulb, seed, stem
Fig	Ficus carica	☼	P	Fruit
Flying dragon	Poncirus trifoliata monstrosa	☼	P	Fruit
Ginger, hardy	Hedychium	●	P	Flavoring, shoot

Common Name	Scientific Name	Light	Life	Edible Use
Goji berry	Lycium barbarum	☀/◐	P	Fruit
Good King Henry	Chenopodium bonushenricus	☀	R	Flower, leaf
Gooseberry	Ribes uva-crispa	☀/◐	P	Fruit
Goumi berry	Elaeagnus multiflora	☀	P	Fruit
Grape	Vitis vinifera	☀	P	Fruit, leaf
Groundcherry	Physalis heterophylla	☀	P	Fruit
Hazelnut (a.k.a. filbert)	Corylus spp.	☀/◐	P	Nut
Honeysuckle	Lonicera caerula edulis	☀	P	Flower, fruit
Horseradish	Armoracia rusticana	☀	P	Flavoring
Huckleberry	Vaccinium (ovatum, parvifolium, ovalifolium, membranaceum)	☀/◐/●	P	Fruit
Jasmine	Jasminum officinale	☀/◐	P	Flower, tea
Jeruselem artichoke	Helianthus tuberosus	☀/◐	P	Root
Jostaberry	Ribes spp.	☀/◐	P	Fruit
Jujube	Ziziphus zizyphus	☀	P	Fruit
Kale	Brassica oleracea, acephala	☀/◐/●	R	Flower, leaf
Kale, tree	Brassica oleracea ramosa	☀/◐	P	Flower, leaf
King's spear	Asphodeline lutea	☀/◐	R	Flower, leaf
Kinnickinnick (bearberry)	Arctostaphylos uva-ursi	☀	P	Fruit
Kiwi, fuzzy	Actinidia deliciosa	☀	P	Fruit
Kiwi, hardy	Actinidia arguta	☀	P	Fruit
Lambsquarter	Chenopodium album	☀/◐/●	R	Leaf, seed
Lavender	Lavandula spp.	☀	P	Flower, leaf
Lemon balm	Melissa officinalis	☀/◐	R	Leaf, flower, oil, pollinator
Lettuce	Lactuca sativa	☀/◐	R	Leaf
Lingonberry	Vaccinium vitis-idaea	☀/◐	P	Fruit
Lovage	Levisticum officinale	☀/◐	P	Leaf, stalk
Mâche	Valerianella locusta	☀/◐	R	Leaf
Magentespreen	Chenopodium gigantium	☀/◐	R	Leaf
Malabar spinach	Basella alba	☀/◐	P	Leaf
Mallow	Hibiscus syriacus	☀	P	Tea
Marjoram	Origanum majorana	☀/◐	P	Flower, leaf
Maypop	Passiflora incarnate	☀	P	Flower, fruit
Medlar	Mespilus germanica	☀	P	Fruit
Mint	Mentha spp.	◐	P	Leaf, tea
Mitsuba	Crytotaenia japonica	●	P	Leaf
Mulberry	Morus alba or nigra	☀	P	Fruit
Mullein	Verbascum thapsus	☀/◐	R	Tea
Mushrooms		●	P	
Mustard	Brassica spp.	☀/◐	R	Leaf, seed
Nasturtium	Trapaeolum minus	☀	R	Flower, leaf, seed pod
Oca	Oxalis tuberose	☀/◐	P	Flower, leaf, root
Onion, Egyptian perennial	Allium cepa proliferium	☀	P	Bulb, leaf, seed
Onion, multiplier	Allium cepa aggregatum	☀	P	Bulb, leaf, seed
Orach	Atriplex hortensis	☀/◐	R	Leaf
Oregano	Origanum spp.	☀/◐	P	Flower, leaf
Oregon grape	Mahonia	◐	P	Fruit
Ostrich fern (fiddlehead)	Matteuccia struthiopteris	◐	P	New shoots only
Parsley	Petroselinum crispum	☀/◐	R	Leaf
Passion flower	Passiflora caerulea	☀	P	Flower, fruit

Common Name	Scientific Name	Light	Life	Edible Use
Paw paw	Asimina trilobata	☀/◐/●	P	Fruit if in full sun
Pea, perennial	Lathyrus latifolius	☀/◐	P	Leaf
Pear, Asian	Pyrus serotina	☀	P	Fruit
Pear, European	Pyrus communis	☀	P	Fruit
Peppercorns, sancho	Xanthoxylum piperitum	☀	P	Fruit, leaf, flavoring
Peppermint	Mentha x piperita vulgaris	◐	P	Flavoring, tea
Persimmon	Diospyros spp.	☀/◐	P	Fruit
Plantain	Plantago major	☀/◐/●	P	Leaf, root
Plum	Prunus spp.	☀	P	Fruit
Poppy	Papaver spp.	☀	R	Flower, seed
Purslane	Portulaca oleracea	☀/◐/●	R	Leaf
Quince	Chaenomeles speciosaor Cydonia oblonga	☀	P	Fruit, flower
Radish	Raphanus sativus	☀	R	Root
Ramps	Allium triccocum	●	P	Bulb, leaf
Raspberry, black	Rubus occidentalis	☀/◐/●	P	Fruit
Raspberry, red	Rubus idaeus	☀/◐	P	Fruit
Rhubarb	Rheum rhabarbarum	☀/◐	P	Stem
Rose	Rosa spp.	☀/◐	P	Flower
Rosehips	Rosa rugosa	☀	P	Flower, fruit, tea
Rosemary	Rosemarinus officinalis	☀	P	Flower, leaf
Saffron crocus	Crocus sativus	☀	P	Flavoring
Sage	Salvia spp.	☀	P	Flower, flavoring, leaf
Salad burnet	Sanguisorba minor	☀/◐	R	Flower, leaf
Salal	Gaultheria shallon	☀/◐/●	P	Fruit
Salt bush	Atriplex halimus	☀/◐	P	Leaf
Saskatoon	Serviceberry	☀/◐	P	Fruit
Savory, summer and winter	Satureja montana	☀	R	Flavoring
Sea buckthorn	Hippophae rhamnoides	☀	P	Fruit
Seakale	Crambe maritima	☀/◐	P	Flower, leaf
Shephard's purse	Capsella bursa-pastoris	☀/◐	R	Leaf, seedpods
Sorrel, French	Rumex scutatus	☀/◐/●	P	Leaf
Sorrel, wood	Oxalis acetosella	◐	P	Leaf
Spearmint	Mentha spicata	◐	R	Flavoring, tea
Stinging nettle	Urtica dioica	☀/◐/●	P	Leaf
Strawberry	Fragaria spp.	☀/◐	P	Fruit
Strawberry tree	Arbutus unedo	☀	P	Fruit
Strawberry, alpine	Fragaria vesca	◐	P	Fruit
Sugar maple	Acer Saccharum	☀/◐	P	Syrup
Staghorn sumac	Rhus typhina	☀	P	Fruit
Sweet cicely	Myrrhis odorata	◐	R	Leaf, seed
Sweet flag	Acorus calamus	☀/◐	P	Leaf, root
Swiss chard, perpetual	Beta vulgaris, cicla	☀/◐	P	Leaf
Tarragon	Artemisia dracunculus	☀/◐/●	P	Leaf
Tea	Camellia sinensis	☀/◐	P	Tea
Thyme	Thymus spp.	☀/◐	P	Flower, leaf
Turkish rocket	Brassica unias orientalis	☀/◐	P	Flower, leaf
Violet	Viola	☀/◐	R	Flower
Walnut, black	Juglans nigra	☀	P	Nut
Walnut, English	Juglans regia	☀	P	Nut
Wapato	Sagittaria latifolia	☀/◐	P	Root
Wild carrot, Queen Anne's lace	Daucus carota	☀/◐	R	Root, seed, pollinator

Common Name	Scientific Name	Light	Life	Edible Use
Wood violet	Viola sororia	☀	R	Leaf, flower
Yacon	Polymnia edulis	☼	P	Root
Yampah	Perideridia gairdneri	☼	P	Root
Yuzu	Yuzu ichandrin	☼	P	Fruit

plants for livestock

Common Name	Scientific Name	Light	Life	Animal Browse
Akebia (chocolate vine)	Akebia quinata	☼/☀	P	Goat
Alfalfa	Medicago sativa	☼	P	Goat, rabbit
Apple fruit and tree	Malus spp.	☼/☀	P	Goat, rabbit
Arborvitae	Arborvitae	☼/☀	P	Goat
Bamboo	Phyllostachys	☼	P	Goat
Barley, Tibetan purple hullless	Hordeum vulgare	●		Bedding, chicken, goat, rabbit
Beans and bean vine	Phaseolus spp.	☼/☀		Goat
Beets, top and root	Beta vulgaris	☼		Goat, rabbit
Birdsfoot trefoil	Lotus corniculatus	☼/☀	P	Chicken, goat
Broccoli	Brassica oleracea, botrytis	☼		Chicken, goat, rabbit
Buckwheat	Fagopyrum esculentum	☼		Chicken, goat, rabbit
Burdock (gobo)	Arctium spp.	☼/☀	P	Goat
Cabbage	Brassica oleracea, capitata	☼		Chicken, goat
Camellias	Camellia	☼/☀/●	P	Goat
Caneberry, canes and leaves	Rubus spp.	☼/☀/●	P	Goat, rabbit
Carrots, roots and tops	Daucus carota var. sativus	☼		Goat, rabbit
Chicory	Cichorium intybus	☼/☀/●	P	Chicken, goat, rabbit
Clover (not sweet)	Trifolium	☼/☀/●		Chicken, goat
Coltstfoot	Trefoil	☼		Rabbit
Comfrey	Symphytum officinale	☼/☀	P	Chicken (not safe for rabbit)
Conifer branches		☼/☀/●	P	Goat
Corn	Zea mays	☼		Chicken, goat, rabbit
Dandelion	Taraxacum officinale	☼/☀/●	P	Chicken, goat, rabbit
Dogwood	Cornus spp.	☼/☀	P	Chicken, goat, rabbit
Fern		☀	P	Goat
Field peas	Pisum sativum	☼/☀		Chicken, goat
Fig tree	Ficus carica	☼	P	Goat
Grape	Vitis vinifera	☼	P	Goat
Grass		☼/☀/●		Chicken, goat, rabbit
Honeysuckle	Lonicera caerula edulis	☼/☀	P	Goat
Ivy	Hedera	☼/☀/●	P	Goat
Jeruselem artichokes	Helianthus tuberosus	☼		Rabbit
Kale	Brassica oleracea, acephala	☼/☀		Rabbit
Kohlrabi	Brassica oleracea, bongylodes	☼/☀		Chicken, rabbit
Linden tree	Tilia spp.	☼/☀	P	Goat
Magnolia	Magnolia	☼/☀/●	P	Goat
Maple tree	Acer	☼/☀/●	P	Goat
Mangel	Beta vulgaris	☼		Goat, chicken

Common Name	Scientific Name	Light	Life	Animal Browse
Morning glory		☼/◐/●	P	Goat
Mountain ash tree	Rowan	☼/◐	P	Goat
Mulberry	Morus alba or nigra	☼	P	Chicken, goat
Mullein	Verbascum thapsus	☼/◐/●	P	Chicken, goat
Mustard	Brassica spp.	☼/◐		Chicken, goat
Nandina	Nandina domestica	☼/◐	P	Goat
Nettles	Urtica	☼/◐/●	P	Goat
Oak tree leaves	Quercus	☼/◐	P	Goat
Oats, Hulless Oats - Terra	Avena Sativa	☼		Bedding, chicken, goat, rabbit
Parsnip	Pastinaca sativa	☼		Rabbit
Pear	Pyrus spp.	☼	P	Goat
Pea	Pisum sativum	☼/◐		Chicken, goat
Photinia	Photinia	☼/◐	P	Goat
Plantain	Plantago major	☼/◐/●	P	Chicken, goat, rabbit
Plum	Prunus spp.	☼/◐	P	Goat
Poplar tree	Populus	☼	P	Goat
Pumpkin, fruit and seed	Cucurbita spp.	☼		Chicken, goat
Rutabaga	Brassica napus	☼		Goat, rabbit
Rye	Secale cereale	☼		Chicken, goat, rabbit
Salad burnet	Sanguisorba minor	☼/◐	R	Chicken, goat, rabbit
Salal	Gaultheria shallon	☼/◐/●	P	Chicken, goat
Saskatoon, serviceberry	Amelanchier alnifolia	☼/◐	P	Chicken
Sea buckthorn	Hippophae rhamnoides	☼	P	Chicken
Siberian pea shrub	Caragana arborescens	☼/◐	P	Chicken, goat
Squash, fruit and seed	Cucurbita spp.	☼		Chicken, goat
Sunflower, leaves and seed	Helianthus annuus	☼		Chicken, goat, rabbit
Turnip	Brassica rapa	☼		Goat, rabbit
Vetch	Vicia	☼/◐		Chicken, goat, rabbit
Vine Maple	Acer circinatum	☼/◐/●	P	Goat
Wax Myrtle	Myrica cerifera	☼/◐/●	P	Goat
Wheat	Triticum spp.	☼		Chicken, goat, rabbit
Willow	Salix	☼/◐	P	Goat, rabbit
Yarrow	Achillea	☼	P	Goat
Yucca	Agavaceae	☼	P	Goat

wild foods

Common Name	Scientific Name	Use
Bamboo	Phyllostachys	Shoots
Barberry	Berberis vulgaris	Fruit, tea
Bittercress	Cardamine hirsuta	Leaf
Black hawthorn	Crataegus douglasii	Fruit
Black walnut	Juglans nigra	Nut
Blackberries	Rubus spp.	Fruit
Borage	Borago offinalis	Flower, leaf, oil
Brook lettuce	Saxifraga micranthidifolia	Leaf
Burdock (gobo)	Arctium spp.	Flower, leaf, root

Common Name	Scientific Name	Use
Camas	Camassia Quamash	Root
Catsear	Hypochoeris radicata	Flower, leaf
Cattail	Typha angustifolia	Pollen, root
Chickweed	Stellaria spp.	Leaf
Chicory	Cichorium intybus	Leaf
Coneflower	Rudbeckia laciniata	Flower
Corn Salad	Valerianella radiate	Leaf
Crabapples	Malus spp.	Fruit
Cranberry, highbush	Elaeagnus multiflora	Fruit
Currant, black	Ribes nigrum	Fruit, tea
Currant, red	Ribes rubrum	Fruit, tea
Dandelion	Taraxacum offinale	Leaf, medicinal root
Dock	Rumex crispa	Leaf
Echinacea	Echinacea angustifolia	Flower, medicinal, root
Elderberry, black	Sambucus nigra	Flower, fruit, medicinal; leaves and bark are toxic, berries must be cooked prior to eating
Elderberry, blue	Sambucus caerulea	Flower, fruit, medicinal; leaves and bark are toxic, berries must be cooked prior to eating
Fiddlehead fern	Circinate vernation	New leaves only
Hazelnut (a.k.a. filbert)	Corylus spp.	Nut
Huckleberry	Vaccinium (ovatum, parvifolium, ovalifolium, membranaceum)	Fruit
Kinnickinnick (bearberry)	Arctostaphylos uva-ursi	Fruit
Lambs quarters	Chenopodium album	Leaf
Medlar	Mespilus germanica	Fruit
Miners lettuce	Claytonia perfoliata	Leaf
Mulberry	Morus alba or nigra	Fruit
Mullein	Verbascum thapsus	Leaf, medicinal, tea
Mushrooms		Many varieties are toxic
Nettles	Urtica spp.	Leaf
Oregon grape	Mahonia	Fruit
Pea, perennial	Lathyrus latifolius	Leaf
Peppergrass	Lepidium virginicum	Leaf
Pigweed	Amaranthus hybridus	Leaf
Plantain	Plantago major	Leaf, root
Purslane	Portulaca oleracea	Leaf
Rose	Rosa spp.	Flower
Rosehips	Rosa rugosa	Fruit, tea
Salal	Gaultheria shallon	Fruit
Salmonberries	Rubus spectabilis	Fruit
Saskatoon, serviceberry	Amelanchier alnifolia	Fruit
Sheep sorrel	Rumex acetosella	Leaf
Shephard's purse	Capsella bursa-pastoris	Leaf, seedpods
Shotweed	Cardamine hirsute	Leaf
Spring cress	Cardamine hirsuta	Flower, leaf
Staghorn sumac	Rhus typhina	Fruit
Stonecrop	Sedum ternatum	Leaf
Strawberry tree	Arbutus unedo	Fruit
Thimbleberry	Rubus parviflorus	Fruit
Thistle	Sonchus oleraceus	Flower, leaf
Watercress	Nasturtium officinale	Flower, leaf

Common Name	Scientific Name	Use
Wild carrot, Queen Anne's lace	Daucus carota	Root, seed; resembles toxic poison hemlock
Wild ginger	Asarum canadense	Root
Wild lettuce	Lactuca graminifolia	Leaf
Wild strawberry	Fragaria virginiana	Fruit
Winter cress	Barbarea vulgaris	Leaf
Wintergreen	Gaultheria procumbens	Fruit, leaf
Wood sorrel	Oxalis acetosella	Leaf
Wood violet	Viola sororia	Flower, leaf
Yarrow	Achillea	Flower

pollinators

Common Name	Scientific Name	Light	Life
Anise hyssop	Agastache foeniculum	☼	
Basil	Ocimum basilicum	☼	
Beebalm	Monarda didyma	☼/◐	P
Bee's friend (Bienen-Freund)	Phacelia tanacetifolia	☼	
Borage	Borago offinalis	☼	R
Buckwheat, perennial	Fagopyrum dibotrys	☼/◐	P
Calendula	Calenula officinalis	☼	R
Cardoon	Cynara cardunculus	☼	P
Cattail	Typha angustifolia	☼/◐	P
Chamomile	Matricaria recutita	☼/◐	R
Clover	Trifolium	☼/◐/●	R
Comfrey	Symphytum officinale	☼/◐	P
Echinacea	Echinacea purpurea	☼	R
Evening primrose	Oenothera spp.	☼	
Good King Henry	Chenopodium bonushenricus	☼	R
Jasmine	Jasminum officinale	☼/◐	P
Lavender	Lavandula spp.	☼	P
Lemon balm	Melissa officinalis	☼/◐	R
Lemon verbena	Aloysia triphylla	☼	
Marjoram	Origanum majorana	☼/◐	P
Nasturtium	Trapaeolum minus	☼	R
Nigella (black cumin)	Nigella sativa	☼	
Passion flower	Passiflora caerulea	☼	P
Poppy	Papaver spp.	☼	R
Rose	Rosa spp.	☼/◐	P
Rosehips	Rosa rugosa	☼	P
Rosemary	Rosemarinus officinalis	☼	P
Sunflowers	Helianthus annuus	☼	
Thyme	Thymus spp.	☼/◐	P
Yarrow	Achillea		

cover crops

Common Name	Scientific Name	When to Sow	Purpose
Alfalfa	Medicago sativa	Sow in April/May	Produces nitrogen plus dry matter
Austrian field pea	Pisum sativum	Sow in August/ early September	Produces nitrogen plus dry matter
Buckwheat	Fagopyrum esculentum	Sow in April through June	Produces phosphorous and organic matter, excellent pollinator, fast growing
Comfrey	Symphytum officinale	Perennial ground cover	Nutrient accumulator
Crimson clover	Trifolium incarnatum	Sow spring, summer or fall	Produces nitrogen
Fava beans	Vicia faba	Sow in fall	Breaks up soil, produces nitrogen and organic matter
Oats	Avena sativa	Sow spring, summer or fall	Produces organic matter
Pea	Pisum sativum	Sow in spring or summer	Fixes nitrogen
Siberian pea shrub	Caragana arborescens	Perennial bush	Fixes nitrogen
White Dutch clover	Trifolium repens	Sow in April/May	Produces nitrogen
Winter rye	Secale cereale	Sow in fall	Breaks up soil, provides dry matter
Yellow sweet clover	Melilotus officinalis	Sow in spring or summer	Breaks up soil, fixes nitrogen

resources

grains

Baking with Whole Grains: Books

Bread: A Baker's Book of Techniques and Recipes, by Jeffrey Hamelman. Hoboken, NJ: Wiley, 2004.

King Arthur Flour Whole Grain Baking: Delicious Recipes Using Nutritious Whole Grains, by King Arthur Flour. Woodstock, VT: Countryman Press, 2006.

The Laurel's Kitchen Bread Book: A Guide to Whole-Grain Breadmaking, by Laurel Robertson, Carol Flinders, and Bronwen Godfrey. Upd. ed. New York: Random House, 2003.

Peter Reinhart's Whole Grain Breads: New Techniques, Extraordinary Flavor, by Peter Reinhart. Berkeley, CA: Ten Speed Press, 2007.

Baking with Whole Grains: Websites

The Fresh Loaf
Forum, information, blogs, and recipes for baking
www.TheFreshLoaf.com/

King Arthur Flour
Norwich, Vermont
800-827-6836
Ingredients and recipes for baking
www.KingArthurFlour.com/

Wild Yeast
Great collection of baking recipes and photos
www.WildYeastBlog.com/

Sources for Whole Grains

Azure Standard
Dufur, Oregon
541-467-2230
Organic farm that grows, repackages, and sells natural foods. They can tell you the source of anything with their private label on it.
www.AzureStandard.com/

Bluebird Grain Farms
Winthrop, Washington
888-232-0331
Grows dark northern winter rye, hard dark northern red wheat, spring soft wheat, emmer farro, flax, and buckwheat.

They sell at farmers markets and have a grain CSA.
www.BluebirdGrainFarms.com/

Bob's Red Mill
Milwaukie, Oregon
800-553-2258
Packages a wide variety of whole grains, flours and legumes. They will tell you the source of all their items if asked.
www.BobsRedMill.com/

King Arthur Flour
Norwich, Vermont
800-827-6836
Specializes in equipment and ingredients for bakers. Products available through retail stores, and website and catalog sales.
www.KingArthurFlour.com

Lentz Spelt Farms
Marlin, Washington
509-345-2483
Private farm that grows spelt, emmer farro, camelina, and einkorn. They sell through retailers and directly to the public. Look for einkorn to be available in 2012.
http://LentzSpelt.com/

Sources for Supplies and Grinders

Everything Kitchens
Springfield, Missouri
866-852-4268
Retail and online store that specializes in kitchen tools and appliances
www.EverythingKitchens.com/

Lehman's
Kidron, Ohio
888-438-5346
Family-run business that sells products geared toward rural living and self-sufficiency, originally founded to serve Amish and others living without electricity
www.Lehmans.com/

Peaceful Valley Farm and Garden Supply
Grass Valley, California
888-784-1722
Wonderful collection of garden and homesteading tools, amendments, and seeds
www.GrowOrganic.com/

Pleasant Hill Grain
Hampton, Nebraska
800-3210-1070
Online store that specializes in a wide variety of kitchen tools and appliances,

including food grade buckets and gamma seal lids for storing grains
www.PleasantHillGrain.com/

The Urban Homemaker
Paonia, Colorado
800-552-7323
Family-run online store with a wide selection of grain mills and other kitchen equipment
www.UrbanHomemaker.com/

Wisemen Trading and Supply
Athens, Alabama
888-891-8411
Online store that specializes in products for rural living and self-sufficiency
www.WisemenTrading.com/

chickens

Raising Chickens: Books

City Chicks: Keeping Micro-flocks of Chickens as Garden Helpers, Compost Makers, Bio-recyclers, and Local Food Producers, by Patricia Foreman. Buena Vista, VA: Good Earth Publications, 2010.

Keep Chickens! Tending Small Flocks in Cities, Suburbs, and Other Small Spaces, by Barbara Kilarski. North Adams, MA: Storey Publishing, 2003.

Raising Chickens: Websites, Forums, and Classes

The American Livestock Breeds Conservancy
Pittsboro, North Carolina
Provides information about heritage chickens and other livestock
www.ALBC-USA.org/

BackyardChickens.com
Pleasant Hill, California
Information and forum for backyard chicken keepers
www.BackyardChickens.com/

Seattle Farm Co-op
Member-based cooperative that promotes sustainable urban farming through classes, supplies, and a member forum.
www.SeattleFarmCoop.com/
groups.Yahoo.com/group/SeattleFarm-Coop/join/

Seattle Tilth
Seattle, Washington
206-633-0451

Nonprofit educational organization with classes on all manner of urban farming from gardening to rainwater harvesting to livestock keeping
http://SeattleTilth.org/

Sources for Chickens

Dunlop Hatchery
Caldwell, Idaho
208-459-9088
Mail order—25 chick minimum (share with friends)
www.DunlapHatchery.net/

Murray McMurray Hatchery
Webster City, Iowa
515-832-3280
Mail order—25 chick minimum
www.McMurrayHatchery.com/

My Pet Chicken
Norwalk, Connecticut
888-460-1529
Mail order—3 chick minimum
www.MyPetChicken.com/

Sand Hill Preservation Center
Calamus, Iowa
563-246-2299
Mail order—25 chick minimum
www.SandHillPreservation.com/

Local feed stores often carry chicks in the spring. No minimum purchase.

Sources for Chicken Feed

Magill Ranch & Cascade Feeds
Wamic, Oregon
541-544-2087
Organic feed, corn- and soy-free
www.MagillRanch.com/

Pastured Sensations
Snohomish, Washington
360-568-5208
Not organic, but corn- and soy- free
www.PasturedSensations.com/

Scratch and Peck Feeds
Bellingham, Washington
360-318-7585
Organic and corn- and soy-free products, made with ingredients from the Pacific Northwest
www.ScratchandPeck.com/

goats

Raising Goats: Books

Natural Goat Care, by Pat Coleby. Austin, TX: Acres U.S.A., 2001.

Raising Goats: Websites

Fias Co Farm
Okemos, Michigan
Information on goat care, including plans for goat housing, and cheesemaking
http://FiasCoFarm.com/

Goat Justice League
Seattle, Washington
Jennie Grant's website dedicated to backyard mini-goats
www.GoatJusticeLeague.org/

Raising Goats: Classes

Seattle Farm Co-op
Member-based cooperative that promotes sustainable urban farming
www.SeattleFarmCoop.com/
groups.Yahoo.com/group/SeattleFarm-Coop/join/

Seattle Tilth
Seattle, Washington
206-633-0451
Nonprofit educational organization with classes on all manner of urban farming from gardening to rainwater harvesting to livestock keeping
http://SeattleTilth.org/

Sources for Goat Care Supplies and Equipment

Caprine Supply
De Soto, Kansas
800-646-7736
Products for raising and milking goats
www.CaprineSupply.com/

Hoegger Supply Company
Fayetteville, Georgia
800-221-4628
Goat care, milking, and cheesemaking supplies
http://HoeggerGoatSupply.com/

cheesemaking and home dairy

Cheesemaking and Home Dairy: Books

200 Easy Homemade Cheese Recipes: From Cheddar and Brie to Butter and Yogurt, by Debra Amrein-Boyes. Toronto: Robert Rose, 2009.

Home Cheese Making: Recipes for 75 Delicious Cheeses, by Ricki Carroll. North Adams, MA: Storey Publishing, 2002.

Cheesemaking: Websites and Forums

Cheese Forum
Cheesemaking Forum
www.CheeseForum.org/

Fankhauser's Cheese Page
Batavia, Ohio
A biology and chemistry professor's personal cheese page, full of helpful photos of simple cheeses made without special equipment—an excellent starting point for the novice cheesemaker
http://biology.clc.uc.edu/fankhauser/cheese/cheese.html

Fias Co Farm
Okemos, Michigan
Information on goat care and cheesemaking
http://FiasCoFarm.com/

Kefir Making Yahoo Group
An international Yahoo group with information on water and dairy kefir grains. You can find members in your area willing to share their kefir grains with you.
groups.Yahoo.com/group/Kefir_making/

Oregon Cheese Guild
Oregon
Nice listing of Oregon artisan and commercial cheesemakers
www.OregonCheeseGuild.org/

Washington Cheese Guild
Washington State
Information, recipes, and a forum for cheesemakers
www.WACheese.com/

Washington State Cheesemakers Association
Nice listing of Washington artisan and commercial cheesemakers
www.WashingtonCheeseMakers.org/

Sources for Cheesemaking and Home Dairy Supplies and Equipment

The Cellar Homebrew
Seattle, Washington
800-342-1871
Cheesemaking classes and limited supplies
www.Cellar-HomeBrew.com/

The Cheesemaker
Cedarburg, Wisconsin
414-745-5483
Cheesemaking supplies and equipment with a focus on blues, brie, and camembert
www.TheCheeseMaker.com/

Cultures for Health
Vancouver, Washington
800-962-1959
Wide selection of cheesemaking cultures
and equipment
www.CulturesForHealth.com/

Dairy Connection
Madison, Wisconsin
608-242-9030
Large selection of cheese cultures, molds,
and forms
www.DairyConnection.com/

The Grape and Granary
Akron, Ohio
800-695-9870
A wide variety of supplies for home
cheesemaking, home brewing, coffee
roasting, and more
www.GrapeandGranary.com/

Hoegger Supply Company
Fayetteville, Georgia
800-221-4628
Goat care, milking, and cheesemaking
supplies
http://HoeggerGoatSupply.com/

Leeners
Northfield, Ohio
800-543-3697
Wide selection of specialty cheese
cultures, including those used in Pav's
"Annette" cheese
www.Leeners.com/

New England Cheesemaking Supply
Company
South Deerfield, Massachusetts
413-397-2012
Ricki Carroll's now famous site, including recipes and troubleshooting
www.CheeseMaking.com/

foraging

City Fruit
Seattle, Washington
Nonprofit that organizes volunteers to
harvest and distribute communal fruit
http://CityFruit.org/

Fat of the Land
Langdon Cook's foraging blog and book
by the same name
*Fat of the Land: Adventures of a 21st Cen-
tury Forager,* by Langdon Cook. Seattle,
WA: Skipstone Press, 2009.
http://Fat-of-the-Land.blogspot.com/

Portland Fruit Tree Project
Portland, Oregon
Nonprofit that organizes volunteers to
harvest and distribute communal fruit
www.PortlandFruit.org/

Urban Edibles
Portland, Oregon
Database of wild food sources in Portland, Oregon
http://UrbanEdibles.org/

Wildman Steve Brill
New York, New York
Comprehensive wild food site
www.WildmanSteveBrill.com/

gardening

Gardening: Books

All New Square Foot Gardening, by Mel
Bartholomew. Brentwood, TN: Cool
Springs Press, 2006.

*Four-Season Harvest: Organic Vegetables
from Your Home Garden All Year Long,*
by Eliot Coleman. White River Junction,
VT: Chelsea Green Publishing, 1999.

*Gaia's Garden: A Guide to Home-Scale
Permaculture,* by Toby Hemenway. 2nd
ed. White River Junction, VT: Chelsea
Green Publishing, 2009.

*Growing Vegetables West of the Cascades:
The complete Guide to Organic Garden-
ing,* by Steve Solomon. 6th ed. Seattle,
WA: Sasquatch Books, 2007.

*The Home Orchard: Growing Your Own
Decidous Fruit and Nut Trees,* by Chuck
A. Ingels, Pamela M. Geisel, and Maxwell
V. Norton. Oakland, CA: University
of California Agriculture and Natural
Resources, 2007.

How to Grow More Vegetables (and
fruits, nuts, berries, grains, and other
crops) *Than You Ever Thought Possible
on Less Land Than You Can Imagine,* by
John Jeavons. 7th ed. Berkeley, CA: Ten
Speed Press, 2006.

*Landscaping with Fruit: Strawberry
Ground Covers, Blueberry Hedges, Grape
Arbors, and 39 Other Luscious Fruits to
Make Your Yard an Edible Paradise,* by
Lee Reich. North Adams, MA: Storey
Publishing, 2009.

*The Maritime Northwest Garden Guide:
Planning Calendar for Year-Round
Organic Gardening,* by Carl Elliott and

Rob Peterson. Seattle, WA: Seattle Tilth
Association, 2009.

*The Organic Gardener's Handbook of
Natural Insect and Disease Control: A
Complete Problem-Solving Guide to
Keeping Your Garden and Yard Healthy
without Chemicals,* by Barbara W. Ellis
and Fern Marshall Bradley. Emmaus, PA:
Rodale Press, 1992.

*Perennial Vegetables: From Artichokes
to Zuiki Taro, A Gardener's Guide to
Over 100 Delicious and Easy to Grow
Edibles,* by Eric Toensmeier. White River
Junction, VT: Chelsea Green Publish-
ing, 2007.

**Gardening: Classes, Websites, Com-
munity Gardens, Planning Software,
Biochar**

Bullocks Permaculture Homestead
Orcas Island, Washington
Information and resources
www.PermaculturePortal.com/

Eugene Permaculture Guild
Eugene, Oregon
News, information, and events put on by
the Eugene Permaculture Guild
www.EugenePermacultureGuild.org/

Gardener's Supply Company
Burlington, Vermont
888-833-1412
Gardening supplies and furniture, plus
some nifty garden plans
www.Gardeners.com/

Gardening with Biochar FAQ
Informative wiki serving as a portal to
many online biochar resources
http://biochar.pbworks.com/

GrowVeg.com
Online garden planner with a free trial
period
www.GrowVeg.com/

Lost Valley Educational Center
Dexter, Oregon
541-937-3351
Permaculture design workshops and
intentional community
www.LostValley.org/

Portland Community Garden Program
Portland, Oregon
503-823-1612
City of Portland's Community Garden
Program. Search for "community gardens" on city website:
www.PortlandOnline.com/

Portland Permaculture Guild
Portland, Oregon
News, information, and events put on by
the Portland Permaculture Guild
www.TheDirt.org/

Seattle BioChar Working Group
(SeaChar)
Seattle, Washington
SeaChar hosts biochar-stove-building
workshops throughout the greater Seattle
area, sometimes at points beyond.
www.SeaChar.org/

Seattle Permaculture Guild
Seattle, Washington
News, information, and events put on by
the Seattle Permaculture Guild
www.SeattlePermacultureGuild.org/

Seattle P-Patch Program
Seattle, Washington
206-684-0264
City of Seattle's Community Garden
Program
www.seattle.gov/neighborhoods/ppatch/

Seattle Tilth
Seattle, Washington
206-633-0451
Seattle Tilth has classes in everything
from gardening to composting to goats.
http://SeattleTilth.org/

Gardening: Soil Tests

A&L Labs
Modesto, California
209-529-4080
Tests for soil nutrients, extra for
contaminants (lead, arsenic). Can write
recommendations based on organic
agricultural principles upon request.
www.AL-Labs-West.com/

Logan Labs
Lakeview, Ohio
888-494-SOIL (7645)
Tests for soil nutrients
www.LoganLabs.com/

Soil Minerals
Soil test interpretation service. After
you've received your soil test results, this
company will translate your test into
understandable language and provide
simple instructions on how to improve
your soil fertility. Soil amendments
ship from Olympia, Washington, and
Modesto, California.
www.SoilMinerals.com/

University of Massachusetts, Soil and
Plant Tissue Testing Laboratory

Amherst, Massachusetts
413-545-2311
Tests for soil nutrients, some contaminants. One of the most affordable labs.
www.UMass.edu/soiltest/

**Gardening: Sources for Soil Amend-
ments, Compost, and Worms**

Black Lake Organic
Olympia, Washington
360-786-0537
Great selection of organic soil amendments and fertilizer blends
www.BlackLakeOrganic.com/

Cedar Grove Composting
Maple Valley, Washington
877-764-5748
Compost, topsoil, mulch and more
www.Cedar-Grove.com/

Concentrates, Inc.
Portland, Oregon
800-388-4870
All manner of livestock feeds and soil
amendments
www.ConcentratesNW.com/

Creekside Gardens (Worm Lady)
155 Nix Road
Chehalis, Washington
360-748-4024
Information on red wiggler worms and
worm bins
www.WormLady.com/

East Multnomah County Manure Connection Program
Near Portland, Oregon
Free or inexpensive sources for animal
manure in the Portland area. Search for
"manure connection."
www.EMSWCD.org/

King County Conservation District
Manure Share Program
Near Seattle, Washington
Free or inexpensive animal manure in
King County, Washington. Search for
"manure share."
www.KingCD.org/

Kitsap E-Z Earth
16952 Clear Creek Road
Poulsbo, Washington
360-779-WORM (9676)
Red wiggler worms and vermicompost
systems
www.KitsapEZEarth.com/wp/

McFarlane's Bark
Milwaukie, Oregon
503-659-4240

Sells compost near Portland, Oregon
www.McFarlanesBark.com/

Northwest Wigglers
Lake Stevens, Washington
206-659-6767
Red wiggler worms and vermicompost
systems
www.NorthWestWigglers.com/

Pacific Topsoils
Various locations in the Seattle metro area
800-884-7645
Compost, topsoil, mulch and more
www.PacificTopSoils.com/

Peaceful Valley Farm and Garden Supply
Grass Valley, California
888-784-1722
Wonderful collection of garden tools,
amendments, and seeds
www.GrowOrganic.com/

Seattle Farm Co-op
Member-based cooperative that sells
mealworms and red wiggler bins
www.SeattleFarmCoop.com/
groups.Yahoo.com/group/SeattleFarm-
Coop/join/

Seattle Tilth
Seattle, Washington
206-633-0451
Red wiggler worms, classes, and hand-
outs on making worm boxes
http://SeattleTilth.org/

Three Trees Farm
Cottage Grove, Oregon
541-942-9033
Worms, worm boxes, and castings
www.RedWiggler.com/

Walt's Organic Fertilizer Company
Seattle, Washington
206-297-9092
Soil fertilizers and amendments in the
Ballard neighborhood
www.WaltsOrganic.com/

We Got Worms
McMinnville, Oregon
503-889-6193
Red wiggler worms, compost tea, and
castings
http://WeGotWorms4U.com/

Yelm Earthworm & Castings Farm
14741 Lawrence Lake Road SE
Yelm, Washington
360-894-0707
Red wiggler worms and vermicompost
systems
www.YelmWorms.com/

Gardening: Sources for Seeds and Plant Starts

Abundant Life Seeds
Cottage Grove, Oregon
541-767-9606
Certified organic sister seed company of
Territorial Seed
www.AbundantLifeSeeds.com/

Cascadian Edible Landscapes
Seattle, Washington
206-708-9298
Plant starts through a CSA plan or sold
at local farmers markets
www.EatYourYard.com/

Irish Eyes Garden Seeds
Ellensburg, Washington
509-933-7150
Large collection of potatoes and early
season vegetable seeds. Nearly all organic
and trialed for the Pacific Northwest
climate.
www.IrishEyesGardenSeeds.com/

Nichols Garden Nursery
Albany, Oregon
800-422-3985
Impressive collection of hard-to-find
perennial and annual seeds, trialed for
the Pacific Northwest climate.
www.NicholsGardenNursery.com/

Peaceful Valley Farm and Garden Supply
Grass Valley, California
888-784-1722
Wonderful collection of garden tools,
amendments, and seeds
www.GrowOrganic.com/

Richters Herb Specialists
Goodwood, Ontario, Canada
905-640-6641
Great source for perennial seeds
www.Richters.com/

Seattle Tilth
Seattle, Washington
206-633-0451
Nonprofit educational organization with
classes on all manner of urban farming
from gardening to rainwater harvesting
to livestock keeping
http://SeattleTilth.org/

Seed Savers Exchange
Decorah, Iowa
563-382-5990
Nonprofit organization that saves and
shares heirloom seeds
www.SeedSavers.org/

Seeds of Change
Rancho Dominguez, California
888-762-7333
Extensive selection of organic seeds
www.SeedsofChange.com/

Seeds of Diversity Canada
Toronto, Ontario, Canada
866-509-SEED (7333)
Nonprofit organization of volunteers
dedicated to saving heritage seeds. Members have access to the seed directory,
which lists seeds available for exchange
between members.
www.Seeds.ca/

Siskiyou Seeds
Williams, Oregon
541-846-9233
Organic seed grower in southern Oregon
www.SiskiyouSeeds.com/

Territorial Seed Company
Cottage Grove, Oregon
800-626-866
Garden supplies and seeds, trialed for
the Pacific Northwest climate
www.TerritorialSeed.com/

Uprising Seeds
Bellingham, Washington
360-778-3749
Open pollinated (OP), organic seeds,
trialed for the Pacific Northwest climate
www.UprisingOrganics.com/

West Coast Seeds
Vancouver, British Columbia, Canada
888-804-8820
Information, classes, and large selection
of organic seeds
www.WestCoastSeeds.com/

Gardening: Sources for Perennials, Fruit Trees, and Bushes

Burnt Ridge Nursery and Orchards
Onalaska, Washington
360-985-2873
Regional source for fruit trees
www.BurntRidgeNursery.com/

Cloud Mountain Farm
Everson, Washington
360-966-5859
Regional source for fruit trees
www.CloudMountainFarm.com/

Food Forest Farm
Holyoke, Massachusetts
Source for hard-to-find perennial vegetable seeds
www.PermacultureNursery.com/

Forest Farm
Williams, Oregon
541-846-7269

Extensive inventory of plants, including
some perennial vegetables
www.ForestFarm.com/

Molbak's
Woodinville, Washington
866-466-5225
Regional source for fruit trees and
vegetable starts
www.Molbaks.com/

Nichols Garden Nursery
Albany, Oregon
800-422-3985
Source for vegetable starts and hard-
to-find seeds, including perennial
vegetables
www.GardenNursery.com/

One Green World
Molalla, Oregon
877-353-4028
Perennial fruit, nut, and berry plants
www.OneGreenWorld.com/

Raintree Nursery
Morton, Washington
800-391-8892
Perennial fruit, nut, and berry plants
www.RaintreeNursery.com/

Rockridge Orchards
Enumclaw, Washington
360-802-6800
Hard-to-find fruit trees and edible plants
by request, from their farm or farmers
markets. They carry tea plants, peppercorn bushes, yuzus, hardy ginger, edible
bamboo, and shiso.
www.RockridgeOrchards.com/

Sky Nursery
Shoreline, Washington
206-546-4851
Regional source for fruit trees and
vegetable starts
www.SkyNursery.com/

Swansons Nursery
Seattle, Washington
206-782-2543
Regional source for fruit trees and
vegetable starts
www.SwansonsNursery.com/

Whitman Farms
Salem, Oregon
503-510-0486
Regional source for fruiting bushes and
trees
www.WhitmanFarms.com/

Gardening: Sources for Irrigation, Greywater, Grow Lights, Grow Tunnels, and Aquaponics Equipment

Backyard Aquaponics
Success, Western Australia
(61) 08 9414-9334
Great informational site and forum
www.BackYardAquaponics.com/

Charley's Greenhouse and Garden
Mt. Vernon, Washington
800-322-4707
Large selection of greenhouse kits and
supplies
www.CharleysGreenHouse.com/

Do It Yourself Aquaponics
Orange Park, Florida
904-707-3201
Information and forum for making your
own aquaponics system
www.DIYAquaponics.com/

Drip Depot
Medford, Oregon
888-525-8874
Irrigation supplies
www.DripDepot.com/

DripWorks
Willits, California
800-522-3747
Irrigation supplies
www.DripWorks.com/

Gardener's Supply Company
Burlington, Vermont
888-833-1412
Gardening supplies and furniture, plus
some nifty garden plans
www.Gardeners.com/

Growing Power
Milwaukee, Wisconsin
414-527-1546
A community food project headed by
Will Allen, national advocate for urban
farming (and former basketball super-
star). Utilizes aquaponics in greenhouses.
www.GrowingPower.org/aquaponics.
htm/

Lee Valley Tools
Retail stores across Canada
From Canada: 1-800-267-8767
From the United States: 1-800-871-8158
Good source for grow tunnels and other
gardening equipment
www.LeeValley.com/

Lilypons Water Gardens
Adamstown, Maryland
800-999-5459
Large selection of fountains, pond supplies, and water plants
www.Lilypons.com/

Oasis Design
Santa Barbara, California
805-967-9956
Information and books on rainwater
harvesting and greywater
www.OasisDesign.net/

Peaceful Valley Farm and Garden Supply
Grass Valley, California
888-784-1722
Wonderful collection of garden tools,
amendments, and seeds
www.GrowOrganic.com/

....

beekeeping: infor-
mation and supplies

....

Ballard Bee Company
Seattle, Washington
206-459-4131
Company will set up bees in your backyard or sell you equipment. Will customize a standard hive if you're interested in
the foundationless method featured in
this book. Our favorite beekeepers Ken
and Rebecca Reid recommend custom-
izing Langstroth-style hives, as these are
the industry standard and use the most
commonly available components.
http://www.BallardBeeCompany.com/

Beemaster Forum
Online forum concerning all styles of
beekeeping
http://Forum.BeeMaster.com/

Bee Source Forum
Huge online forum concerning all styles
of beekeeping
www.BeeSource.com/

Bee Thinking
Portland, Oregon
Online retailer of beekeeping products.
Specialist in top bar beekeeping.
www.BeeThinking.com/

Bush Farms
Greenwood, Nebraska
Website devoted to promoting various
foundationless beekeeping methods
www.BushFarms.com/bees.htm

Natural Beekeeping Network Online
forum concerning various forms of
foundationless beekeeping. Click on the
"forum" tab.
www.BioBees.com/

Reid's Bees
12763 39th Avenue NE

Seattle, Washington 98125
206-786-3804 (Ken's cell)
206-579-4449 (Rebecca's cell) Ken and
Rebecca Reid will extract the bees infest-
ing your Seattle-area attic and use them
to populate new beehives.

Ruhl Bee Supply
Gladstone, Oregon
503-657-5399
Online and brick-and-mortar retailer of
beekeeping products. Will customize a
standard Langstroth-style hive if you're
interested in the foundationless method
featured in this book.
www.Bee-Outside.com/

....

food preservation

....

Food Preservation: Books

*Ball Complete Book of Home Preserving:
400 Delicious and Creative Recipes for
Today,* Judi Kingry and Lauren Devine,
eds. Toronto: Robert Rose, 2006.

*The Big Book of Preserving the Harvest:
150 Recipes for Freezing, Canning, Drying
and Pickling Fruits and Vegetables,* by
Carol W. Costenbader. North Adams,
MA: Storey Publishing, 2002.

*Mary Bell's Complete Dehydrator Cook-
book,* By Mary Bell. New York: William
Morrow and Company, 1994.

*Preserving Food Without Freezing or
Canning: Traditional Techniques Using
Salt, Oil, Sugar, Alcohol, Vinegar, Drying,
Cold Storage, and Lactic Fermentation,*
by The Gardeners and Farmers of Centre
Terre Vivante and Deborah Madison.
White River Junction, VT: Chelsea Green
Publishing, 1999.

*Wild Fermentation: The Flavor, Nutri-
tion, and Craft of Live-Culture Foods,* by
Sandor Katz. White River Junction, VT:
Chelsea Green Publishing, 2003.

Food Preservation: Forums

Fresh Preserving
Forum and website hosted by Jarden
Home Brands, the parent company of
Ball, known for its canning jars
www.FreshPreserving.com/

Homesteading Today
Active forum with threads on any animal
you can keep in the city plus fiber, crafting, soap making, and food preservation:

all manner of homesteading
www.HomesteadingToday.com/

Food Preservation: Sources for Equipment

Amazon
Online retailer with all manner of homesteading supplies and books
www.Amazon.com/

Canning Pantry
Hyrum, Utah
800-285-9044
All manner of canning supplies
www.CanningPantry.com/

Lehman's
Kidron, Ohio
888-438-5346
Family-run business that sells products geared towards rural living and self-sufficiency
www.Lehmans.com/

Peaceful Valley Farm and Garden Supply
Grass Valley, California
888-784-1722
Wonderful collection of food preservation equipment, garden tools, amendments, and seeds
www.GrowOrganic.com/

local farmers, farmers markets and csa programs, buying clubs

Eatwild
Online directory of pastured meats, dairy and produce in the United States and Canada
www.Eatwild.com/

Local Harvest
Online directory of local foods, farms, and farmers markets in the United States
www.LocalHarvest.org/

Oregon Department of Agriculture
Commodity Inspection Division
503-986-4620
Issues licenses for cash buyers of produce—for buying clubs in Oregon
http://oregon.gov/ODA/CID/http://oregon.gov/ODA/CID/description_of_licenses.shtml/

Sustainable Table
Online directory of fresh, locally grown,

and sustainably produced food in the United States and Canada
www.SustainableTable.com/

United States Department of Agriculture, Agricultural Marketing Service Perishable Agricultural Commodities Act (PACA), Fair Trading Regulations
800-495-7222
USDA requires a PACA license when a buying club's activities grow beyond certain thresholds.
www.ams.usda.gov/AMSv1.0/paca/

Washington State Department of Agriculture, Commission Merchants Program
360-902-1857
Issues licenses for cash buyers of produce—for buying clubs in Washington State
http://agr.wa.gov/inspection/CommissionMerchants/

....

meat

....

Meat: Books

The Art of Making Fermented Sausages, by Stanley Marianski and Adam Marianski. Seminole, FL: Bookmagic, 2009.

Bruce Aidells' Complete Sausage Book: Recipes from America's Premium Sausage Maker, by Bruce Aidells and Denis Kelly. Berkeley, CA: Ten Speed Press, 2000.

Charcuterie: The Craft of Salting, Smoking and Curing, by Michael Ruhlman and Brian Polcyn. New York: W. W. Norton & Company, 2005.

The Complete Book of Butchering, Smoking, Curing, and Sausage Making: How to Harvest Your Livestock and Wild Game, by Philip Hasheider. Minneapolis, MN: Voyageur Press, 2010.

The River Cottage Meat Book, by Hugh Fearnley-Whittingstall. Berkeley, CA: Ten Speed Press, 2007.

Meat: Sources for Curing Salts, Ferments, and Sausage Casings
Butcher & Packer
Madison Heights, Michigan
248-583-1250
Full line of meat curing ingredients, meat grinders, and sausage stuffers
www.Butcher-Packer.com/

The Sausage Maker
Buffalo, New York

888-490-8525
Full line of meat curing ingredients, meat grinders, and sausage stuffers
www.SausageMaker.com

Meat: Ranchers and Sources for Heritage Small Animals

Abundant Acres Farm
Toledo, Washington
Rabbit, turkeys, duck, geese, pork, and heritage chickens fed local grains
http://AbundantAcres-Farm.com/

Eatwild
Directory of pasture-based farms
www.Eatwild.com/

Ebey Farm
Everett, Washington
206-940-4980
Farmer Bruce King sells hogs, chickens, turkeys, and lamb at Ebey Farm. We like his hogs. He avoids over-reliance on industry-standard corn and soy feeds by choosing unconventional feed sources, such as truckloads of rejected vegetables from Walmart stores.
http://ebeyfarm.blogspot.com/

Pastured Sensations
Snohomish, Washington
360-568-5208
Family-run business that raises chickens, turkeys, pork, and grass-fed beef. Chickens are Cornish Cross but raised without soy or corn.
www.PasturedSensations.com/

Meat: Rabbit Keeping Forums

Homesteading Today
Active forum with threads on any animal you can keep in the city plus fiber, crafting, soap making, and food preservation: all manner of homesteading
www.HomesteadingToday.com/

Meat Rabbits Yahoo Group
Very active forum on raising meat rabbits
Pets.groups.Yahoo.com/group/Meatrabbits/

Rabbit Talk
Active forum with a focus on meat rabbits
www.RabbitTalk.com/

Meat: Sources for Live Rabbits, Equipment, and Housing

Abundant Acres Farm
Toledo, Washington
Rabbit, turkeys, duck, geese, pork and

heritage chickens fed local grains. Farmer Brad will also sell you rabbit breeding stock and supplies upon request.
http://AbundantAcres-Farm.com/

Petco
San Diego, California
877-738-6742
Large pet supply retailer with stores across the country and online
www.Petco.com/

The Rabbit House
UK website with lots of photos of rabbit housing
www.TheRabbitHouse.com/

Rabbit Mart
Farmington Hills, Michigan
866-331-1920
All manner of rabbit equipment
www.RabbitMart.com/

soaps and lotions

Soaps and Lotions: Books

Handcrafted Soap, by Delores Boone. Cincinnati, OH: North Light Books, 2002.

Soaps and Lotions: Forums

Homesteading Today
Active forum with threads on any animal you can keep in the city plus fiber, crafting, soap and lotion making, and food preservation: all manner of homesteading
www.HomesteadingToday.com/

Soap Making Forum
Active forum covering soap, lotions, and other products
www.SoapMakingForum.com/forum/

Teach Soap Forum
Forum with information on soap and lotion making
www.TeachSoap.com/forum/

Soaps and Lotions: Sources for Supplies

Bramble Berry
Bellingham, Washington
877-627-7883
Soap and lotion making supplies and classes
www.BrambleBerry.com/

GloryBee Foods
Eugene, Oregon
800-456-7923
Soap and lotion making supplies
www.GloryBeeFoods.com/

cooking with real food: books

The Art of Simple Food: Notes, Lessons, and Recipes from a Delicious Revolution, by Alice Waters. New York: Clarkson Potter, 2007.

Forgotten Skills of Cooking: The Time-Honored Ways Are the Best—Over 700 Recipes Show You Why, by Darina Allen. Great Britain: Kyle Books, 2009.

The Herbfarm Cookbook, by Jerry Traunfeld. New York: Scribner, 2000.

The Lost Art of Real Cooking: Rediscovering the Pleasures of Traditional Food One Recipe at a Time, by Ken Albala and Rosanna Nafziger. New York: Perigee, 2010.

Nourishing Traditions: The Cookbook that Challenges Politically Correct Nutrition and the Diet Dictocrats, by Sally Fallon. Washington, DC: NewTrends Publishing, 2001.

index

mulching, 132–133
mustard, 159, 244–245

N

nest boxes, 60–61, 64
nitrogen, 124, 126, 135
nixtamalization, 37–38
North Carolina Vinegar Sauce,
    263

O

oats, 36
omega-3 enhanced eggs, 55
onions, 213
open pollinated seeds, 156
orchard, 173–175
Oregon grape, 200
organic bread, 24
organic eggs, 54
organic produce, 141–143
ostriches, 284–285
oyster shell, 62

P

pac choi, 208
Pan Roasted New Potatoes, 192–
    193
parsnips, 206
pasta sauce, 241–242
pasteurized milk, 74
pastured chickens, 55
peaches, 216, 233–235
pear cider, 326–327
pear tree, 174
pears, 216
peas, 208
pectin, 226–227
pepperoni sausage, 289–290
Perishable Agricultural
    Commodities Act, 259
permaculture, 144–145
perpetual gardening, 166,
    172–173, 361–365
personal care products, 339–341
pests, 177–178, 180–182
pickled beets, 239

pickled pepper cornbread,
    264–265
pies
    berries and fruits for, 199–200
    Grandma Judy's Rhubarb
        Custard Pie, 100
    Heirloom Apple Pie with
        Whipped Cream, 267
pie crust, 101
pigeons, 320–321
pigs. See hogs
pizza, 47–49
plant(s)
    edible, 356–360
    for livestock, 365–366
    non-edible, 360–361
    pollinators, 368
    water, 321
plant varieties
    early maturing, 167–168
    selection of, 163
    for winter gardening, 206–207
planting schedule, 104–105
plums, 233
polenta, 19–20
pollinators, plants for, 368
polycultures, 170–171
potatoes, 192–193, 213
potting soil, 111
power pancakes, 41–42
pre-ferment, 42
premix, 309
preserving
    canning, 226–229
    dehydrating, 215–216
    fermenting, 217–224
    freezing, 212
    overview of, 211
    resources regarding, 375–376
pricking seedlings, 155
produce
    bulk buying of, 252–257
    eating plan, 104–105
    organic versus local, 141–142
    overview of, 103–104
    sources for, 203

pudding, 69–70
purple hull-less barley, 36

Q

quince jelly, 232

R

rabbit(s)
    Alsatian Rabbit, 303–305
    Lapin en Daube à la Provençale,
        18–19
    raising, 298–303
    recipes for, 303–305
    slaughtering of, 284–285
rabbit hutch, 299
raised garden beds, 109–110
raw milk, 74
recipes
    Apple Breakfast Sausage, 288
    apple cider, 326–327
    applesauce, 236–237
    Apricot Glazed Ham, 287–288
    beef jerky, 289
    Better than Canned Baked
        Beans, 265–266
    beverage, 326–332
    bone broth, 291–292
    bread and butter cucumber
        slices, 237–238
    Canadian Bacon, 286–287
    canning, 232–245
    caramelized onion jam, 241
    cheese, 90–93
    Chèvre Polenta, 19–20
    Cock 'n' Beer, 317–319
    corned beef, 290–291
    crisp whole grain crackers,
        49–50
    Cucumbers with Dill and Chive
        Crème Fraîche, 193
    dairy, 84–89
    dandelion coffee, 328
    dill pickle spears or slices, 238
    egg, 69–71
    elderberry syrup, 330–331
    for fall, 261–267

about the authors

Annette Cottrell is the author of the popular blog www.SustainableEats.com. She had canned, gardened, and pined for a hobby farm for more than twenty years. Then in December of 2008, she developed a midlife food crisis and, as a result, she stopped buying industrial food altogether and transformed her one-fifth-acre Seattle city lot into an edible oasis and urban farm. After finishing this book, she decided to move to small acreage just outside the city, where she now raises food for a handful of Seattle-area families.

Annette takes particular delight in proving how strong in-city food security can be, creating compact garden plans and focusing on shade-loving edibles and perennial vegetables. Her efforts have been featured in a variety of media, including a television pilot, "Urban Tomato," and she has spoken at Sustainable NE Seattle's "Planet Home" event and Seattle's Hardy Plant Society.

When not raising and making food for her husband and two children, Annette, who has a background in finance, runs an online store and support site for infant reflux, www.Pollywog Baby.com.

Joshua McNichols is a 37-year-old journalist who loves finding food outside the grocery store system. He has reported for Seattle public radio station KUOW and for nationally syndicated public radio programs, including "Weekend America" and "The Splendid Table." He currently produces a podcast on composting for Seattle Tilth.

Joshua traces his love of home-grown food to his days as a latchkey kid in Washington State, when having lost his house key, he spent many afternoons eating ripe fruit in an ancient plum tree until his parents came home. Though trained as an architect, his propensity for asking questions eventually led him into journalism. Today, the local food movement allows him to explore fundamental questions about our relationship to food. His favorite stories feature memorable characters connecting through their food and community; it's these stories that have infected him with a passion for urban farming.

A seasoned gardener and certified master composter, Joshua lives and farms in Seattle's Ballard neighborhood with his wife and two children. He still has quite a thing for plums.

Harley Soltes is a photojournalist with a deep appreciation of farming and farmers. Working as a staff photographer for *The Seattle Times* for over twenty years he has shot world events, celebrities, sports, fashion, and everyday life. His work has been published in the *New York Times*, *Sports Illustrated*, *Time*, *Life*, and *National Geographic*. He resides on an organic farm in Bow, Washington. See more of his work at www.harleysoltes.com.